Twin Star Exorcists

ONMYOJI

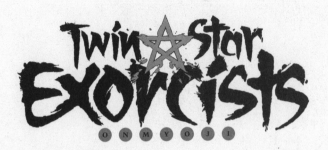

Twin ☆ Star Exorcists

O N M Y O J I

12

STORY & ART
YOSHIAKI SUKENO

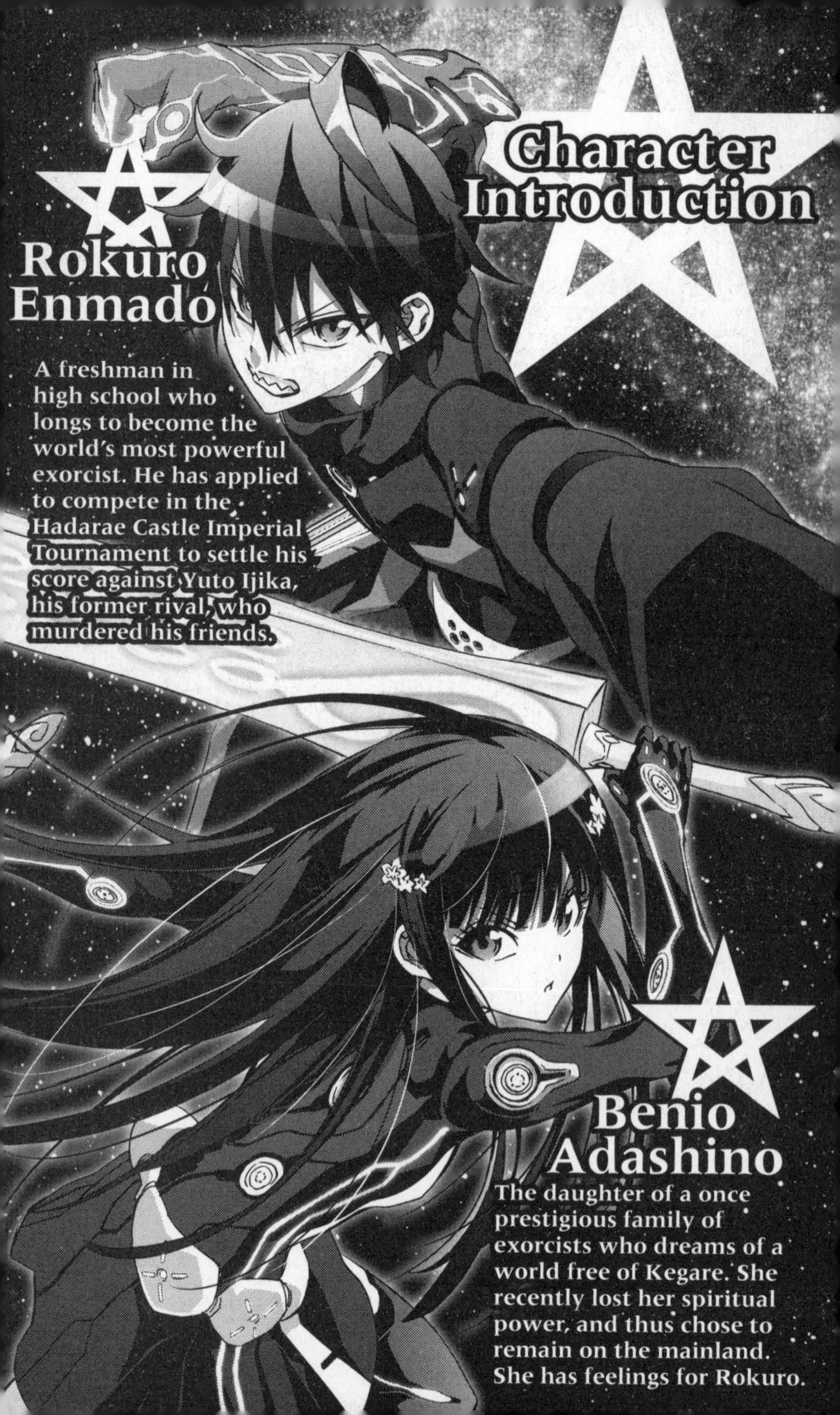
Character Introduction
Rokuro Enmado
A freshman in high school who longs to become the world's most powerful exorcist. He has applied to compete in the Hadarae Castle Imperial Tournament to settle his score against Yuto Ijika, his former rival, who murdered his friends.
Benio Adashino
The daughter of a once prestigious family of exorcists who dreams of a world free of Kegare. She recently lost her spiritual power, and thus chose to remain on the mainland. She has feelings for Rokuro.

Mayura Otomi

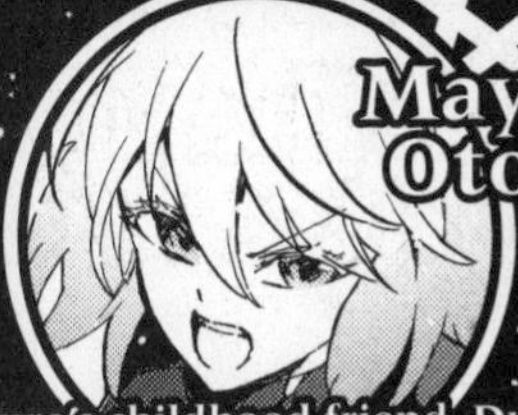

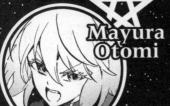

Rokuro's childhood friend. During a fierce battle in Magano, her commitment to protecting others earned her the spiritual protector White Tiger. She is now the new head of the Amawaka Family.

Arimori Tsuchimikado

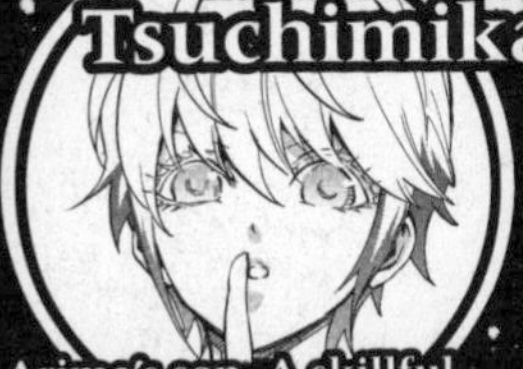

Arima's son. A skillful wielder of shikigami. He joined the Enmado Clan to get his father's attention.

Shizuru Ioroi

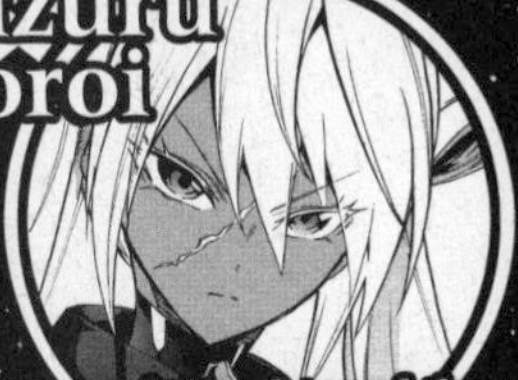

The second daughter of the Ioroi Family, one of the Twelve Guardian Families entrusted with Golden Snake. She is athletic and outspoken.

Kinako

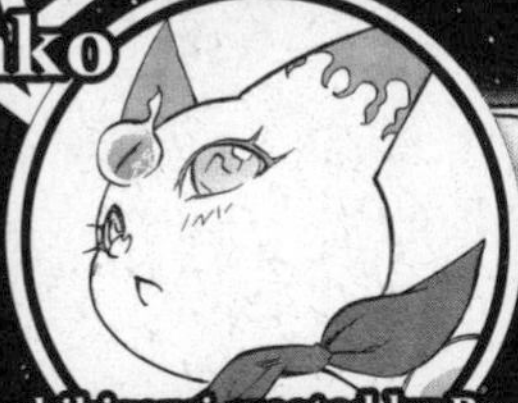

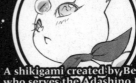

A shikigami created by Benio who serves the Adashino Family and remains on their estate awaiting her return.

Kankuro Mitosaka

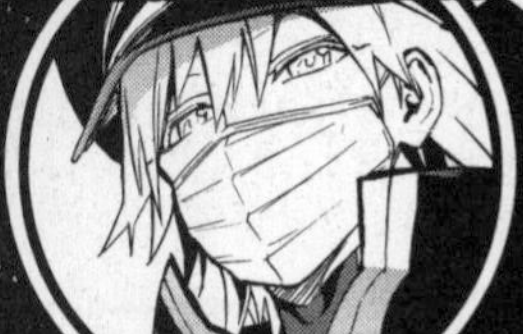

A doctor and the head of the Mitosaka Family. He is the Azure Dragon, one of the strongest of the Twelve Guardians.

Arima Tsuchimikado

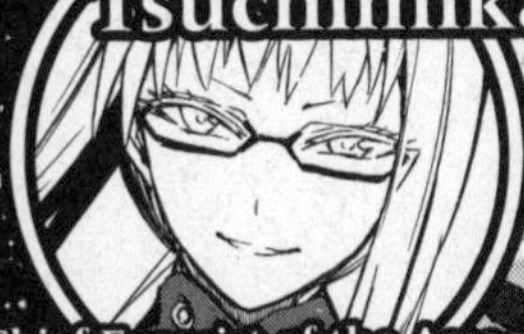

The Chief Exorcist of the Association of Unified Exorcists, the organization that presides over all exorcists. To fulfill a prophecy, he is determined to get Rokuro and Benio together.

Story Thus Far...

Kegare are creatures from Magano, the underworld, and it is the duty of an exorcist to hunt, exorcise and purify them. Rokuro and Benio are the Twin Star Exorcists, fated to bear the Prophesied Child who will defeat the Kegare. Their goal was to go to Tsuchimikado Island to get revenge on Yuto, the mastermind behind the Hinatsuki Tragedy and Benio's brother.

After two years, Rokuro qualifies to go to the island, but Benio loses her spiritual power in battle. Leaving her behind, Rokuro instead moves to the island with his childhood friend and newbie exorcist Mayura. The Amawaka family promptly appoints Mayura as their new family head. Rokuro founds his own Enmado family at the abandoned Adashino family home with the aid of Benio's shikigami Kinako. With the help of Arimori Tsuchimikado, he is able to enter a tournament in hopes of qualifying to join a mission to take out Yuto. But first his team must win the tournament...

EXORCISMS

#41	**Women's Battle, Part 1**	007
#42	**Women's Battle, Part 2**	053
#43	**Dreams and Aspirations**	099
#44	**Burning Down Hadarae Castle!**	145

12

ONMYOJI have worked for the Imperial Court since the Heian era.
In addition to exorcising evil spirits, as civil servants they performed a
variety of roles, including advising nobles by foretelling the future, creating
the calendar, observing the movements of the stars, measuring time…

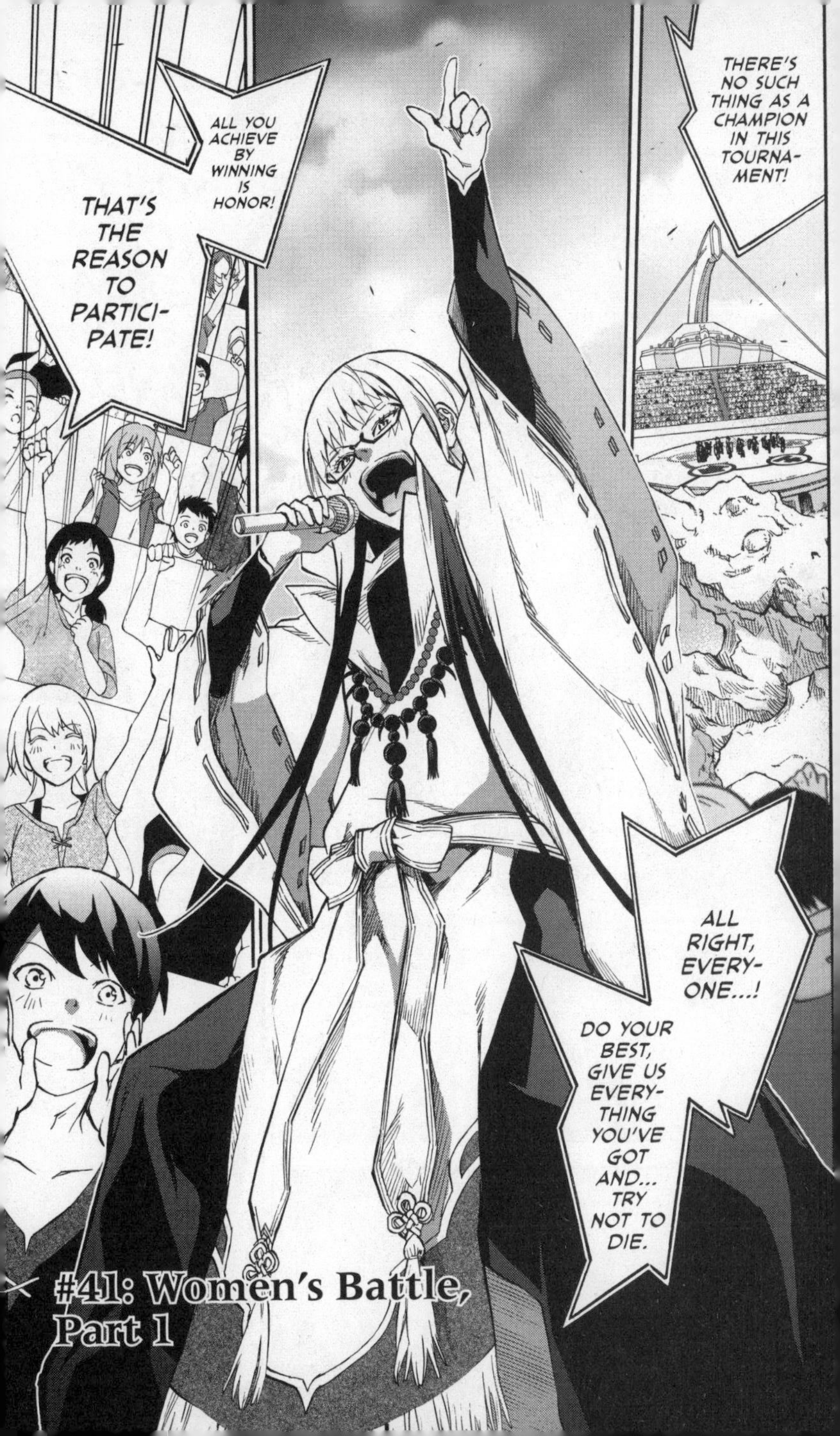
THERE'S NO SUCH THING AS A CHAMPION IN THIS TOURNAMENT!
ALL YOU ACHIEVE BY WINNING IS HONOR!
THAT'S THE REASON TO PARTICIPATE!
ALL RIGHT, EVERYONE...!
DO YOUR BEST, GIVE US EVERYTHING YOU'VE GOT AND... TRY NOT TO DIE.

#41: Women's Battle, Part 1

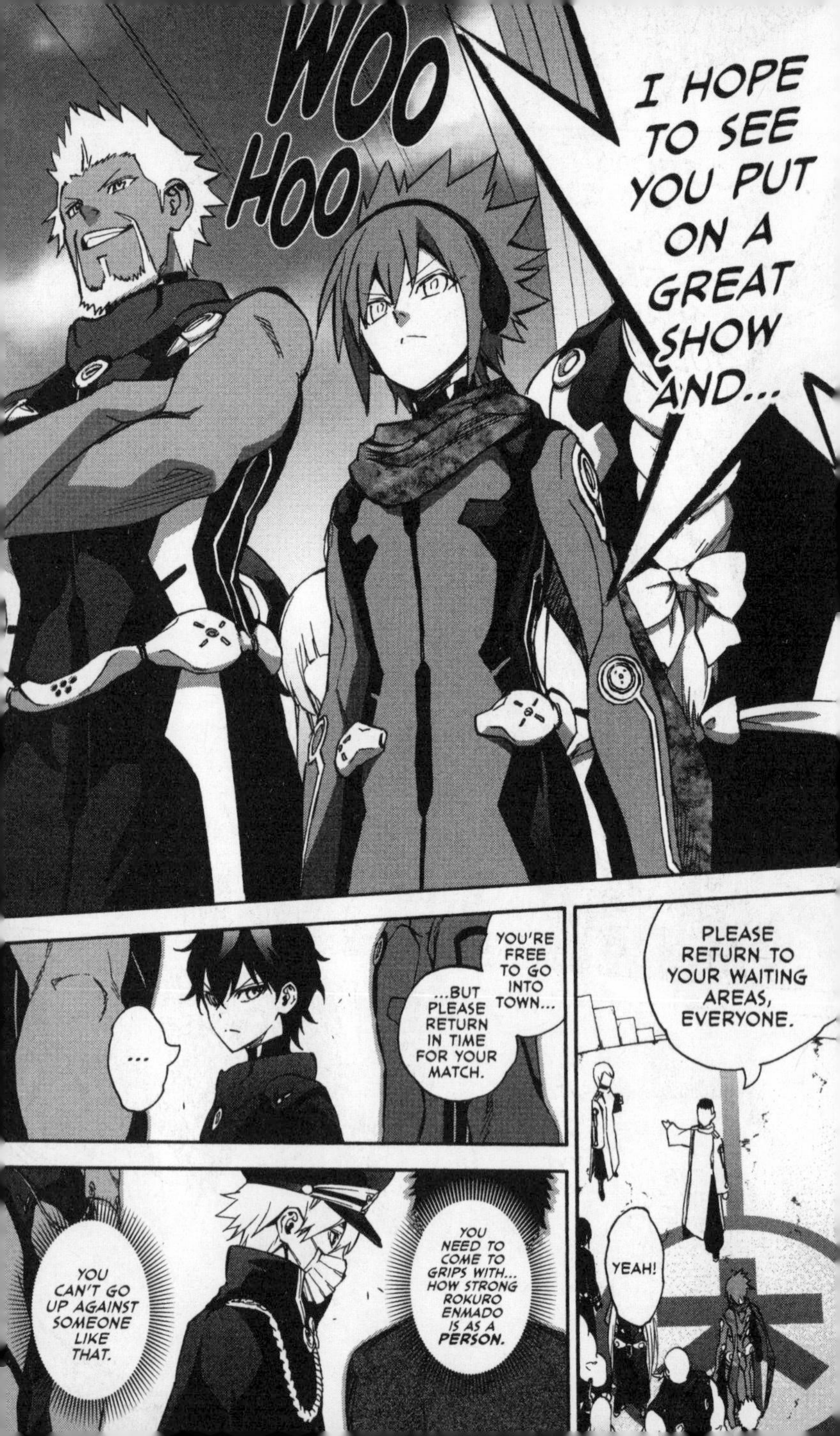
I HOPE TO SEE YOU PUT ON A GREAT SHOW AND...
WOO HOO
PLEASE RETURN TO YOUR WAITING AREAS, EVERYONE.
YEAH!
YOU'RE FREE TO GO INTO TOWN...
...BUT PLEASE RETURN IN TIME FOR YOUR MATCH.
...
YOU NEED TO COME TO GRIPS WITH... HOW STRONG ROKURO ENMADO IS AS A PERSON.
YOU CAN'T GO UP AGAINST SOMEONE LIKE THAT.

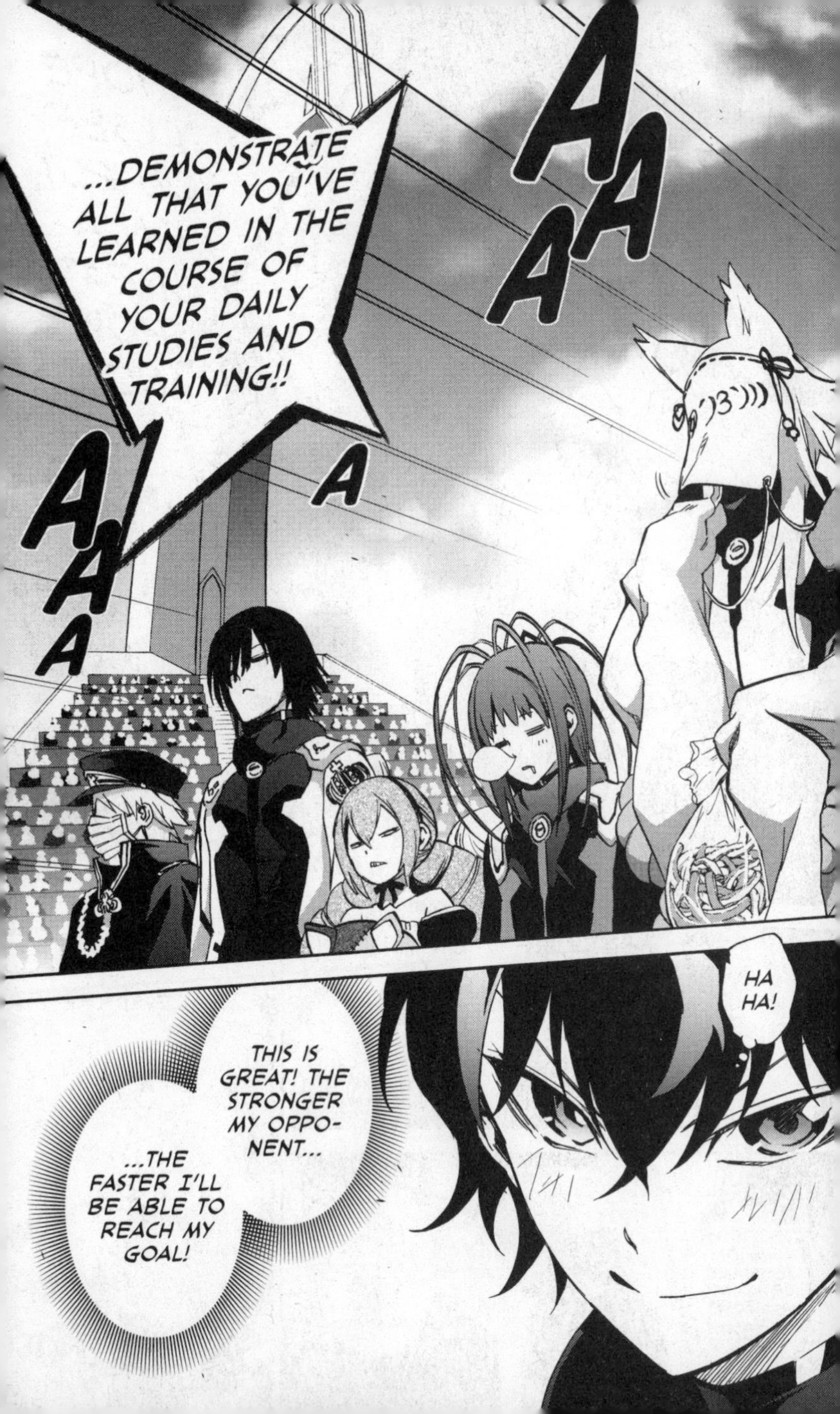
...DEMONSTRATE ALL THAT YOU'VE LEARNED IN THE COURSE OF YOUR DAILY STUDIES AND TRAINING!!
AAAA
A
AAAA
HA HA!
THIS IS GREAT! THE STRONGER MY OPPO-NENT...
...THE FASTER I'LL BE ABLE TO REACH MY GOAL!

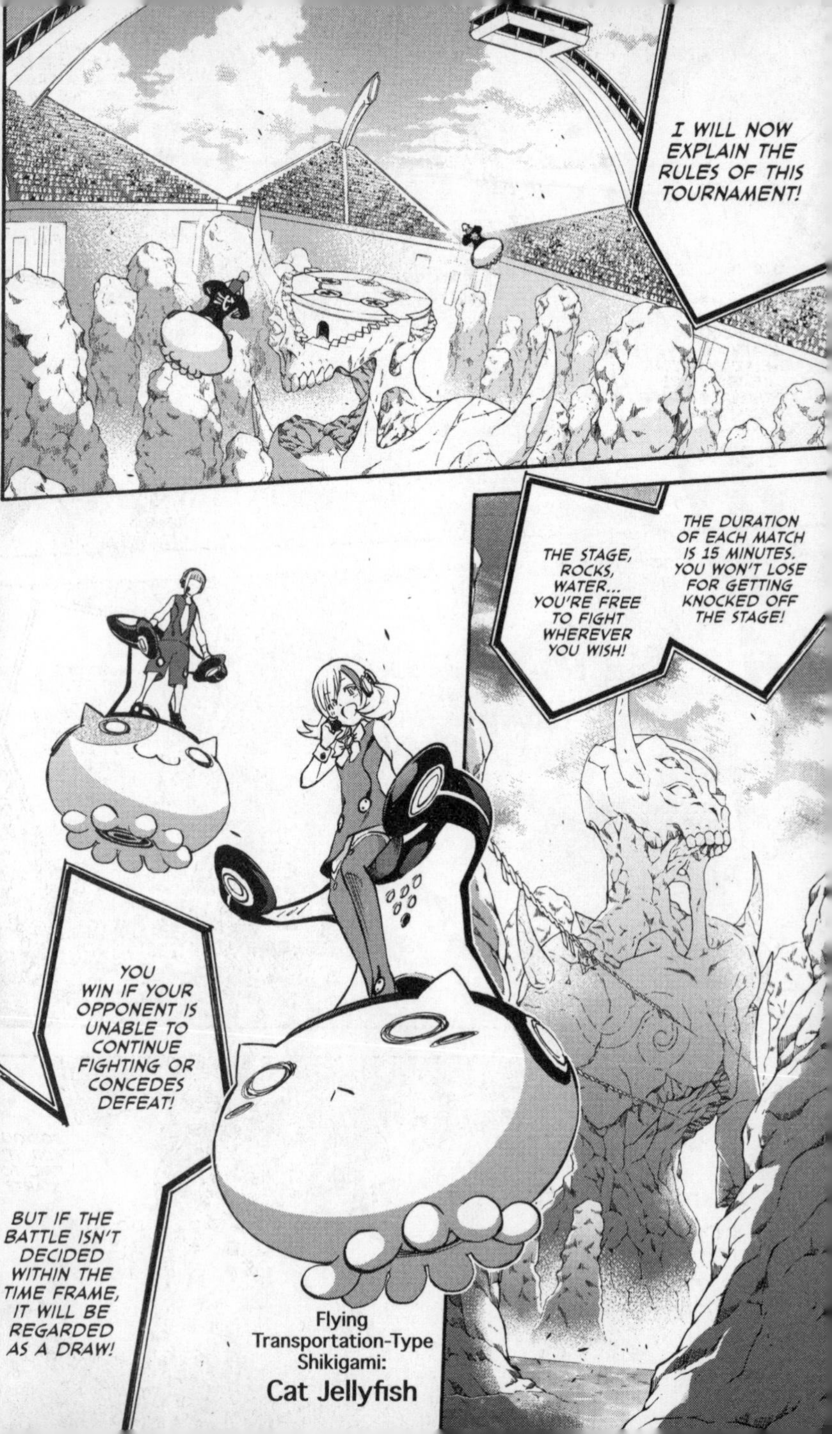
I WILL NOW EXPLAIN THE RULES OF THIS TOURNAMENT!
THE DURATION OF EACH MATCH IS 15 MINUTES. YOU WON'T LOSE FOR GETTING KNOCKED OFF THE STAGE!
THE STAGE, ROCKS, WATER... YOU'RE FREE TO FIGHT WHEREVER YOU WISH!
YOU WIN IF YOUR OPPONENT IS UNABLE TO CONTINUE FIGHTING OR CONCEDES DEFEAT!
BUT IF THE BATTLE ISN'T DECIDED WITHIN THE TIME FRAME, IT WILL BE REGARDED AS A DRAW!
Flying Transportation-Type Shikigami:
Cat Jellyfish

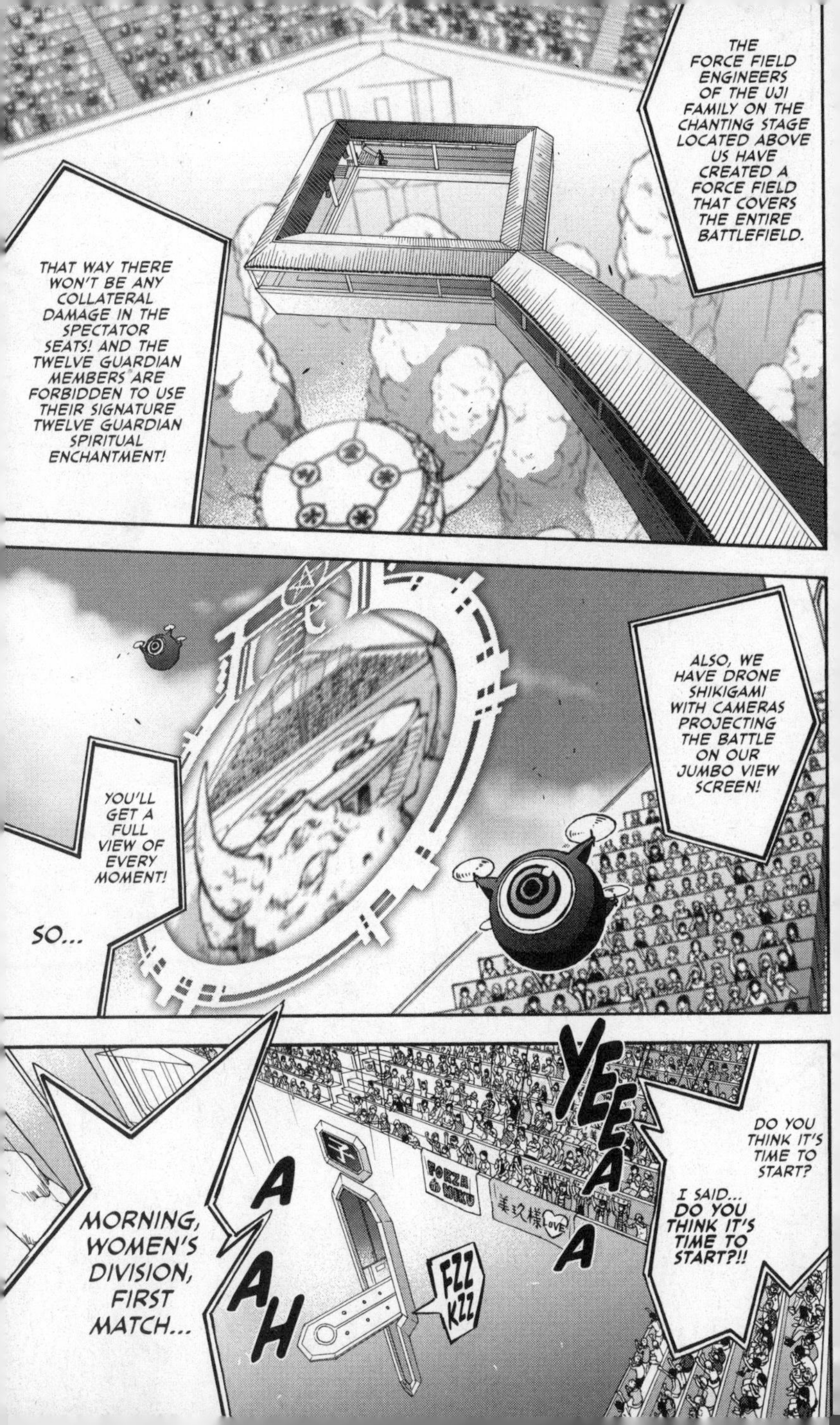

THE FORCE FIELD ENGINEERS OF THE UJI FAMILY ON THE CHANTING STAGE LOCATED ABOVE US HAVE CREATED A FORCE FIELD THAT COVERS THE ENTIRE BATTLEFIELD.
THAT WAY THERE WON'T BE ANY COLLATERAL DAMAGE IN THE SPECTATOR SEATS! AND THE TWELVE GUARDIAN MEMBERS ARE FORBIDDEN TO USE THEIR SIGNATURE TWELVE GUARDIAN SPIRITUAL ENCHANTMENT!
ALSO, WE HAVE DRONE SHIKIGAMI WITH CAMERAS PROJECTING THE BATTLE ON OUR JUMBO VIEW SCREEN!
YOU'LL GET A FULL VIEW OF EVERY MOMENT!
SO...
DO YOU THINK IT'S TIME TO START?
I SAID... DO YOU THINK IT'S TIME TO START?!!
YEEAAA
A
FORZA MIKU
美玖様 LOVE
FZZ KZZ
AAH
MORNING, WOMEN'S DIVISION, FIRST MATCH...

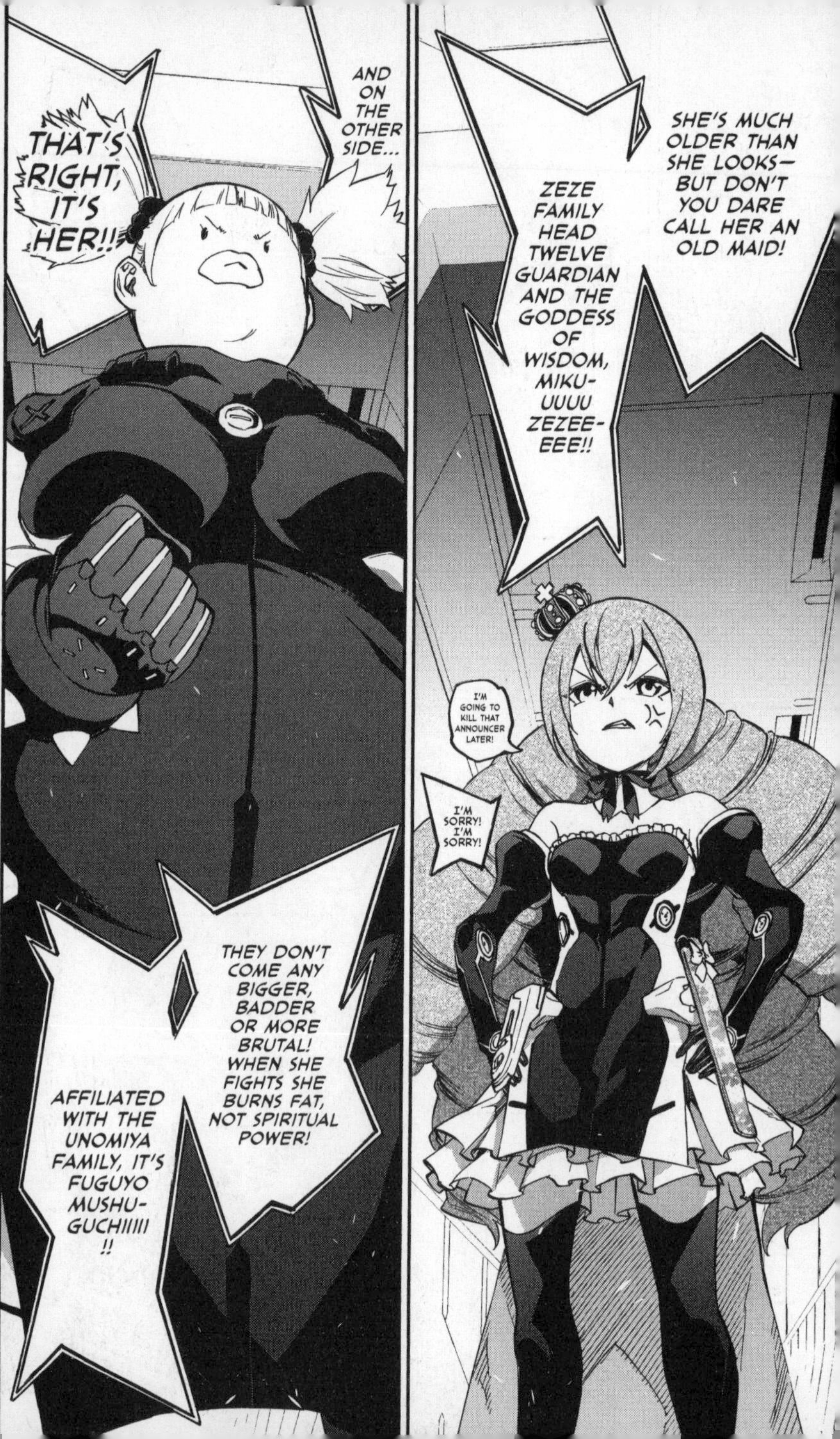
SHE'S MUCH OLDER THAN SHE LOOKS—BUT DON'T YOU DARE CALL HER AN OLD MAID!
ZEZE FAMILY HEAD TWELVE GUARDIAN AND THE GODDESS OF WISDOM, MIKU-UUUU ZEZEE-EEE!!
I'M GOING TO KILL THAT ANNOUNCER LATER!
I'M SORRY! I'M SORRY!
AND ON THE OTHER SIDE...
THAT'S RIGHT, IT'S HER!!
THEY DON'T COME ANY BIGGER, BADDER OR MORE BRUTAL! WHEN SHE FIGHTS SHE BURNS FAT, NOT SPIRITUAL POWER!
AFFILIATED WITH THE UNOMIYA FAMILY, IT'S FUGUYO MUSHU-GUCHIIIII !!

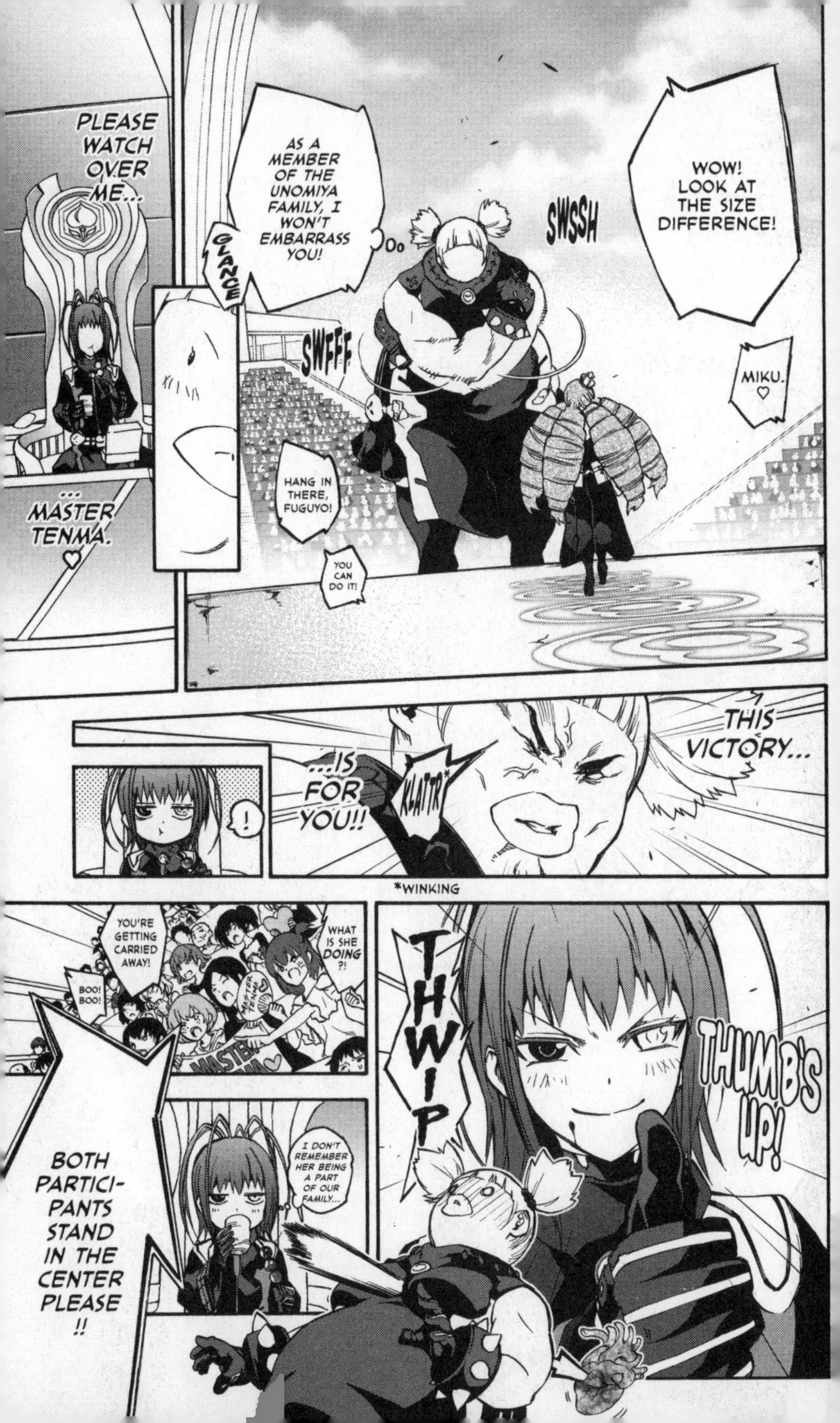
WOW! LOOK AT THE SIZE DIFFERENCE!
SWSSH
MIKU. ♡
AS A MEMBER OF THE UNOMIYA FAMILY, I WON'T EMBARRASS YOU!
SWFFF
HANG IN THERE, FUGUYO!
YOU CAN DO IT!
GLANCE
PLEASE WATCH OVER ME...
...MASTER TENMA. ♡
THIS VICTORY...
...IS FOR YOU!!
KLATTR*
!
*WINKING
THUMB'S UP!
THWIP
WHAT IS SHE DOING?!
YOU'RE GETTING CARRIED AWAY!
BOO! BOO!
MASTER TENMA
I DON'T REMEMBER HER BEING A PART OF OUR FAMILY...
BOTH PARTICI-PANTS STAND IN THE CENTER PLEASE!!

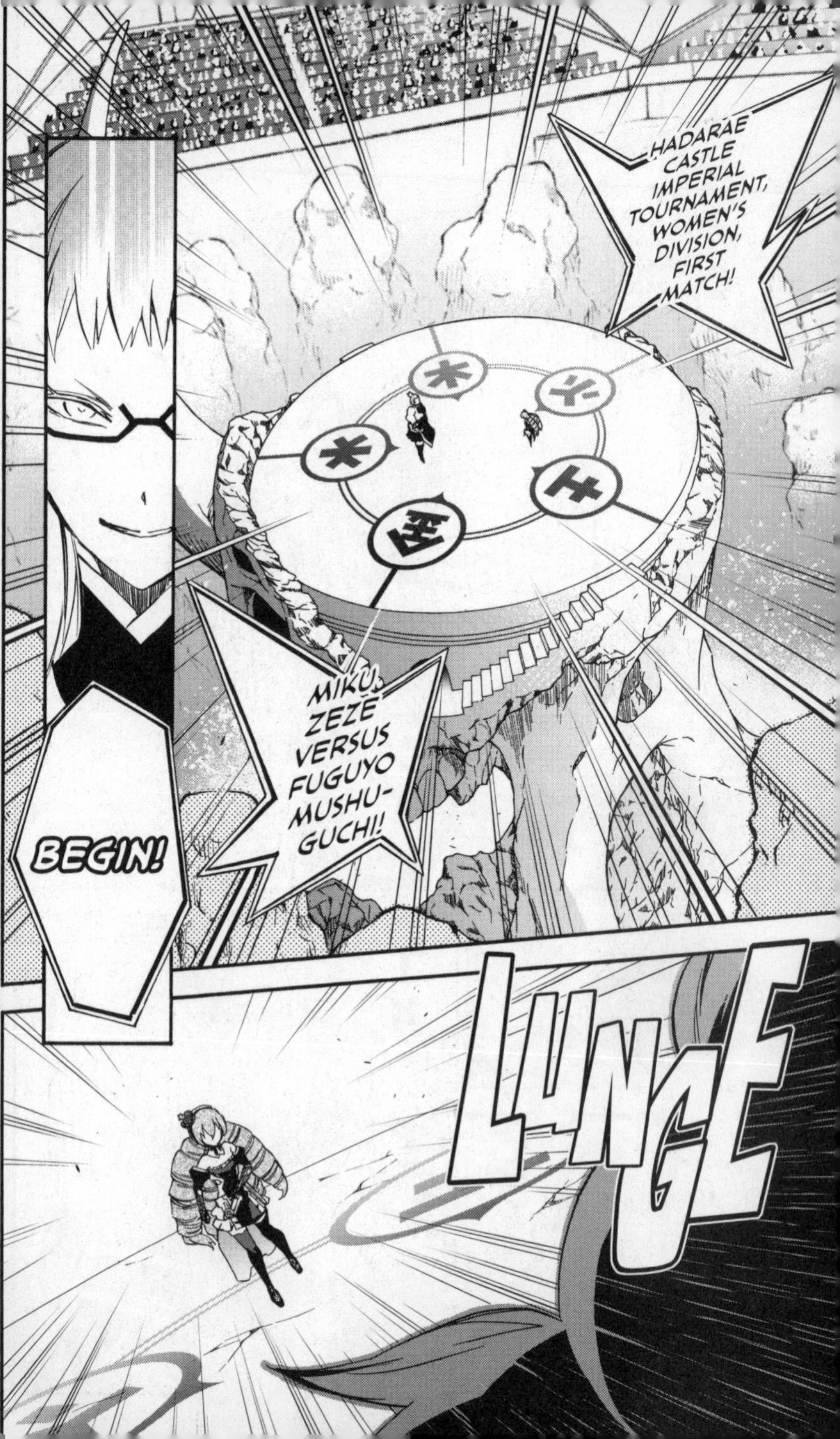
HADARAE CASTLE IMPERIAL TOURNAMENT, WOMEN'S DIVISION, FIRST MATCH!
MIKU ZEZE VERSUS FUGUYO MUSHU-GUCHI!!
LUNGE
BEGIN!

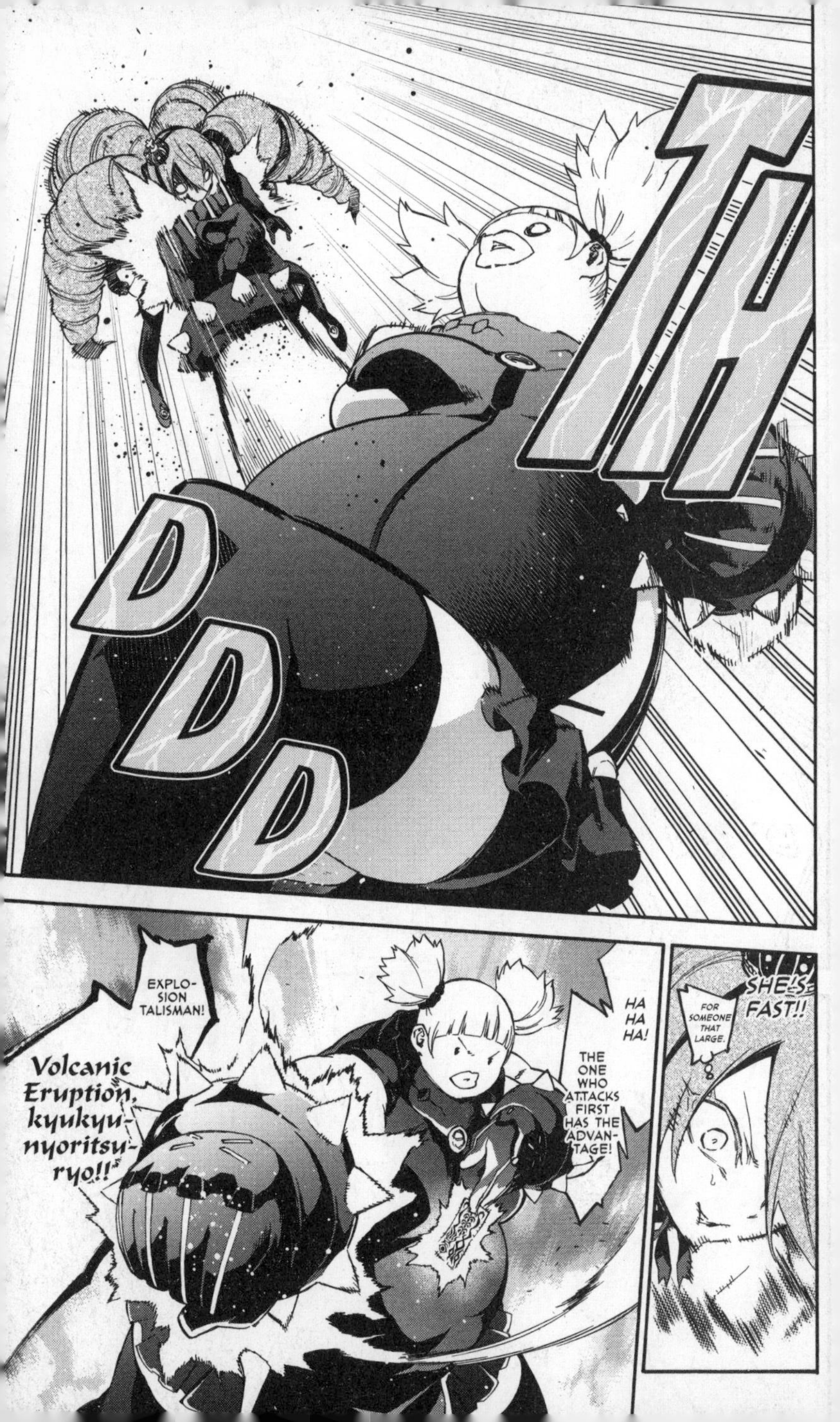
TA
DDD
SHE'S FAST!!
FOR SOMEONE THAT LARGE.
HA HA HA!
THE ONE WHO ATTACKS FIRST HAS THE ADVANTAGE!
EXPLOSION TALISMAN!
Volcanic Eruption, kyukyu-nyoritsu-ryo!!

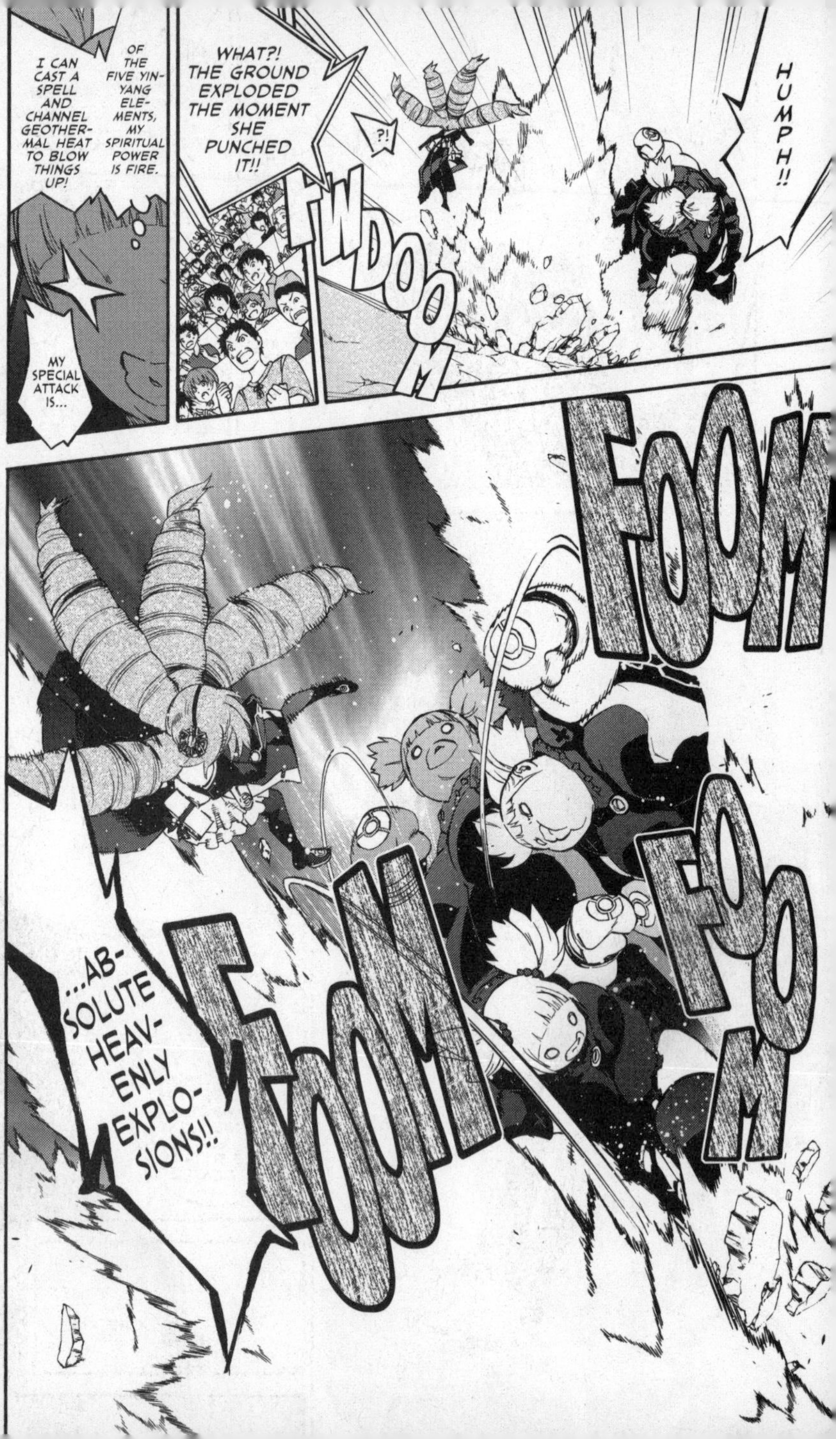

HUMPH!!
FWDOOOM
WHAT?! THE GROUND EXPLODED THE MOMENT SHE PUNCHED IT!!
?!
OF THE FIVE YIN-YANG ELEMENTS, MY SPIRITUAL POWER IS FIRE.
I CAN CAST A SPELL AND CHANNEL GEOTHERMAL HEAT TO BLOW THINGS UP!
MY SPECIAL ATTACK IS...
FOOM
FOOM
FOOM
...ABSOLUTE HEAVENLY EXPLOSIONS!!

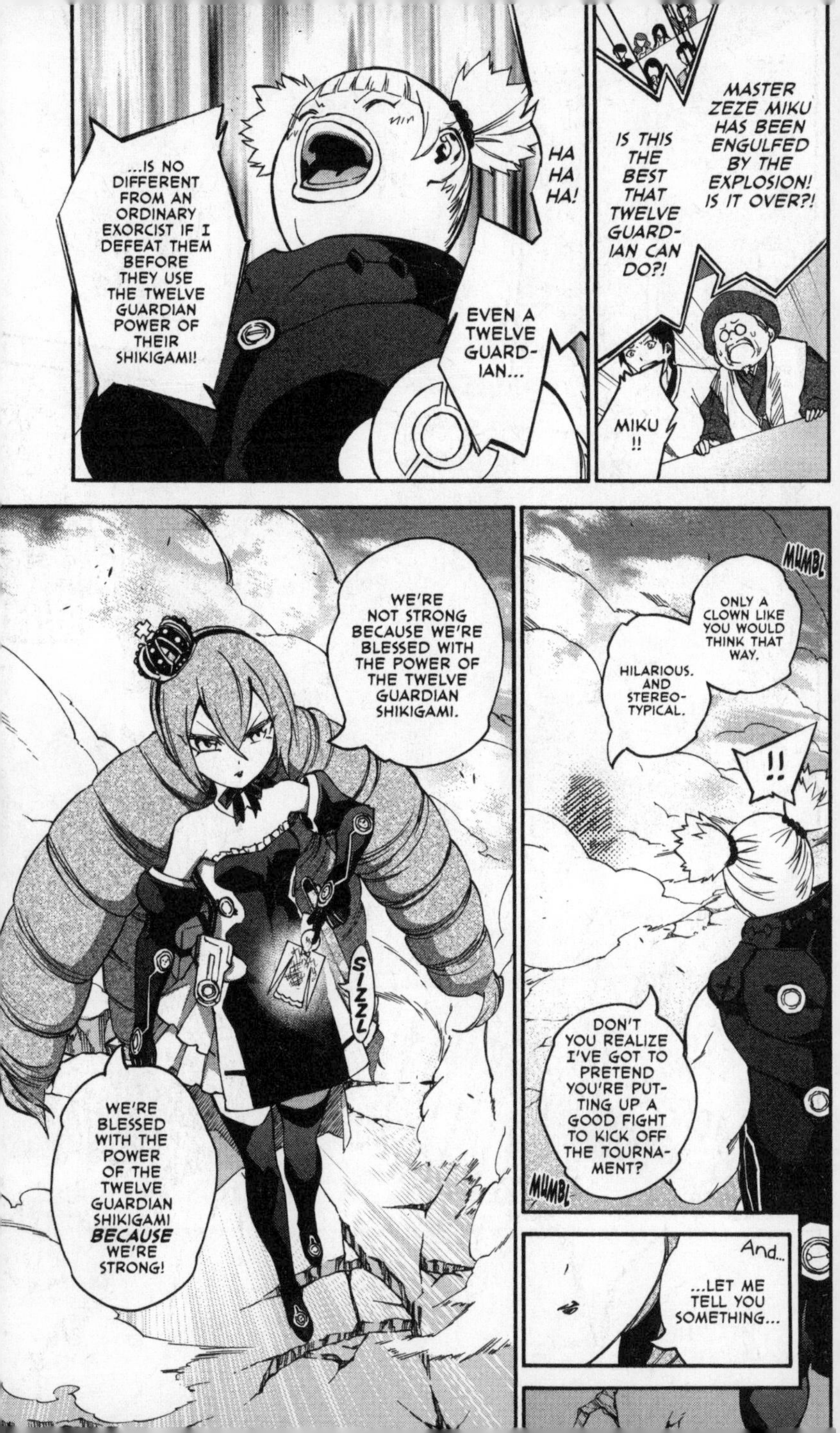
MASTER ZEZE MIKU HAS BEEN ENGULFED BY THE EXPLOSION! IS IT OVER?!
IS THIS THE BEST THAT TWELVE GUARDIAN CAN DO?!
MIKU !!
HA HA HA!
EVEN A TWELVE GUARDIAN...
...IS NO DIFFERENT FROM AN ORDINARY EXORCIST IF I DEFEAT THEM BEFORE THEY USE THE TWELVE GUARDIAN POWER OF THEIR SHIKIGAMI!
MUMBL
ONLY A CLOWN LIKE YOU WOULD THINK THAT WAY.
HILARIOUS. AND STEREOTYPICAL.
!!
DON'T YOU REALIZE I'VE GOT TO PRETEND YOU'RE PUTTING UP A GOOD FIGHT TO KICK OFF THE TOURNAMENT?
MUMBL
And...
...LET ME TELL YOU SOMETHING...
WE'RE NOT STRONG BECAUSE WE'RE BLESSED WITH THE POWER OF THE TWELVE GUARDIAN SHIKIGAMI.
SIZZL
WE'RE BLESSED WITH THE POWER OF THE TWELVE GUARDIAN SHIKIGAMI *BECAUSE* WE'RE STRONG!

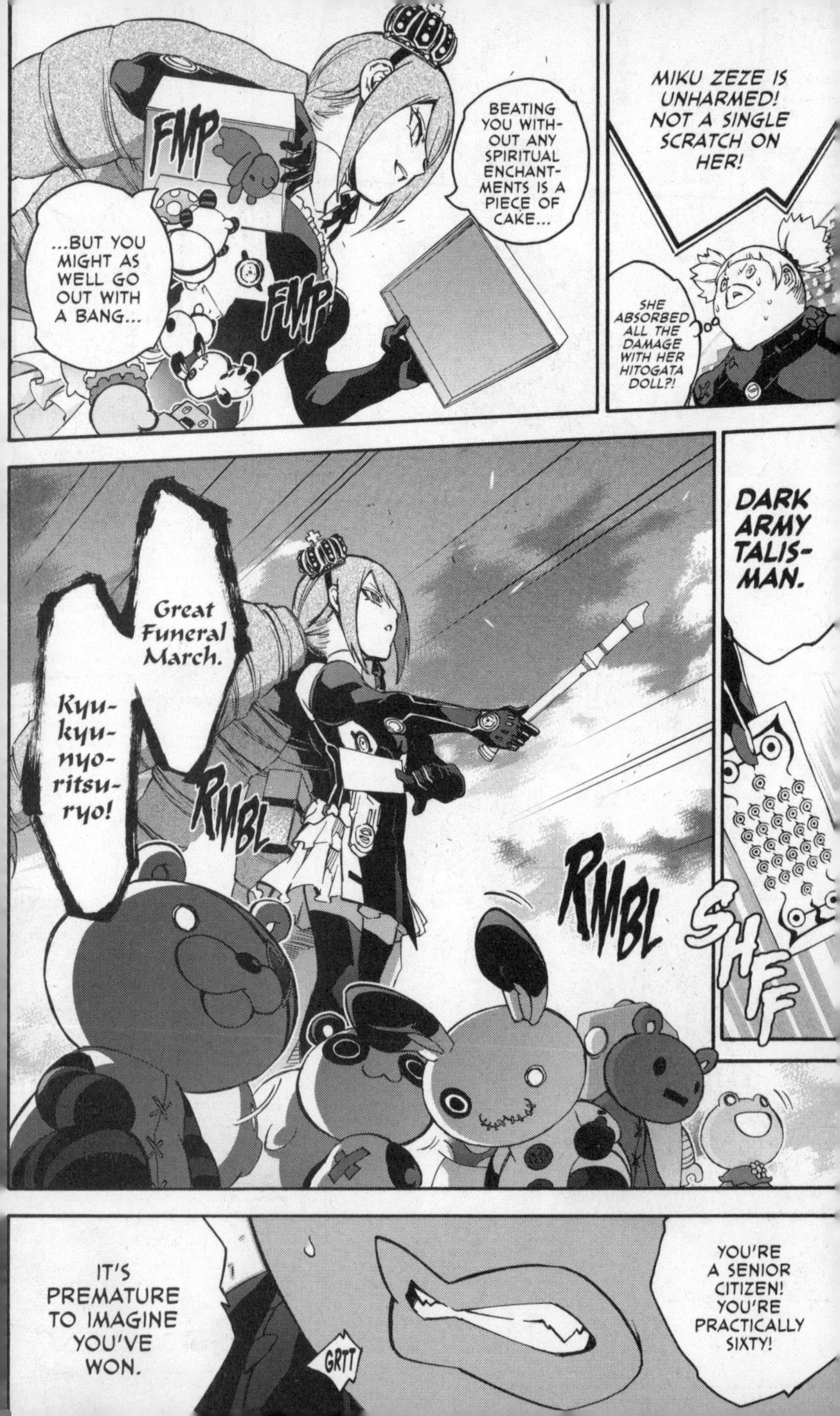
MIKU ZEZE IS UNHARMED! NOT A SINGLE SCRATCH ON HER!
SHE ABSORBED ALL THE DAMAGE WITH HER HITOGATA DOLL?!
BEATING YOU WITHOUT ANY SPIRITUAL ENCHANTMENTS IS A PIECE OF CAKE...
FMP
...BUT YOU MIGHT AS WELL GO OUT WITH A BANG...
FMP
DARK ARMY TALISMAN.
SHF
Great Funeral March.
Kyukyunyoritsuryo!
RMBL
RMBL
YOU'RE A SENIOR CITIZEN! YOU'RE PRACTICALLY SIXTY!
GRTT
IT'S PREMATURE TO IMAGINE YOU'VE WON.

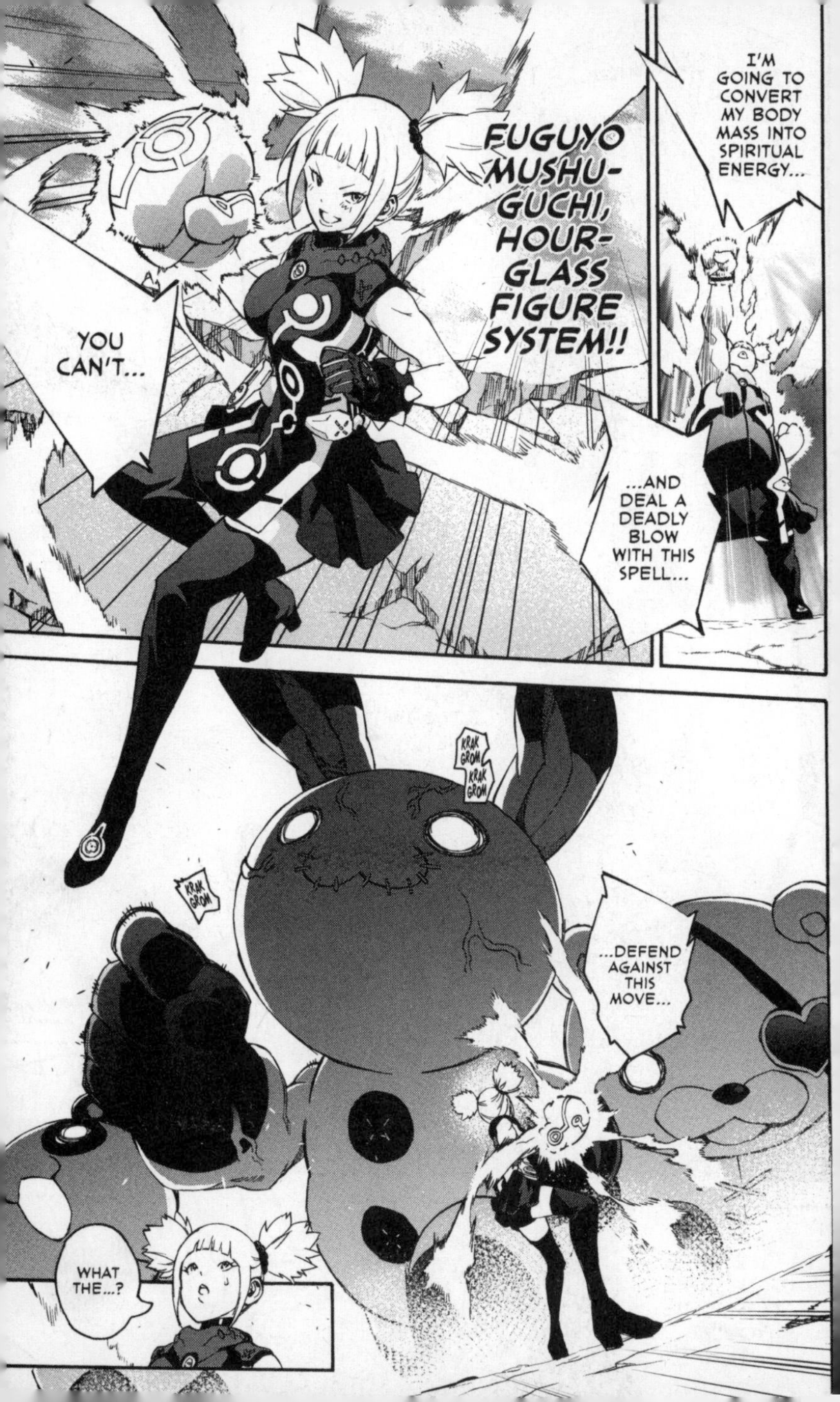

I'M GOING TO CONVERT MY BODY MASS INTO SPIRITUAL ENERGY...
...AND DEAL A DEADLY BLOW WITH THIS SPELL...
FUGUYO MUSHU-GUCHI, HOUR-GLASS FIGURE SYSTEM!!
YOU CAN'T...
KRAK GROM KRAK GROM
...DEFEND AGAINST THIS MOVE...
KRAK GROM
WHAT THE...?

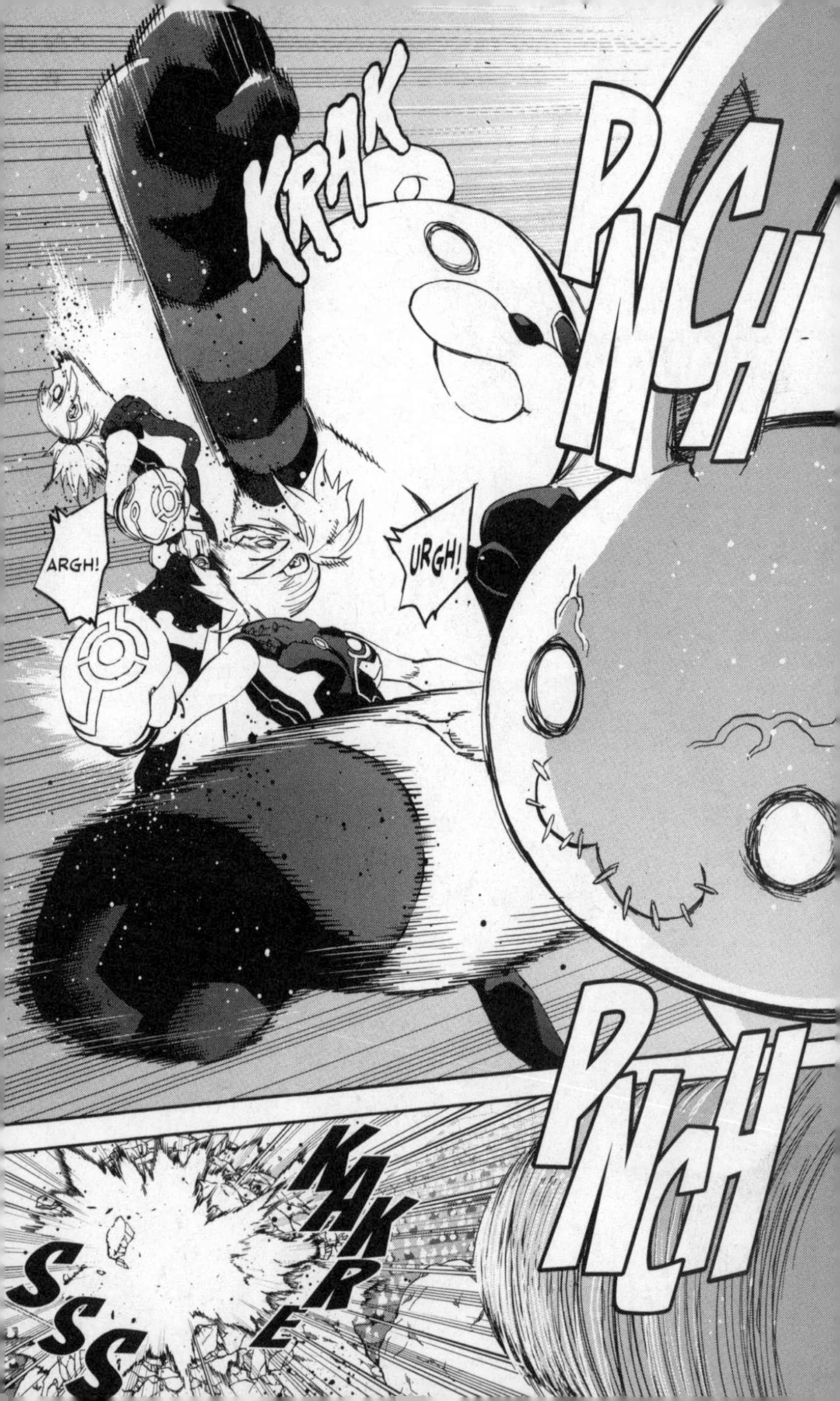
PNCH
KRAK
URGH!
ARGH!
PNCH
SSS

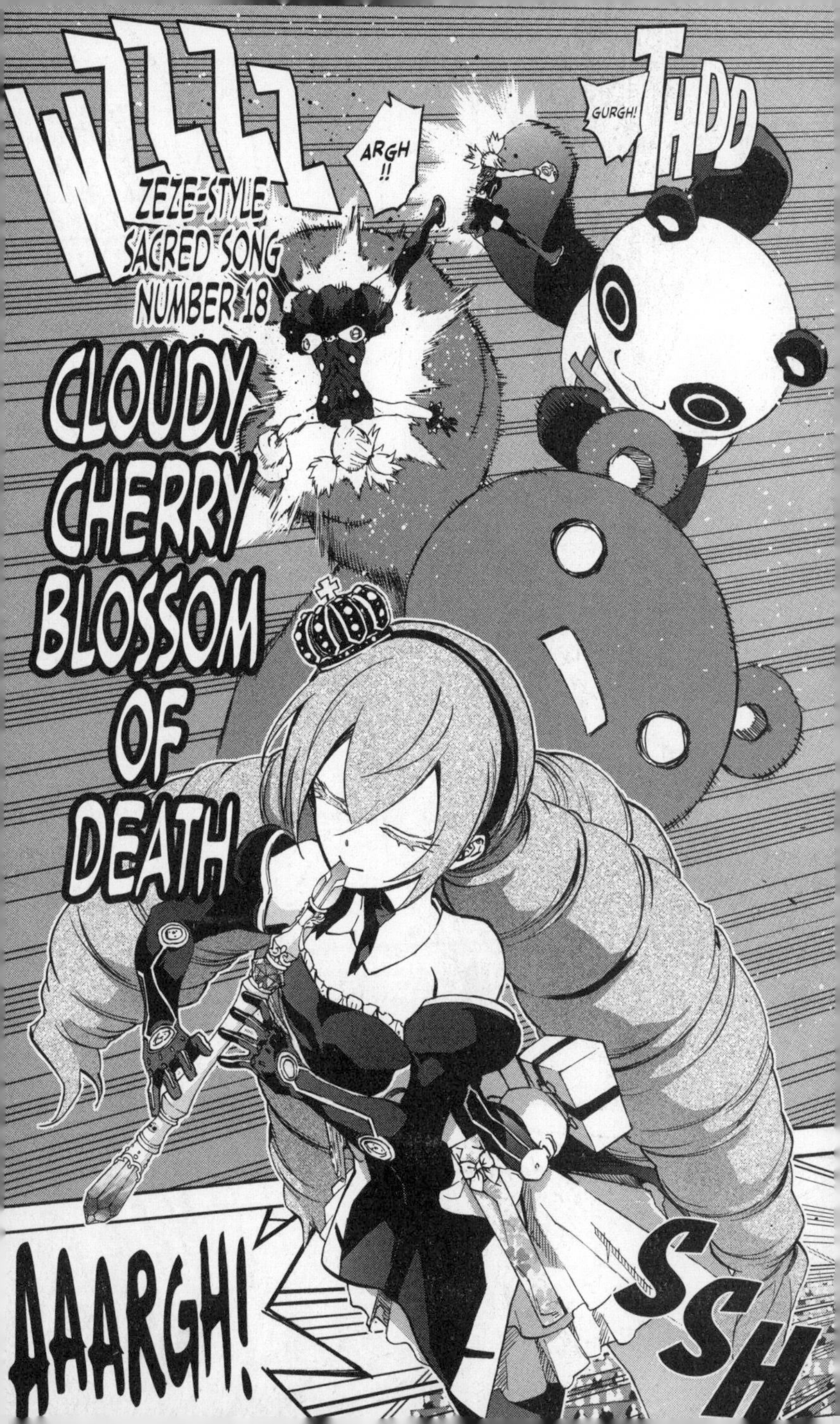
THDD
GURGH!
ARGH!!
WZZZZZ
ZEZE-STYLE SACRED SONG NUMBER 18
CLOUDY CHERRY BLOSSOM OF DEATH
SSH
AAARGH!

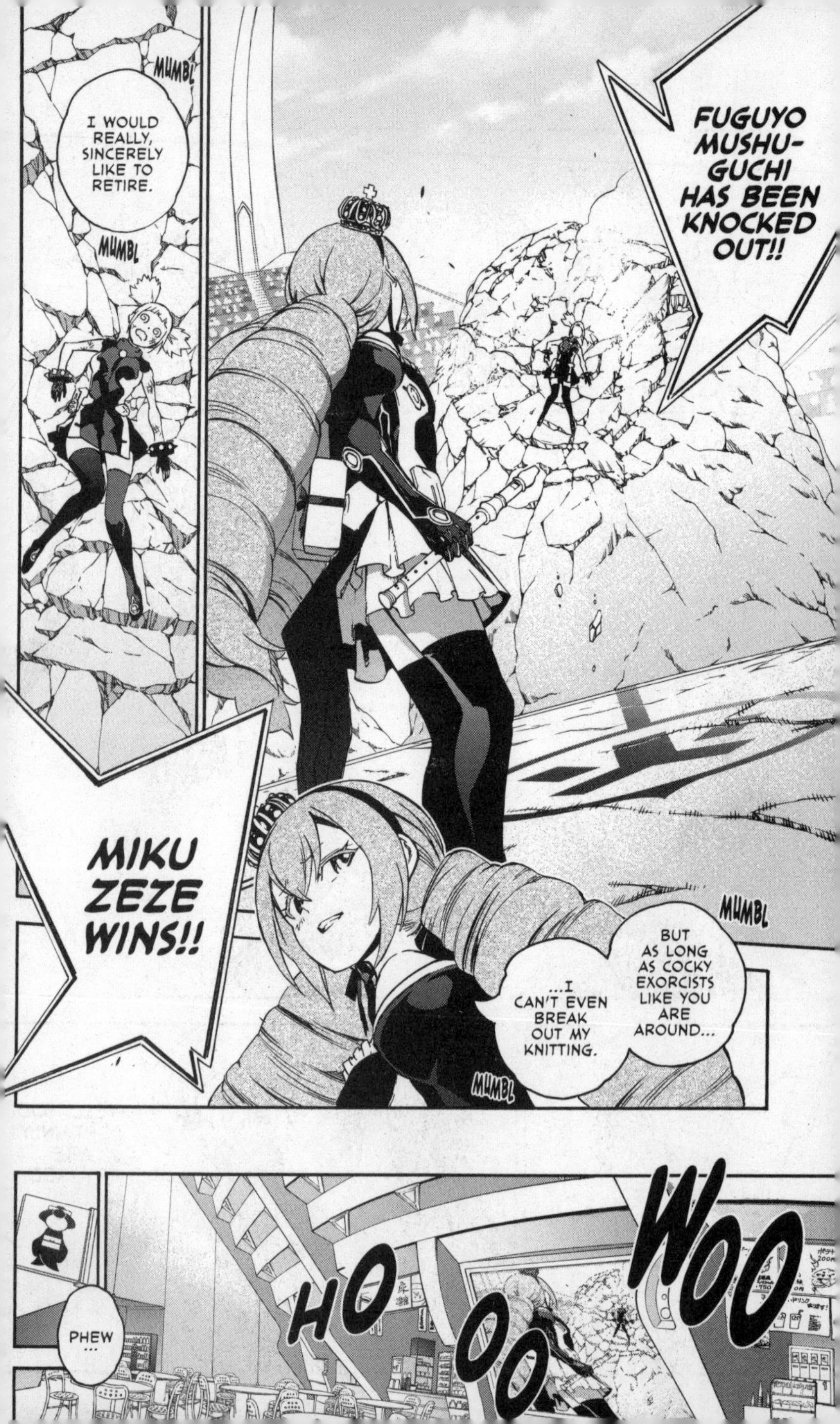
FUGUYO MUSHU-GUCHI HAS BEEN KNOCKED OUT!!
MUMBL
I WOULD REALLY, SINCERELY LIKE TO RETIRE.
MUMBL
MIKU ZEZE WINS!!
MUMBL
BUT AS LONG AS COCKY EXORCISTS LIKE YOU ARE AROUND...
...I CAN'T EVEN BREAK OUT MY KNITTING.
MUMBL
WOO
HOOOOO
PHEW...

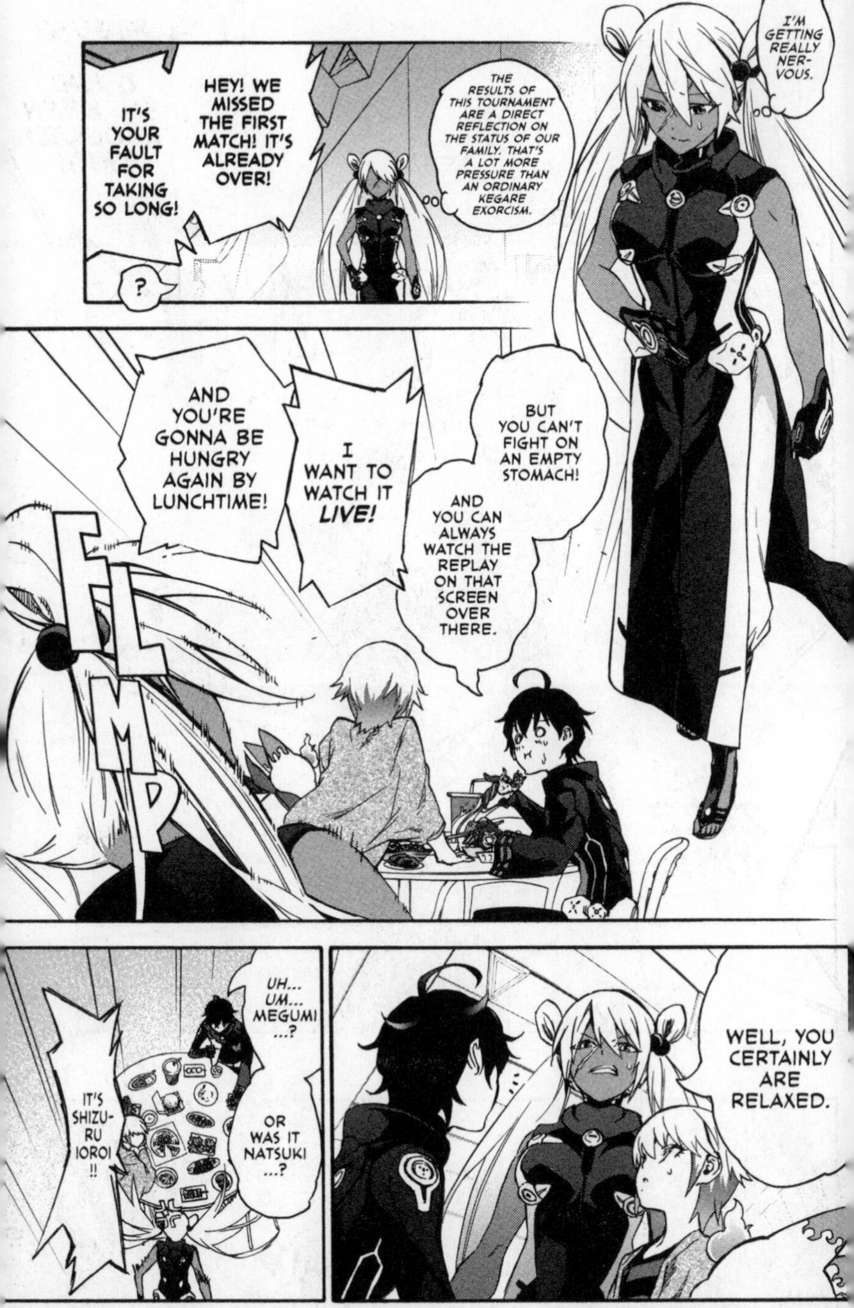
I'M GETTING REALLY NER-VOUS.
THE RESULTS OF THIS TOURNAMENT ARE A DIRECT REFLECTION ON THE STATUS OF OUR FAMILY. THAT'S A LOT MORE PRESSURE THAN AN ORDINARY KEGARE EXORCISM.
HEY! WE MISSED THE FIRST MATCH! IT'S ALREADY OVER!
IT'S YOUR FAULT FOR TAKING SO LONG!
?
BUT YOU CAN'T FIGHT ON AN EMPTY STOMACH!
AND YOU CAN ALWAYS WATCH THE REPLAY ON THAT SCREEN OVER THERE.
I WANT TO WATCH IT *LIVE!*
AND YOU'RE GONNA BE HUNGRY AGAIN BY LUNCHTIME!
FLMP
WELL, YOU CERTAINLY ARE RELAXED.
UH... UM... MEGUMI ...?
OR WAS IT NATSUKI ...?
IT'S SHIZU-RU IOROI !!

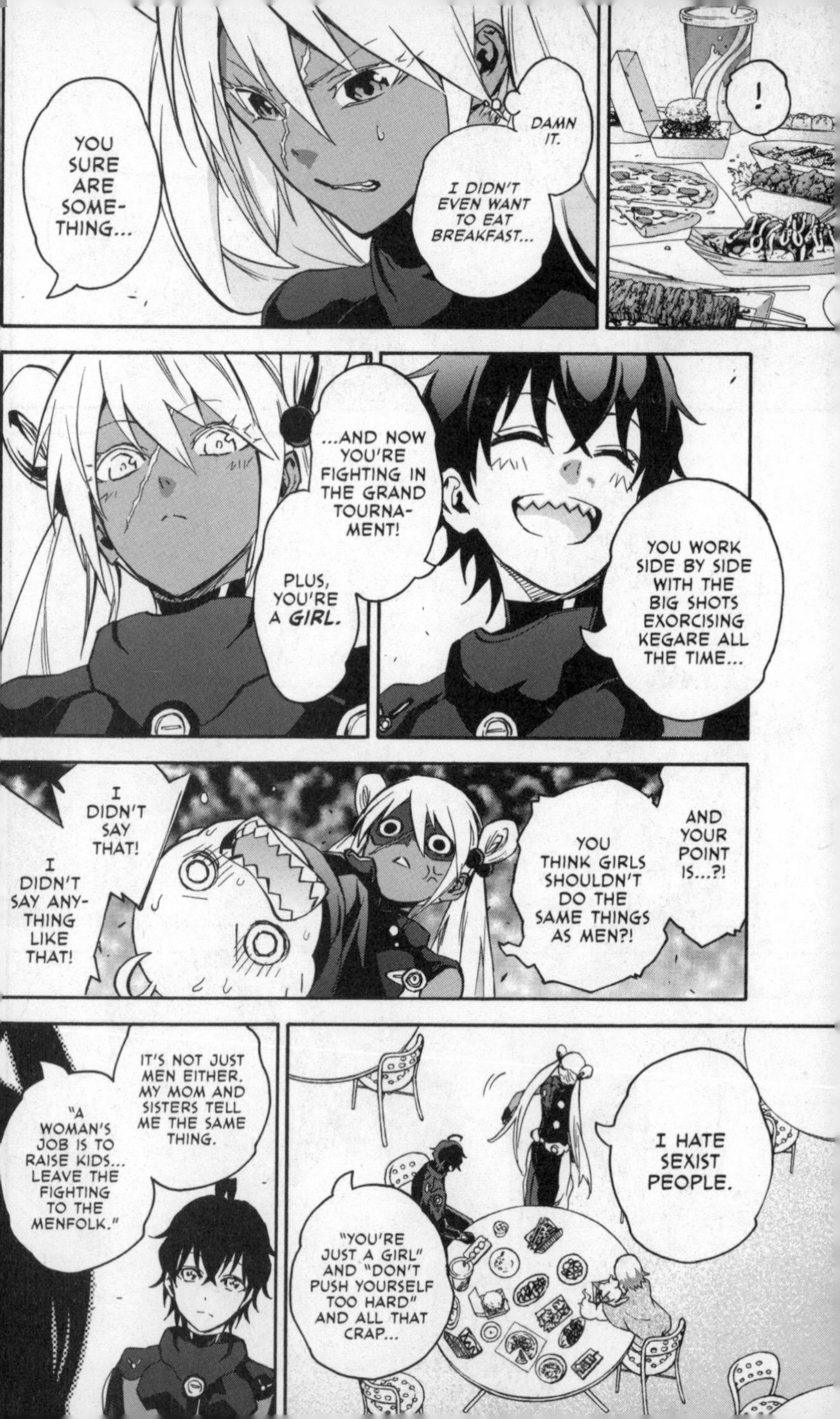
!
DAMN IT.
I DIDN'T EVEN WANT TO EAT BREAKFAST...
YOU SURE ARE SOME-THING...
YOU WORK SIDE BY SIDE WITH THE BIG SHOTS EXORCISING KEGARE ALL THE TIME...
...AND NOW YOU'RE FIGHTING IN THE GRAND TOURNA-MENT!
PLUS, YOU'RE A *GIRL.*
AND YOUR POINT IS...?!
YOU THINK GIRLS SHOULDN'T DO THE SAME THINGS AS MEN?!
I DIDN'T SAY THAT!
I DIDN'T SAY ANY-THING LIKE THAT!
I HATE SEXIST PEOPLE.
"YOU'RE JUST A GIRL" AND "DON'T PUSH YOURSELF TOO HARD" AND ALL THAT CRAP...
IT'S NOT JUST MEN EITHER. MY MOM AND SISTERS TELL ME THE SAME THING.
"A WOMAN'S JOB IS TO RAISE KIDS... LEAVE THE FIGHTING TO THE MENFOLK."

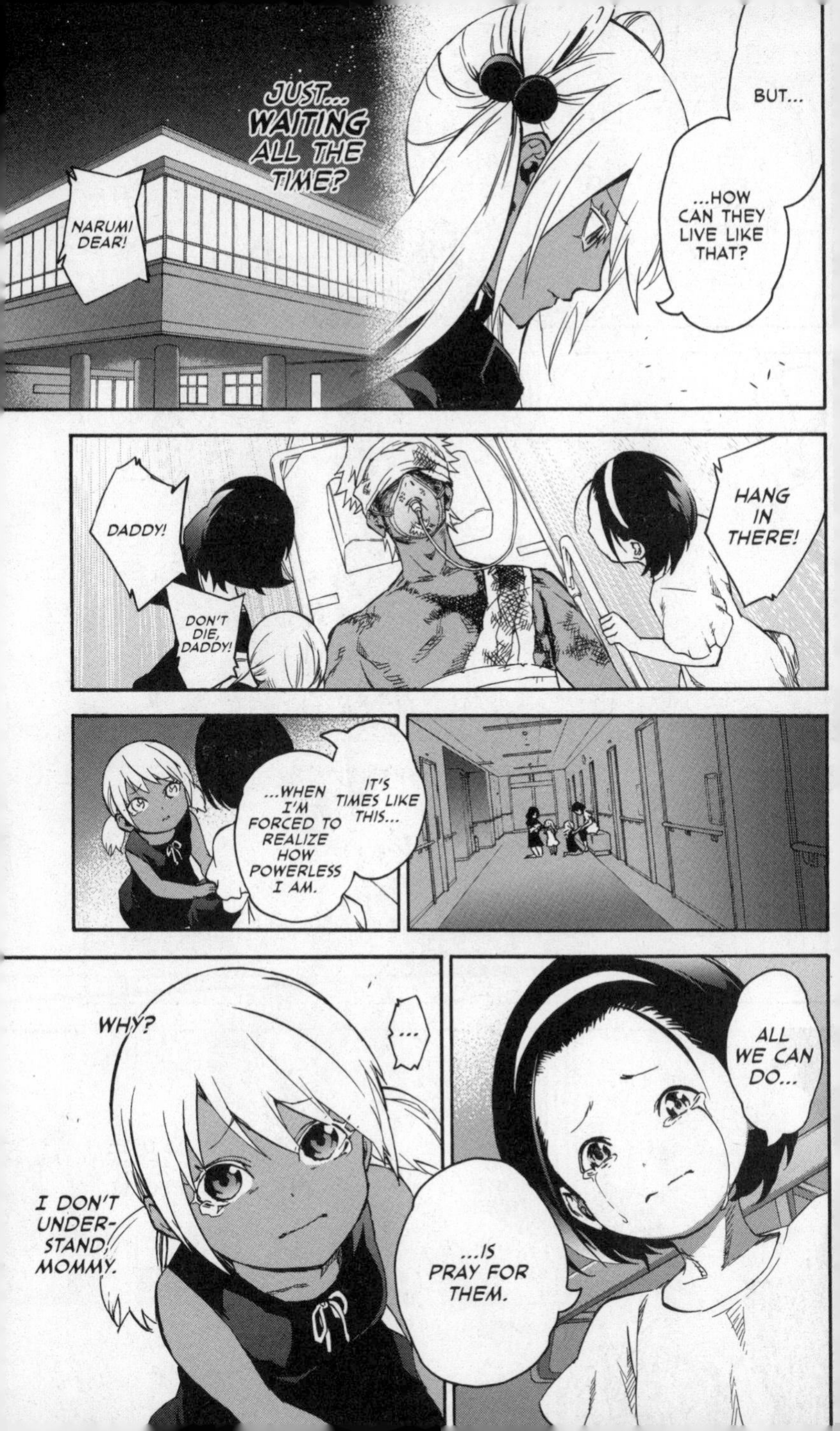
BUT...
...HOW CAN THEY LIVE LIKE THAT?
JUST... WAITING ALL THE TIME?
NARUMI DEAR!
HANG IN THERE!
DADDY!
DON'T DIE, DADDY!
IT'S TIMES LIKE THIS...
...WHEN I'M FORCED TO REALIZE HOW POWERLESS I AM.
ALL WE CAN DO...
...IS PRAY FOR THEM.
...
WHY?
I DON'T UNDER-STAND, MOMMY.

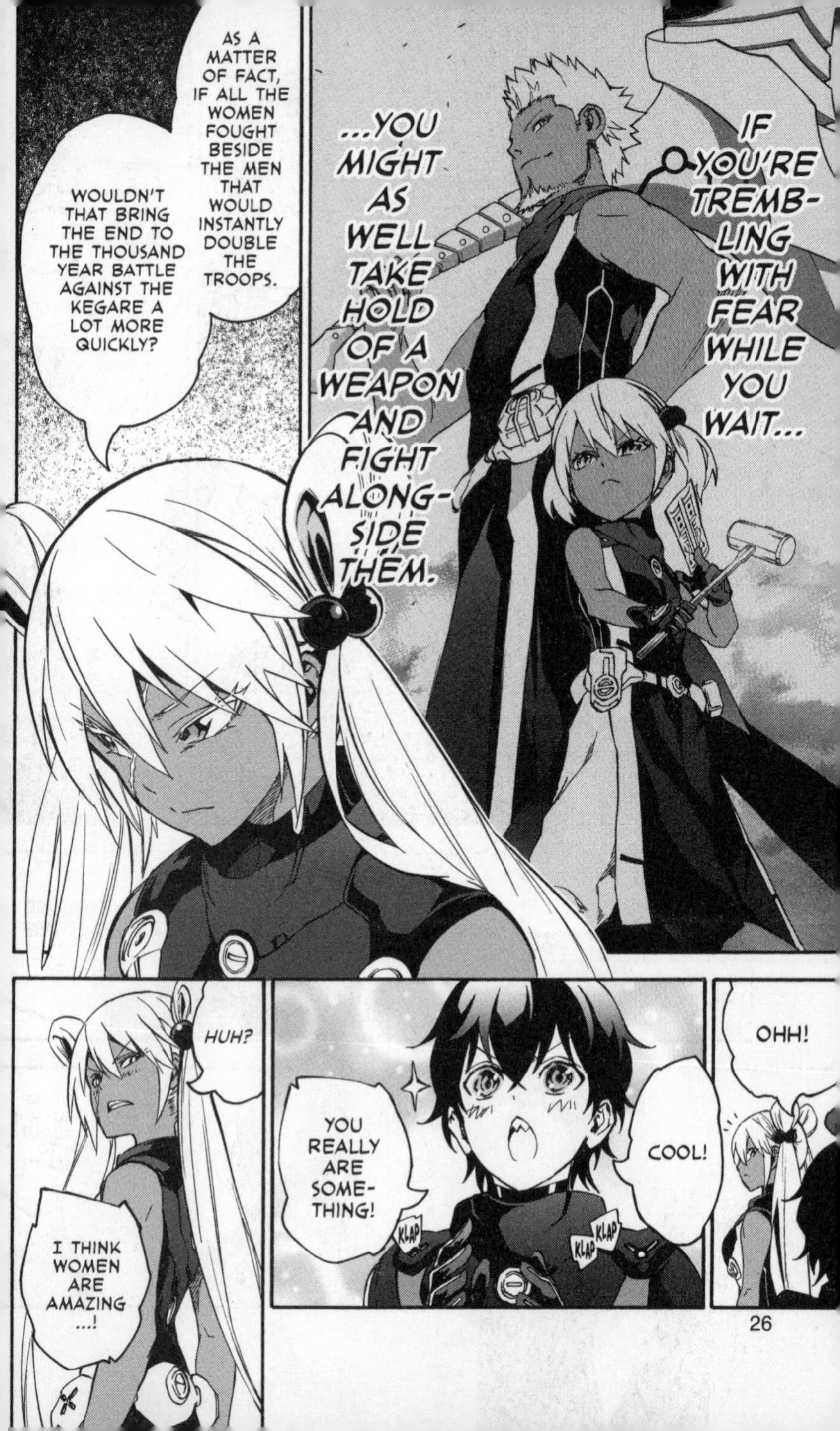
IF YOU'RE TREMBLING WITH FEAR WHILE YOU WAIT...
...YOU MIGHT AS WELL TAKE HOLD OF A WEAPON AND FIGHT ALONGSIDE THEM.
AS A MATTER OF FACT, IF ALL THE WOMEN FOUGHT BESIDE THE MEN THAT WOULD INSTANTLY DOUBLE THE TROOPS.
WOULDN'T THAT BRING THE END TO THE THOUSAND YEAR BATTLE AGAINST THE KEGARE A LOT MORE QUICKLY?
OHH!
COOL!
YOU REALLY ARE SOMETHING!
KLAP
KLAP
KLAP
HUH?
I THINK WOMEN ARE AMAZING ...!

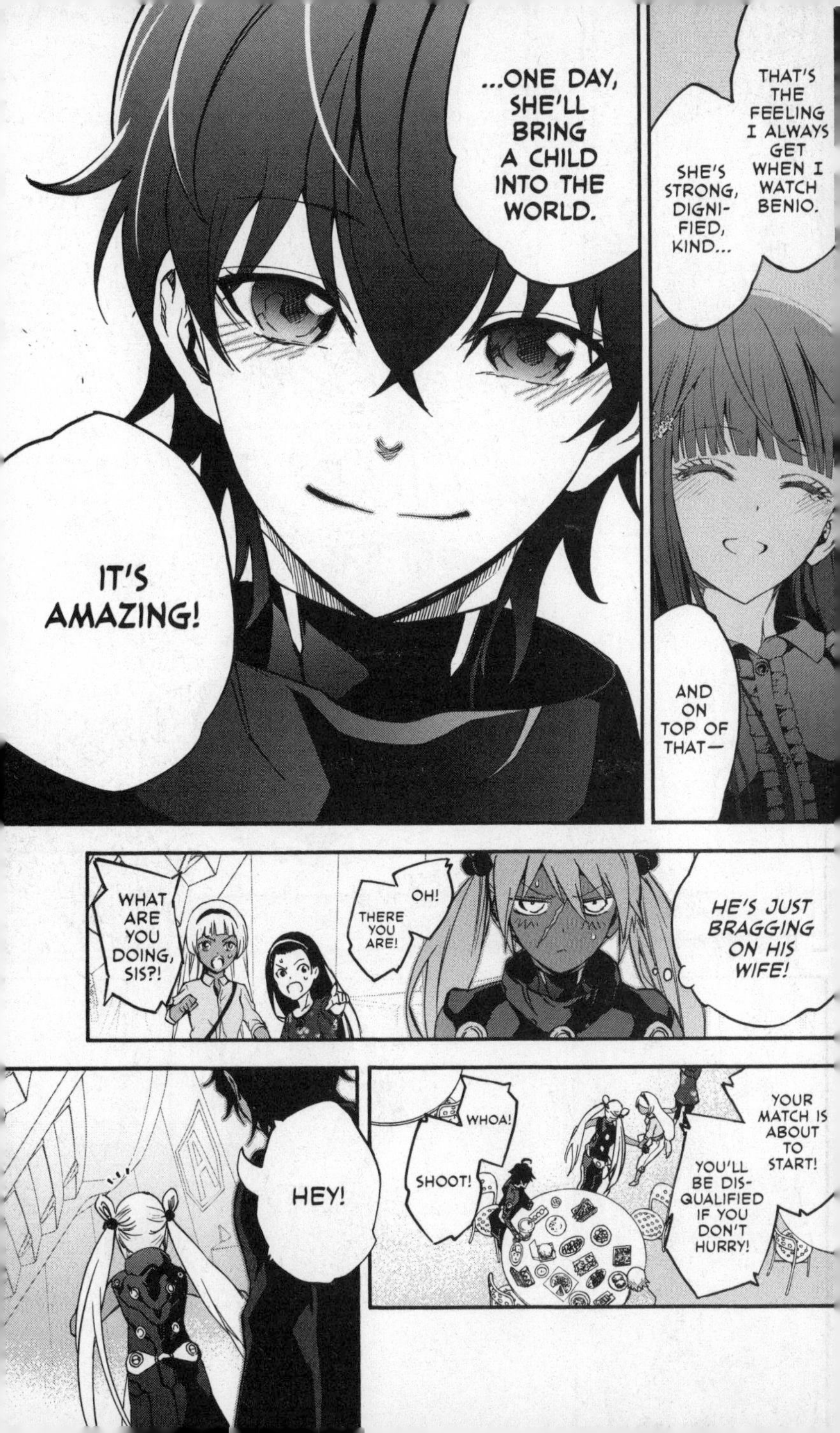
THAT'S THE FEELING I ALWAYS GET WHEN I WATCH BENIO.
SHE'S STRONG, DIGNIFIED, KIND...
AND ON TOP OF THAT—
...ONE DAY, SHE'LL BRING A CHILD INTO THE WORLD.
IT'S AMAZING!
HE'S JUST BRAGGING ON HIS WIFE!
OH! THERE YOU ARE!
WHAT ARE YOU DOING, SIS?!
YOUR MATCH IS ABOUT TO START!
YOU'LL BE DISQUALIFIED IF YOU DON'T HURRY!
SHOOT!
WHOA!
HEY!

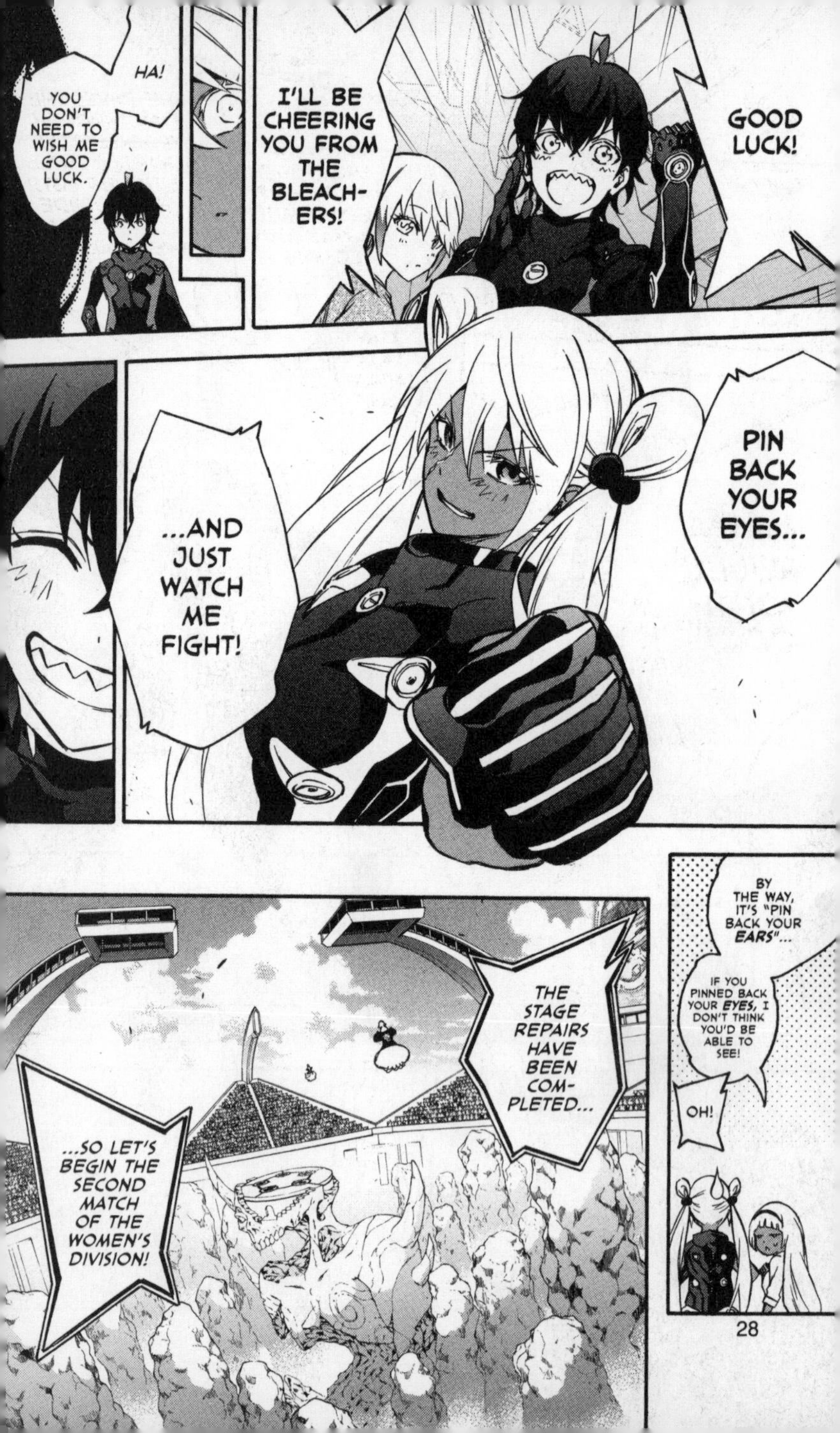
GOOD LUCK!
I'LL BE CHEERING YOU FROM THE BLEACHERS!
HA!
YOU DON'T NEED TO WISH ME GOOD LUCK.
PIN BACK YOUR EYES...
...AND JUST WATCH ME FIGHT!
BY THE WAY, IT'S "PIN BACK YOUR *EARS*"...
IF YOU PINNED BACK YOUR *EYES*, I DON'T THINK YOU'D BE ABLE TO SEE!
OH!
THE STAGE REPAIRS HAVE BEEN COMPLETED...
...SO LET'S BEGIN THE SECOND MATCH OF THE WOMEN'S DIVISION!

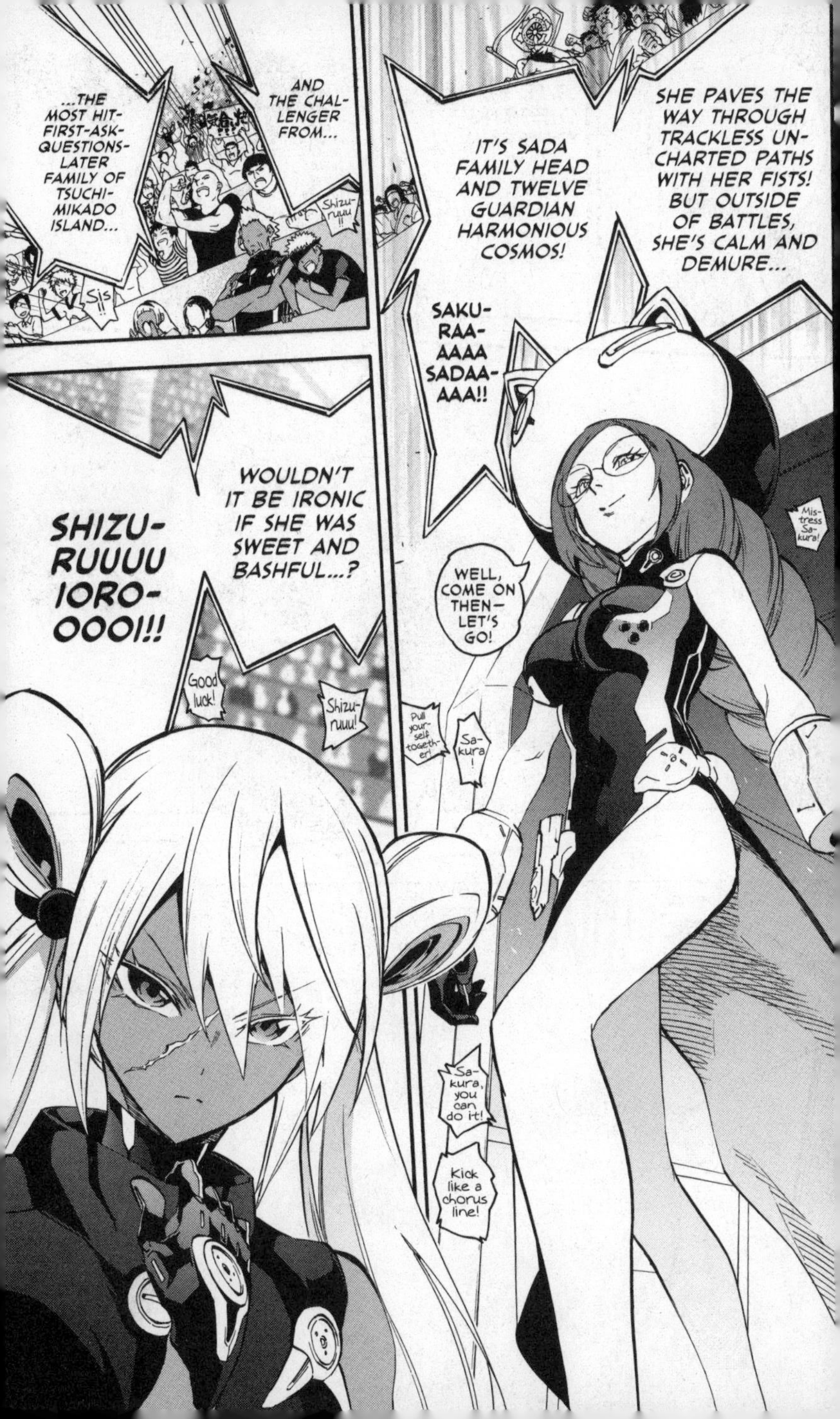
SHE PAVES THE WAY THROUGH TRACKLESS UNCHARTED PATHS WITH HER FISTS! BUT OUTSIDE OF BATTLES, SHE'S CALM AND DEMURE...
IT'S SADA FAMILY HEAD AND TWELVE GUARDIAN HARMONIOUS COSMOS!
SAKURAAAAAA SADAAAAA!!
Mistress Sakura!
WELL, COME ON THEN—LET'S GO!
Sakura!
Pull yourself together!
Sakura, you can do it!
Kick like a chorus line!
AND THE CHALLENGER FROM...
...THE MOST HIT-FIRST-ASK-QUESTIONS-LATER FAMILY OF TSUCHIMIKADO ISLAND...
Shizuruuu!!
Sis!!
WOULDN'T IT BE IRONIC IF SHE WAS SWEET AND BASHFUL...?
SHIZURUUUU IOROOOOI!!
Shizuruuu!
Good luck!

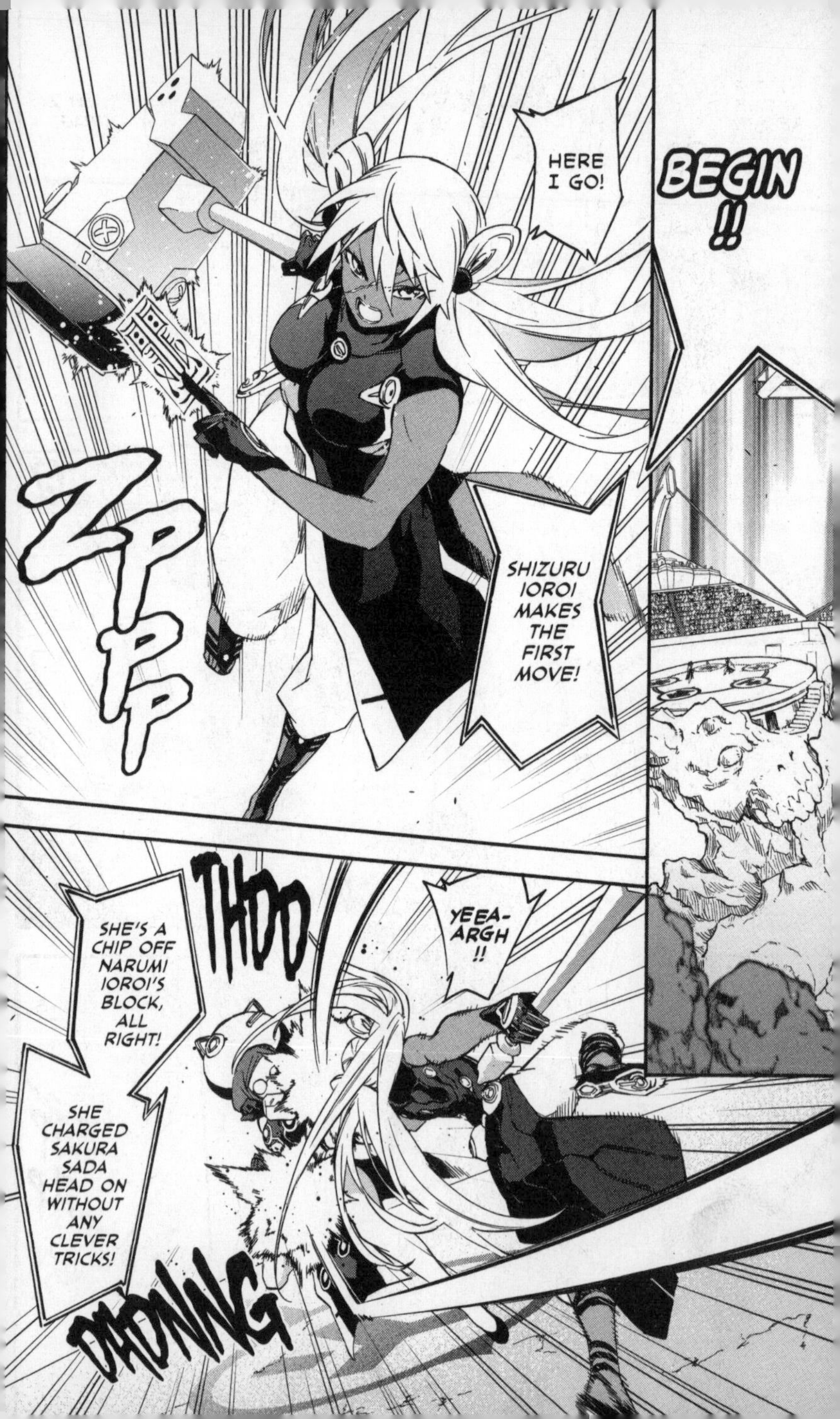

BEGIN !!
HERE I GO!
SHIZURU IOROI MAKES THE FIRST MOVE!
ZIPPP
YEEA-ARGH !!
THDD
SHE'S A CHIP OFF NARUMI IOROI'S BLOCK, ALL RIGHT!
SHE CHARGED SAKURA SADA HEAD ON WITHOUT ANY CLEVER TRICKS!
DADNNG

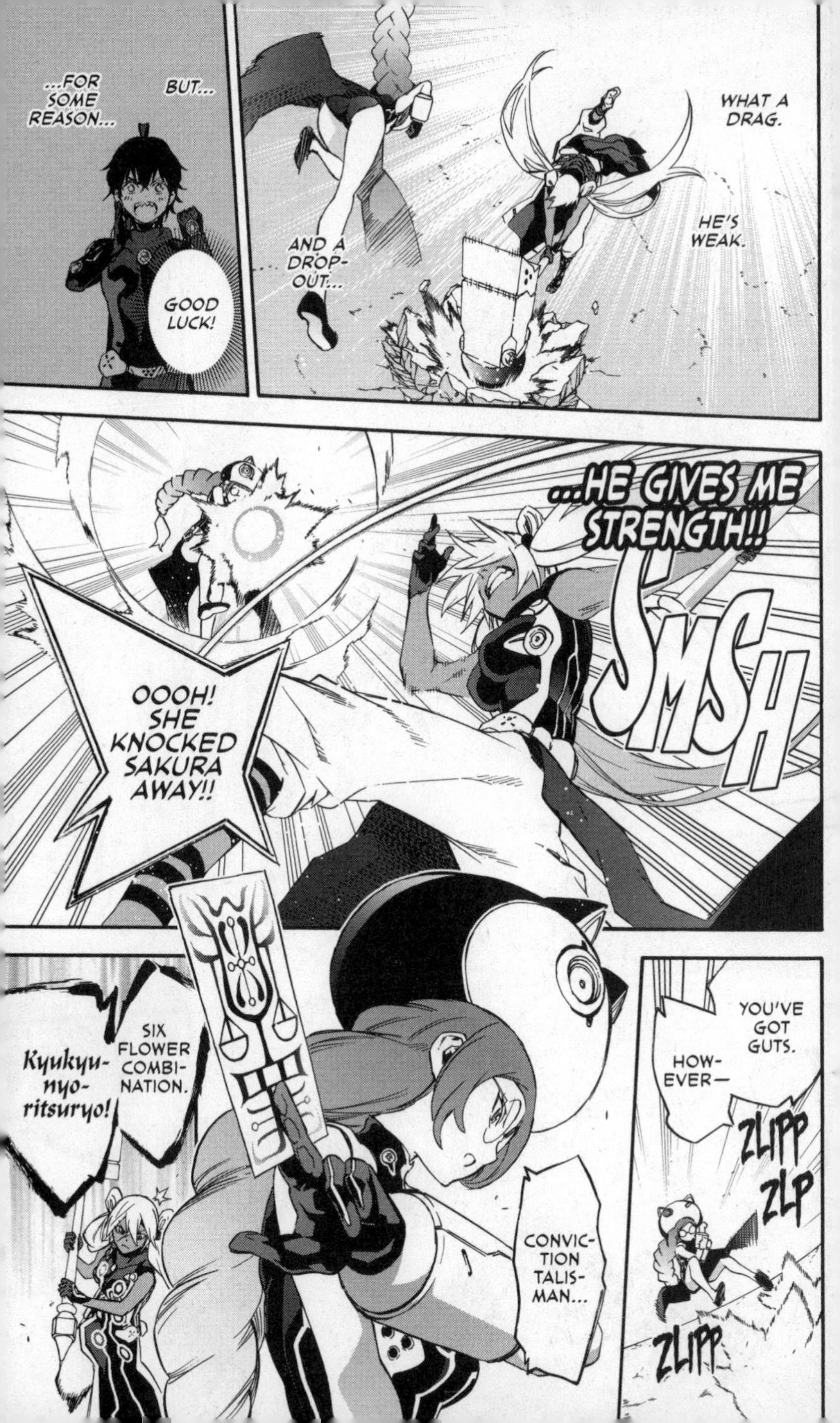
WHAT A DRAG.
HE'S WEAK.
AND A DROP-OUT...
BUT...
...FOR SOME REASON...
GOOD LUCK!
...HE GIVES ME STRENGTH!!
SMSH
OOOH! SHE KNOCKED SAKURA AWAY!!
YOU'VE GOT GUTS.
HOW-EVER—
ZLIPP
ZLP
ZLIPP
SIX FLOWER COMBI-NATION.
Kyukyu-nyo-ritsuryo!
CONVIC-TION TALIS-MAN...

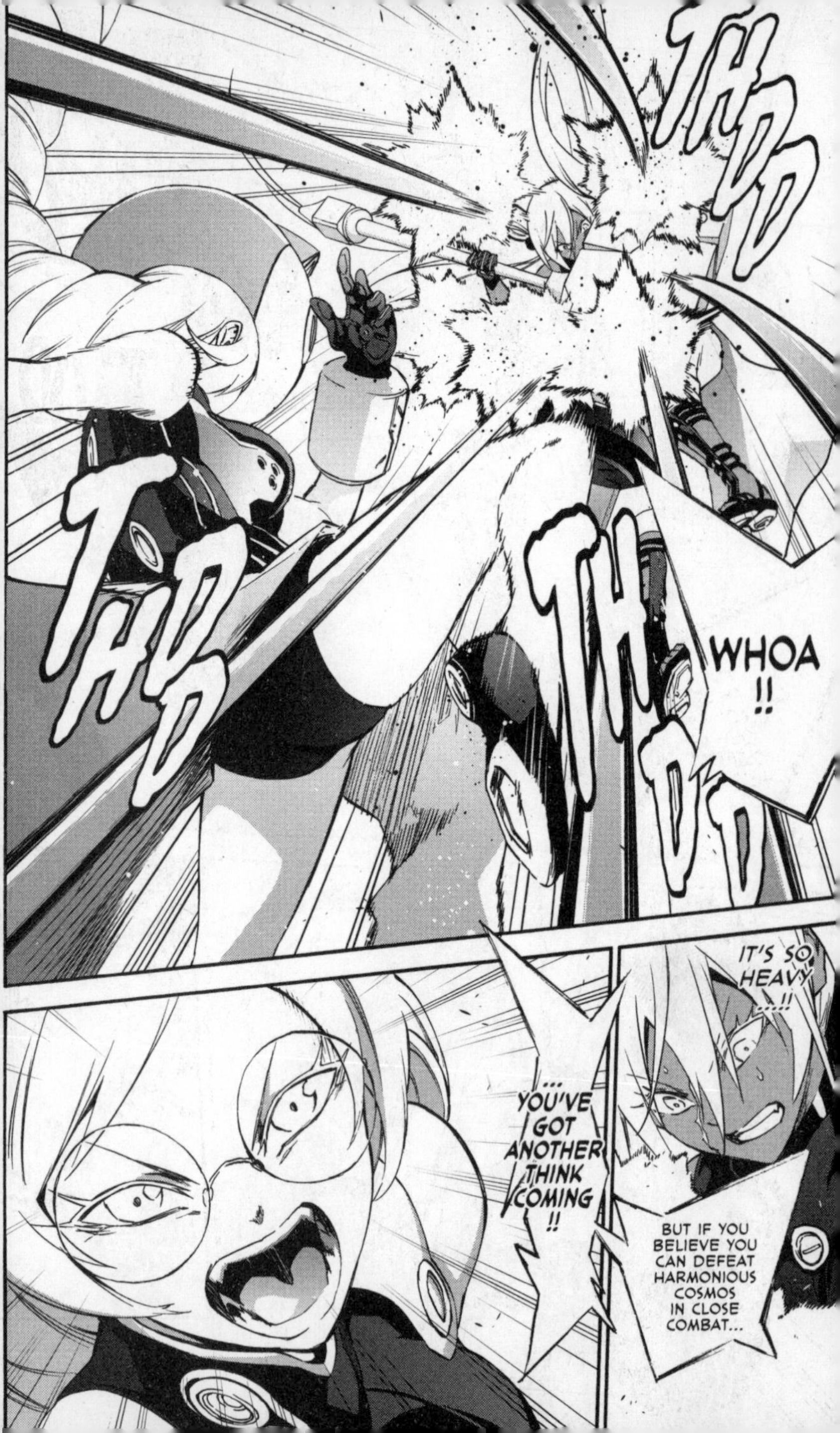
THUD
WHOA!!
THUD
THUD
IT'S SO HEAVY...!!
BUT IF YOU BELIEVE YOU CAN DEFEAT HARMONIOUS COSMOS IN CLOSE COMBAT...
...YOU'VE GOT ANOTHER THINK COMING!!

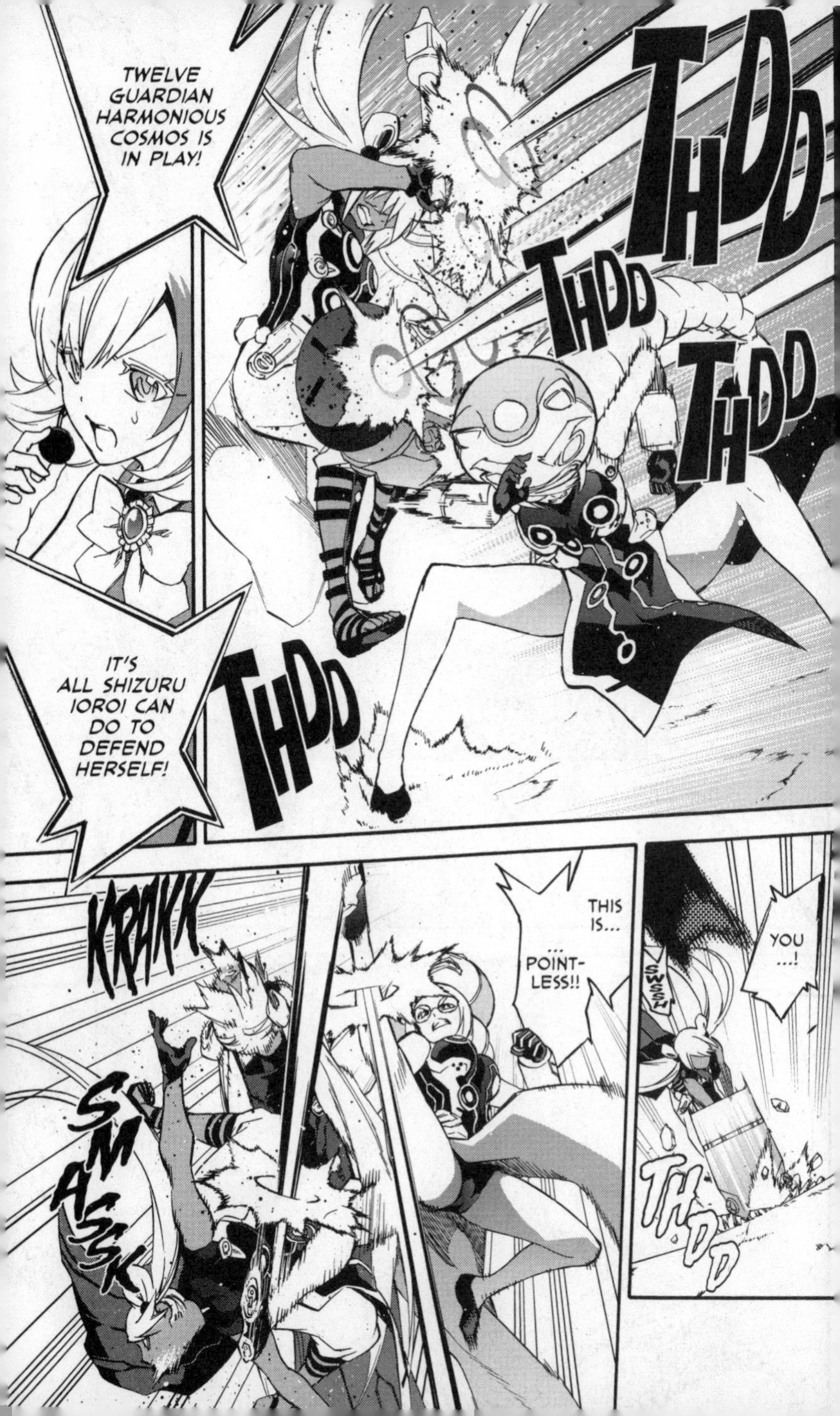
THDD
THDD
THDD
THDD
TWELVE GUARDIAN HARMONIOUS COSMOS IS IN PLAY!
IT'S ALL SHIZURU IOROI CAN DO TO DEFEND HERSELF!
THDD
YOU ...!
SWSSH
THDD
THIS IS...
...POINTLESS!!
KRAKK
SMASSK

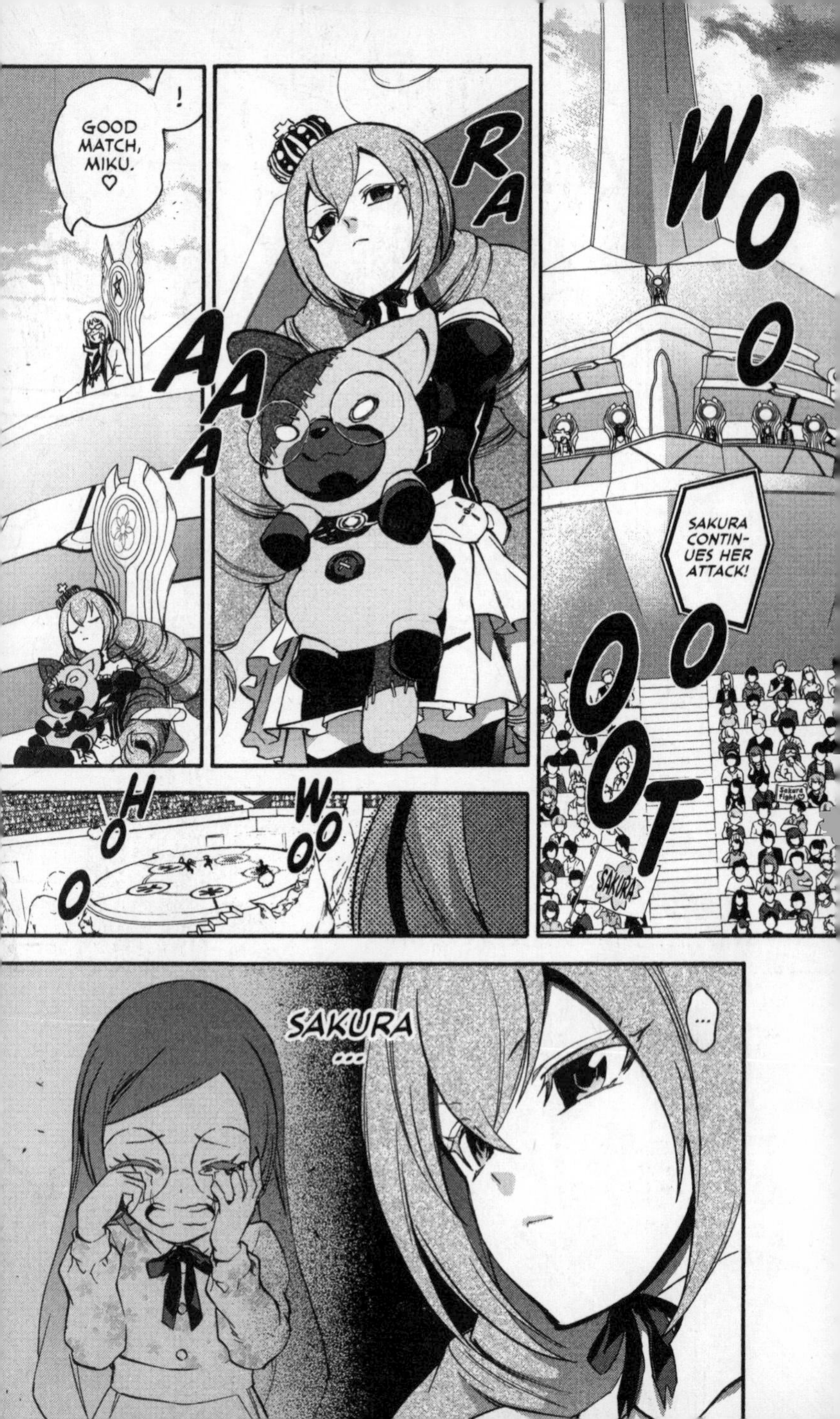
WOOOOOOOOT
SAKURA CONTIN-UES HER ATTACK!
Sakura Fight♡
SAKURA
RAAAA
!
GOOD MATCH, MIKU. ♡
WOOO
HOOO
...
SAKURA ...

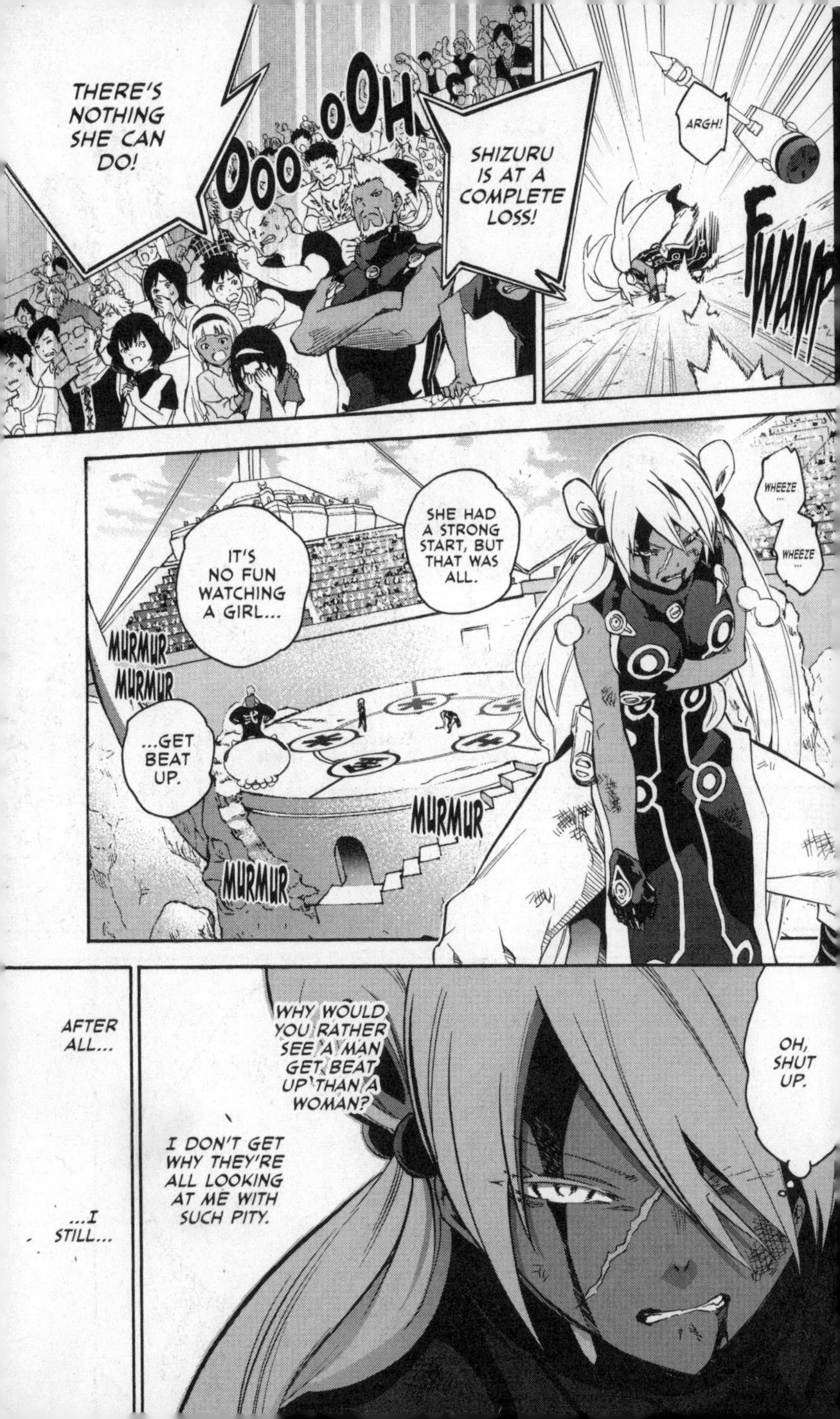
ARGH!
FWUMP
SHIZURU IS AT A COMPLETE LOSS!
OOOOOOH
THERE'S NOTHING SHE CAN DO!
WHEEZE...
WHEEZE...
SHE HAD A STRONG START, BUT THAT WAS ALL.
IT'S NO FUN WATCHING A GIRL...
MURMUR
MURMUR
...GET BEAT UP.
MURMUR
MURMUR
OH, SHUT UP.
WHY WOULD YOU RATHER SEE A MAN GET BEAT UP THAN A WOMAN?
I DON'T GET WHY THEY'RE ALL LOOKING AT ME WITH SUCH PITY.
AFTER ALL...
...I STILL...

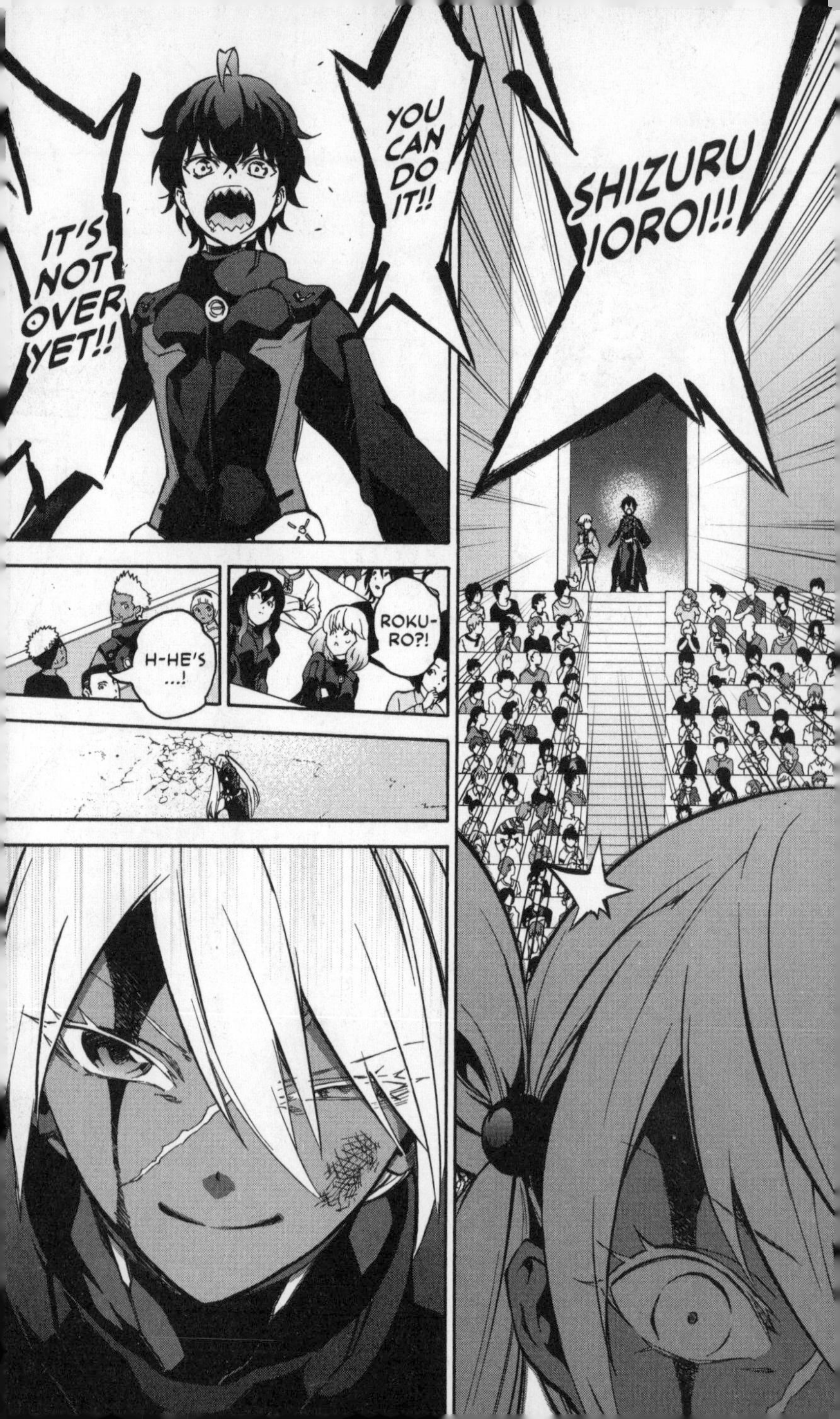
SHIZURU IOROI!!
YOU CAN DO IT!!
IT'S NOT OVER YET!!
ROKU-RO?!
H-HE'S ...!

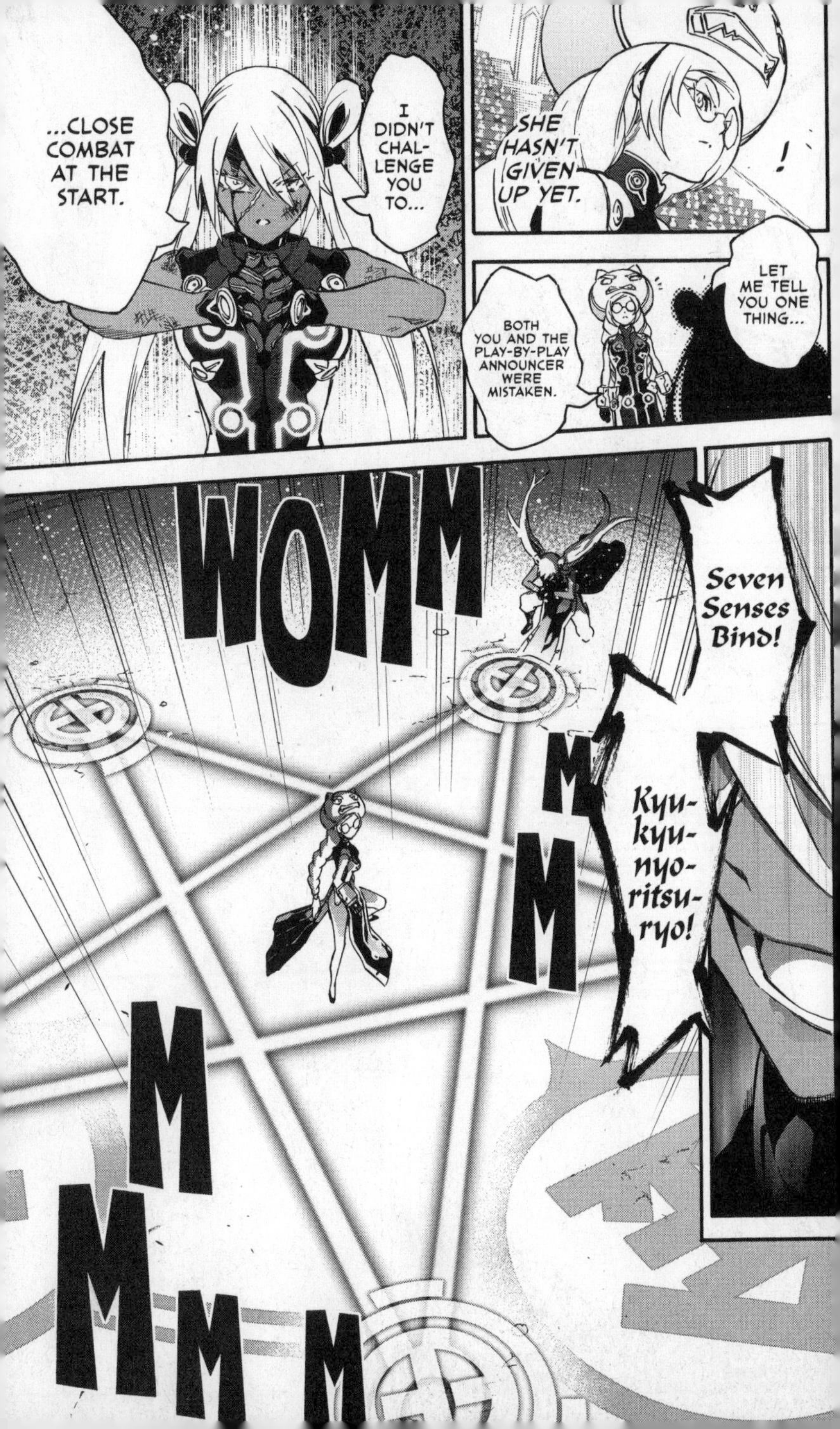
SHE HASN'T GIVEN UP YET.
!
LET ME TELL YOU ONE THING...
BOTH YOU AND THE PLAY-BY-PLAY ANNOUNCER WERE MISTAKEN.
I DIDN'T CHAL-LENGE YOU TO...
...CLOSE COMBAT AT THE START.
Seven Senses Bind!
Kyu-kyu-nyo-ritsu-ryo!
WOMM
MM
MMMMM

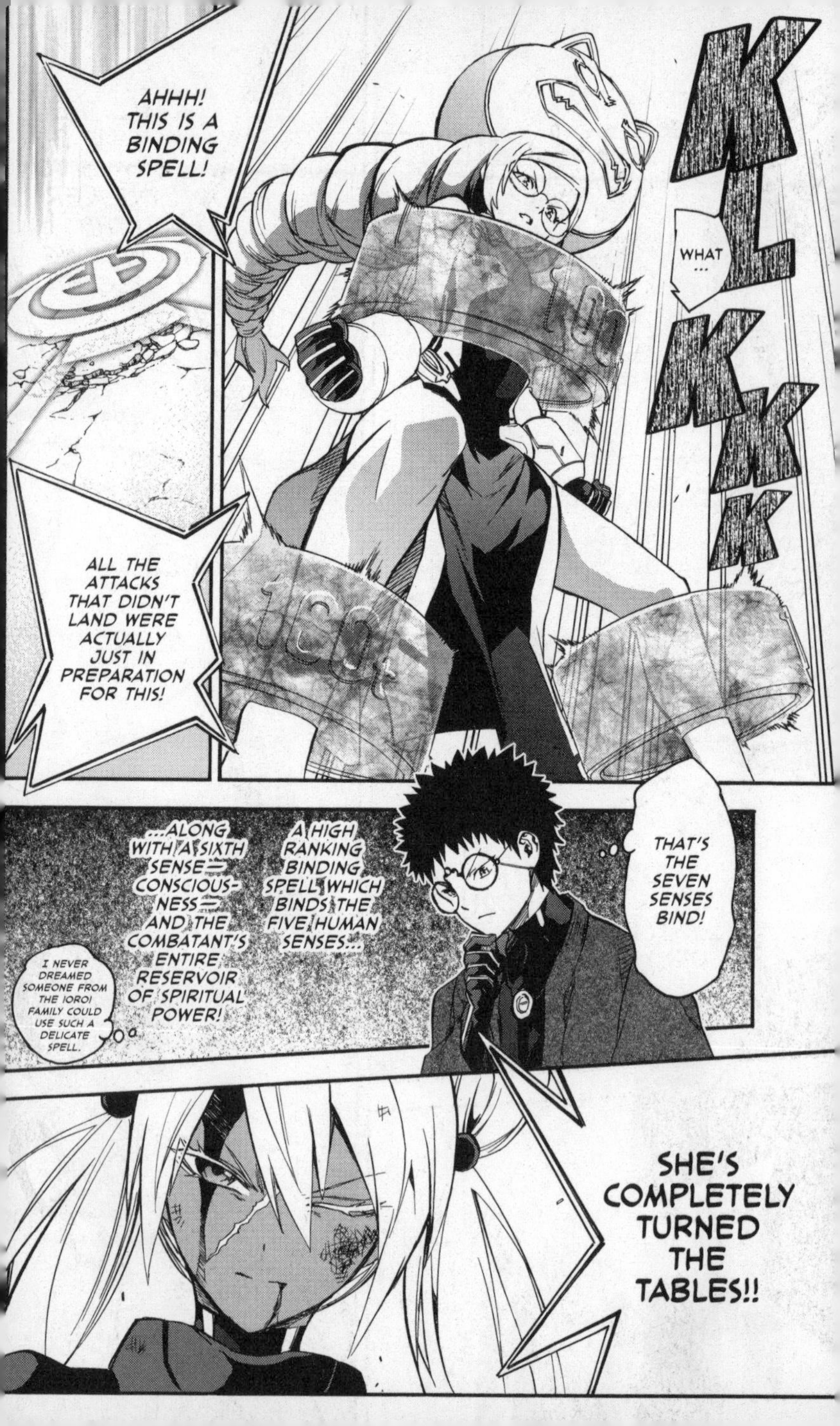
KLKKKK
WHAT...
AHHH! THIS IS A BINDING SPELL!
ALL THE ATTACKS THAT DIDN'T LAND WERE ACTUALLY JUST IN PREPARATION FOR THIS!
THAT'S THE SEVEN SENSES BIND!
A HIGH RANKING BINDING SPELL WHICH BINDS THE FIVE HUMAN SENSES...
...ALONG WITH A SIXTH SENSE=CONSCIOUSNESS=AND THE COMBATANT'S ENTIRE RESERVOIR OF SPIRITUAL POWER!
I NEVER DREAMED SOMEONE FROM THE IOROI FAMILY COULD USE SUCH A DELICATE SPELL.
SHE'S COMPLETELY TURNED THE TABLES!!

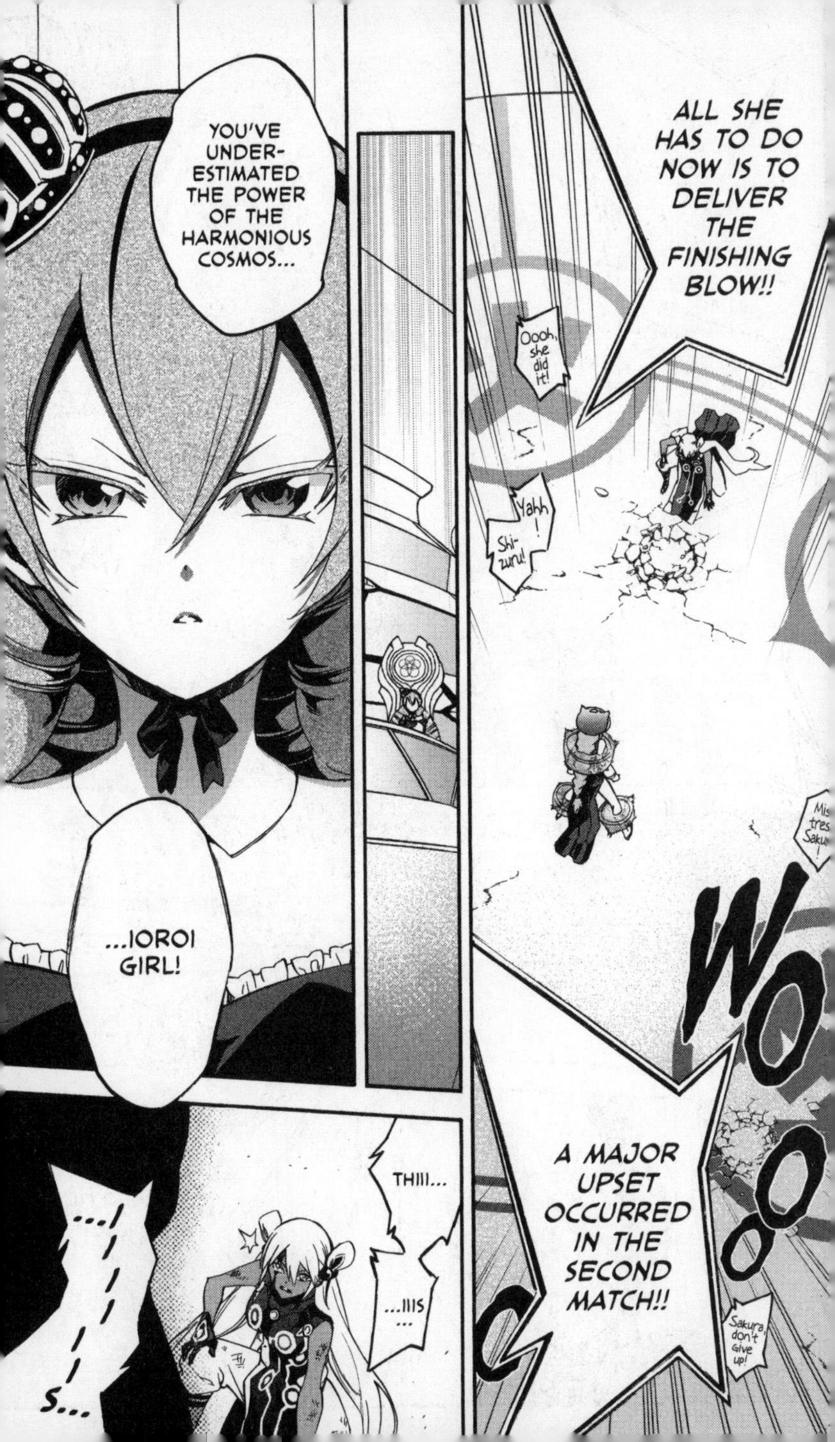
ALL SHE HAS TO DO NOW IS TO DELIVER THE FINISHING BLOW!!
Oooh, she did it!
Yahh! Shi-zuru!
WOOO
A MAJOR UPSET OCCURRED IN THE SECOND MATCH!!
Sakura, don't give up!
YOU'VE UNDER-ESTIMATED THE POWER OF THE HARMONIOUS COSMOS...
...IOROI GIRL!
THIII...
...IIIS...
...IIIIIIIS...

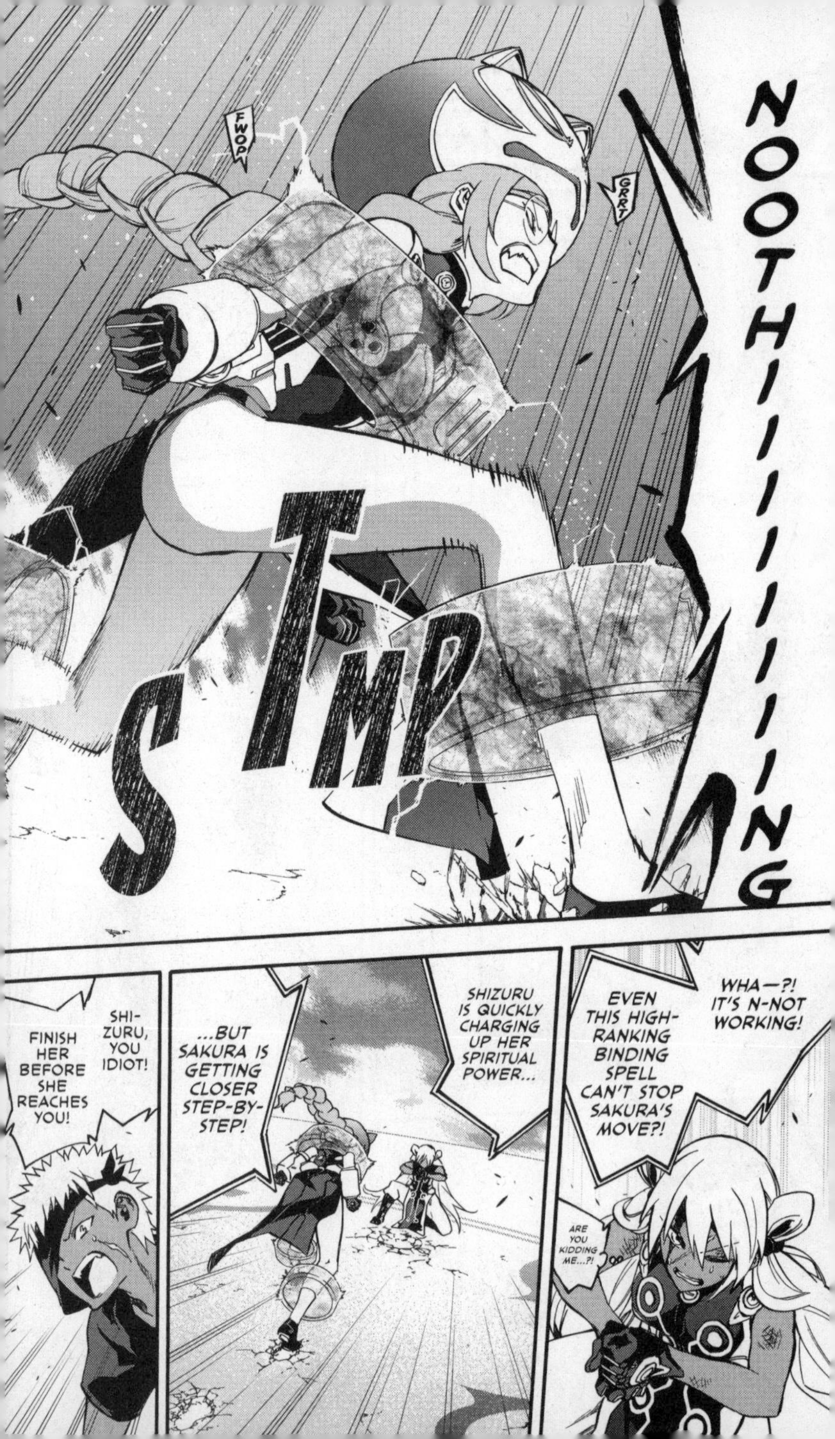
NOOTHIIIIIIIING
GRRT
FWOP
STMP
WHA—?! IT'S N-NOT WORKING!
EVEN THIS HIGH-RANKING BINDING SPELL CAN'T STOP SAKURA'S MOVE?!
ARE YOU KIDDING ME...?!
SHIZURU IS QUICKLY CHARGING UP HER SPIRITUAL POWER...
...BUT SAKURA IS GETTING CLOSER STEP-BY-STEP!
SHI-ZURU, YOU IDIOT!
FINISH HER BEFORE SHE REACHES YOU!

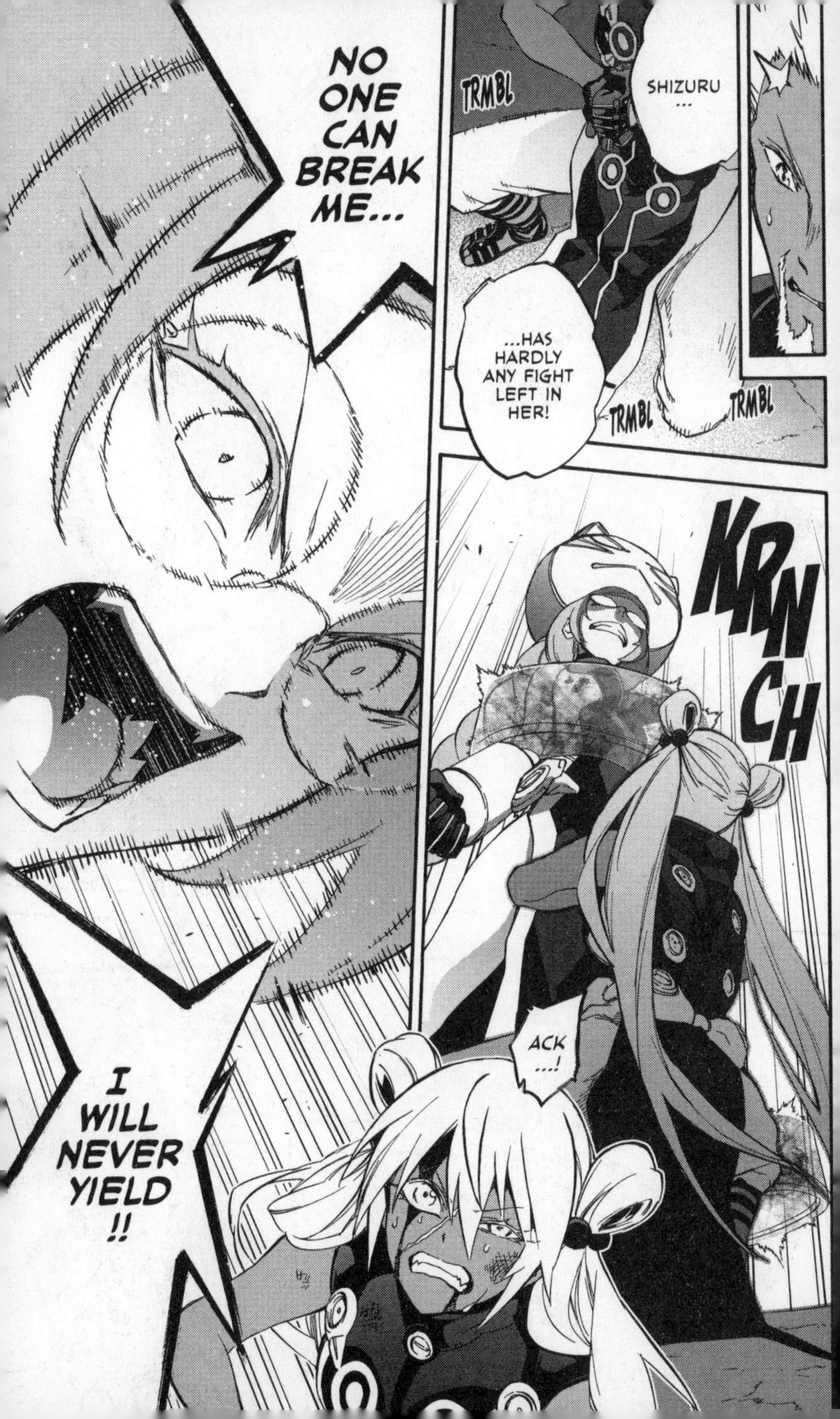
SHIZURU...
TRMBL
...HAS HARDLY ANY FIGHT LEFT IN HER!
TRMBL
TRMBL
KRNCH
ACK...!
NO ONE CAN BREAK ME...
I WILL NEVER YIELD!!

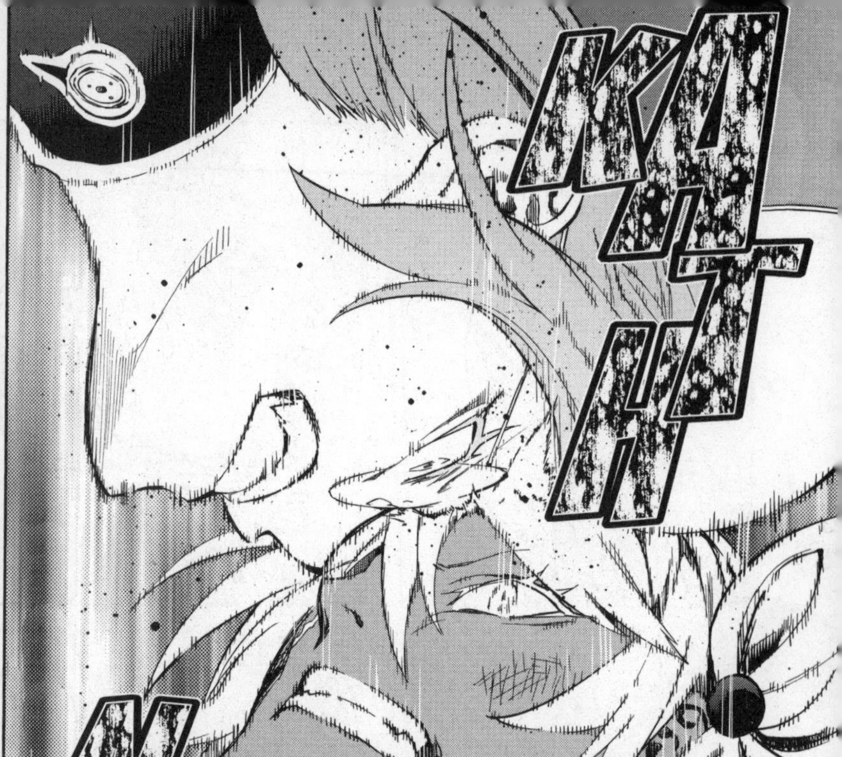
KATH
NNNK

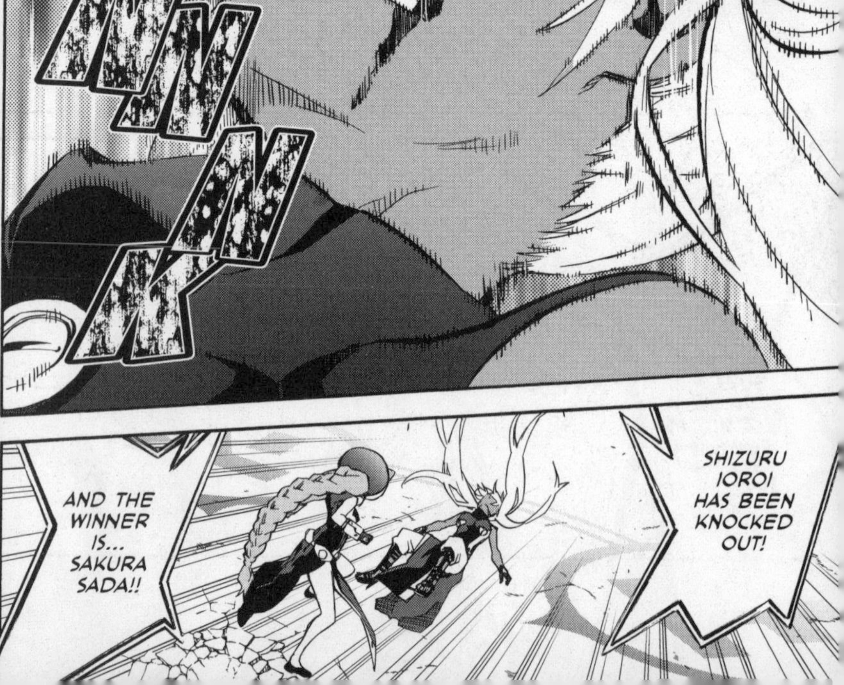
SHIZURU IOROI HAS BEEN KNOCKED OUT!
AND THE WINNER IS... SAKURA SADA!!

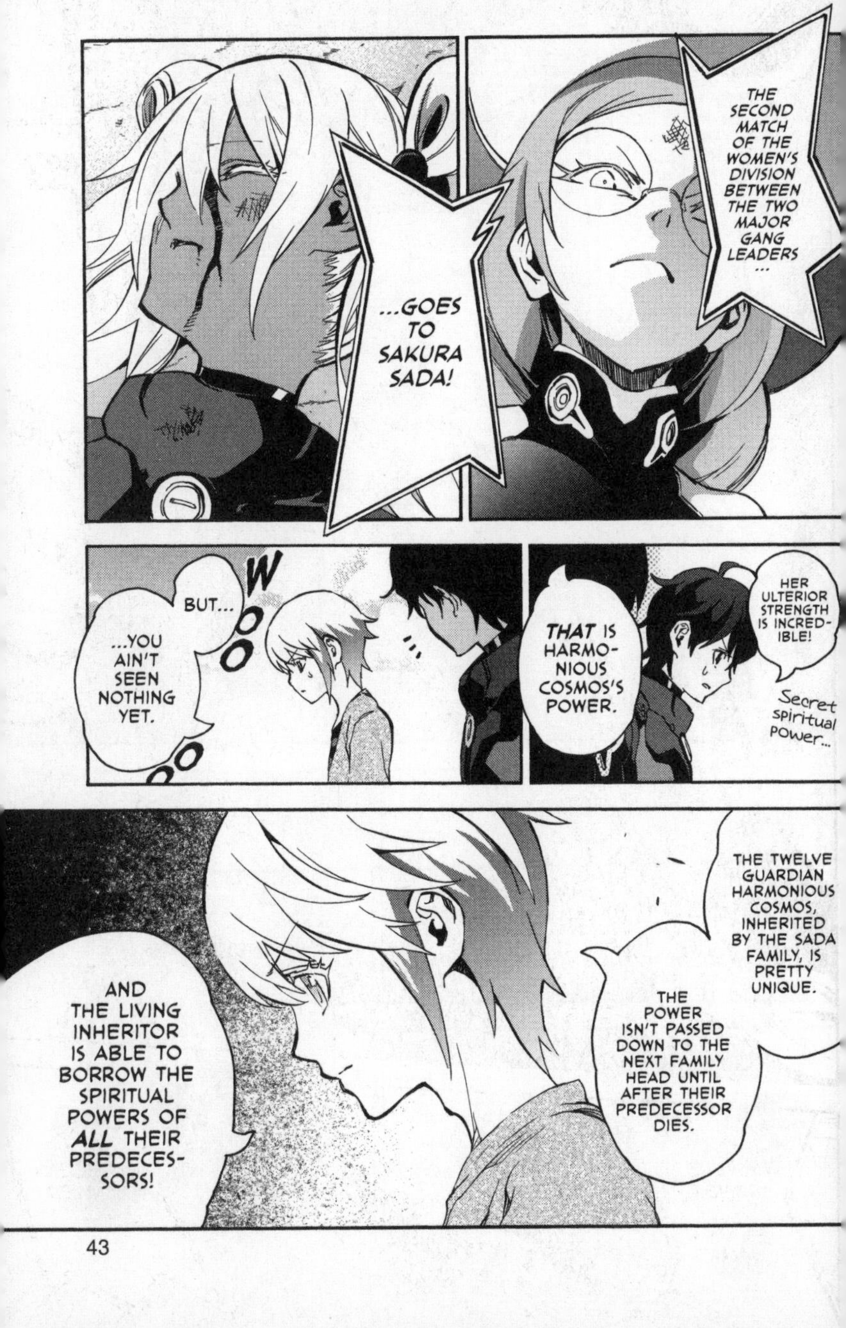
THE SECOND MATCH OF THE WOMEN'S DIVISION BETWEEN THE TWO MAJOR GANG LEADERS...
...GOES TO SAKURA SADA!
HER ULTERIOR STRENGTH IS INCREDIBLE!
Secret spiritual power...
THAT IS HARMONIOUS COSMOS'S POWER.
...
BUT...
...YOU AIN'T SEEN NOTHING YET.
WOOOOO
THE TWELVE GUARDIAN HARMONIOUS COSMOS, INHERITED BY THE SADA FAMILY, IS PRETTY UNIQUE.
THE POWER ISN'T PASSED DOWN TO THE NEXT FAMILY HEAD UNTIL AFTER THEIR PREDECESSOR DIES.
AND THE LIVING INHERITOR IS ABLE TO BORROW THE SPIRITUAL POWERS OF ALL THEIR PREDECES-SORS!

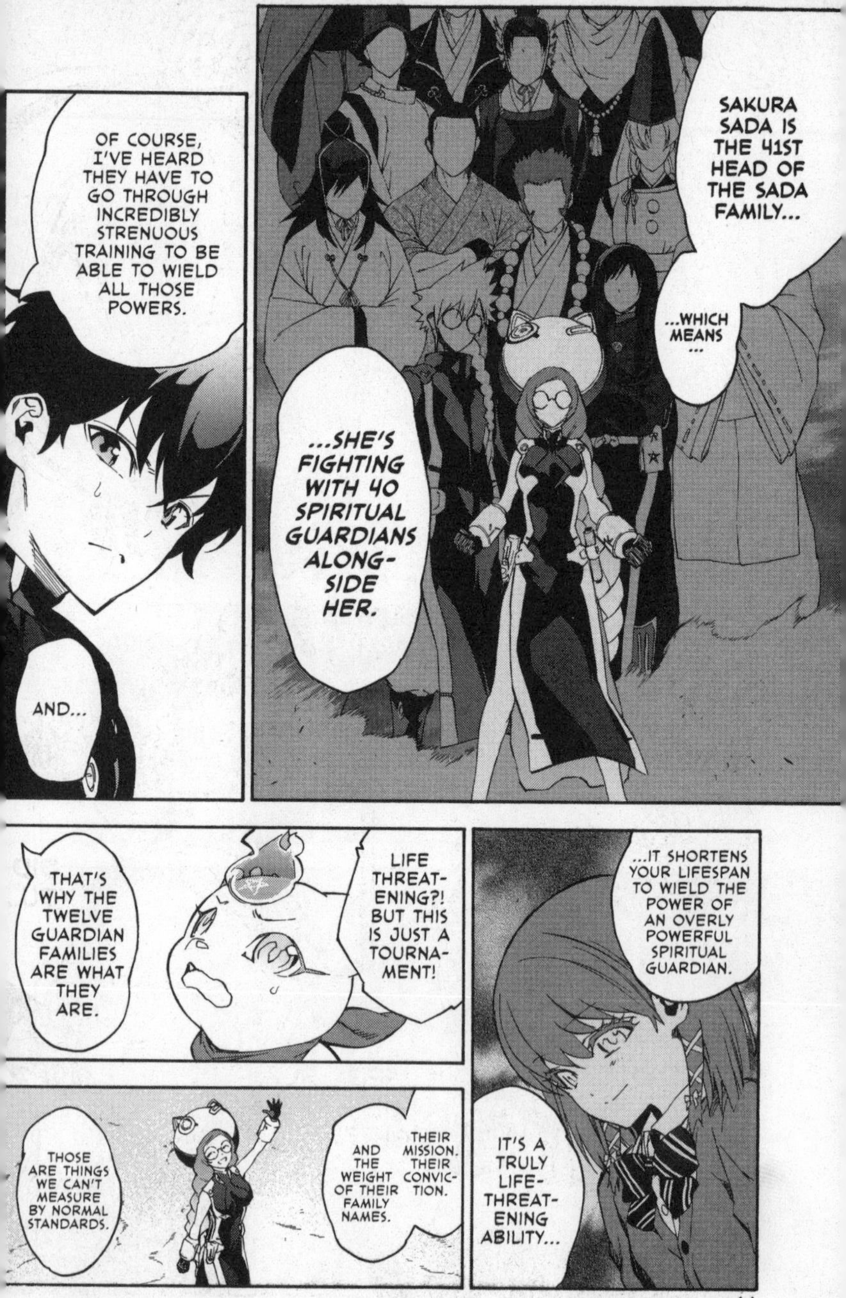
SAKURA SADA IS THE 41ST HEAD OF THE SADA FAMILY...
...WHICH MEANS ...
...SHE'S FIGHTING WITH 40 SPIRITUAL GUARDIANS ALONG-SIDE HER.
OF COURSE, I'VE HEARD THEY HAVE TO GO THROUGH INCREDIBLY STRENUOUS TRAINING TO BE ABLE TO WIELD ALL THOSE POWERS.
AND...
...IT SHORTENS YOUR LIFESPAN TO WIELD THE POWER OF AN OVERLY POWERFUL SPIRITUAL GUARDIAN.
IT'S A TRULY LIFE-THREAT-ENING ABILITY...
LIFE THREAT-ENING?! BUT THIS IS JUST A TOURNA-MENT!
THAT'S WHY THE TWELVE GUARDIAN FAMILIES ARE WHAT THEY ARE.
THEIR MISSION. THEIR CONVIC-TION.
AND THE WEIGHT OF THEIR FAMILY NAMES.
THOSE ARE THINGS WE CAN'T MEASURE BY NORMAL STANDARDS.

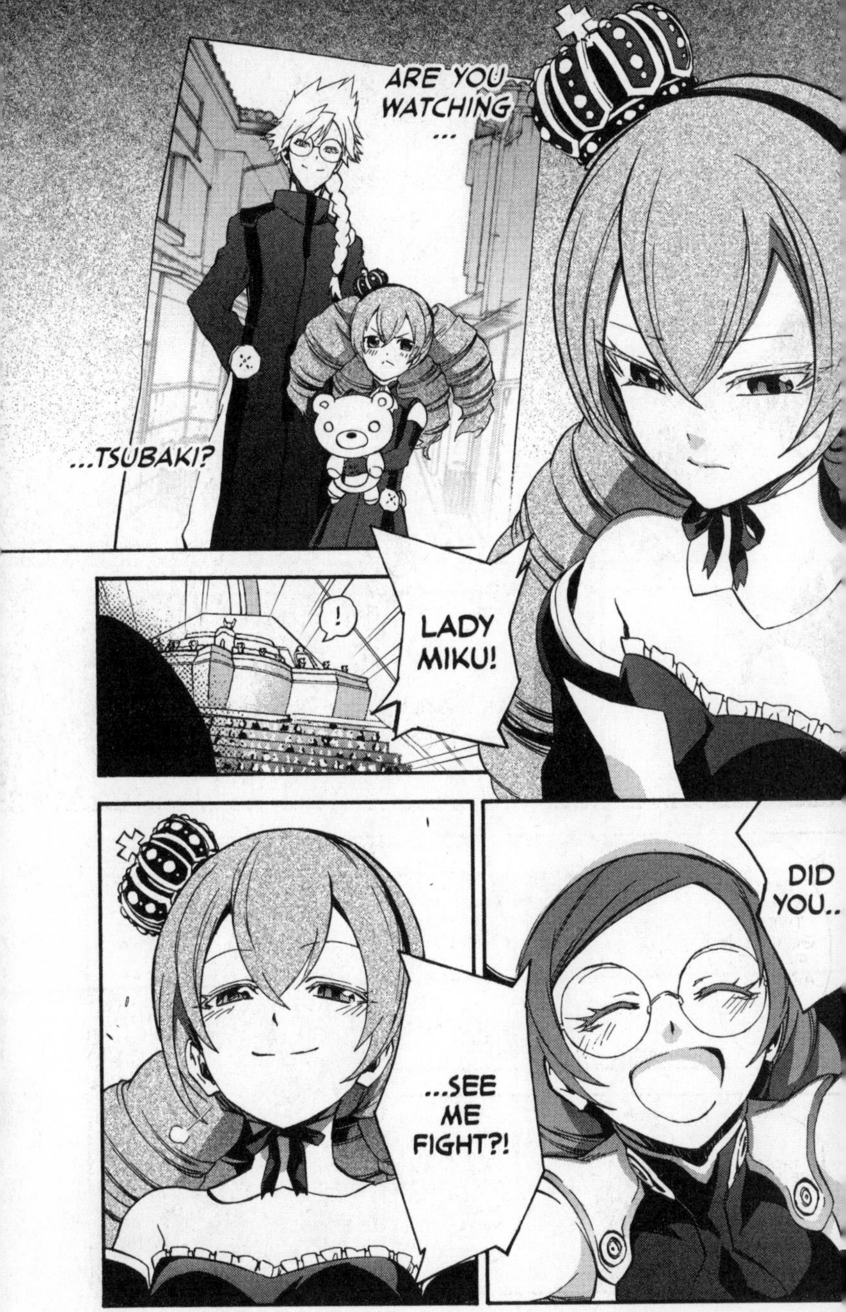
ARE YOU WATCHING ...
...TSUBAKI?
LADY MIKU!
!
DID YOU...
...SEE ME FIGHT?!

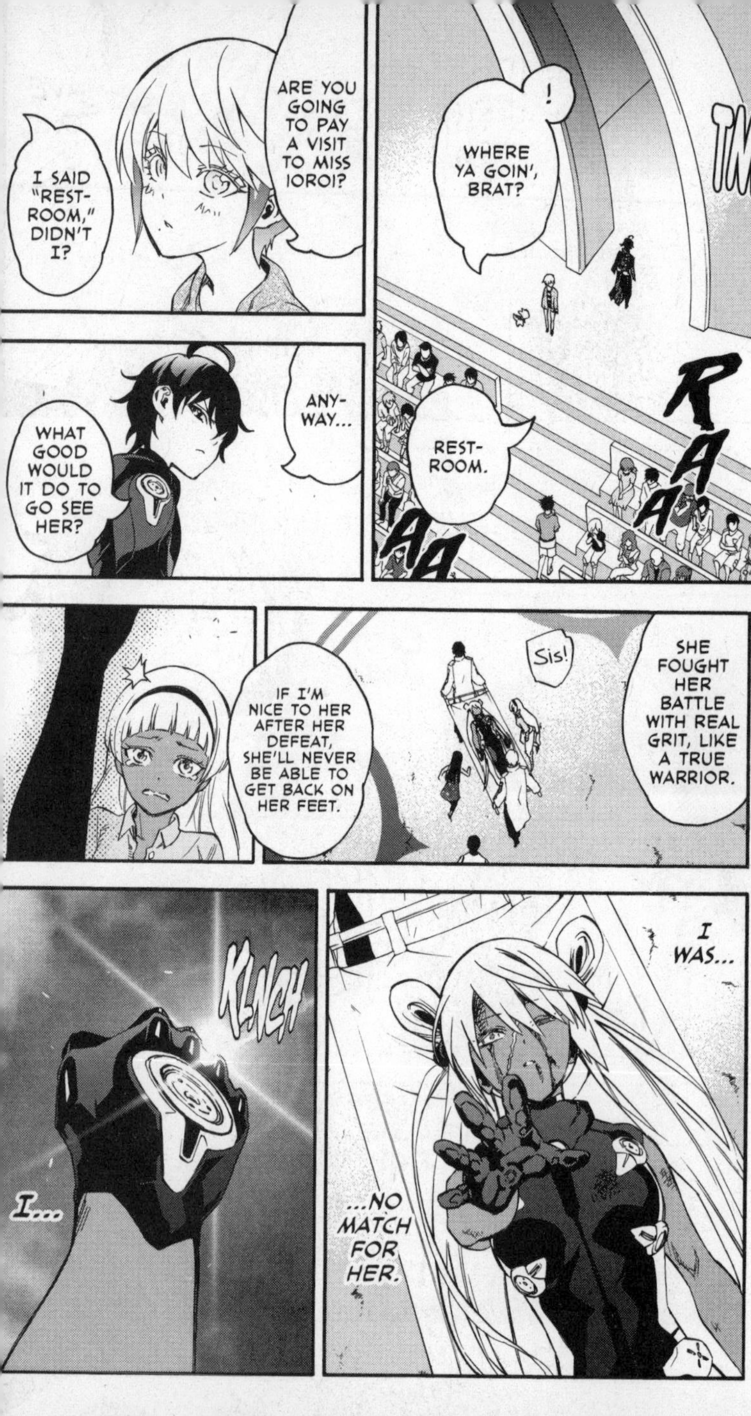

!
WHERE YA GOIN', BRAT?
TMP
REST-ROOM.
RAAAAA
ARE YOU GOING TO PAY A VISIT TO MISS IOROI?
I SAID "REST-ROOM," DIDN'T I?
ANY-WAY...
WHAT GOOD WOULD IT DO TO GO SEE HER?
SHE FOUGHT HER BATTLE WITH REAL GRIT, LIKE A TRUE WARRIOR.
Sis!
IF I'M NICE TO HER AFTER HER DEFEAT, SHE'LL NEVER BE ABLE TO GET BACK ON HER FEET.
I WAS...
...NO MATCH FOR HER.
KLNCH
I...

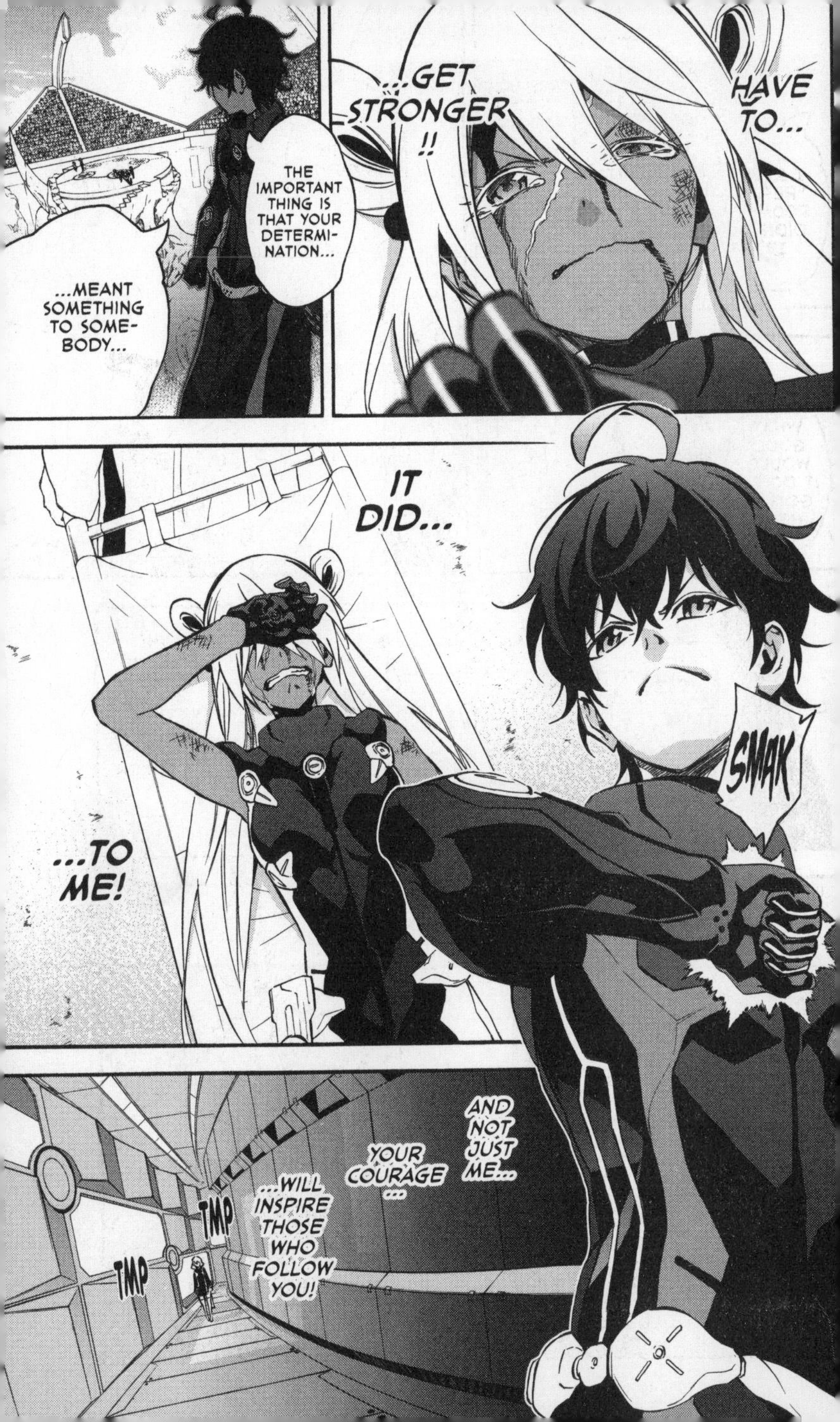
HAVE TO...
...GET STRONGER!!
THE IMPORTANT THING IS THAT YOUR DETERMINATION...
...MEANT SOMETHING TO SOMEBODY...
IT DID...
SMAK
...TO ME!
AND NOT JUST ME...
YOUR COURAGE...
...WILL INSPIRE THOSE WHO FOLLOW YOU!
TMP
TMP

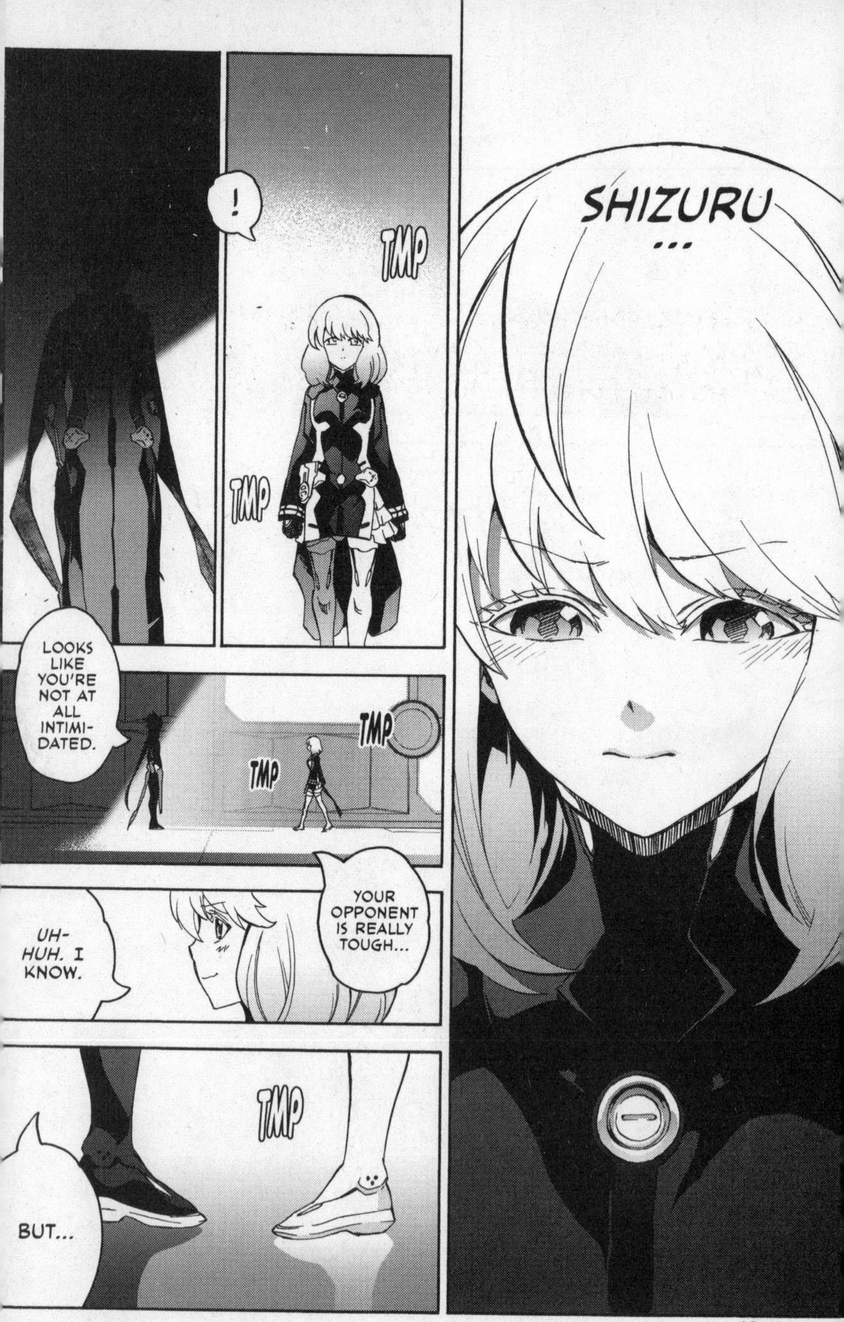
SHIZURU ...
!
TMP
TMP
LOOKS LIKE YOU'RE NOT AT ALL INTIMI-DATED.
TMP
TMP
YOUR OPPONENT IS REALLY TOUGH...
UH-HUH. I KNOW.
TMP
BUT...

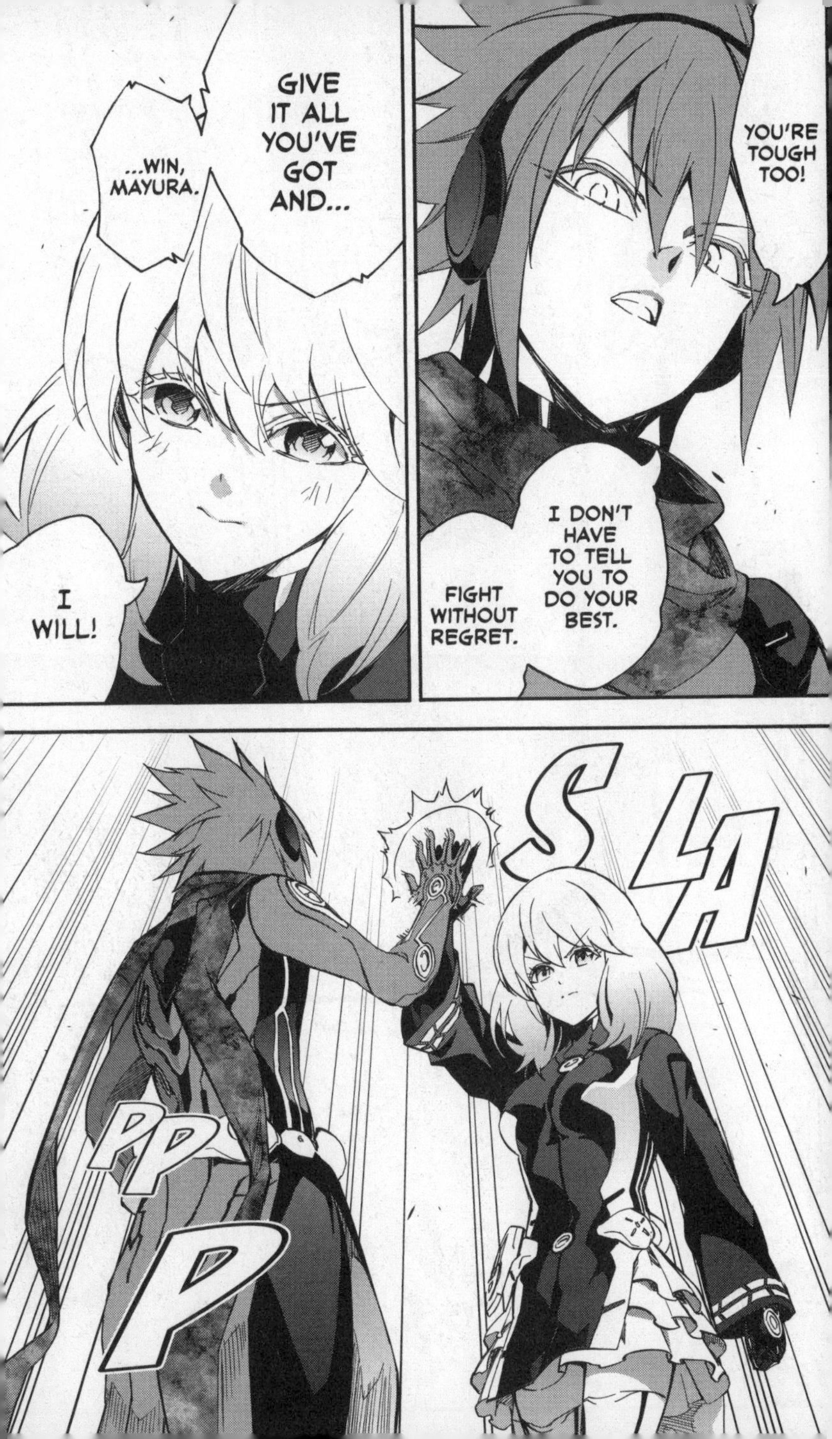
YOU'RE TOUGH TOO!
I DON'T HAVE TO TELL YOU TO DO YOUR BEST.
FIGHT WITHOUT REGRET.
GIVE IT ALL YOU'VE GOT AND...
...WIN, MAYURA.
I WILL!
SLA
PPP

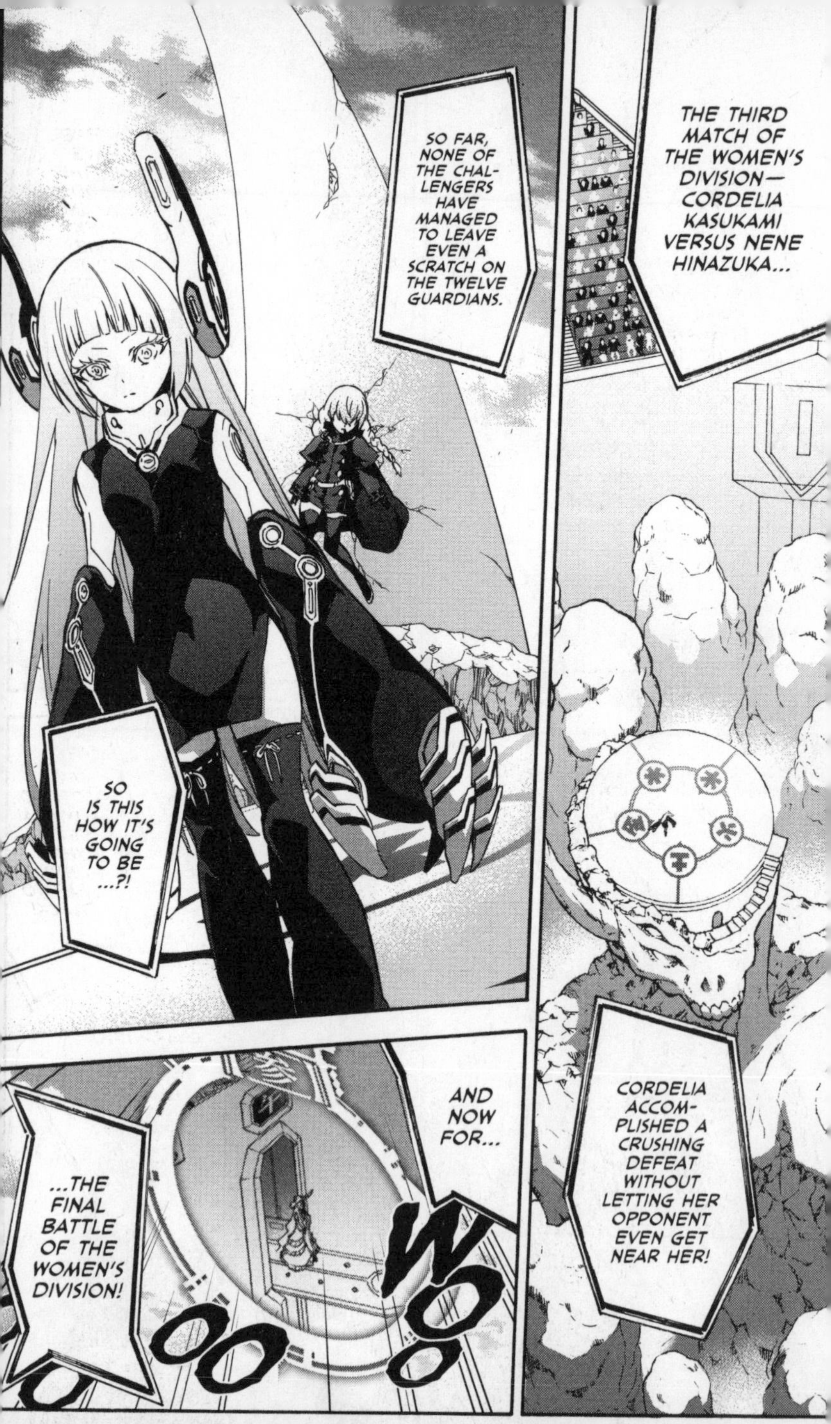
THE THIRD MATCH OF THE WOMEN'S DIVISION—CORDELIA KASUKAMI VERSUS NENE HINAZUKA...
CORDELIA ACCOMPLISHED A CRUSHING DEFEAT WITHOUT LETTING HER OPPONENT EVEN GET NEAR HER!
SO FAR, NONE OF THE CHALLENGERS HAVE MANAGED TO LEAVE EVEN A SCRATCH ON THE TWELVE GUARDIANS.
SO IS THIS HOW IT'S GOING TO BE ...?!
AND NOW FOR...
...THE FINAL BATTLE OF THE WOMEN'S DIVISION!
WOOOOO

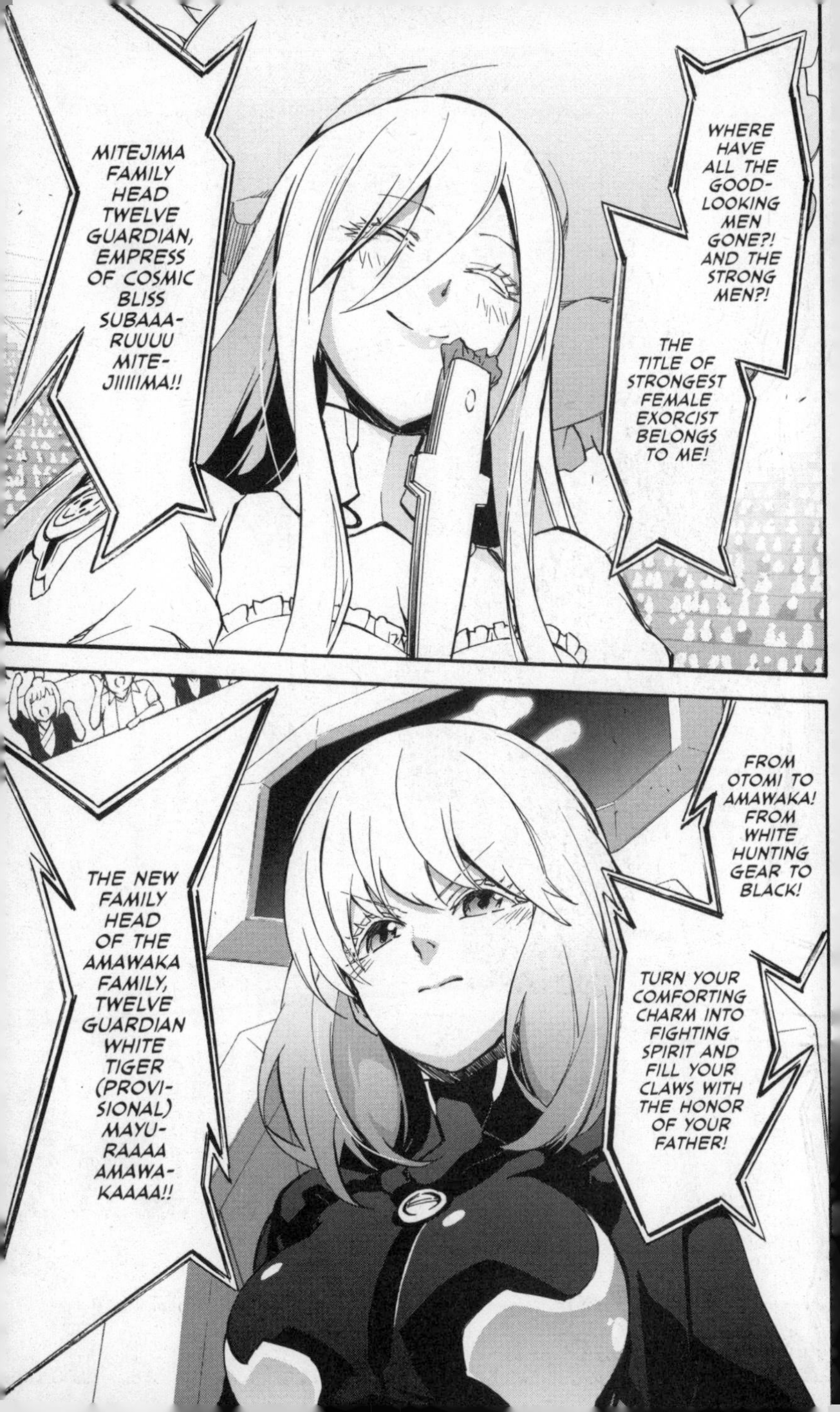
WHERE HAVE ALL THE GOOD-LOOKING MEN GONE?! AND THE STRONG MEN?!
THE TITLE OF STRONGEST FEMALE EXORCIST BELONGS TO ME!
MITEJIMA FAMILY HEAD TWELVE GUARDIAN, EMPRESS OF COSMIC BLISS SUBAAA-RUUUU MITE-JIIIIMA!!
FROM OTOMI TO AMAWAKA! FROM WHITE HUNTING GEAR TO BLACK!
TURN YOUR COMFORTING CHARM INTO FIGHTING SPIRIT AND FILL YOUR CLAWS WITH THE HONOR OF YOUR FATHER!
THE NEW FAMILY HEAD OF THE AMAWAKA FAMILY, TWELVE GUARDIAN WHITE TIGER (PROVI-SIONAL) MAYU-RAAAA AMAWA-KAAAA!!

The 167th Hadarae Castle Imperial Tournament

Morning—Women's Division

1st Match:
Miku Zeze
(Zeze Family)
vs.
Fuguyo Mushuguchi
(Unomiya Family)

2nd Match:
Sakura Sada
(Sada Family)
vs.
Shizuru Ioroi
(Ioroi Family)

3rd Match:
Cordelia Kasukami
(Kasukami Family)
vs.
Nene Hinazuka
(Mitosaka Family)

4th Match:
Subaru Mitejima
(Mitejima Family)
vs.
Mayura Amawaka
(Amawaka Family)

Afternoon—Men's Division

1st Match:
Kengo Uji
(Uji Family)
vs.
Danma Kurozu
(Sada Family)

2nd Match:
Soma Todoromi
(Inanaki Family)
vs.
Danri Nimyo
(Nimyo Family)

3rd Match:
Jinya Yosami
(Amawaka Family)
vs.
Juzo Nakiri
(Zeze Family)

4th Match:
Keiji Ikaruga
(Ikaruga Family)
vs.
Gunki Ioroi
(Ioroi Family)

5th Match:
Tatara
(Hagusa Family)
vs.
Hayatonosuke Inami
(Mitejima Family)

6th Match:
Kankuro Mitosaka
(Mitosaka Family)
vs.
Rokuro Enmado
(Enmado Family)

7th Match:
Shozan Saragi
(Kasukami Family)
vs.
Izumi Kujinogawa
(Uji Family)

8th Match:
Shusuke Gein
(Unomiya Family)
vs.
Sanai Iwamuro
(Iwamuro Family)

9th Match:
Narumi Ioroi
(Ioroi Family)
vs.
Arata Inanaki
(Inanaki Family)

10th Match:
Tenma Unomiya
(Unomiya Family)
vs.
Shimon Ikaruga
(Ikaruga Family)

#42: Women's Battle, Part 2

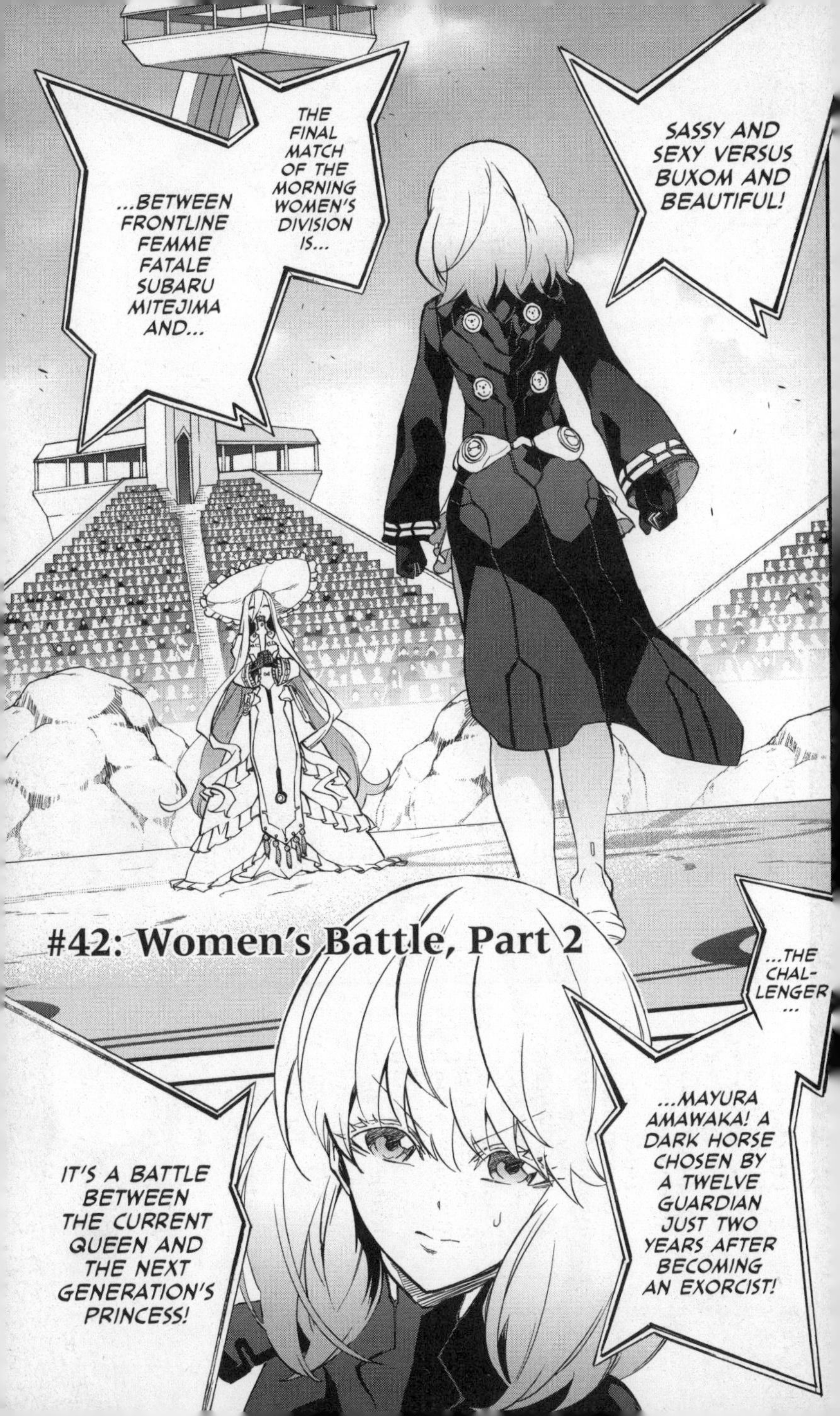
SASSY AND SEXY VERSUS BUXOM AND BEAUTIFUL!
THE FINAL MATCH OF THE MORNING WOMEN'S DIVISION IS...
...BETWEEN FRONTLINE FEMME FATALE SUBARU MITEJIMA AND...
...THE CHAL-LENGER...
...MAYURA AMAWAKA! A DARK HORSE CHOSEN BY A TWELVE GUARDIAN JUST TWO YEARS AFTER BECOMING AN EXORCIST!
IT'S A BATTLE BETWEEN THE CURRENT QUEEN AND THE NEXT GENERATION'S PRINCESS!

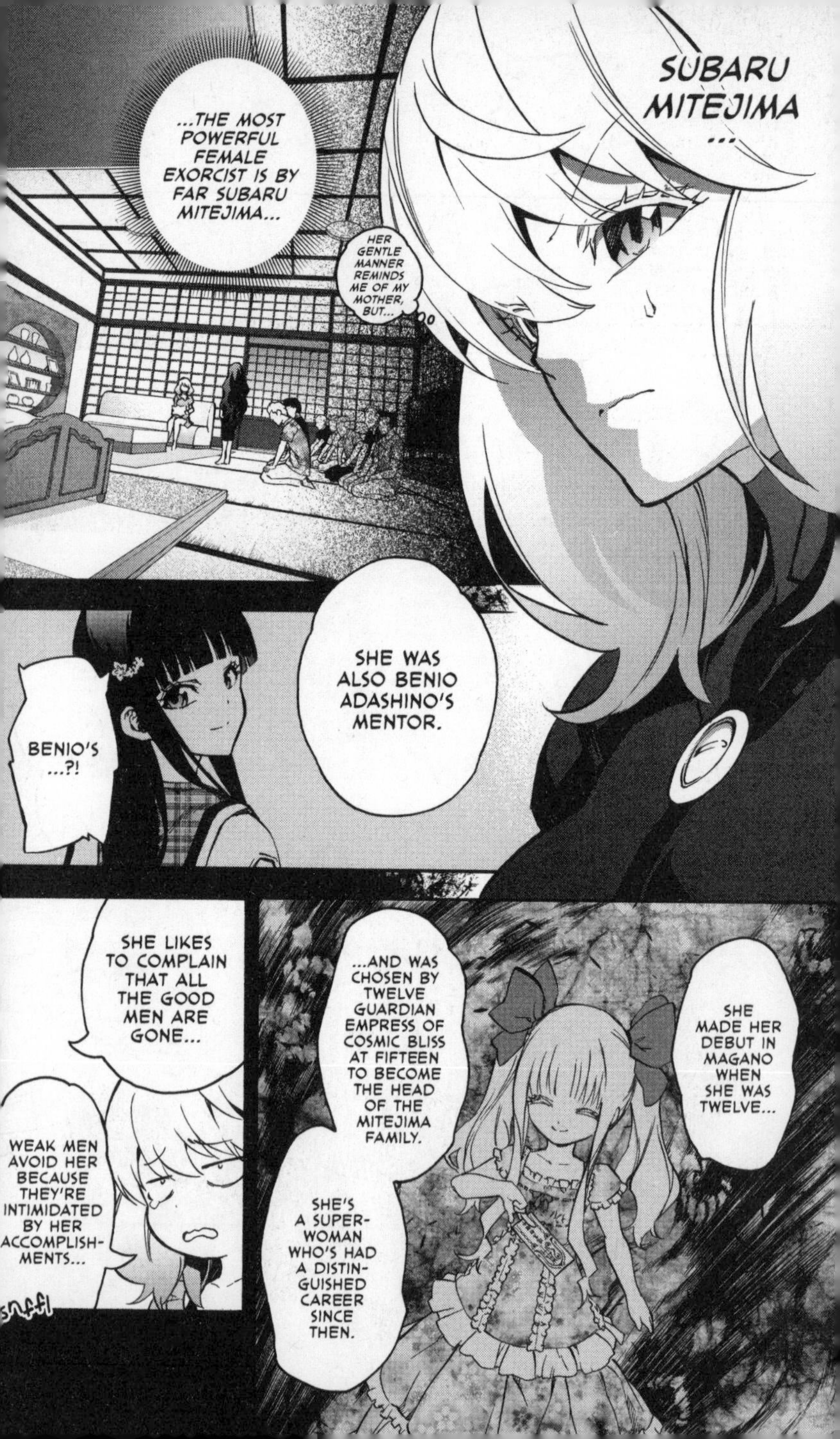
SUBARU MITEJIMA ...
HER GENTLE MANNER REMINDS ME OF MY MOTHER, BUT...
SHE WAS ALSO BENIO ADASHINO'S MENTOR.
...THE MOST POWERFUL FEMALE EXORCIST IS BY FAR SUBARU MITEJIMA...
BENIO'S ...?!
SHE MADE HER DEBUT IN MAGANO WHEN SHE WAS TWELVE...
...AND WAS CHOSEN BY TWELVE GUARDIAN EMPRESS OF COSMIC BLISS AT FIFTEEN TO BECOME THE HEAD OF THE MITEJIMA FAMILY.
SHE'S A SUPER-WOMAN WHO'S HAD A DISTIN-GUISHED CAREER SINCE THEN.
SHE LIKES TO COMPLAIN THAT ALL THE GOOD MEN ARE GONE...
WEAK MEN AVOID HER BECAUSE THEY'RE INTIMIDATED BY HER ACCOMPLISH-MENTS...
snffl

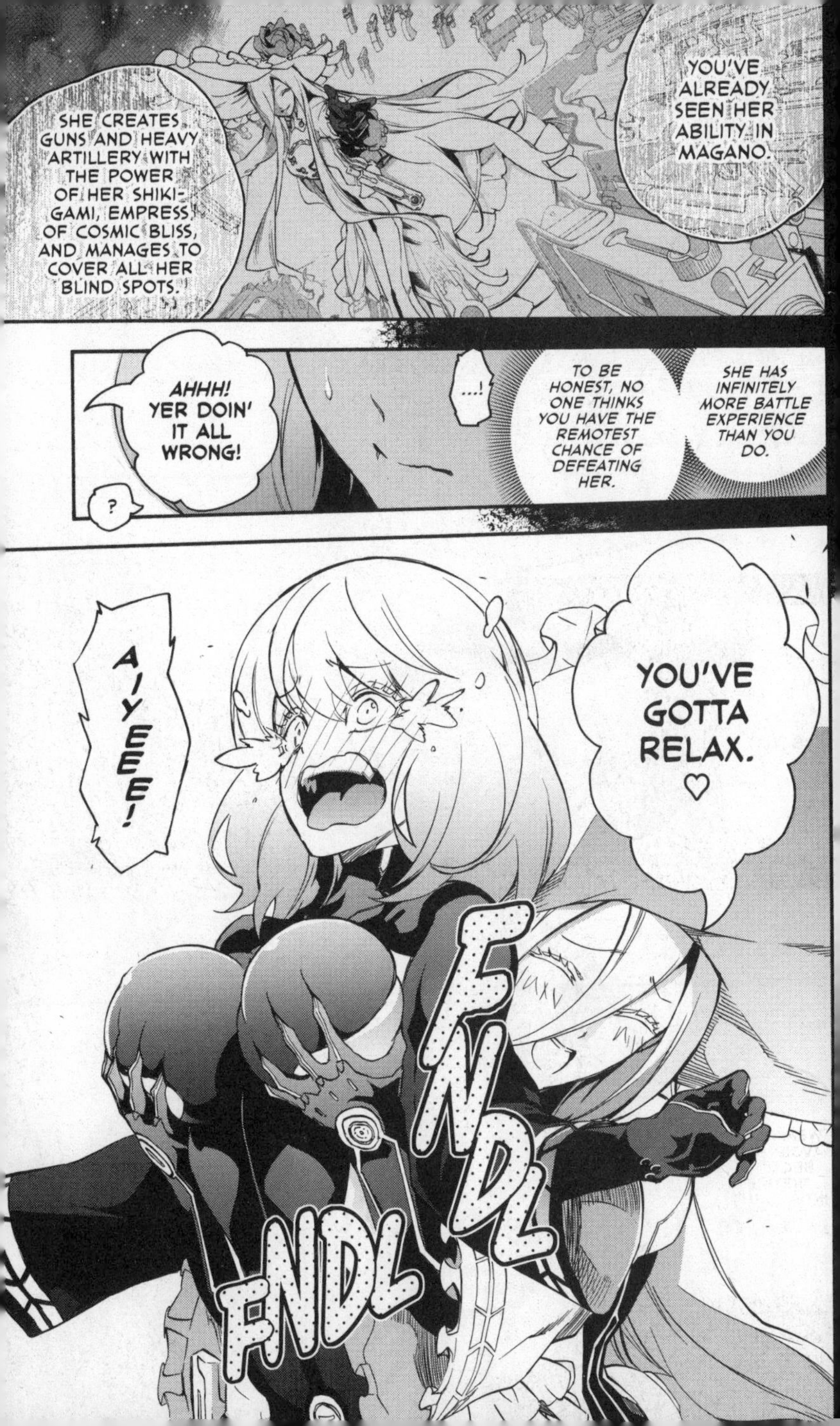
YOU'VE ALREADY SEEN HER ABILITY IN MAGANO.
SHE CREATES GUNS AND HEAVY ARTILLERY WITH THE POWER OF HER SHIKIGAMI, EMPRESS OF COSMIC BLISS, AND MANAGES TO COVER ALL HER BLIND SPOTS.
SHE HAS INFINITELY MORE BATTLE EXPERIENCE THAN YOU DO.
TO BE HONEST, NO ONE THINKS YOU HAVE THE REMOTEST CHANCE OF DEFEATING HER.
...!
AHHH! YER DOIN' IT ALL WRONG!
?
YOU'VE GOTTA RELAX. ♥
AIYEEE!
FNDL
FNDL

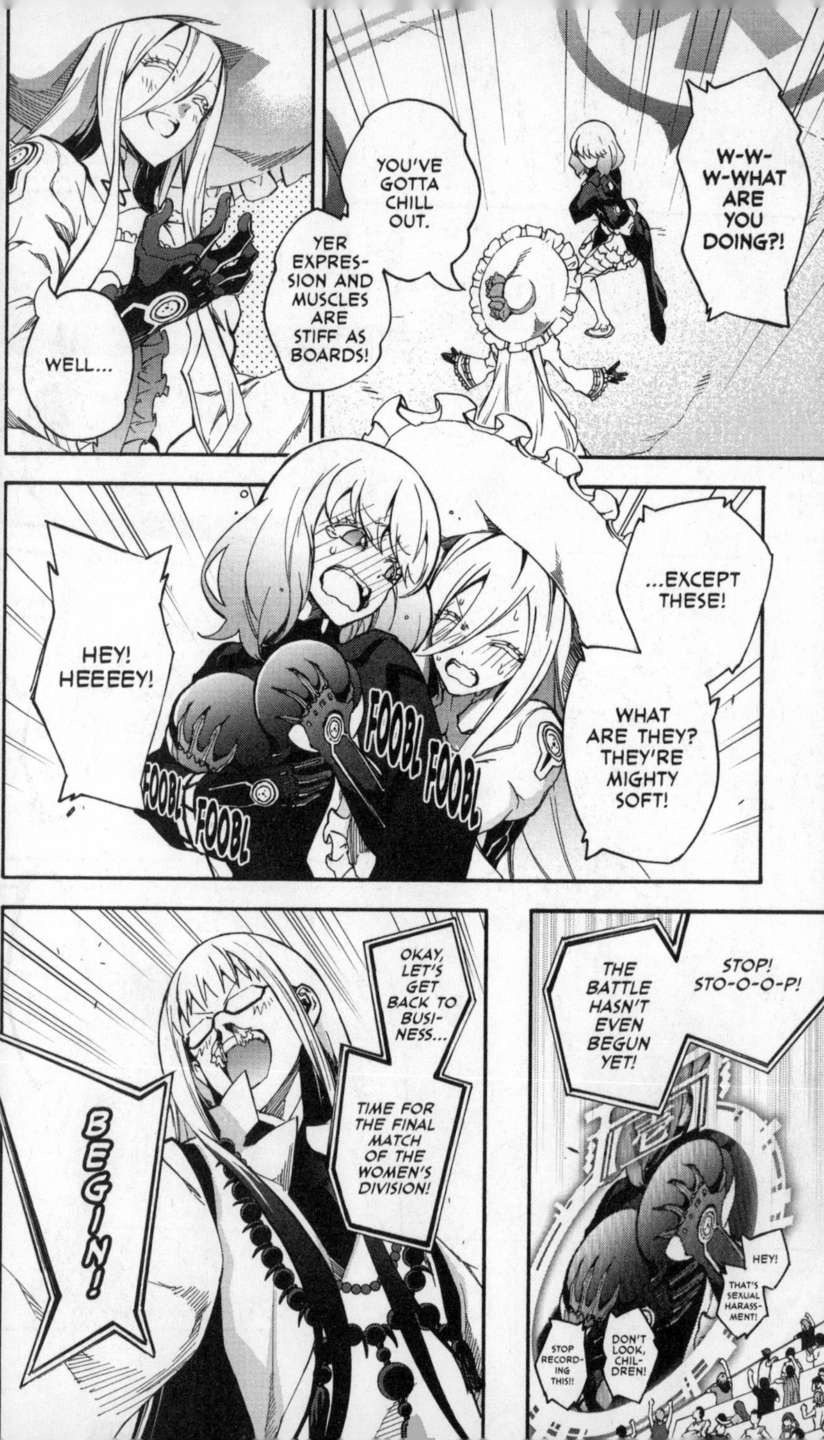
W-W-W-WHAT ARE YOU DOING?!
YOU'VE GOTTA CHILL OUT.
YER EXPRESSION AND MUSCLES ARE STIFF AS BOARDS!
WELL...
...EXCEPT THESE!
WHAT ARE THEY? THEY'RE MIGHTY SOFT!
FOOBL FOOBL
FOOBL FOOBL
HEY! HEEEEY!
STOP! STO-O-O-P!
THE BATTLE HASN'T EVEN BEGUN YET!
HEY!
THAT'S SEXUAL HARASSMENT!
DON'T LOOK, CHILDREN!
STOP RECORDING THIS!!
OKAY, LET'S GET BACK TO BUSINESS...
TIME FOR THE FINAL MATCH OF THE WOMEN'S DIVISION!
BEGIN!

*FOOBL – FONDLE + BOOB

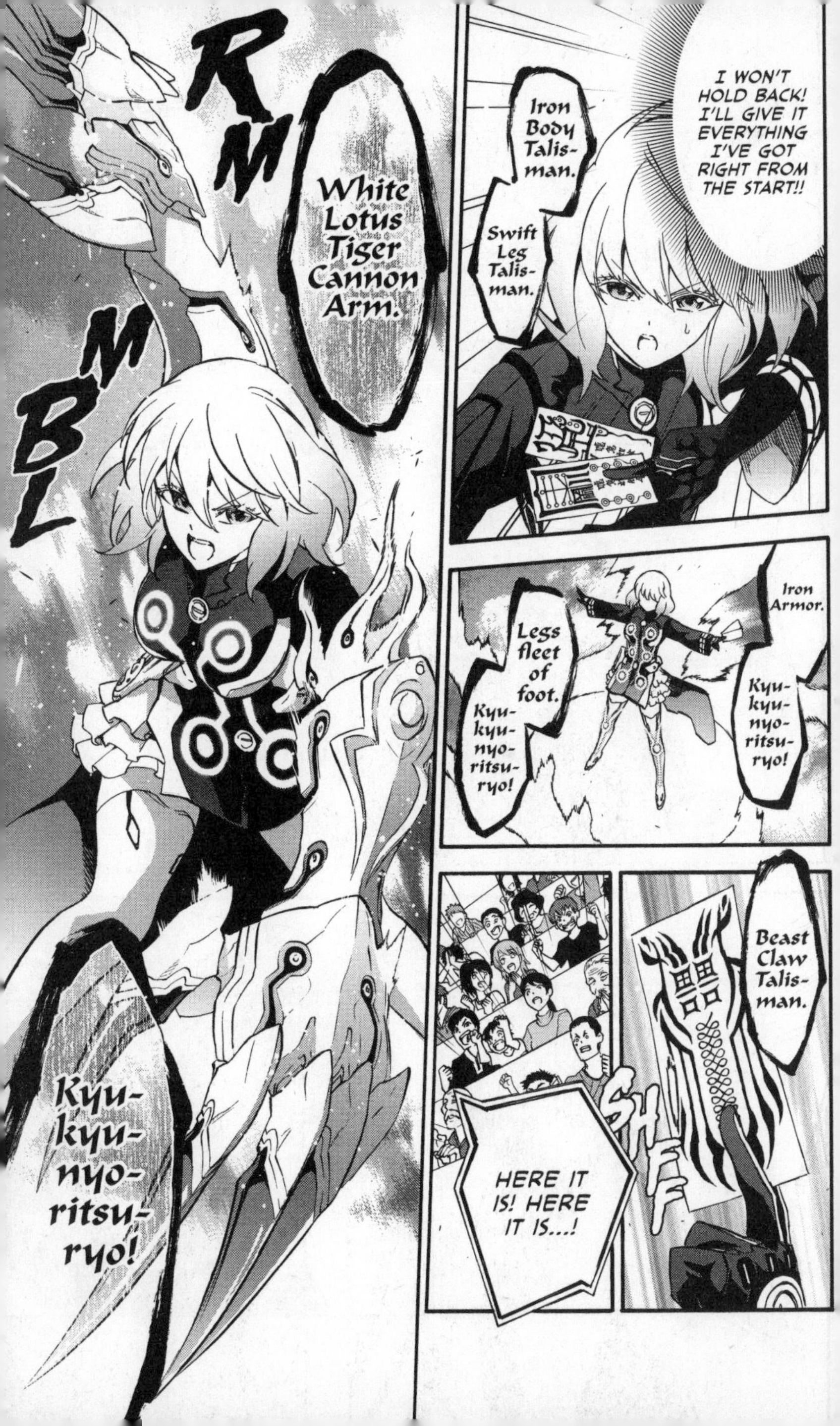
I WON'T HOLD BACK! I'LL GIVE IT EVERYTHING I'VE GOT RIGHT FROM THE START!!
Iron Body Talisman.
Swift Leg Talisman.
Iron Armor.
Kyu-kyu-nyo-ritsu-ryo!
Legs fleet of foot.
Kyu-kyu-nyo-ritsu-ryo!
Beast Claw Talisman.
SHF
HERE IT IS! HERE IT IS...!
RMMBL
White Lotus Tiger Cannon Arm.
Kyu-kyu-nyo-ritsu-ryo!

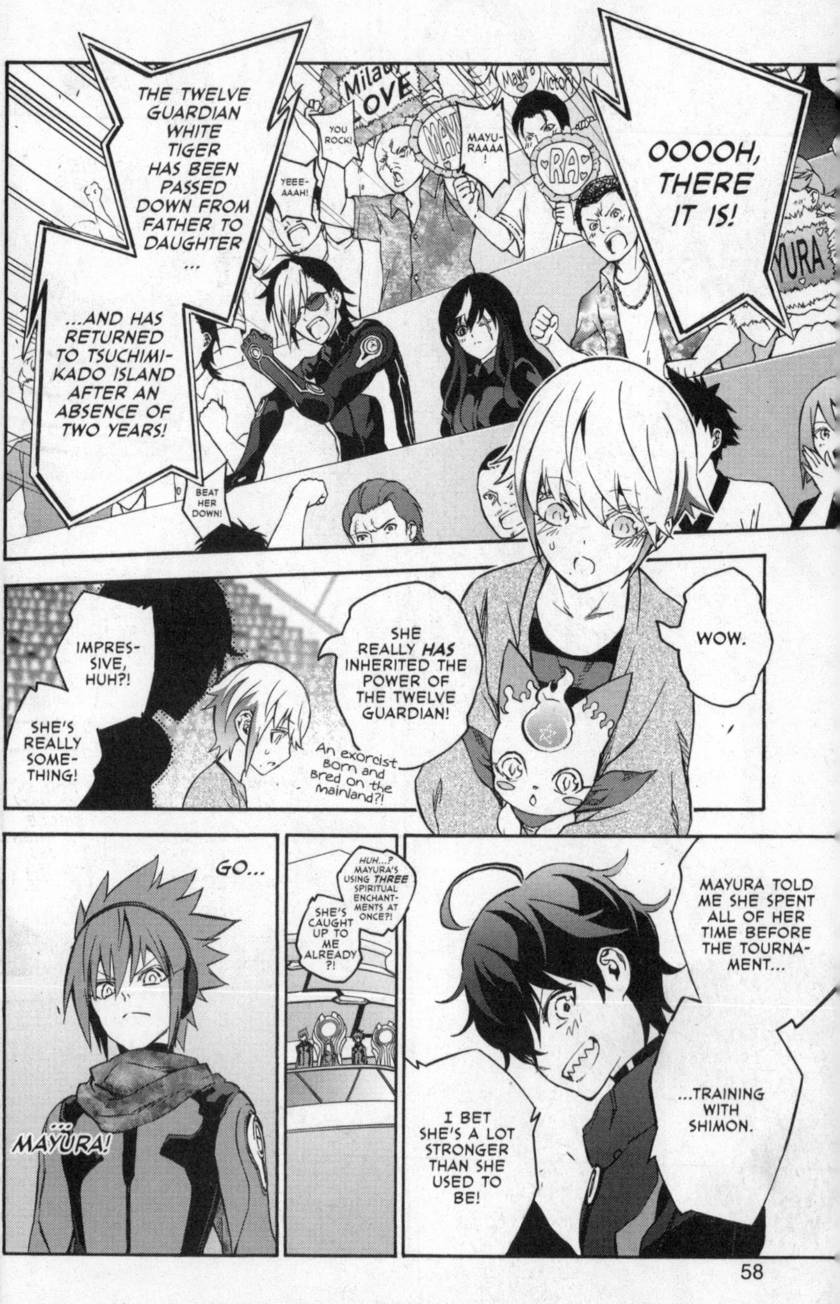

OOOOH, THERE IT IS!
YURA
Victor
Mayura
MAYU-RAAAA!
RA
MA
YOU ROCK!
Milady LOVE
YEEE-AAAH!
THE TWELVE GUARDIAN WHITE TIGER HAS BEEN PASSED DOWN FROM FATHER TO DAUGHTER...
...AND HAS RETURNED TO TSUCHIMIKADO ISLAND AFTER AN ABSENCE OF TWO YEARS!
BEAT HER DOWN!
WOW.
SHE REALLY HAS INHERITED THE POWER OF THE TWELVE GUARDIAN!
An exorcist born and bred on the mainland?!
IMPRESSIVE, HUH?!
SHE'S REALLY SOMETHING!
MAYURA TOLD ME SHE SPENT ALL OF HER TIME BEFORE THE TOURNAMENT...
...TRAINING WITH SHIMON.
I BET SHE'S A LOT STRONGER THAN SHE USED TO BE!
HUH...? MAYURA'S USING THREE SPIRITUAL ENCHANTMENTS AT ONCE?!
SHE'S CAUGHT UP TO ME ALREADY?!
GO...
...MAYURA!

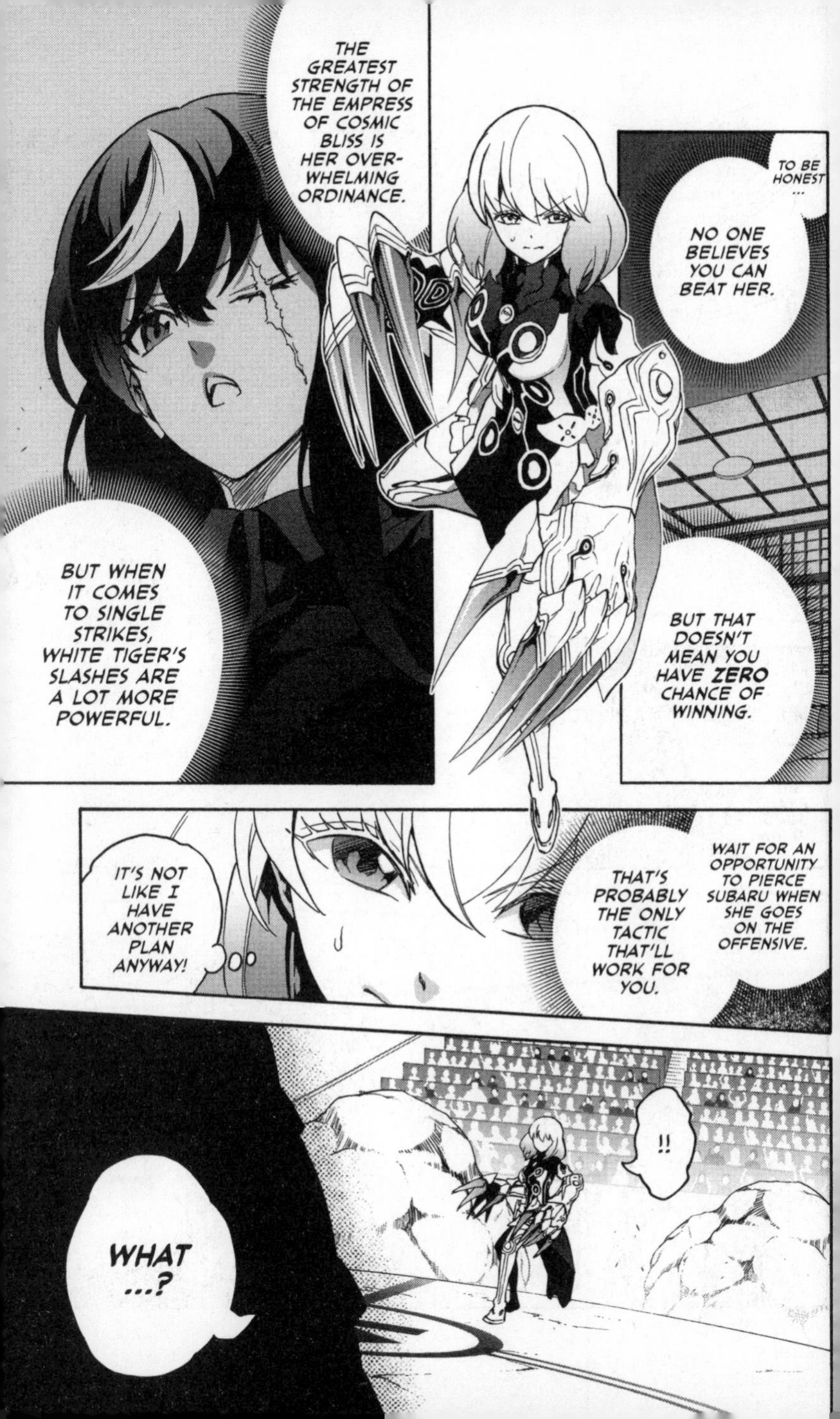
TO BE HONEST ...
NO ONE BELIEVES YOU CAN BEAT HER.
BUT THAT DOESN'T MEAN YOU HAVE **ZERO** CHANCE OF WINNING.
THE GREATEST STRENGTH OF THE EMPRESS OF COSMIC BLISS IS HER OVER-WHELMING ORDINANCE.
BUT WHEN IT COMES TO SINGLE STRIKES, WHITE TIGER'S SLASHES ARE A LOT MORE POWERFUL.
WAIT FOR AN OPPORTUNITY TO PIERCE SUBARU WHEN SHE GOES ON THE OFFENSIVE.
THAT'S PROBABLY THE ONLY TACTIC THAT'LL WORK FOR YOU.
IT'S NOT LIKE I HAVE ANOTHER PLAN ANYWAY!
!!
WHAT ...?

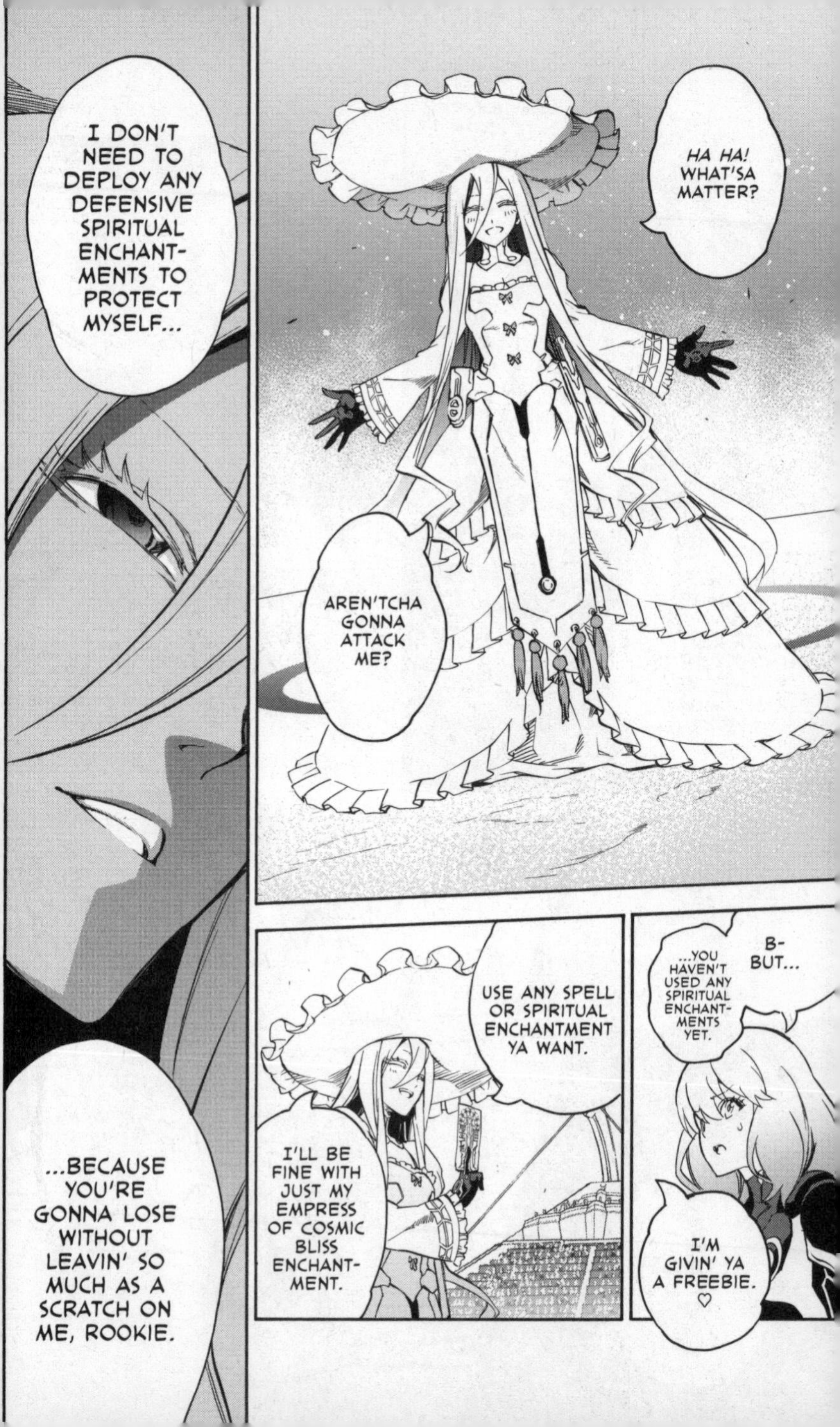
HA HA! WHAT'SA MATTER?
AREN'TCHA GONNA ATTACK ME?
B- BUT...
...YOU HAVEN'T USED ANY SPIRITUAL ENCHANT-MENTS YET.
I'M GIVIN' YA A FREEBIE. ♡
USE ANY SPELL OR SPIRITUAL ENCHANTMENT YA WANT.
I'LL BE FINE WITH JUST MY EMPRESS OF COSMIC BLISS ENCHANT-MENT.
I DON'T NEED TO DEPLOY ANY DEFENSIVE SPIRITUAL ENCHANT-MENTS TO PROTECT MYSELF...
...BECAUSE YOU'RE GONNA LOSE WITHOUT LEAVIN' SO MUCH AS A SCRATCH ON ME, ROOKIE.

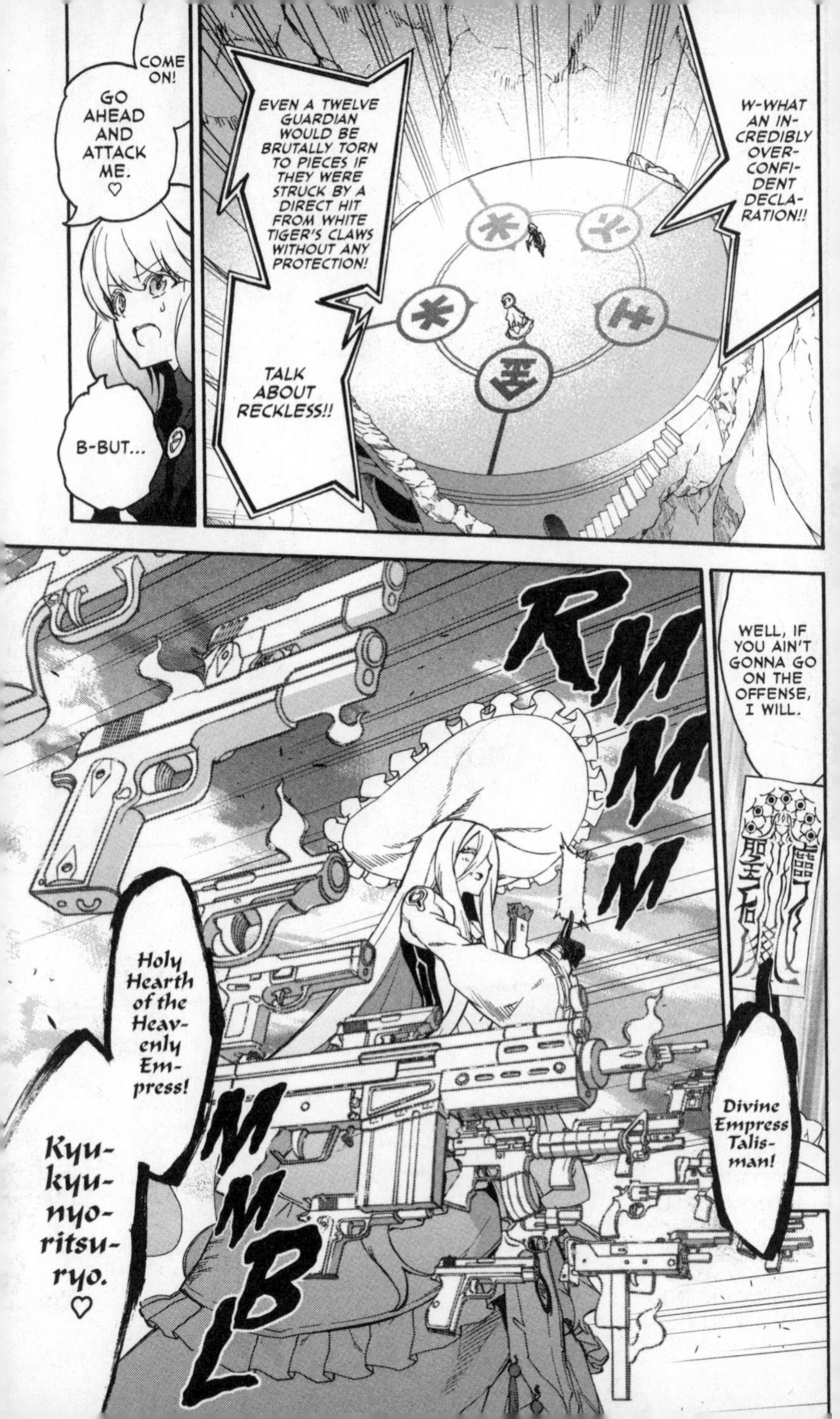
W-WHAT AN INCREDIBLY OVERCONFIDENT DECLARATION!!
EVEN A TWELVE GUARDIAN WOULD BE BRUTALLY TORN TO PIECES IF THEY WERE STRUCK BY A DIRECT HIT FROM WHITE TIGER'S CLAWS WITHOUT ANY PROTECTION!
TALK ABOUT RECKLESS!!
COME ON!
GO AHEAD AND ATTACK ME. ♡
B-BUT...
WELL, IF YOU AIN'T GONNA GO ON THE OFFENSE, I WILL.
Divine Empress Talisman!
RMMMMMMBL
Holy Hearth of the Heavenly Empress!
Kyukyunyoritsuryo. ♡

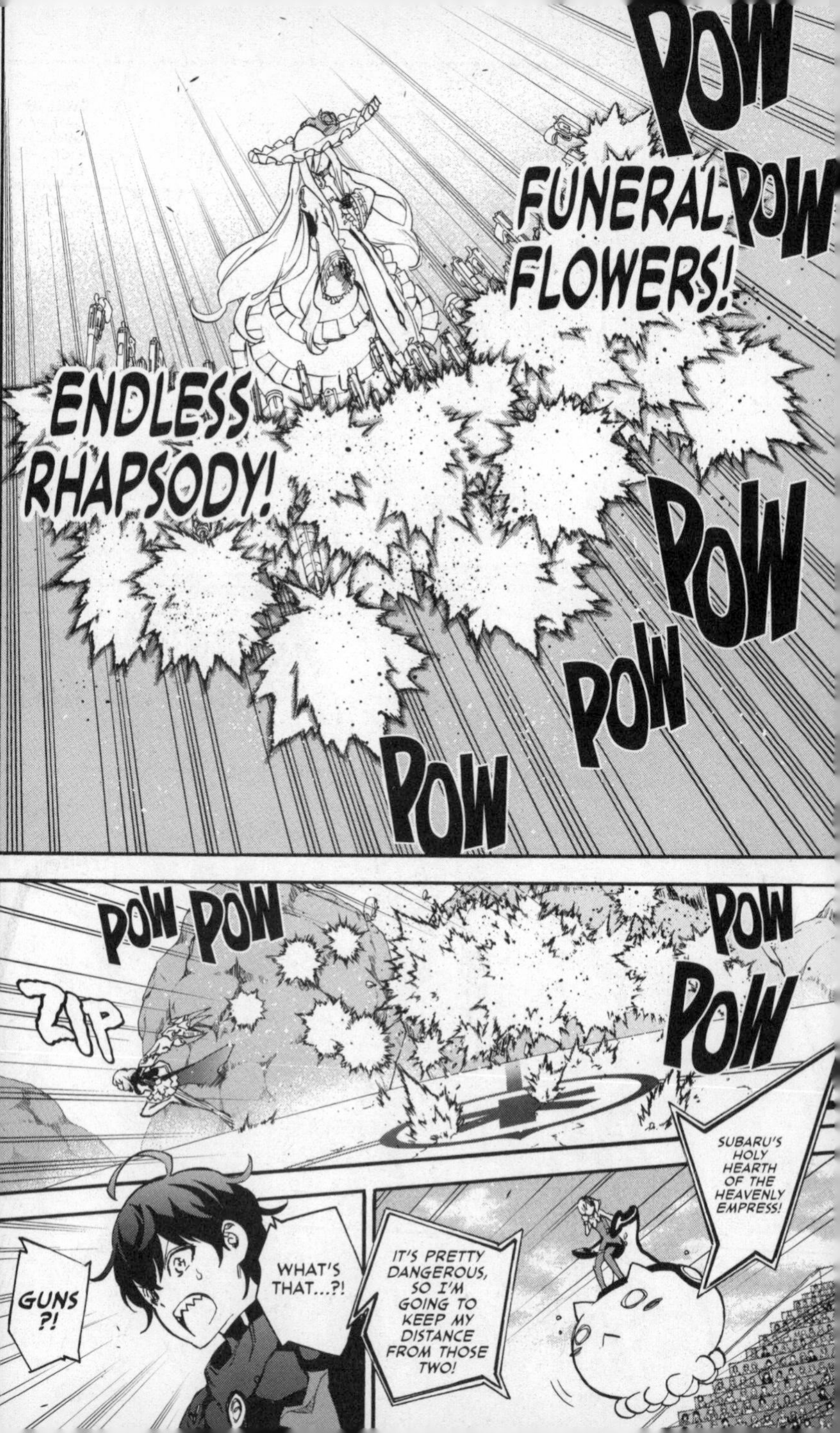
POW
FUNERAL FLOWERS!
POW
ENDLESS RHAPSODY!
POW
POW
POW
POW POW
POW POW
ZIP
SUBARU'S HOLY HEARTH OF THE HEAVENLY EMPRESS!
IT'S PRETTY DANGEROUS, SO I'M GOING TO KEEP MY DISTANCE FROM THOSE TWO!
WHAT'S THAT...?!
GUNS ?!

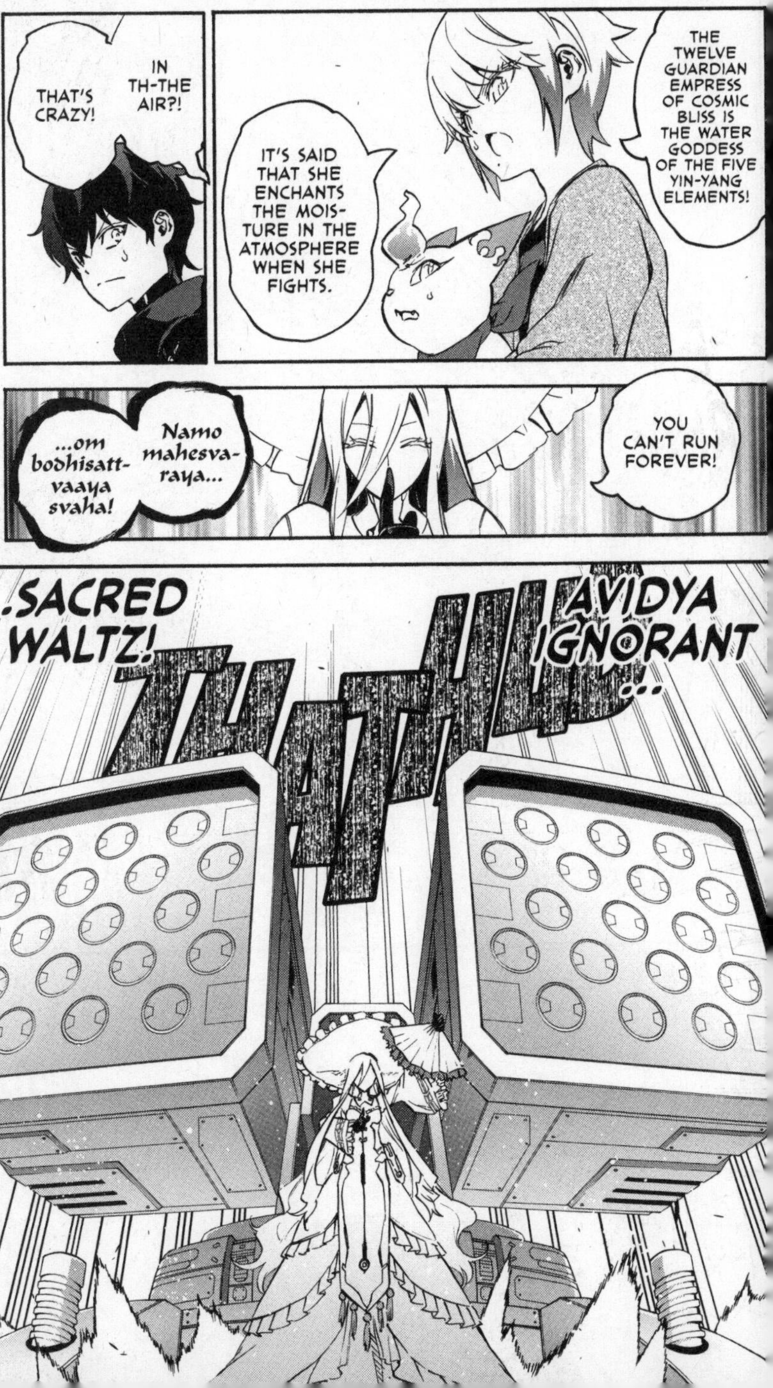
THE TWELVE GUARDIAN EMPRESS OF COSMIC BLISS IS THE WATER GODDESS OF THE FIVE YIN-YANG ELEMENTS!
IT'S SAID THAT SHE ENCHANTS THE MOIS-TURE IN THE ATMOSPHERE WHEN SHE FIGHTS.
IN TH-THE AIR?!
THAT'S CRAZY!
YOU CAN'T RUN FOREVER!
Namo mahesva-raya...
...om bodhisatt-vaaya svaha!
AVIDYA IGNORANT...
...SACRED WALTZ!

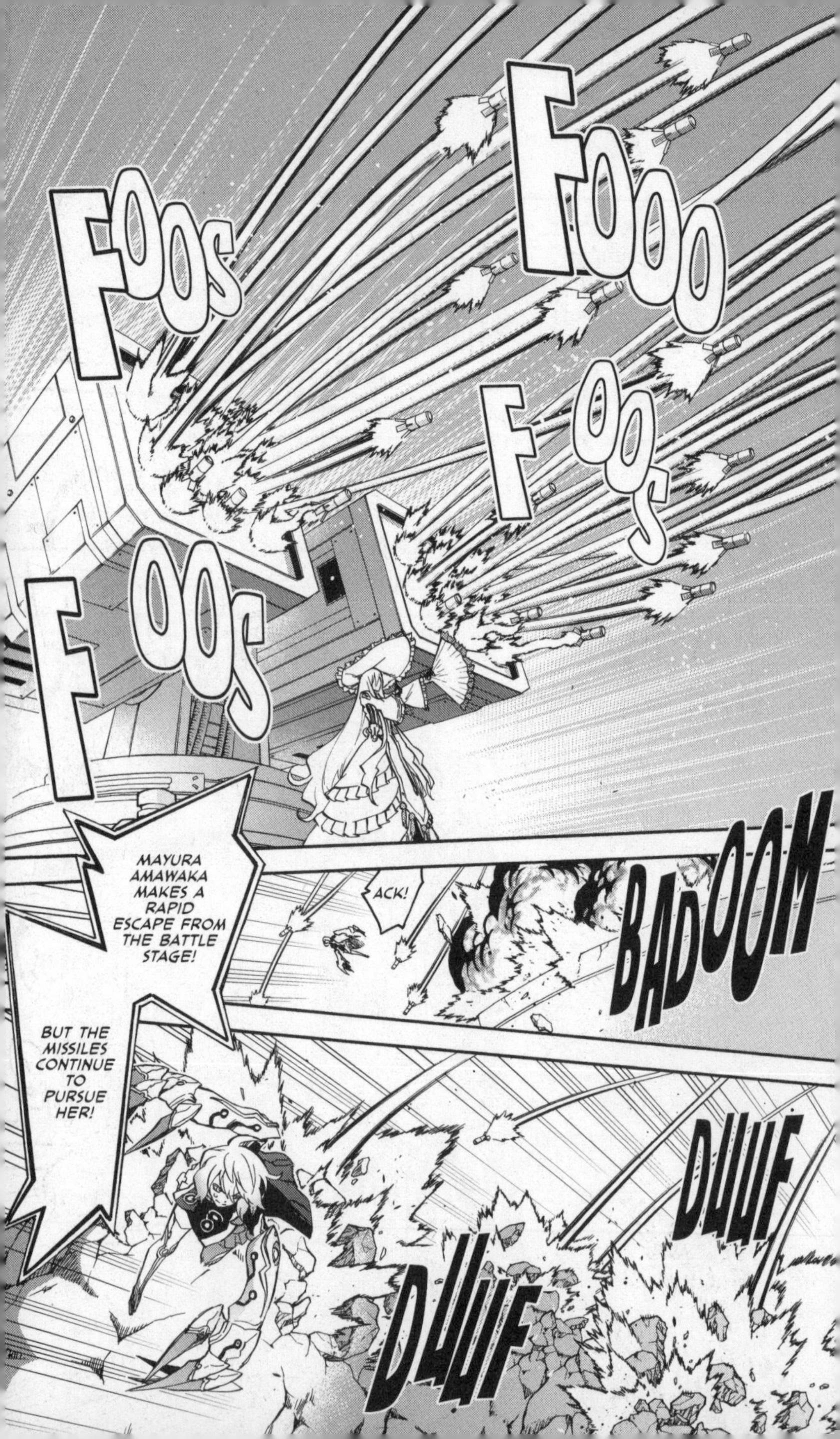
FOOOO
FOOS
FOOS
FOOS
BADOOM
ACK!
MAYURA AMAWAKA MAKES A RAPID ESCAPE FROM THE BATTLE STAGE!
DUUF
DUUF
BUT THE MISSILES CONTINUE TO PURSUE HER!

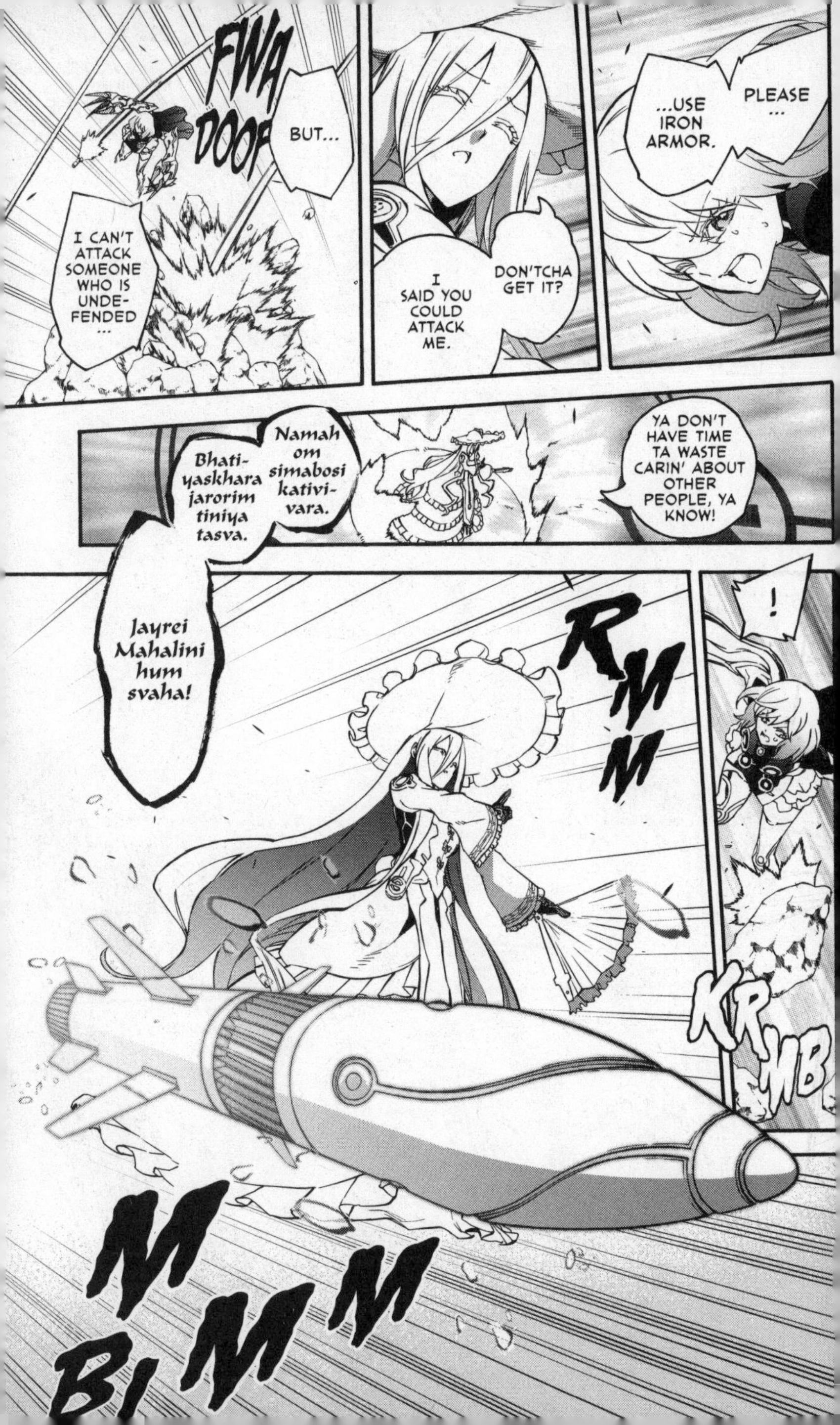
PLEASE...
...USE IRON ARMOR.
DON'TCHA GET IT?
I SAID YOU COULD ATTACK ME.
BUT...
FWA DOOF
I CAN'T ATTACK SOMEONE WHO IS UNDE-FENDED...
YA DON'T HAVE TIME TA WASTE CARIN' ABOUT OTHER PEOPLE, YA KNOW!
Namah om simabosi kativi-vara.
Bhati-yaskhara jarorim tiniya tasva.
!
KRMB
RMM
Jayrei Mahalini hum svaha!
BIMMM

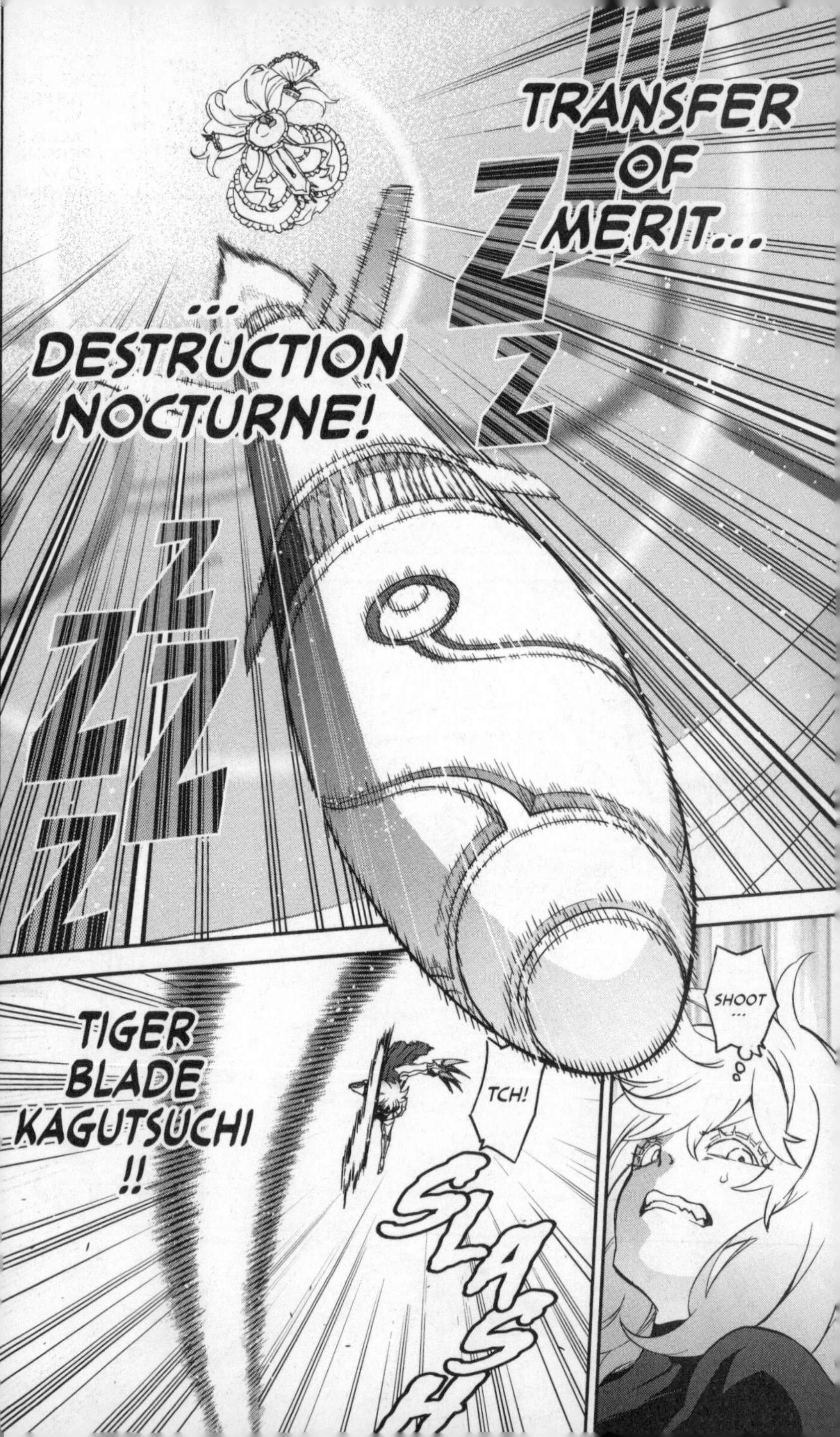
TRANSFER OF MERIT...
ZZZ
...DESTRUCTION NOCTURNE!
ZZZZZ
SHOOT...
TCH!
TIGER BLADE KAGUTSUCHI !!
SLASH

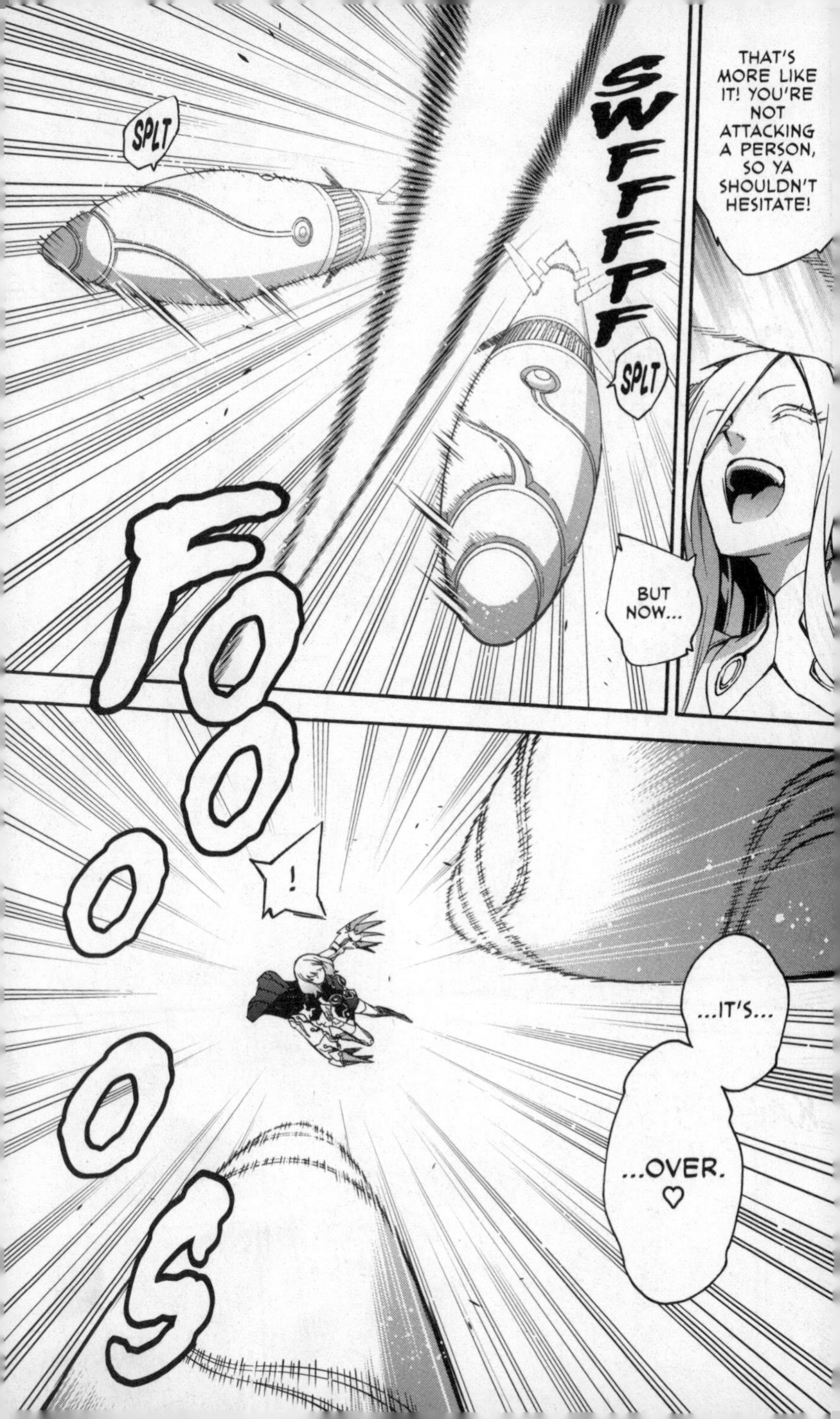
THAT'S MORE LIKE IT! YOU'RE NOT ATTACKING A PERSON, SO YA SHOULDN'T HESITATE!
BUT NOW...
SWFFFPF
SPLT
SPLT
...IT'S...
...OVER. ♡
!
FOOOOS

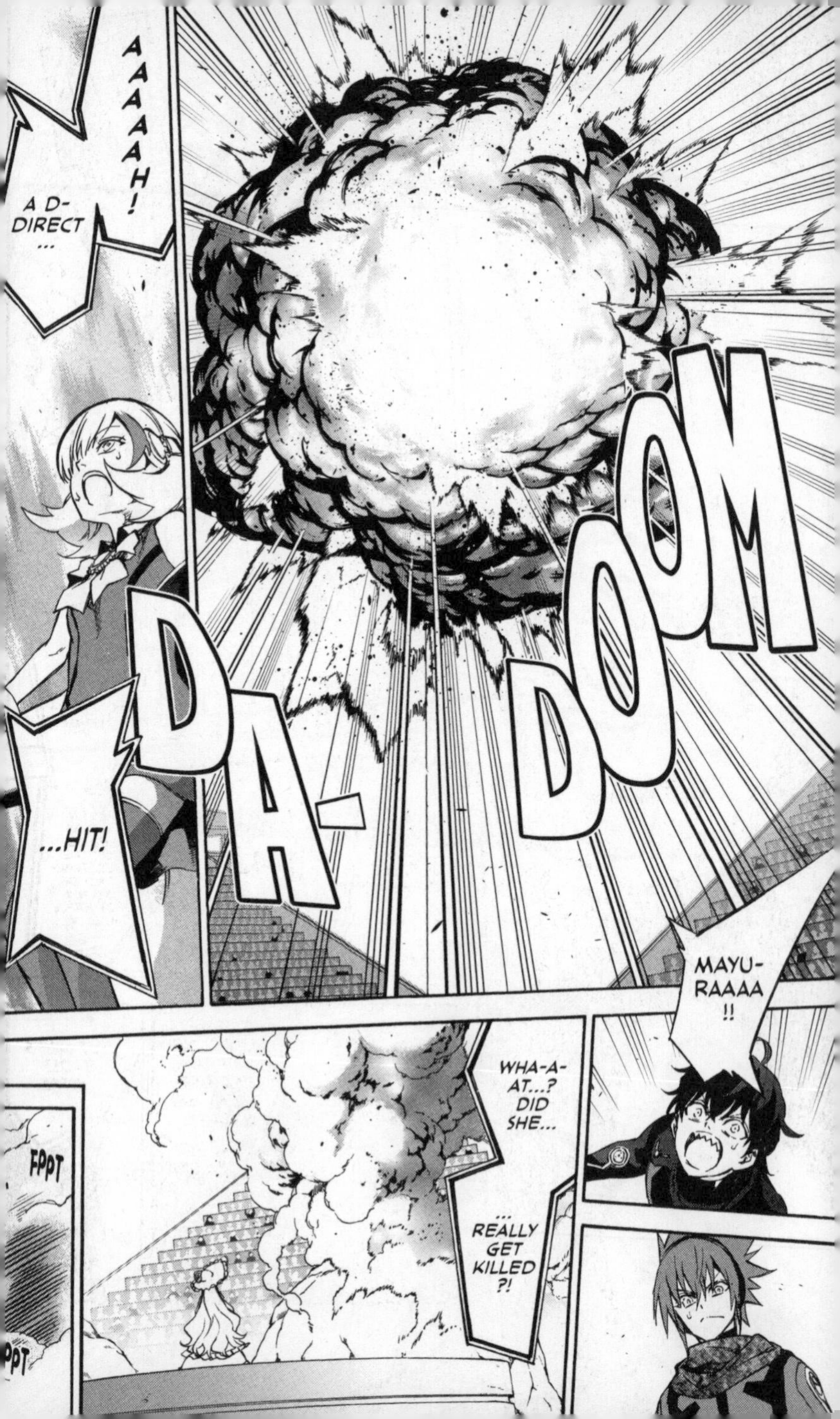
DA-DOOM
AAAAAAH!
A D-DIRECT...
...HIT!
MAYU-RAAAA!!
WHA-A-AT...? DID SHE...
...REALLY GET KILLED?!
FPPT
PPT

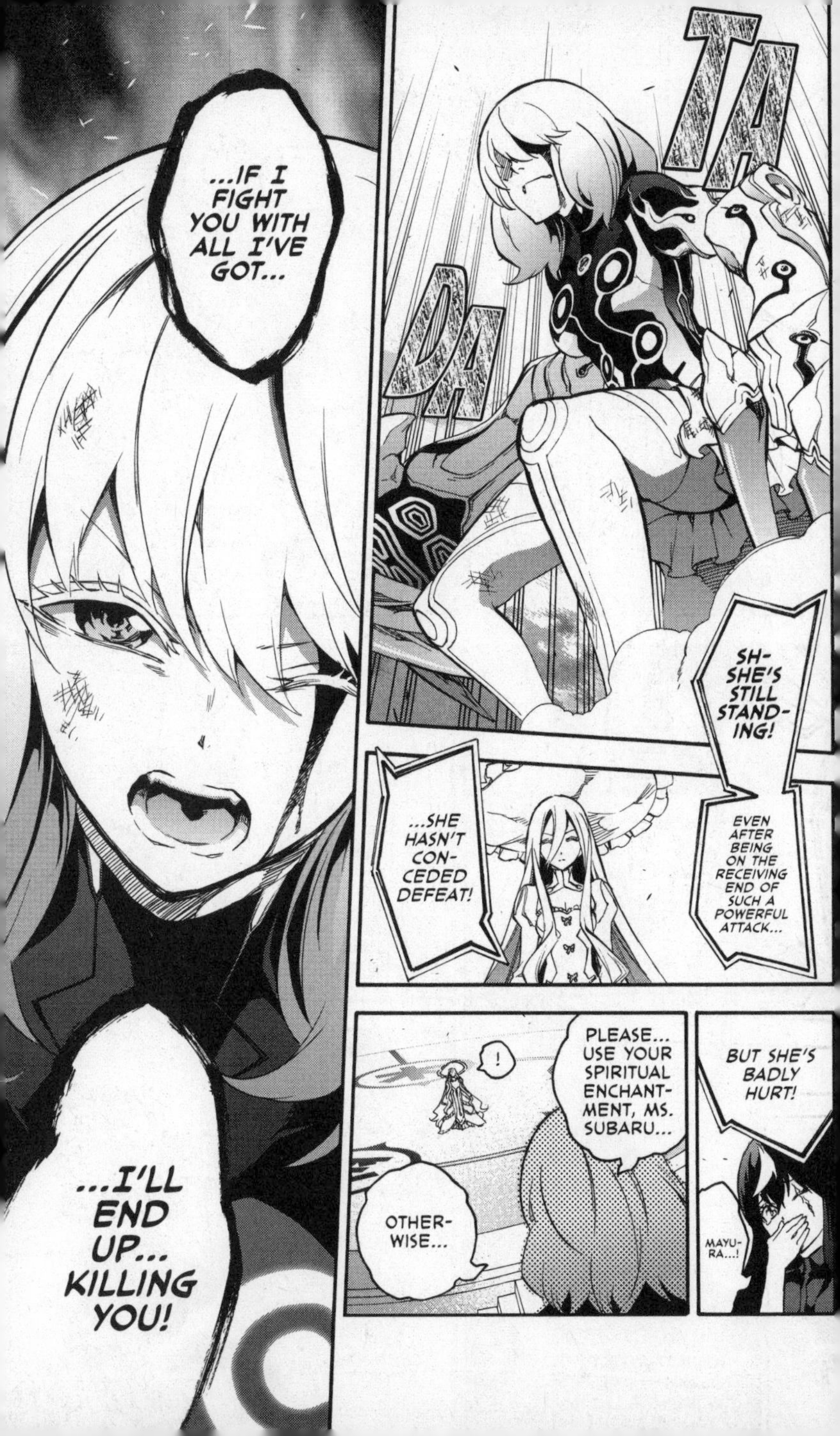
TA
DA
SH-SHE'S STILL STANDING!
EVEN AFTER BEING ON THE RECEIVING END OF SUCH A POWERFUL ATTACK...
...SHE HASN'T CONCEDED DEFEAT!
BUT SHE'S BADLY HURT!
MAYURA...!
!
PLEASE... USE YOUR SPIRITUAL ENCHANTMENT, MS. SUBARU...
OTHERWISE...
...IF I FIGHT YOU WITH ALL I'VE GOT...
...I'LL END UP... KILLING YOU!

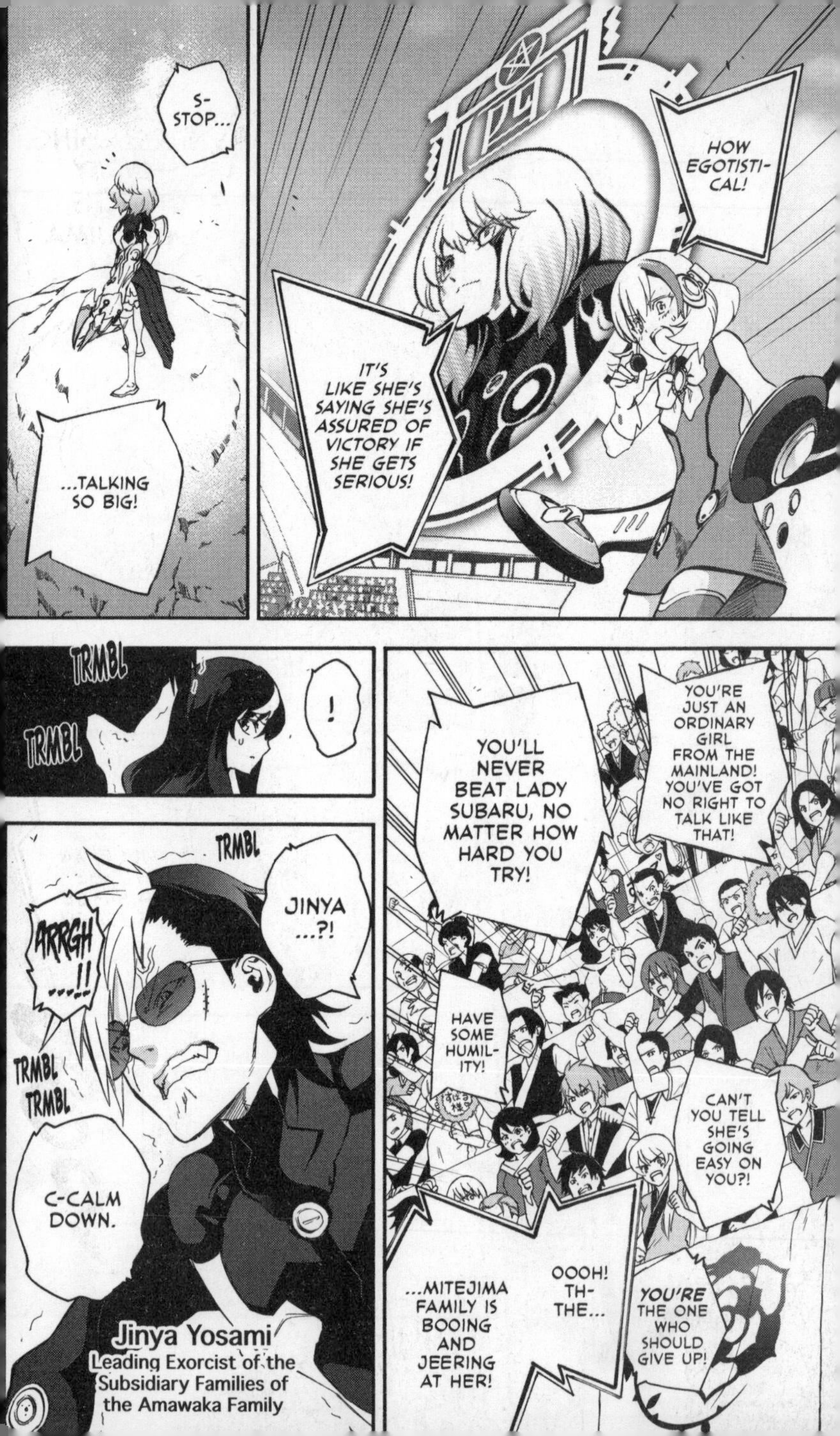
HOW EGOTISTI-CAL!
IT'S LIKE SHE'S SAYING SHE'S ASSURED OF VICTORY IF SHE GETS SERIOUS!
S-STOP...
...TALKING SO BIG!
YOU'RE JUST AN ORDINARY GIRL FROM THE MAINLAND! YOU'VE GOT NO RIGHT TO TALK LIKE THAT!
YOU'LL NEVER BEAT LADY SUBARU, NO MATTER HOW HARD YOU TRY!
HAVE SOME HUMIL-ITY!
CAN'T YOU TELL SHE'S GOING EASY ON YOU?!
YOU'RE THE ONE WHO SHOULD GIVE UP!
OOOH! TH-THE...
...MITEJIMA FAMILY IS BOOING AND JEERING AT HER!
TRMBL
TRMBL
!
JINYA ...?!
TRMBL
ARRGH!! ...!!
TRMBL TRMBL
C-CALM DOWN.
Jinya Yosami
Leading Exorcist of the Subsidiary Families of the Amawaka Family

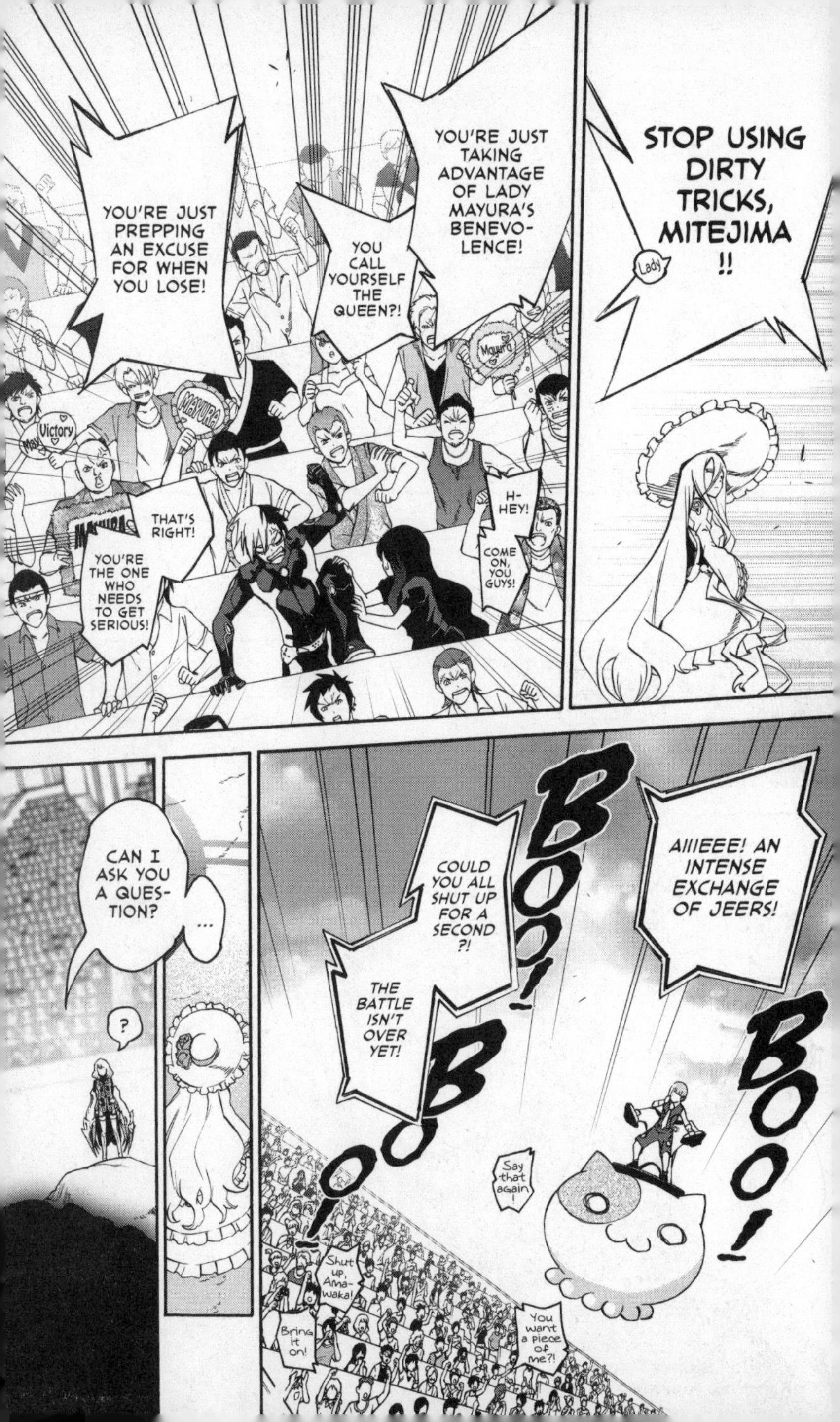

Lady
STOP USING DIRTY TRICKS, MITEJIMA !!
YOU'RE JUST TAKING ADVANTAGE OF LADY MAYURA'S BENEVO-LENCE!
YOU CALL YOURSELF THE QUEEN?!
YOU'RE JUST PREPPING AN EXCUSE FOR WHEN YOU LOSE!
Mayura
MAYURA
Victory
May
H-HEY!
COME ON, YOU GUYS!
THAT'S RIGHT!
YOU'RE THE ONE WHO NEEDS TO GET SERIOUS!
AIIIEEE! AN INTENSE EXCHANGE OF JEERS!
BOOO!
COULD YOU ALL SHUT UP FOR A SECOND ?!
THE BATTLE ISN'T OVER YET!
BOOO!
BOOO!
Say that again!
You want a piece of me?!
Shut up, Ama-waka!
Bring it on!
...
CAN I ASK YOU A QUES-TION?
?

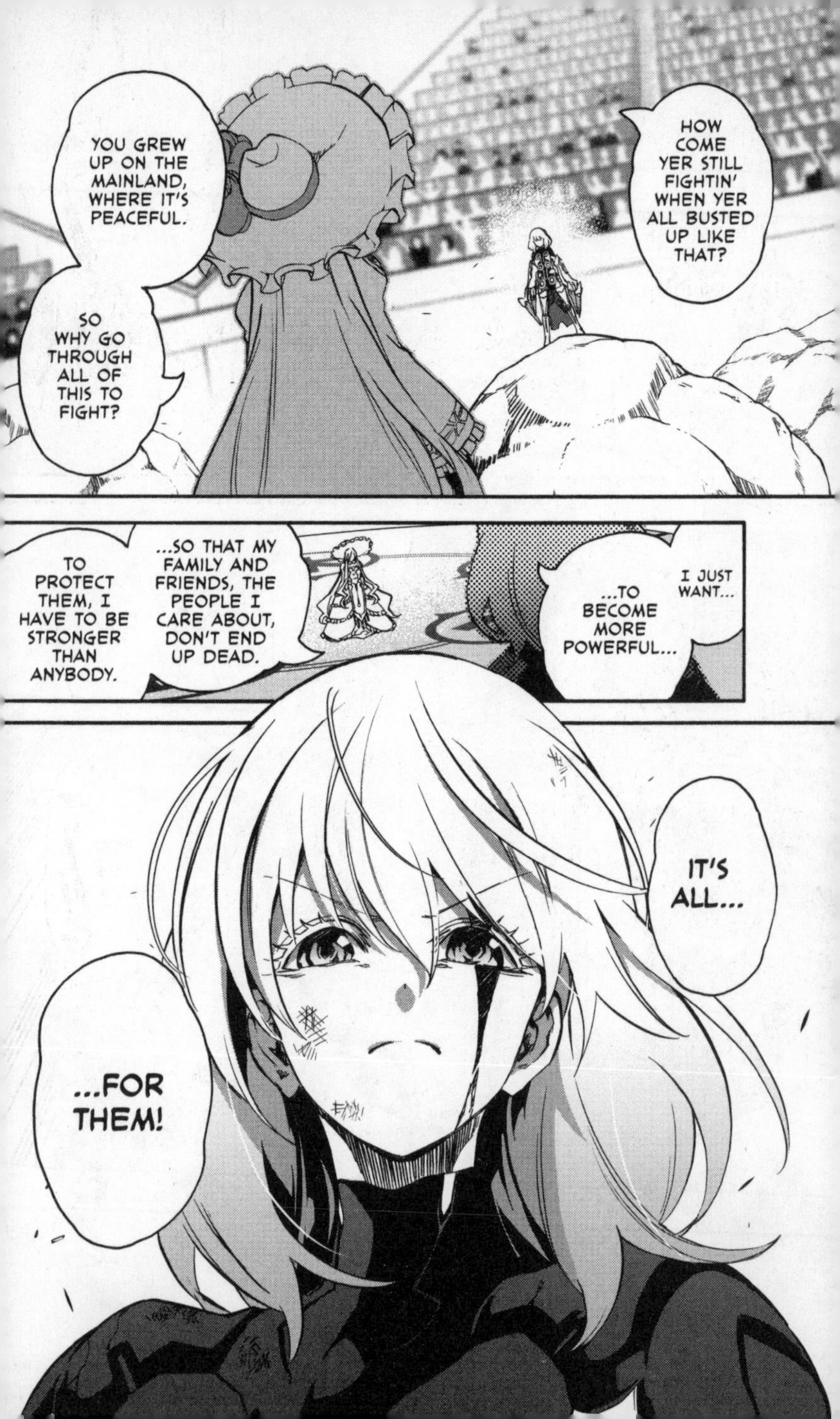
HOW COME YER STILL FIGHTIN' WHEN YER ALL BUSTED UP LIKE THAT?
YOU GREW UP ON THE MAINLAND, WHERE IT'S PEACEFUL.
SO WHY GO THROUGH ALL OF THIS TO FIGHT?
I JUST WANT...
...TO BECOME MORE POWERFUL...
...SO THAT MY FAMILY AND FRIENDS, THE PEOPLE I CARE ABOUT, DON'T END UP DEAD.
TO PROTECT THEM, I HAVE TO BE STRONGER THAN ANYBODY.
IT'S ALL...
...FOR THEM!

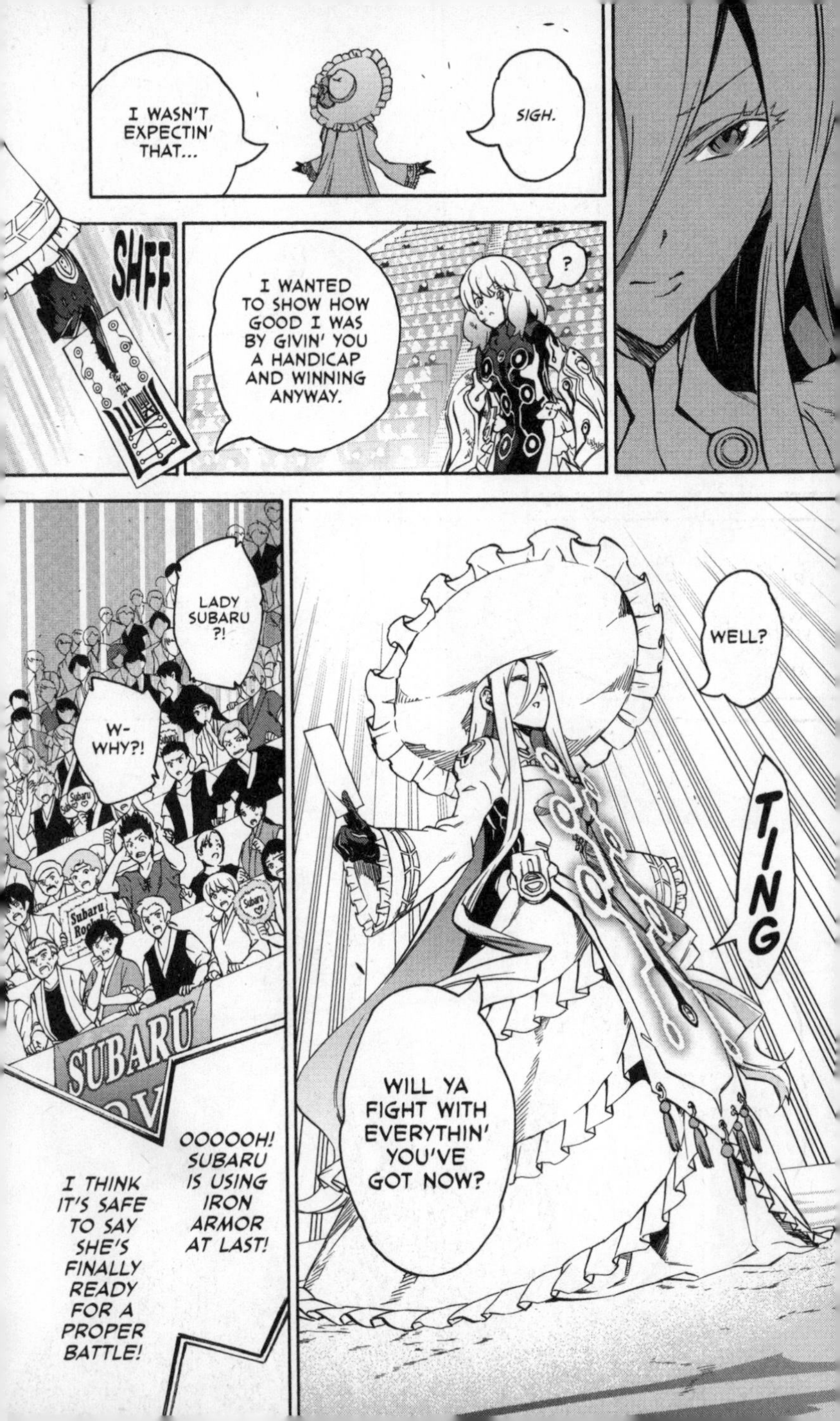
SIGH.
I WASN'T EXPECTIN' THAT...
?
I WANTED TO SHOW HOW GOOD I WAS BY GIVIN' YOU A HANDICAP AND WINNING ANYWAY.
SHFF
WELL?
TING
WILL YA FIGHT WITH EVERYTHIN' YOU'VE GOT NOW?
LADY SUBARU ?!
W- WHY?!
SUBARU
OOOOOH! SUBARU IS USING IRON ARMOR AT LAST!
I THINK IT'S SAFE TO SAY SHE'S FINALLY READY FOR A PROPER BATTLE!

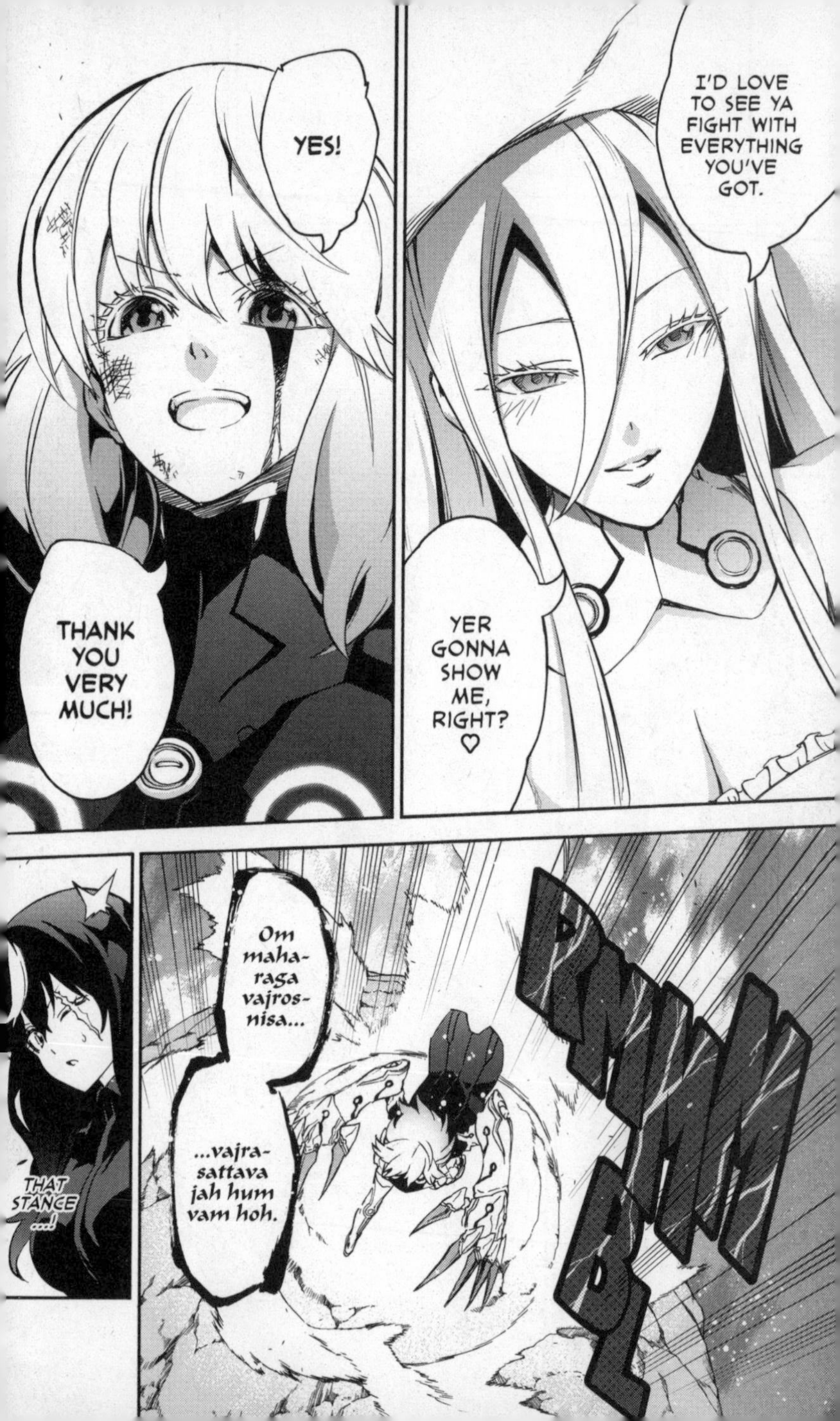
I'D LOVE TO SEE YA FIGHT WITH EVERYTHING YOU'VE GOT.
YER GONNA SHOW ME, RIGHT? ♡
YES!
THANK YOU VERY MUCH!
Om maha-raga vajros-nisa...
...vajra-sattava jah hum vam hoh.
THAT STANCE ...!

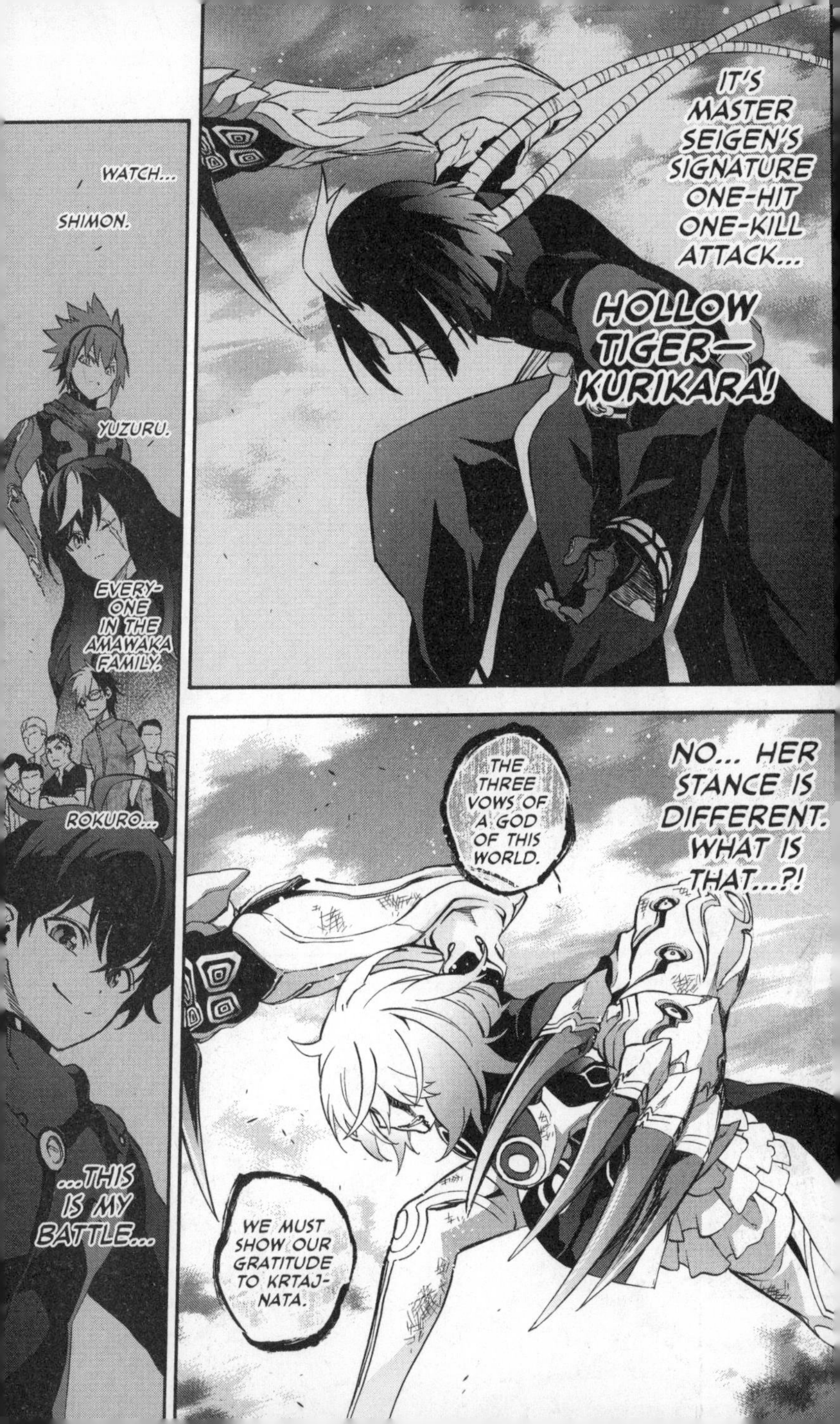
IT'S MASTER SEIGEN'S SIGNATURE ONE-HIT ONE-KILL ATTACK...
HOLLOW TIGER—KURIKARA!
NO... HER STANCE IS DIFFERENT. WHAT IS THAT...?!
THE THREE VOWS OF A GOD OF THIS WORLD.
WE MUST SHOW OUR GRATITUDE TO KRTAJ-NATA.
WATCH...
SHIMON.
YUZURU.
EVERY-ONE IN THE AMAWAKA FAMILY.
ROKURO...
...THIS IS MY BATTLE...

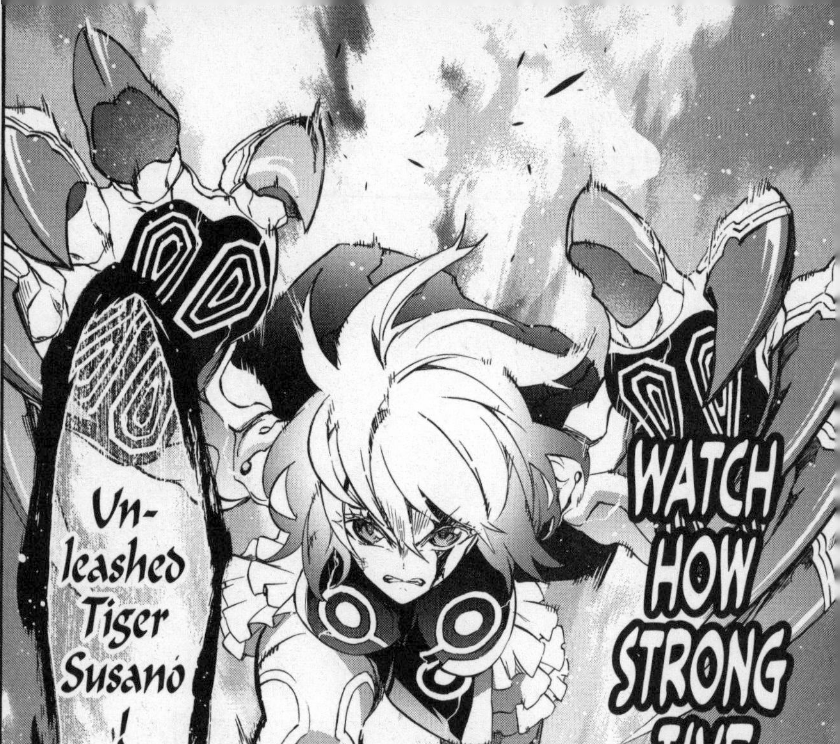
WATCH HOW STRONG I'VE BECOME!
Unleashed Tiger Susanó!
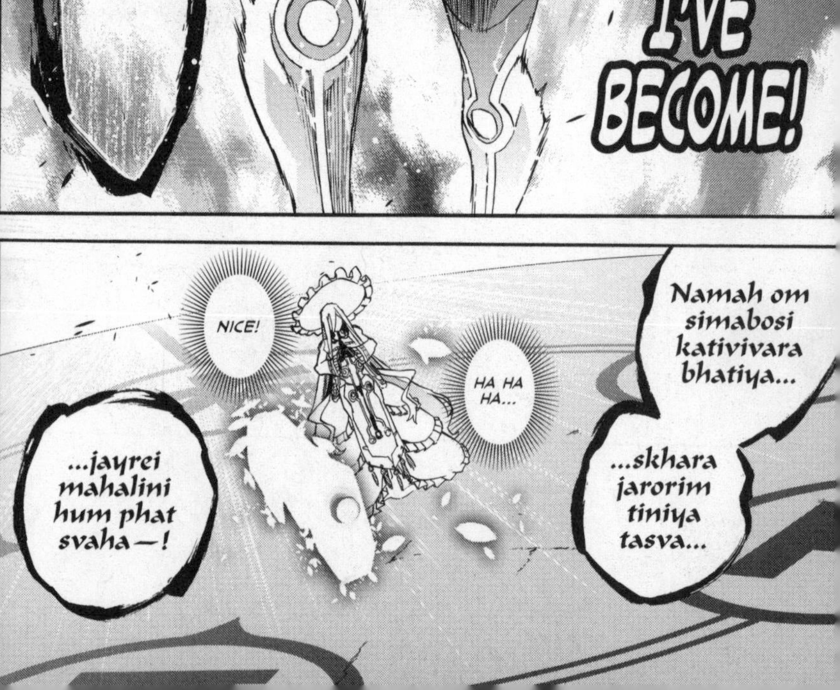
Namah om simabosi kativivara bhatiya...
...skhara jarorim tiniya tasva...
HA HA HA...
NICE!
...jayrei mahalini hum phat svaha—!

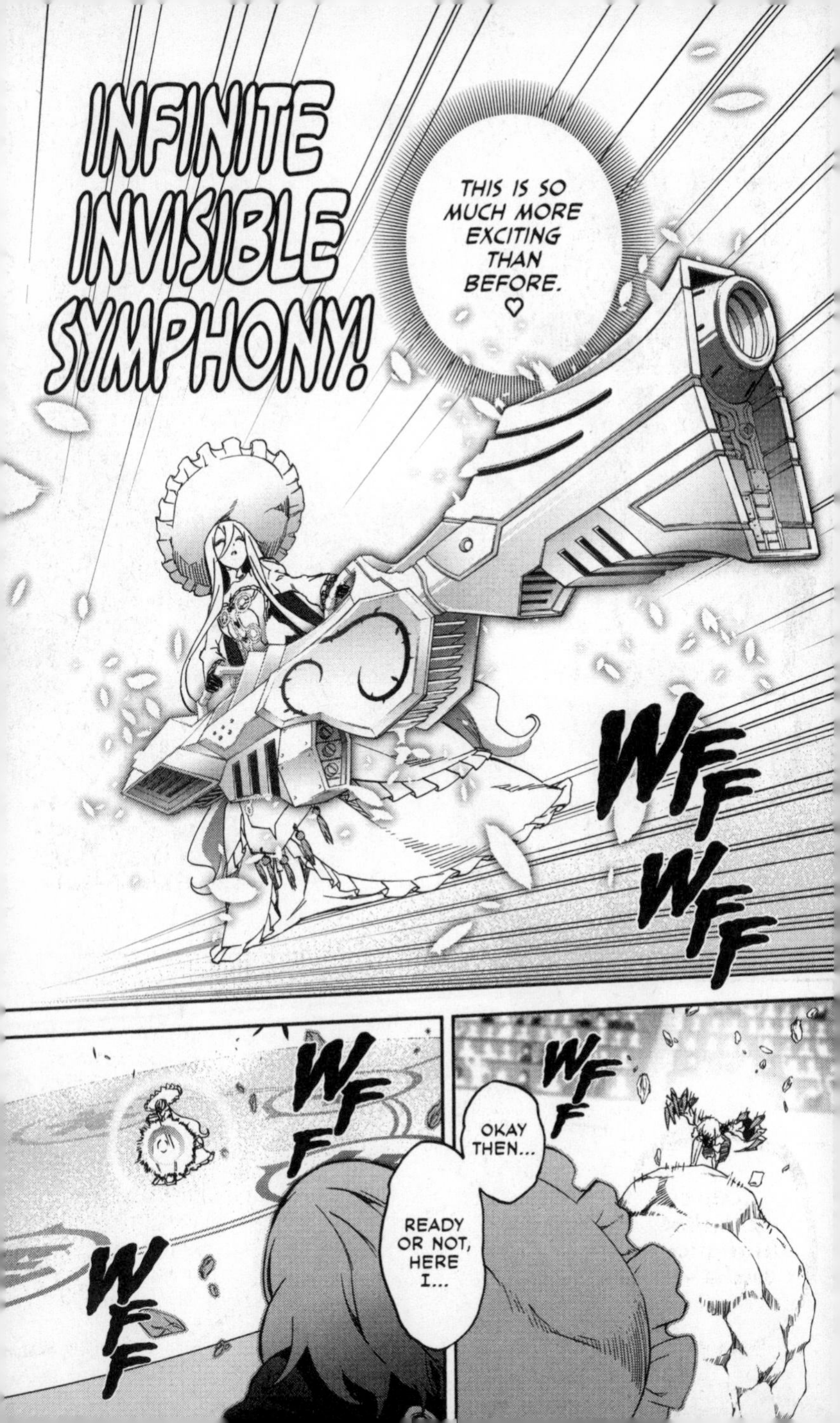
THIS IS SO MUCH MORE EXCITING THAN BEFORE. ♡
INFINITE INVISIBLE SYMPHONY!
WFF
WFF
WFF
OKAY THEN...
READY OR NOT, HERE I...
WFF
WFF

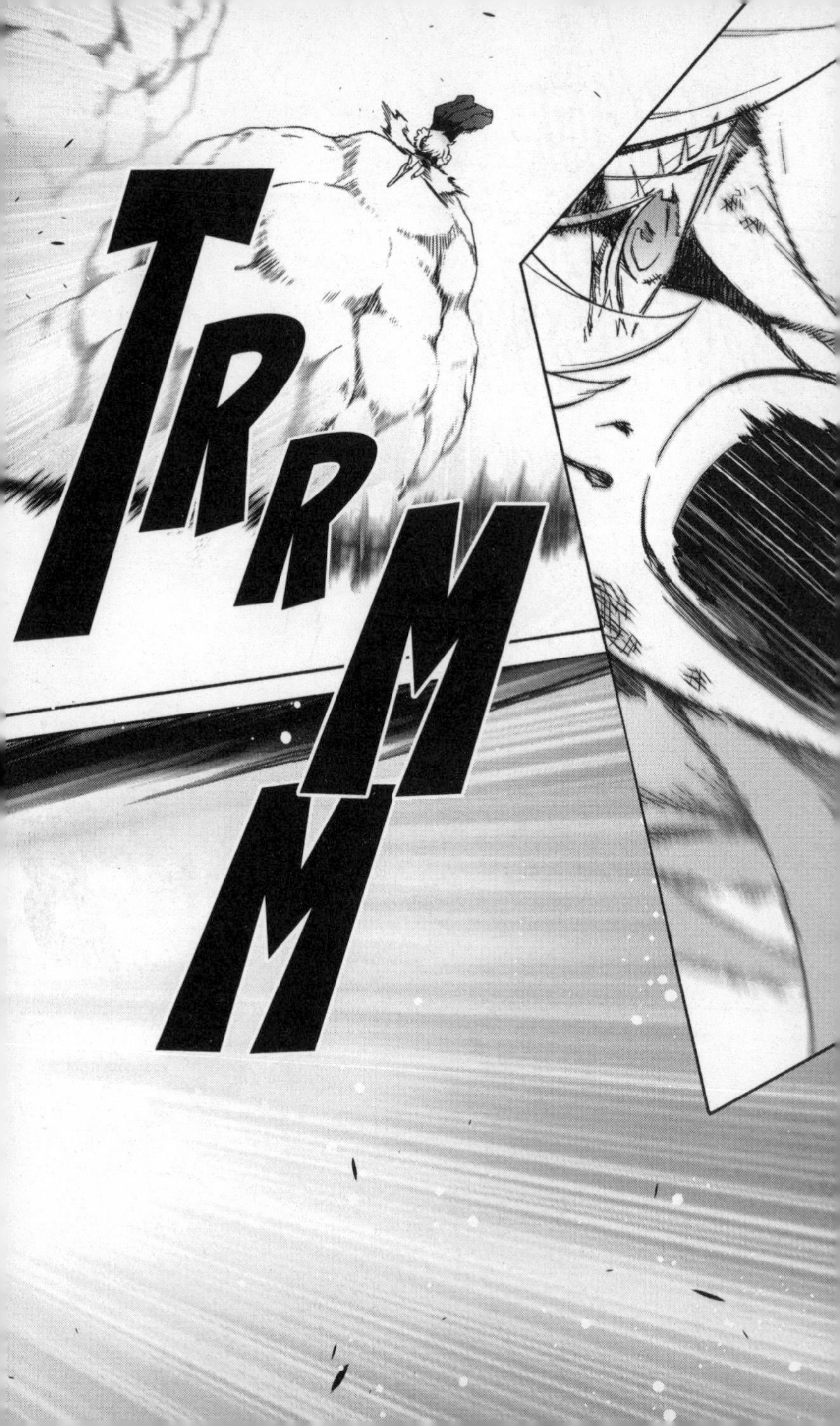
TRRMMM

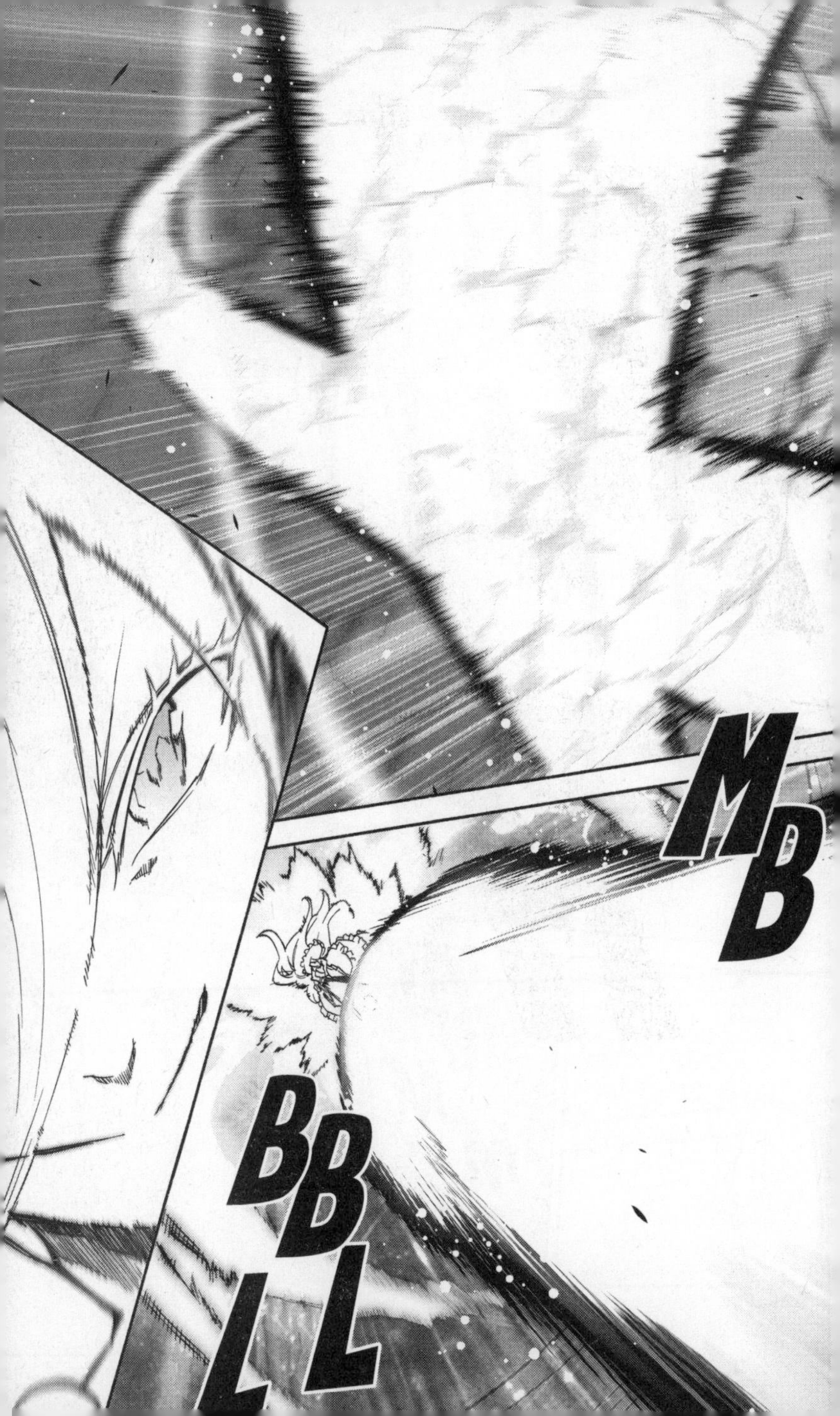
MBB
BBBLL

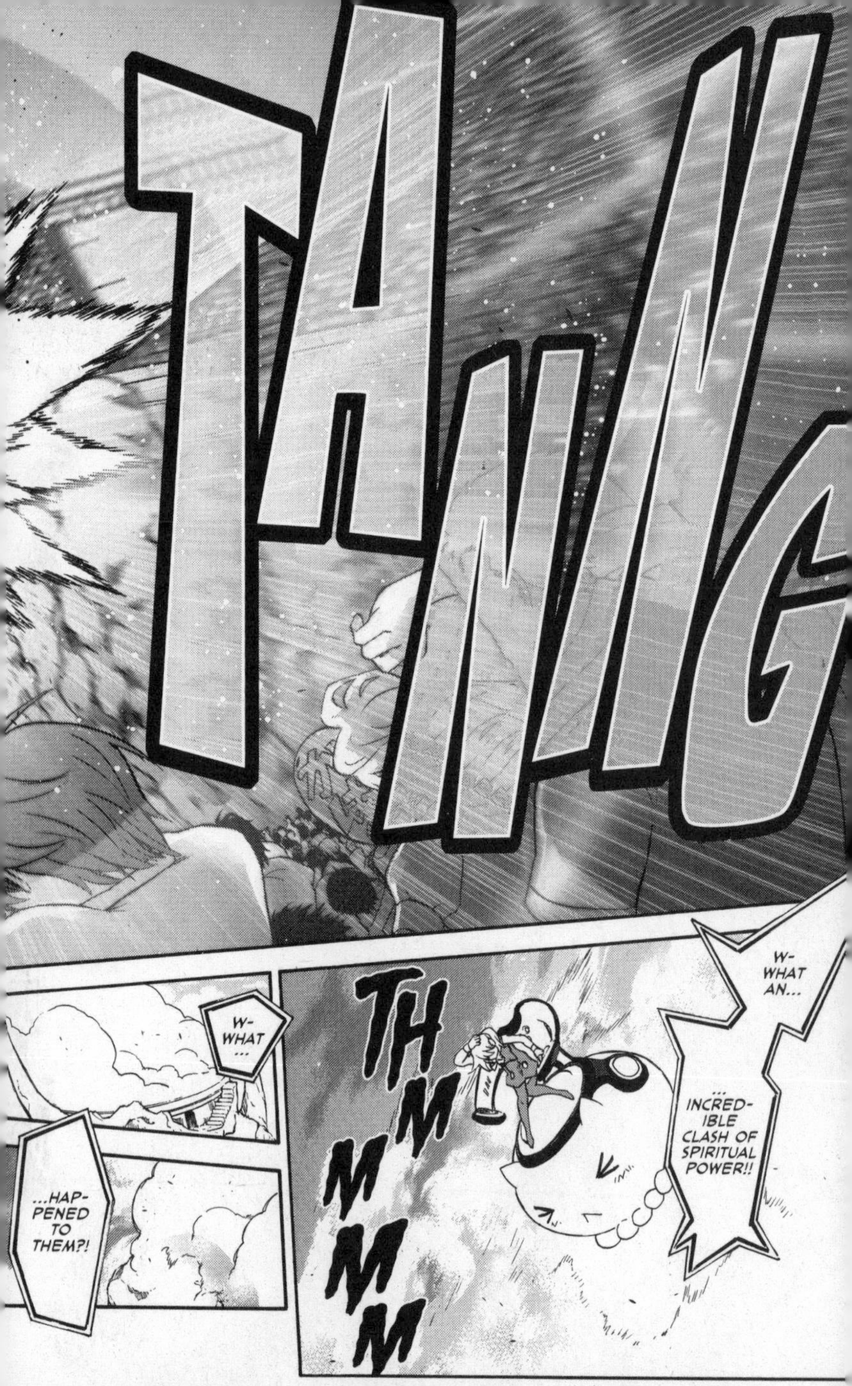
TANNG
W-WHAT AN... ...INCREDIBLE CLASH OF SPIRITUAL POWER!!
THMMMM
W-WHAT...
...HAPPENED TO THEM?!

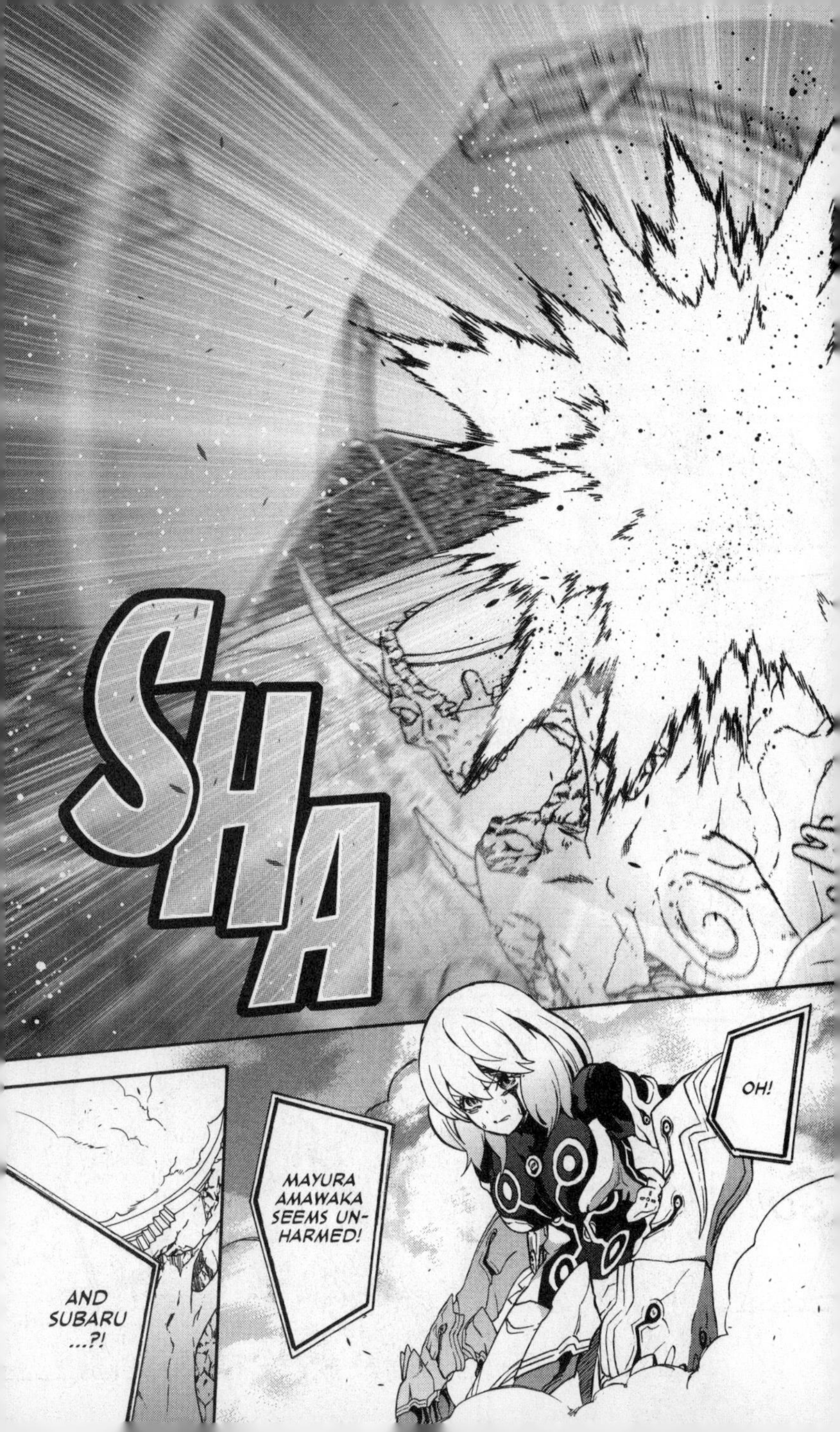
SHA
OH!
MAYURA AMAWAKA SEEMS UN-HARMED!
AND SUBARU ...?!

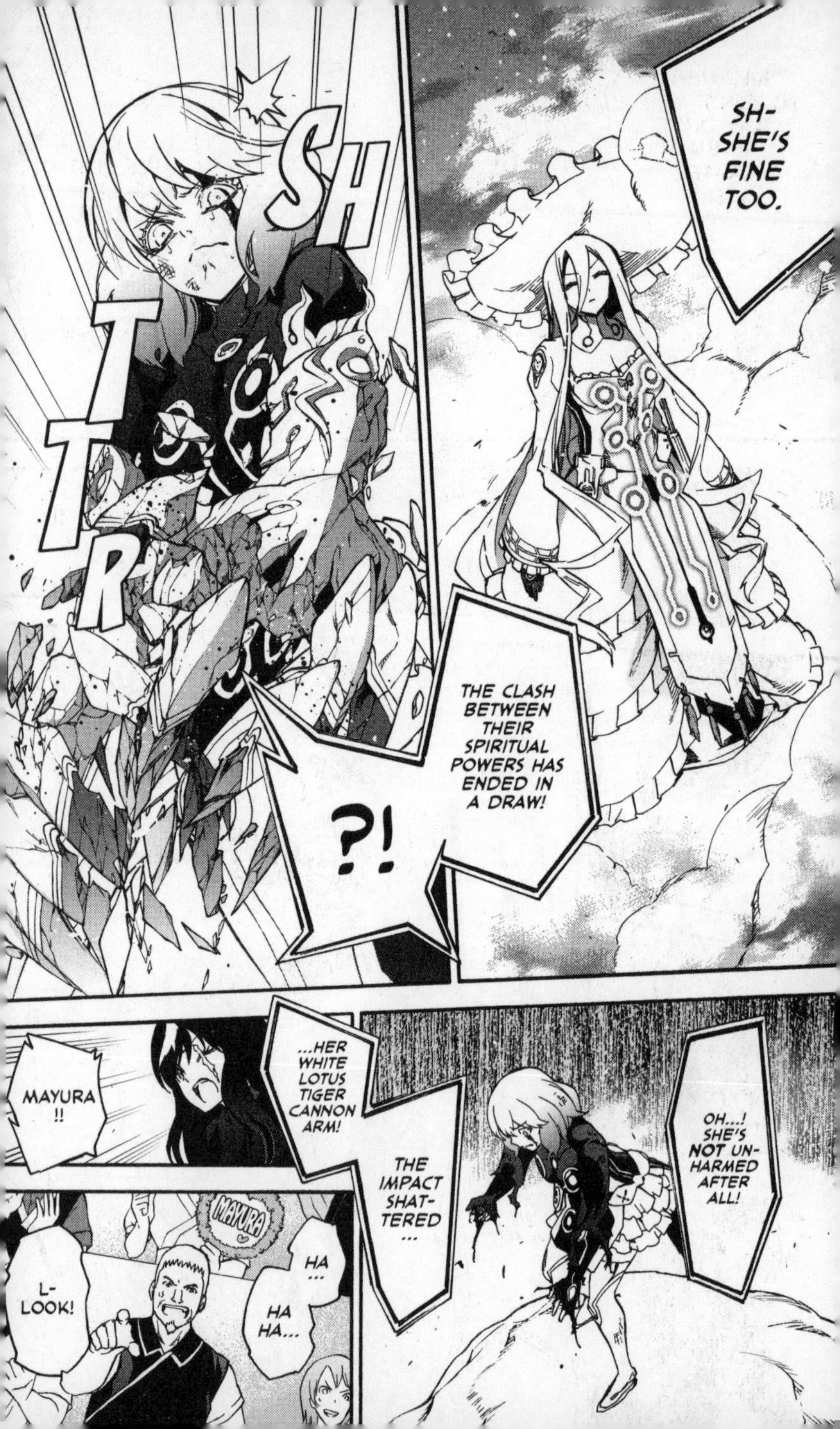
SH-SHE'S FINE TOO.
THE CLASH BETWEEN THEIR SPIRITUAL POWERS HAS ENDED IN A DRAW!
SH
TTR
?!
OH...! SHE'S NOT UNHARMED AFTER ALL!
THE IMPACT SHATTERED...
...HER WHITE LOTUS TIGER CANNON ARM!
MAYURA!!
HA... HA HA...
MAYURA
L-LOOK!

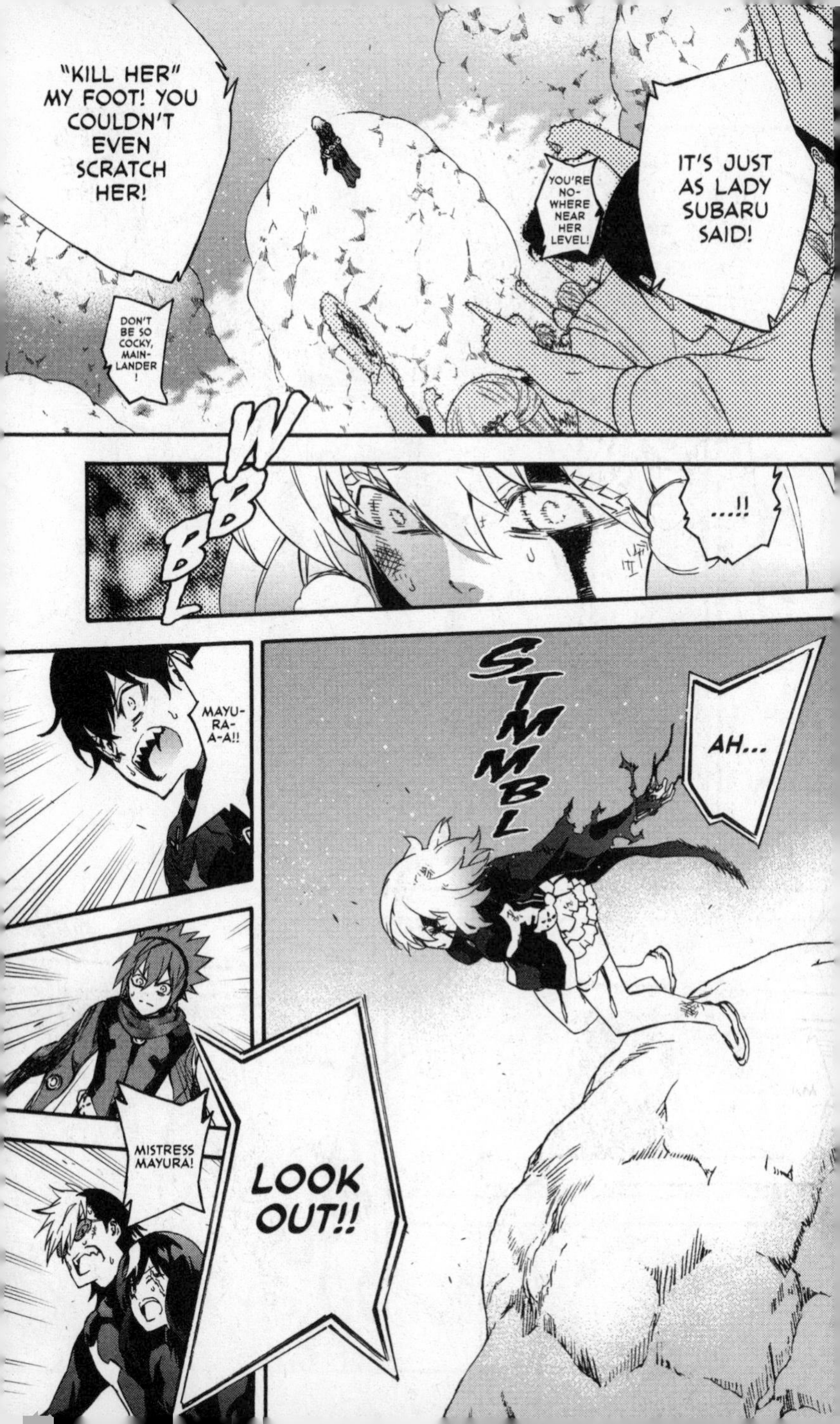
IT'S JUST AS LADY SUBARU SAID!
YOU'RE NO-WHERE NEAR HER LEVEL!
"KILL HER" MY FOOT! YOU COULDN'T EVEN SCRATCH HER!
DON'T BE SO COCKY, MAIN-LANDER!
...!!
WBBL
STMMBL
AH...
MAYU-RA-A-A!!
MISTRESS MAYURA!
LOOK OUT!!

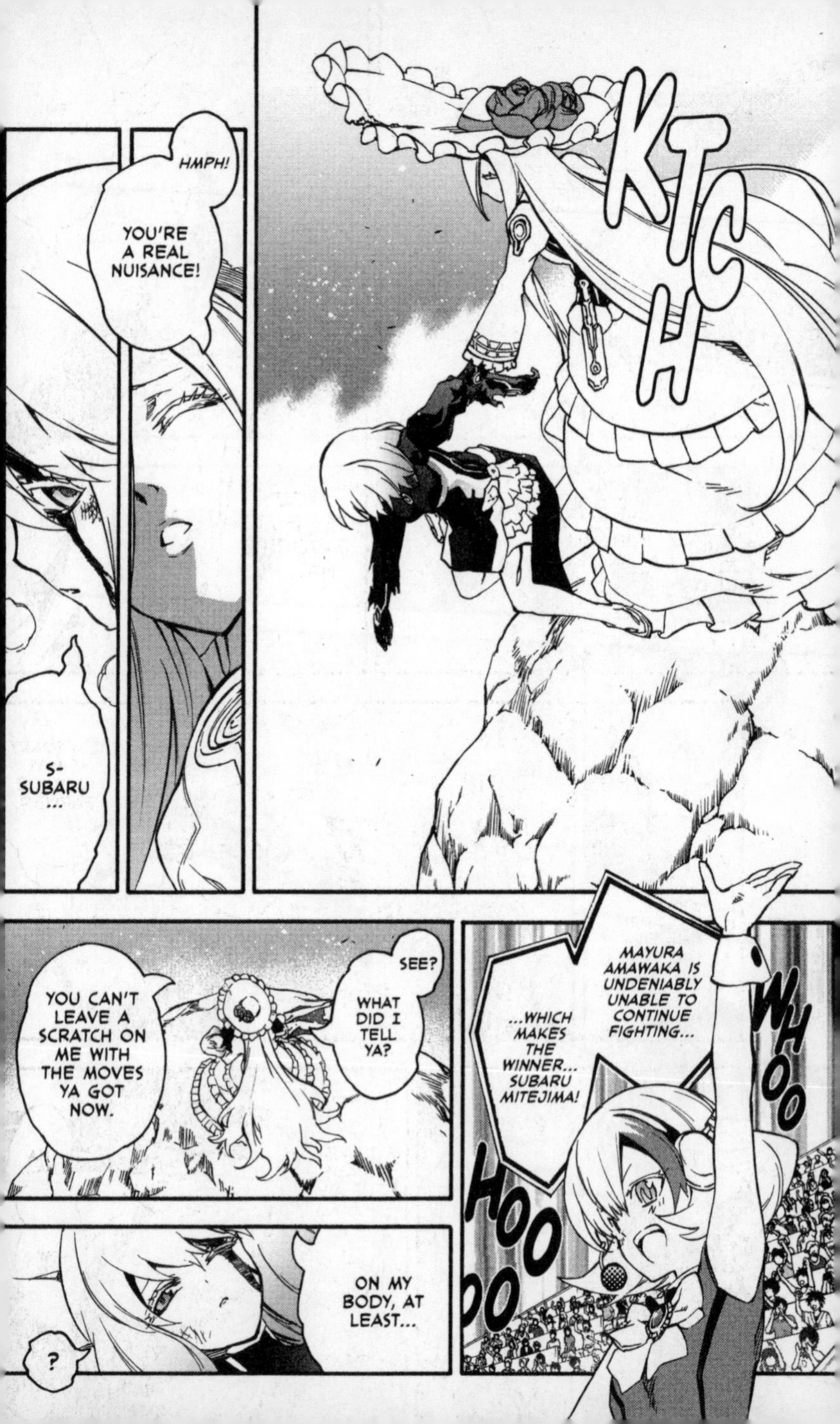
KTCH
HMPH!
YOU'RE A REAL NUISANCE!
S-SUBARU...
MAYURA AMAWAKA IS UNDENIABLY UNABLE TO CONTINUE FIGHTING...
...WHICH MAKES THE WINNER... SUBARU MITEJIMA!
WHOO
HOOOOO
SEE?
WHAT DID I TELL YA?
YOU CAN'T LEAVE A SCRATCH ON ME WITH THE MOVES YA GOT NOW.
ON MY BODY, AT LEAST...
?

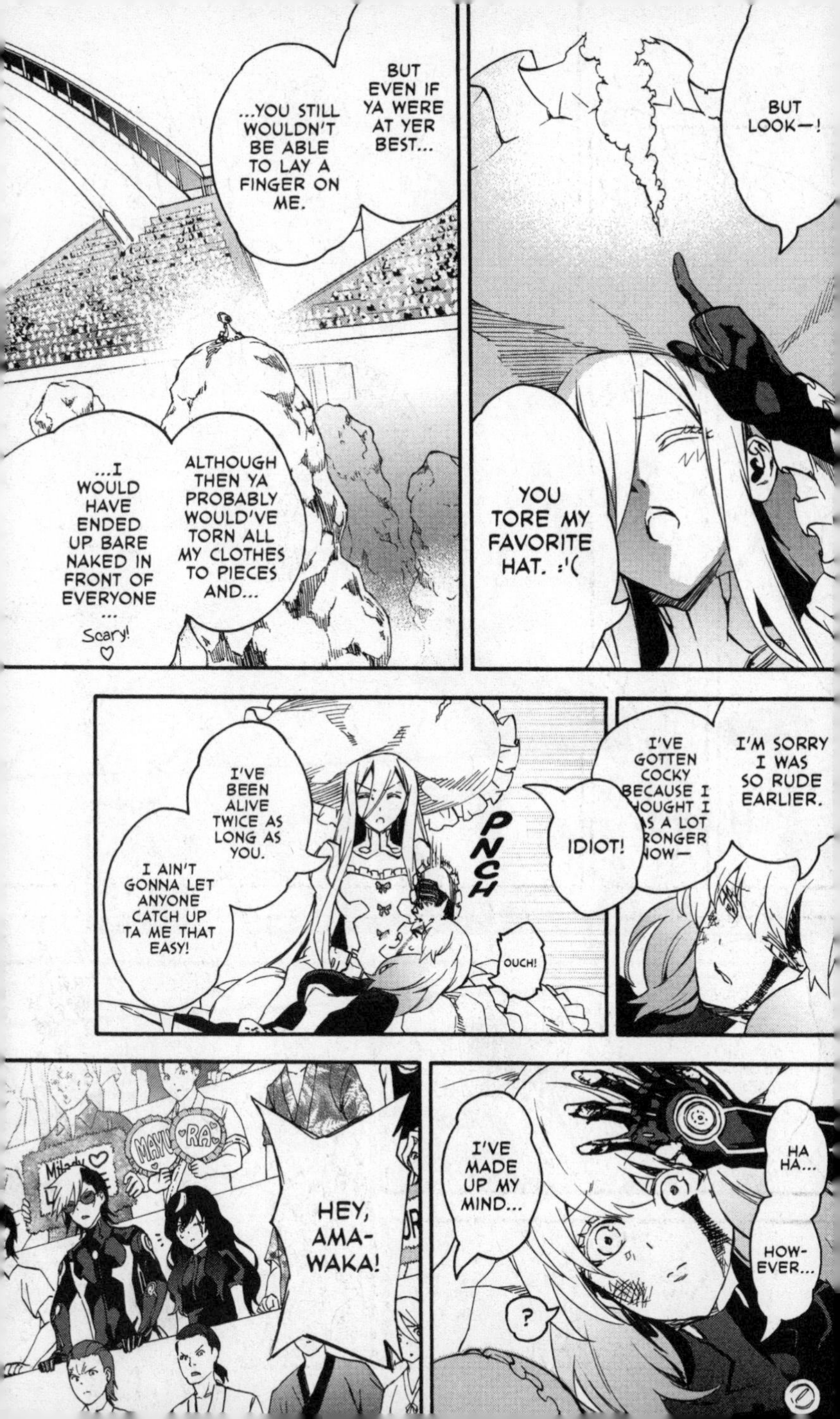
BUT LOOK—!
YOU TORE MY FAVORITE HAT. :'(
BUT EVEN IF YA WERE AT YER BEST...
...YOU STILL WOULDN'T BE ABLE TO LAY A FINGER ON ME.
ALTHOUGH THEN YA PROBABLY WOULD'VE TORN ALL MY CLOTHES TO PIECES AND...
...I WOULD HAVE ENDED UP BARE NAKED IN FRONT OF EVERYONE...
Scary! ♡
I'M SORRY I WAS SO RUDE EARLIER.
I'VE GOTTEN COCKY BECAUSE I HOUGHT I AS A LOT RONGER NOW—
IDIOT!
PNCH
OUCH!
I'VE BEEN ALIVE TWICE AS LONG AS YOU.
I AIN'T GONNA LET ANYONE CATCH UP TA ME THAT EASY!
HA HA...
HOW-EVER...
I'VE MADE UP MY MIND...
?
HEY, AMA-WAKA!
Milady ♡
MAYU
RA

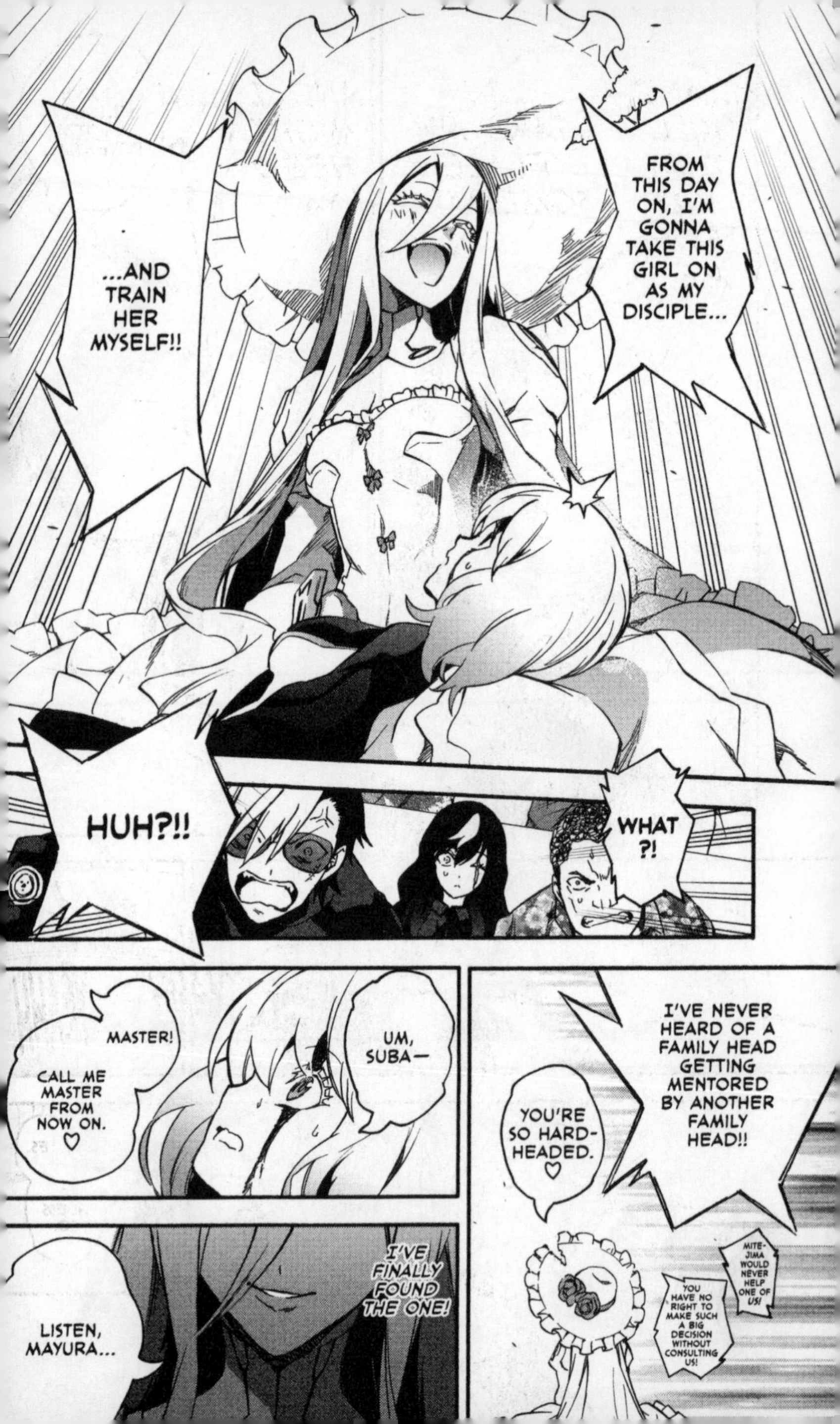
FROM THIS DAY ON, I'M GONNA TAKE THIS GIRL ON AS MY DISCIPLE...
...AND TRAIN HER MYSELF!!
WHAT?!
HUH?!!
I'VE NEVER HEARD OF A FAMILY HEAD GETTING MENTORED BY ANOTHER FAMILY HEAD!!
YOU'RE SO HARD-HEADED. ♡
UM, SUBA—
MASTER!
CALL ME MASTER FROM NOW ON. ♡
MITE-JIMA WOULD NEVER HELP ONE OF US!
YOU HAVE NO RIGHT TO MAKE SUCH A BIG DECISION WITHOUT CONSULTING US!
I'VE FINALLY FOUND THE ONE!
LISTEN, MAYURA...

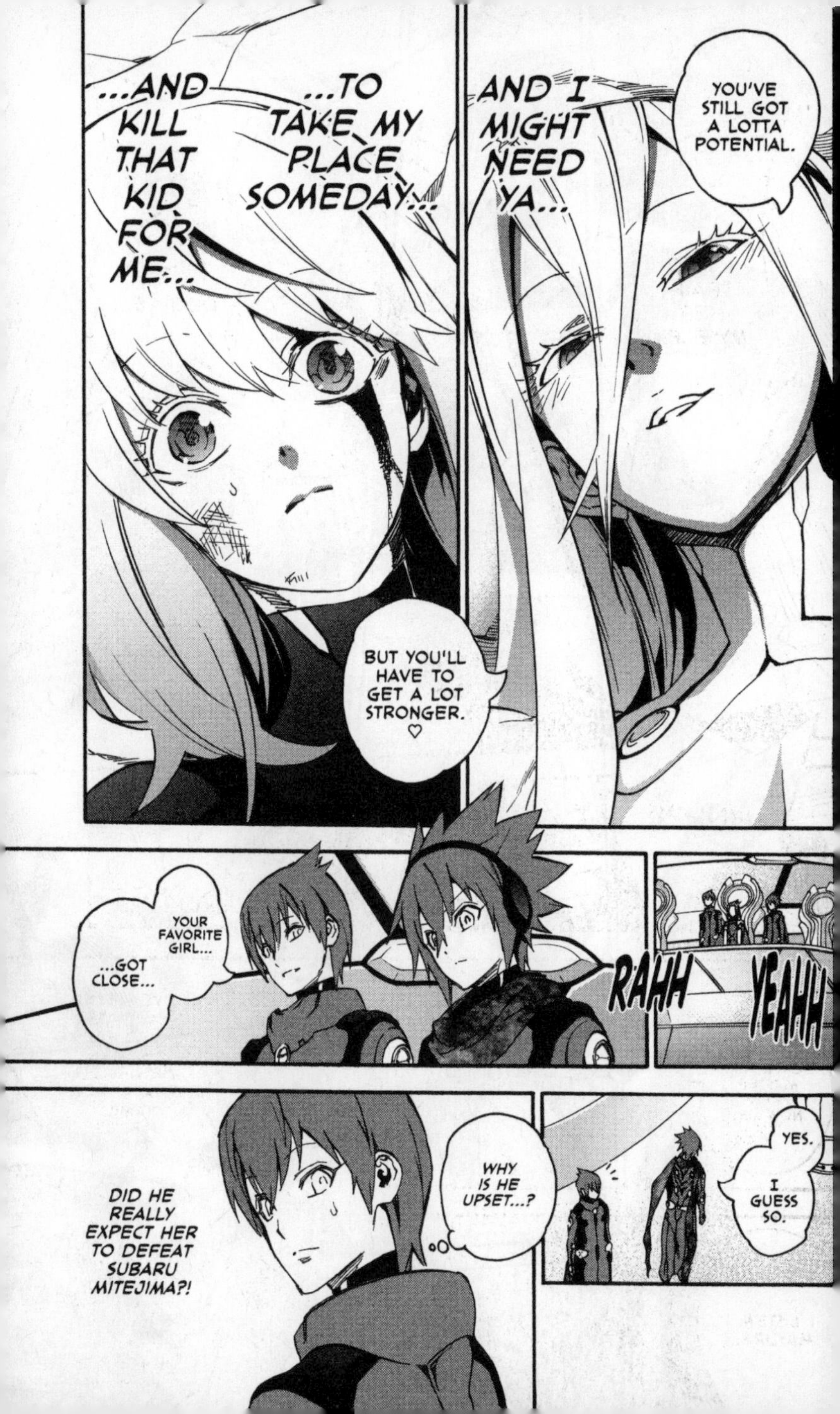
YOU'VE STILL GOT A LOTTA POTENTIAL.
AND I MIGHT NEED YA...
...TO TAKE MY PLACE SOMEDAY...
...AND KILL THAT KID FOR ME...
BUT YOU'LL HAVE TO GET A LOT STRONGER. ♡
YEAHH
RAHH
YOUR FAVORITE GIRL...
...GOT CLOSE...
YES.
I GUESS SO.
WHY IS HE UPSET...?
DID HE REALLY EXPECT HER TO DEFEAT SUBARU MITEJIMA?!

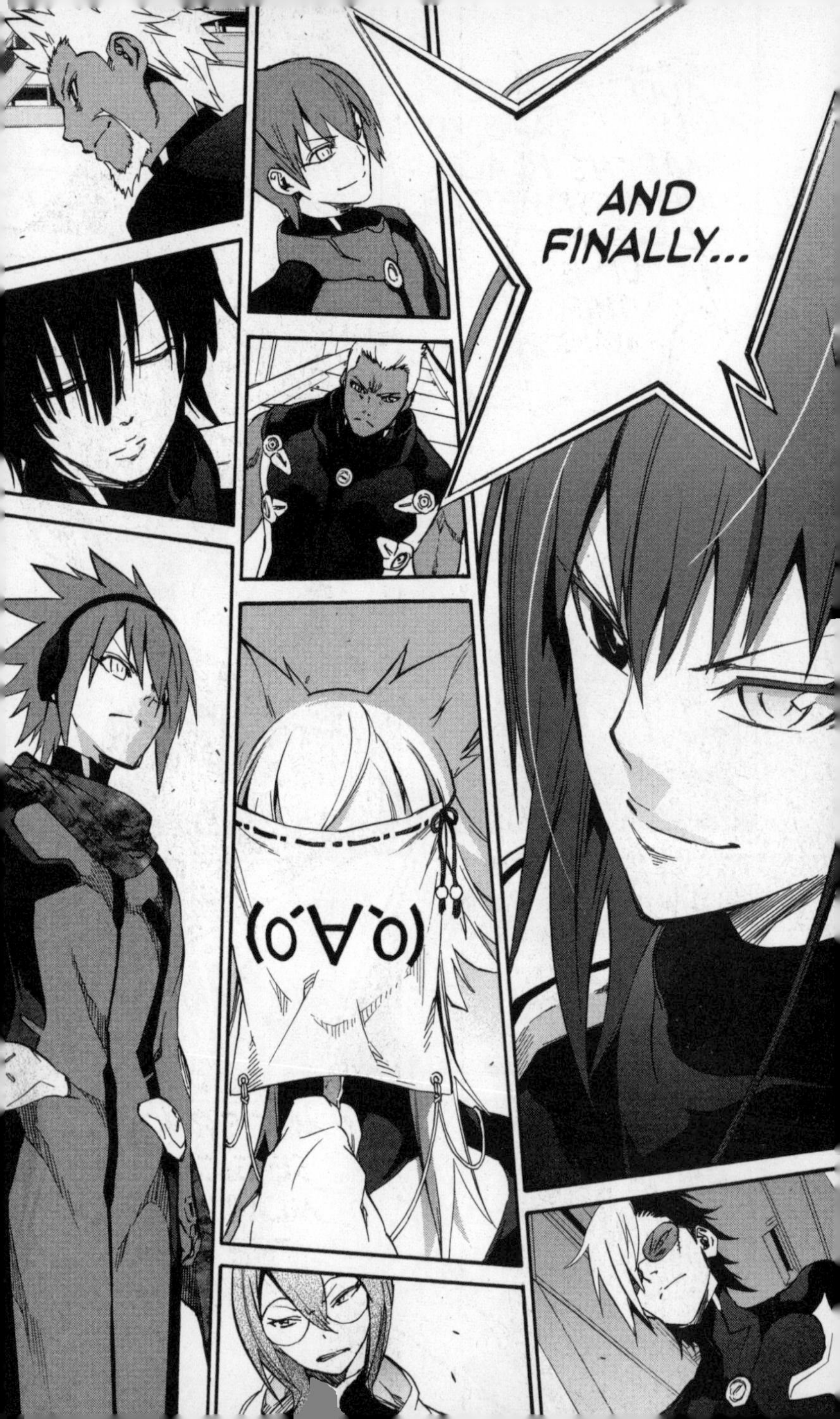
AND FINALLY...
(O_A_O)

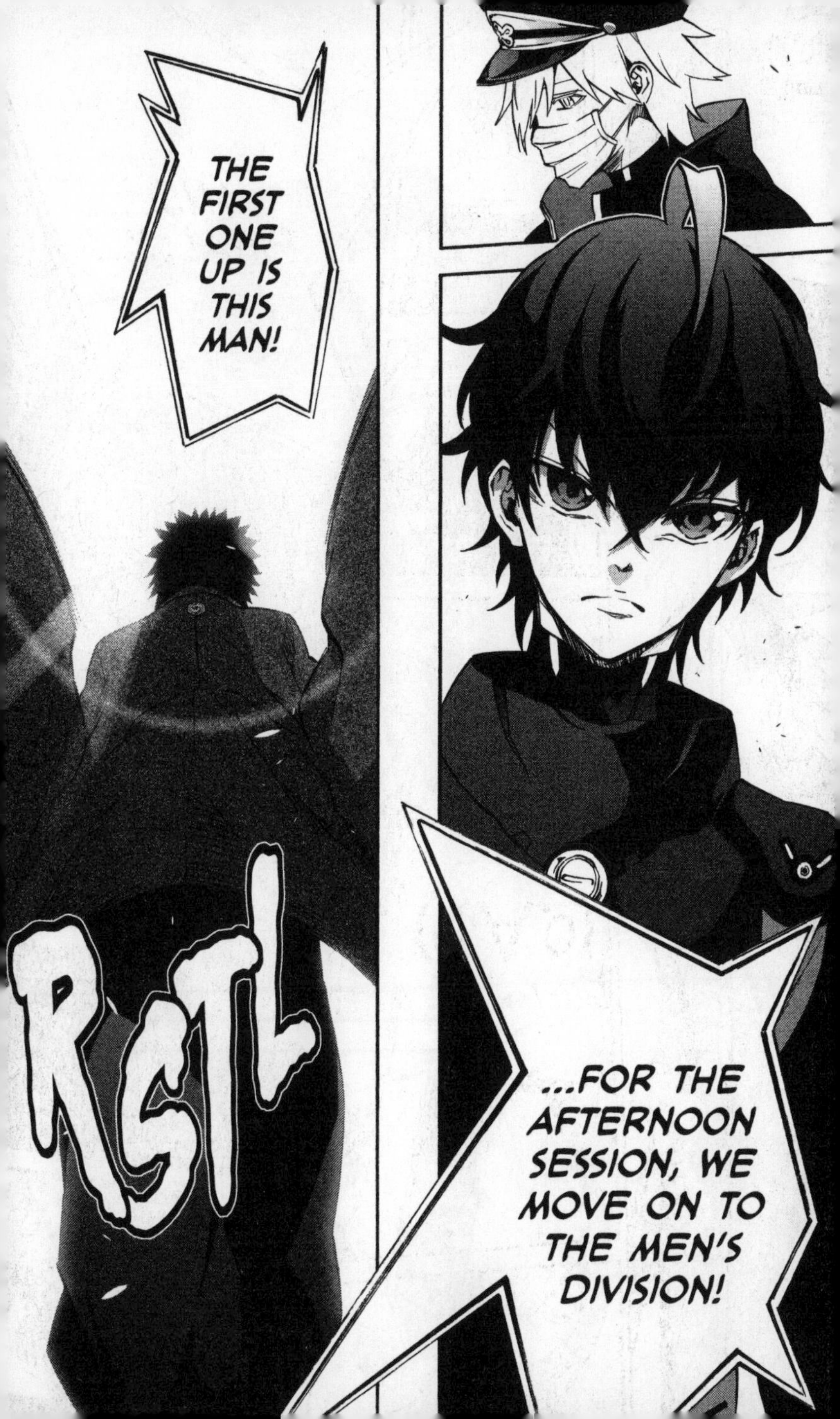
...FOR THE AFTERNOON SESSION, WE MOVE ON TO THE MEN'S DIVISION!
THE FIRST ONE UP IS THIS MAN!
RSTL

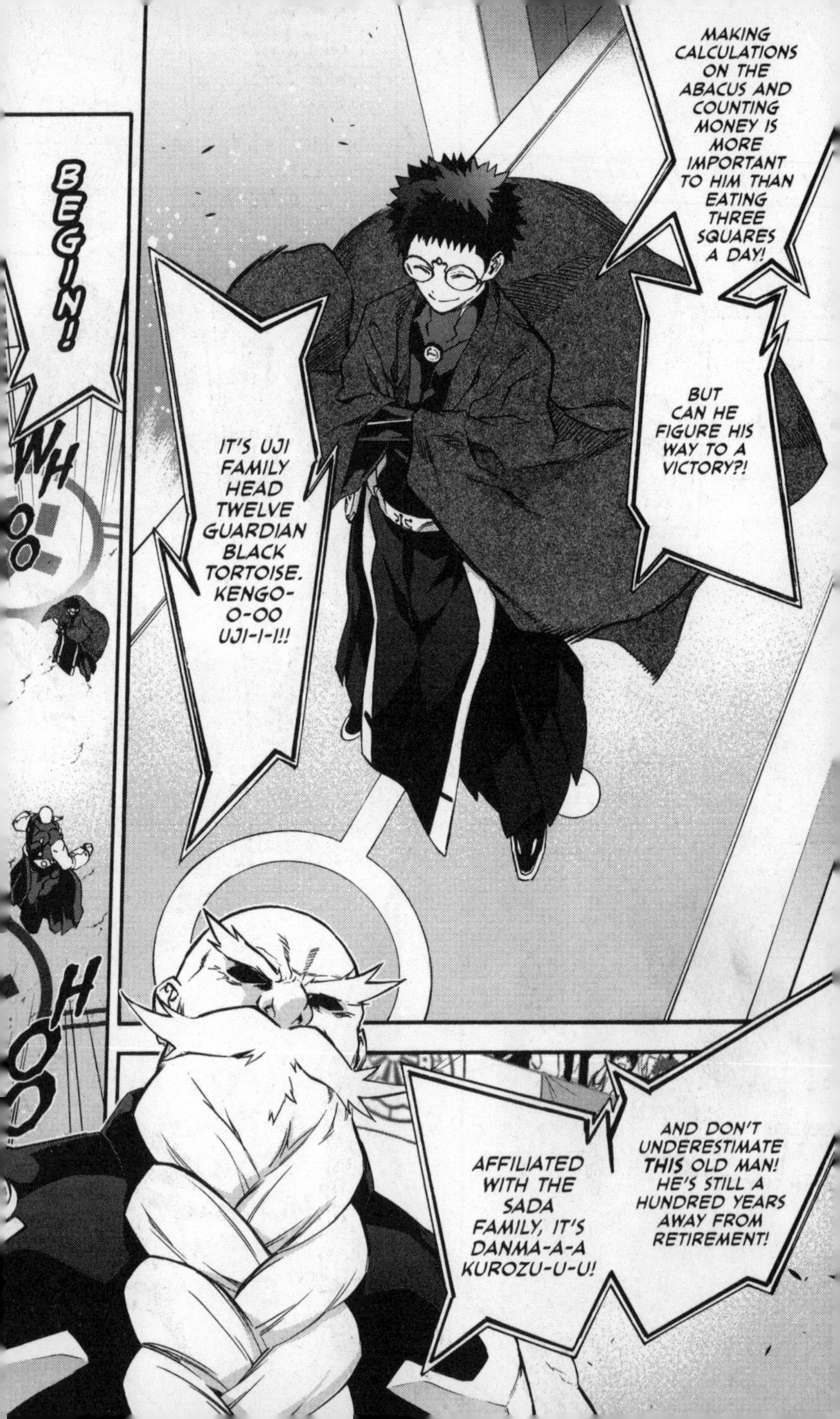
IT'S UJI FAMILY HEAD TWELVE GUARDIAN BLACK TORTOISE. KENGO-O-OO UJI-I-I!!
MAKING CALCULATIONS ON THE ABACUS AND COUNTING MONEY IS MORE IMPORTANT TO HIM THAN EATING THREE SQUARES A DAY!
BUT CAN HE FIGURE HIS WAY TO A VICTORY?!
AFFILIATED WITH THE SADA FAMILY, IT'S DANMA-A-A KUROZU-U-U!
AND DON'T UNDERESTIMATE THIS OLD MAN! HE'S STILL A HUNDRED YEARS AWAY FROM RETIREMENT!
BEGIN!
WHOOO
HOOO

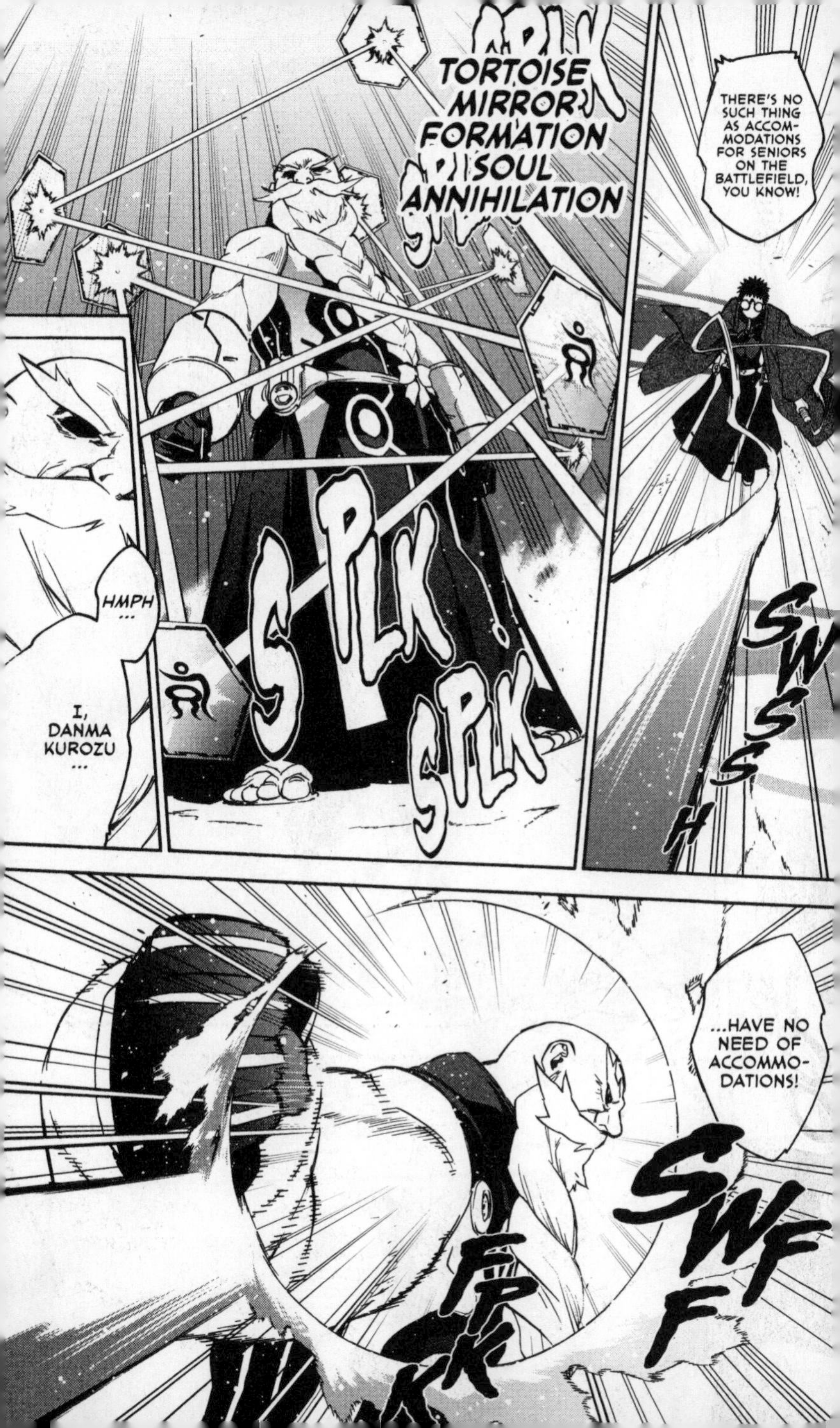
THERE'S NO SUCH THING AS ACCOM-MODATIONS FOR SENIORS ON THE BATTLEFIELD, YOU KNOW!
SWSSSH
TORTOISE MIRROR FORMATION SOUL ANNIHILATION
SPLK
SPLK
HMPH...
I, DANMA KUROZU...
...HAVE NO NEED OF ACCOMMO-DATIONS!
SWFF
FPKK

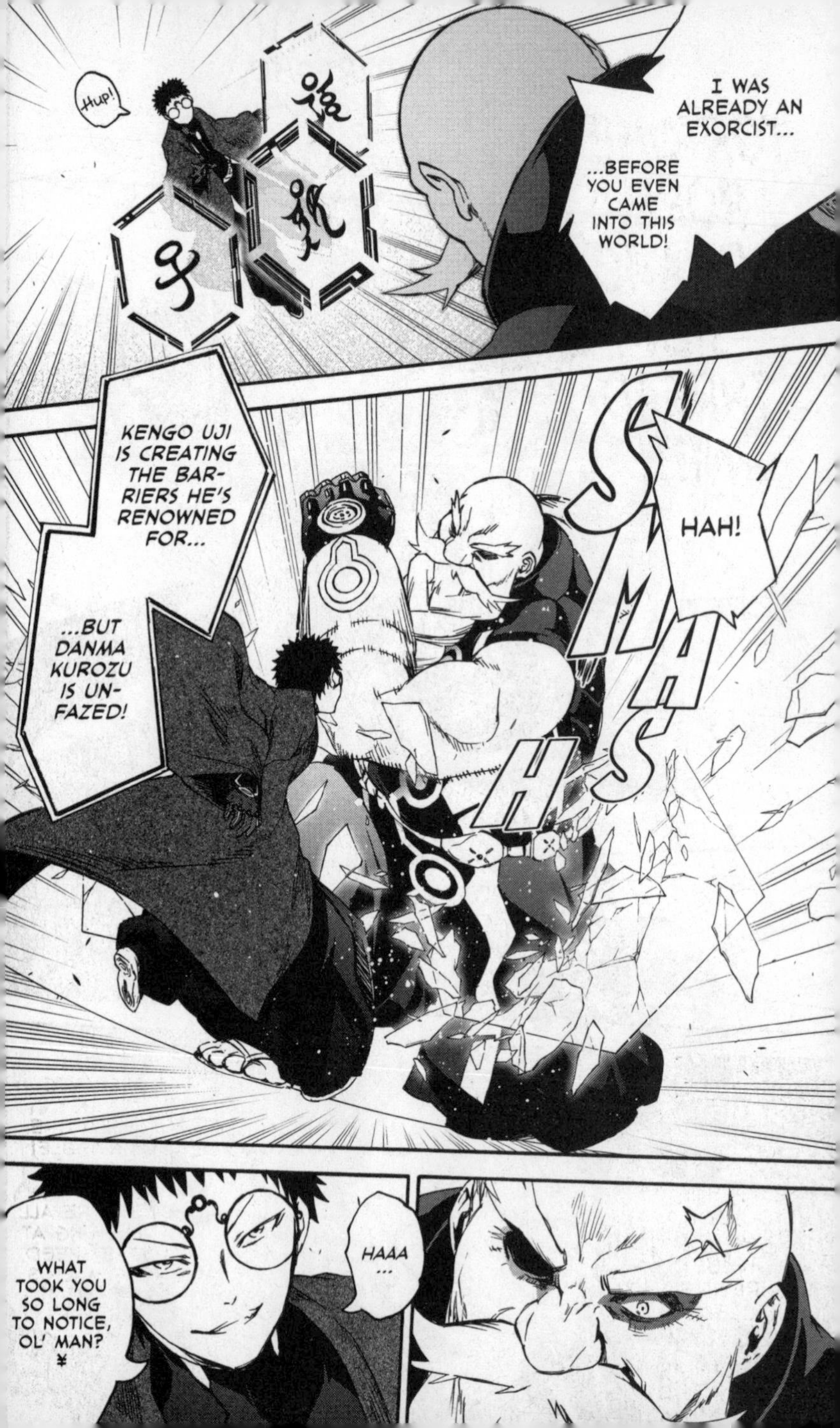
I WAS ALREADY AN EXORCIST...
...BEFORE YOU EVEN CAME INTO THIS WORLD!
Hup!
SMASH
HAH!
KENGO UJI IS CREATING THE BARRIERS HE'S RENOWNED FOR...
...BUT DANMA KUROZU IS UNFAZED!
HAAA...
WHAT TOOK YOU SO LONG TO NOTICE, OL' MAN?

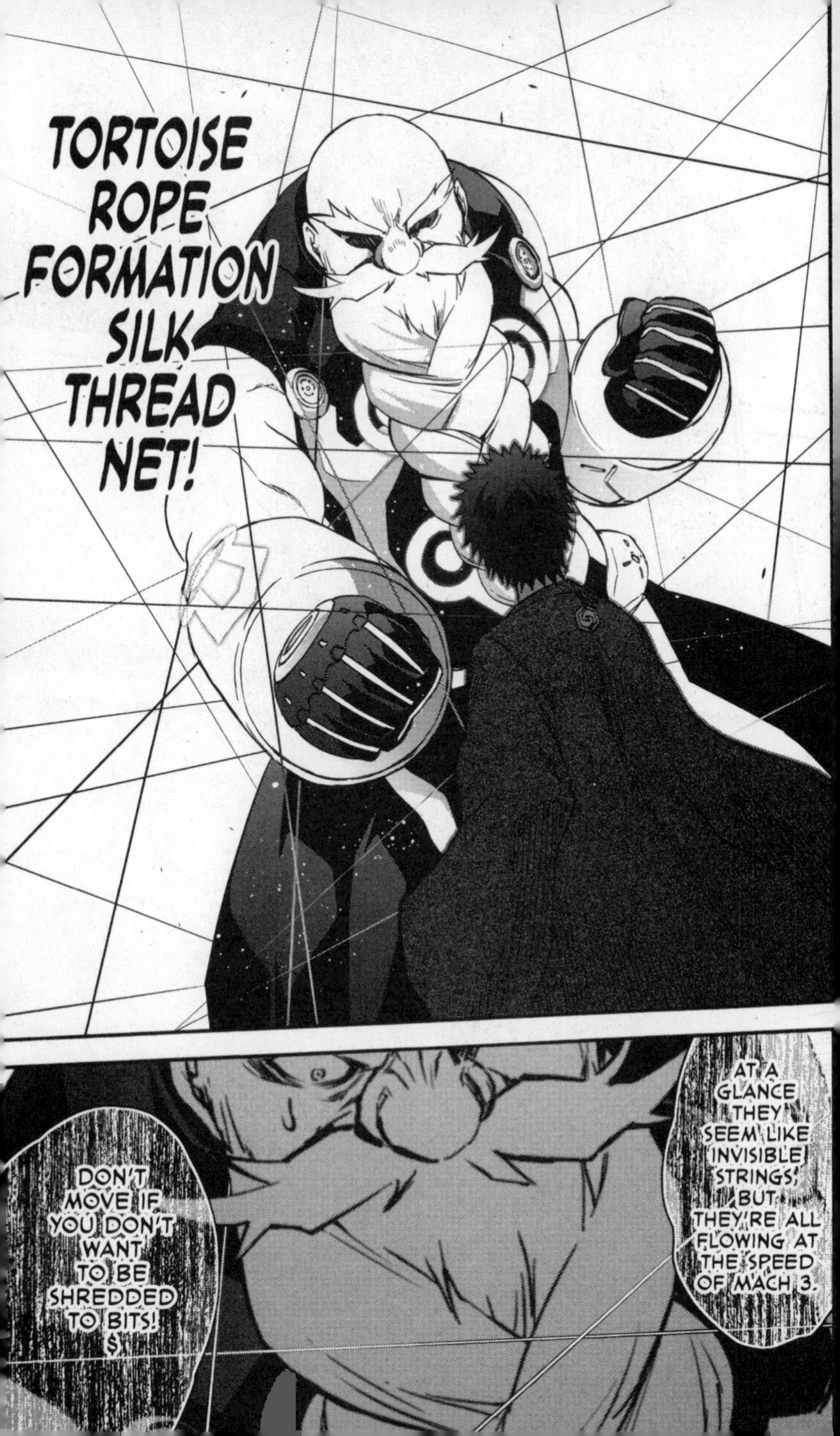
TORTOISE ROPE FORMATION SILK THREAD NET!
AT A GLANCE THEY SEEM LIKE INVISIBLE STRINGS, BUT THEY'RE ALL FLOWING AT THE SPEED OF MACH 3.
DON'T MOVE IF YOU DON'T WANT TO BE SHREDDED TO BITS!

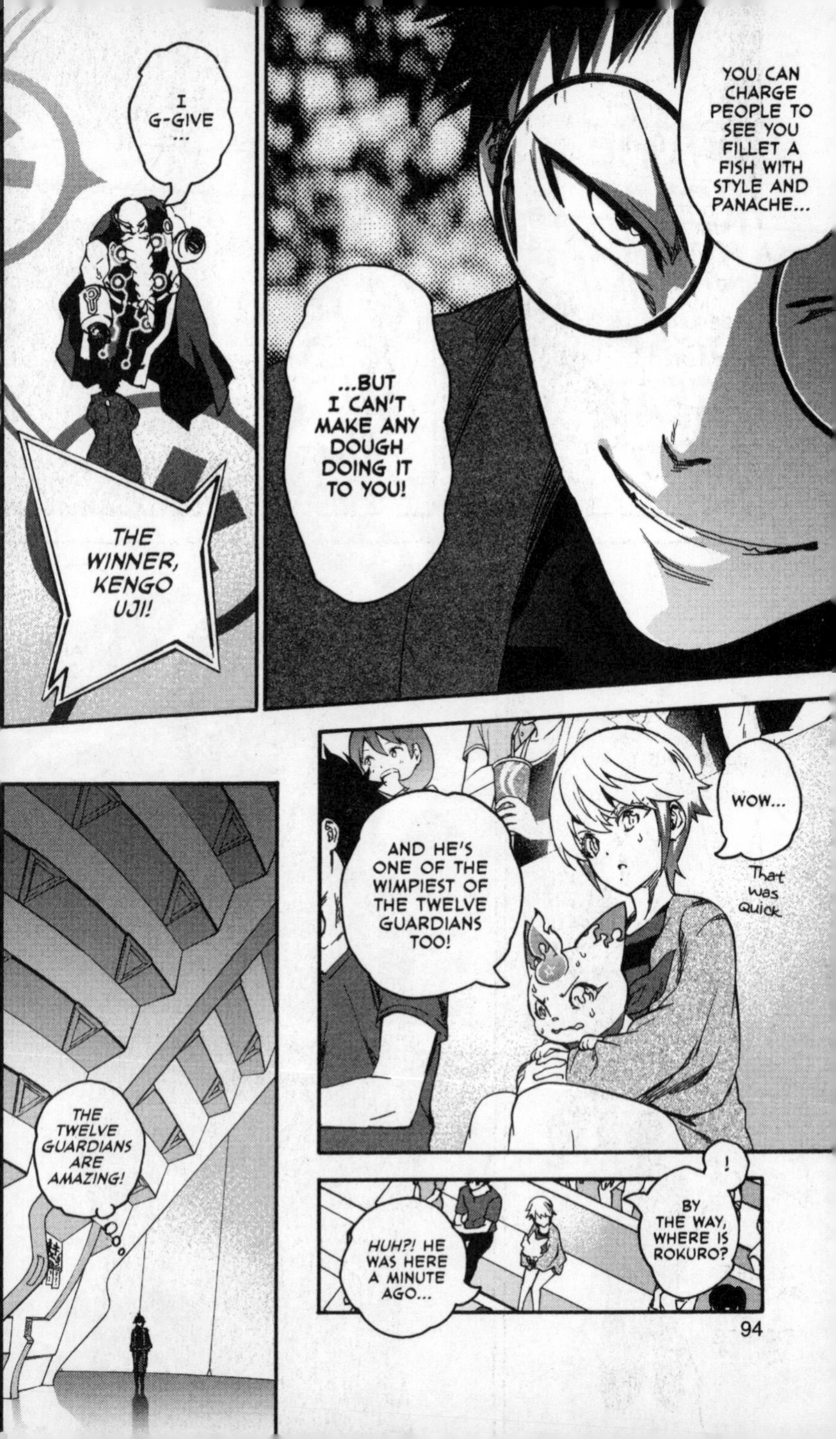
YOU CAN CHARGE PEOPLE TO SEE YOU FILLET A FISH WITH STYLE AND PANACHE...
...BUT I CAN'T MAKE ANY DOUGH DOING IT TO YOU!
I G-GIVE...
THE WINNER, KENGO UJI!
WOW...
That was Quick
AND HE'S ONE OF THE WIMPIEST OF THE TWELVE GUARDIANS TOO!
!
BY THE WAY, WHERE IS ROKURO?
HUH?! HE WAS HERE A MINUTE AGO...
THE TWELVE GUARDIANS ARE AMAZING!

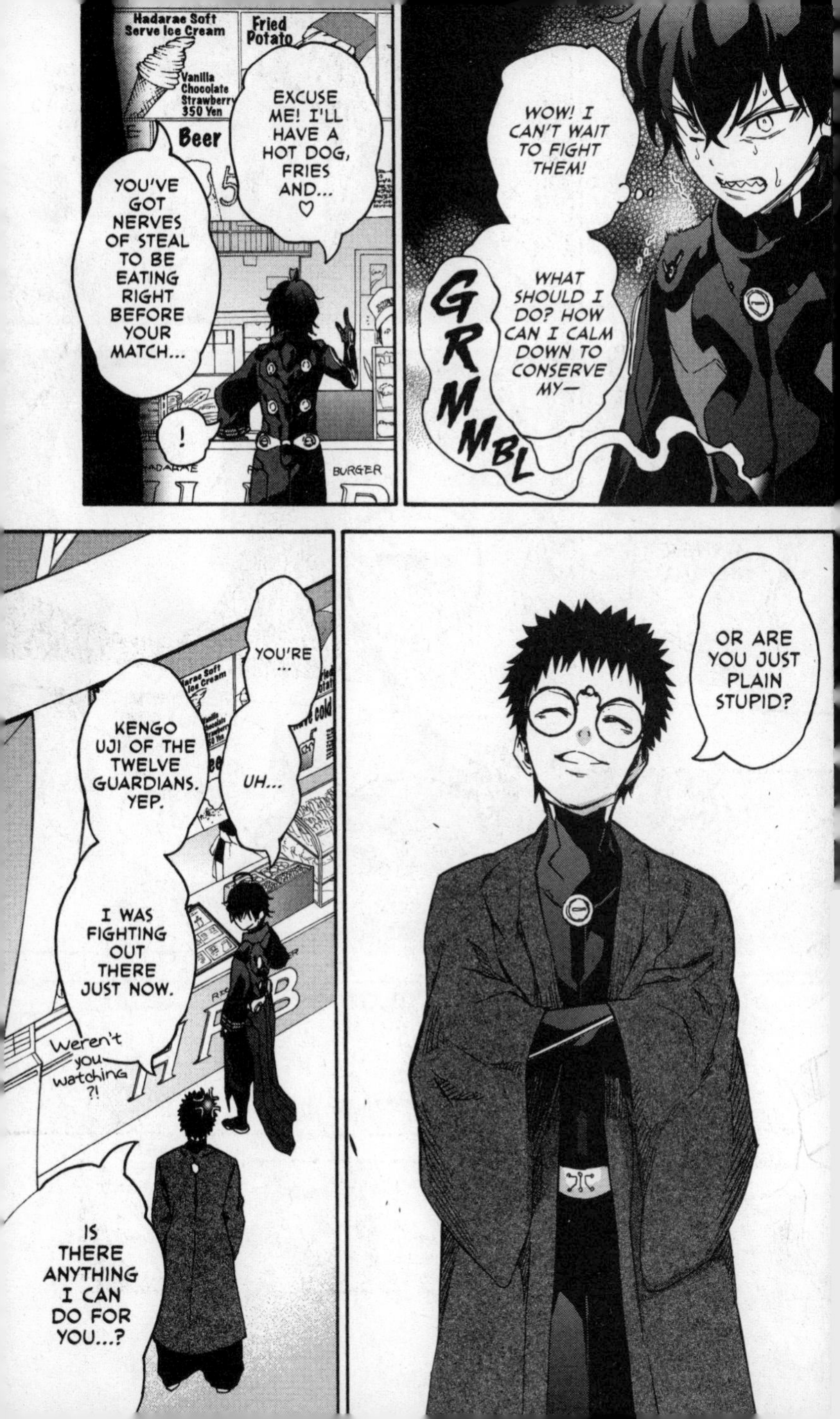
WOW! I CAN'T WAIT TO FIGHT THEM!
WHAT SHOULD I DO? HOW CAN I CALM DOWN TO CONSERVE MY—
GRMMBL
Hadarae Soft Serve Ice Cream
Fried Potato
Vanilla Chocolate Strawberry 350 Yen
Beer
EXCUSE ME! I'LL HAVE A HOT DOG, FRIES AND... ♡
YOU'VE GOT NERVES OF STEAL TO BE EATING RIGHT BEFORE YOUR MATCH...
!
BURGER
OR ARE YOU JUST PLAIN STUPID?
YOU'RE ...
KENGO UJI OF THE TWELVE GUARDIANS. YEP.
UH...
I WAS FIGHTING OUT THERE JUST NOW.
Weren't you watching?!
IS THERE ANYTHING I CAN DO FOR YOU...?

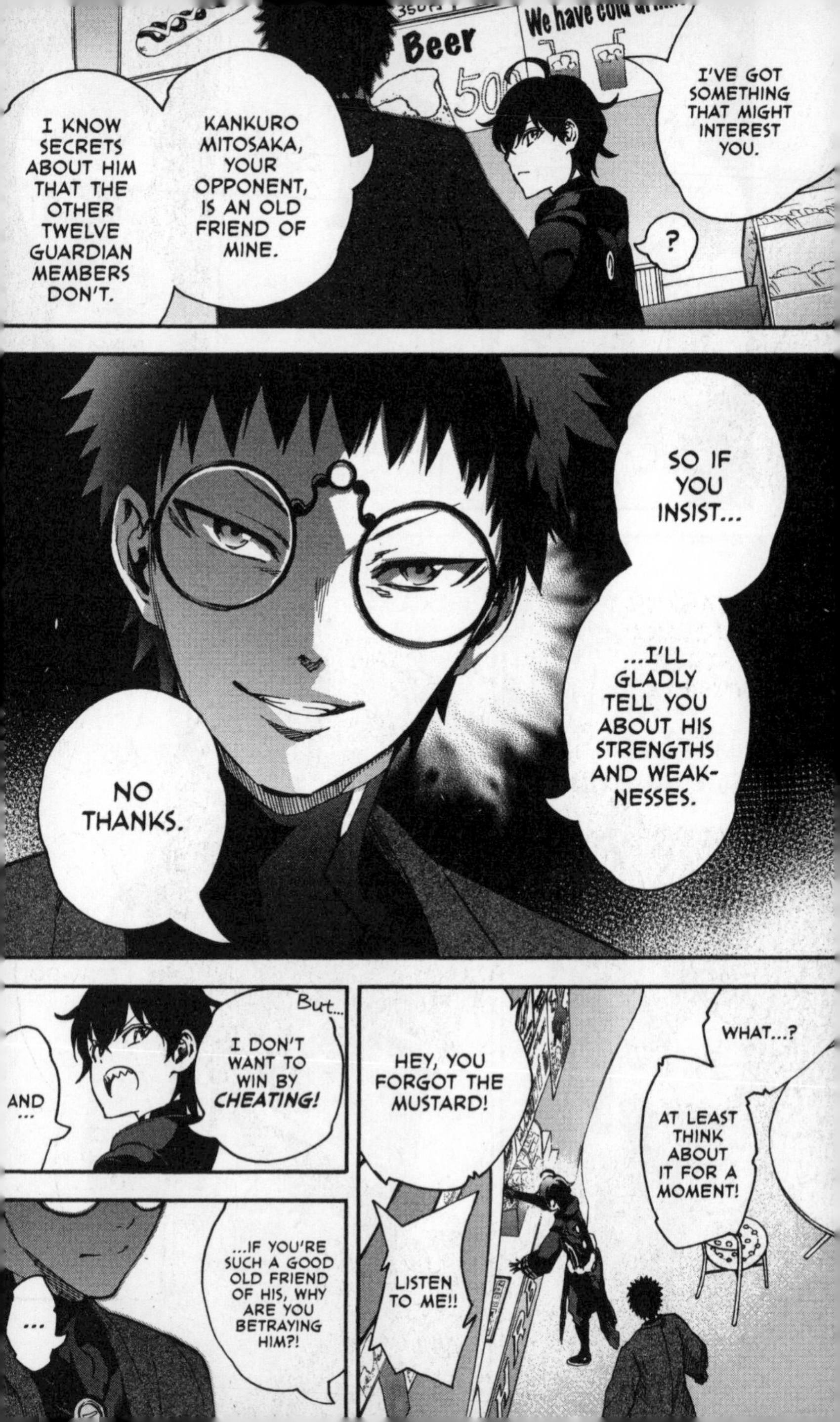
Beer
I'VE GOT SOMETHING THAT MIGHT INTEREST YOU.
?
KANKURO MITOSAKA, YOUR OPPONENT, IS AN OLD FRIEND OF MINE.
I KNOW SECRETS ABOUT HIM THAT THE OTHER TWELVE GUARDIAN MEMBERS DON'T.
SO IF YOU INSIST...
...I'LL GLADLY TELL YOU ABOUT HIS STRENGTHS AND WEAKNESSES.
NO THANKS.
But...
I DON'T WANT TO WIN BY *CHEATING!*
AND ...
...IF YOU'RE SUCH A GOOD OLD FRIEND OF HIS, WHY ARE YOU BETRAYING HIM?!
...
WHAT...?
HEY, YOU FORGOT THE MUSTARD!
AT LEAST THINK ABOUT IT FOR A MOMENT!
LISTEN TO ME!!

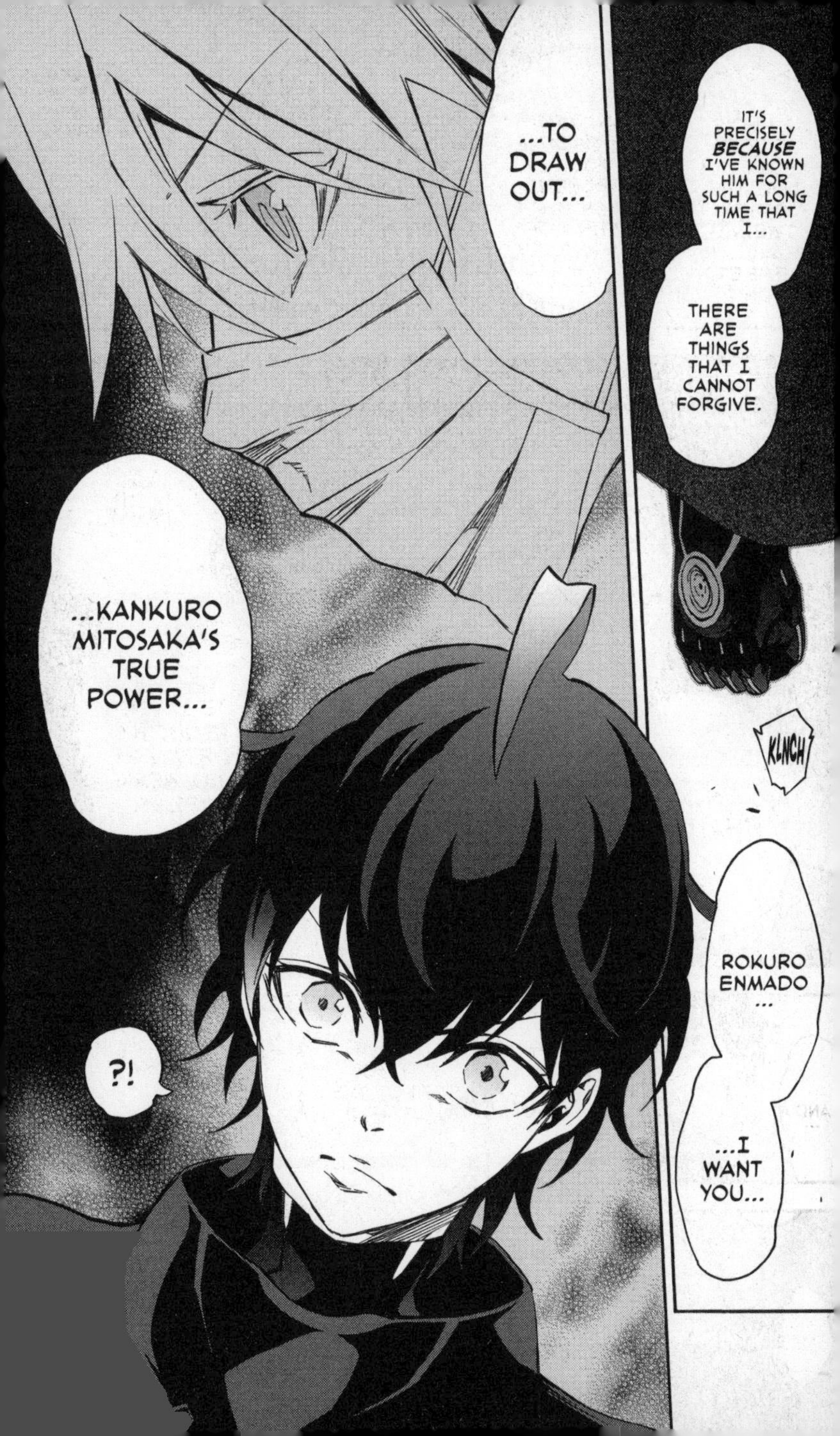
IT'S PRECISELY ***BECAUSE*** I'VE KNOWN HIM FOR SUCH A LONG TIME THAT I...
THERE ARE THINGS THAT I CANNOT FORGIVE.
KLNCH
ROKURO ENMADO...
...I WANT YOU...
...TO DRAW OUT...
...KANKURO MITOSAKA'S TRUE POWER...
?!

CHARACTER PROFILE 3

The third of this series, and the next one after volume 10.
Here I'll introduce the characters warming-up this tournament.

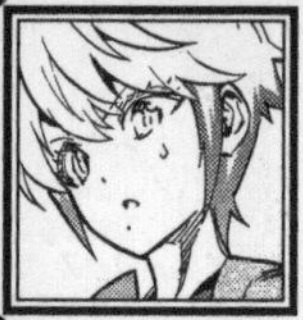

Arimori Tsuchimikado (12 years old)

Birthday: July 7 Blood type: A Height: 4'11" Weight: 95 lbs.
Likes: Father, mother, McDonald's
Dislikes: People who treat him like his parents' dog, green peppers

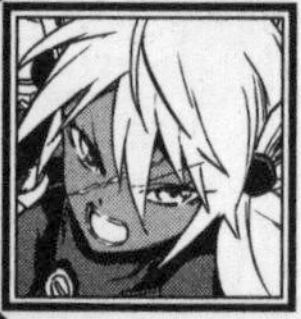

Shizuru Ioroi (17 years old)

Birthday: August 31 Blood type: B Height: 5'7" Weight: 132 lbs.
Likes: Family, his mother's fried chicken
Dislikes: Pickled plums, indecisive people

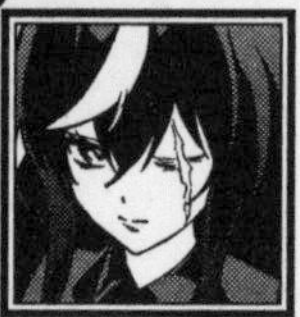

Yuzuru Amawaka (38 years old)

Birthday: October 25 Blood type: A Height: 5'2" Weight: 117 lbs.
Likes: Seigen, root vegetables
Dislikes: Amawaka family (in the old days), romantic movies (so gross)

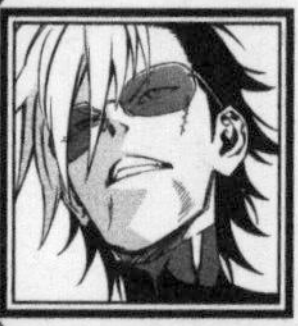

Jinya Yosami (31 years old)

Birthday: November 19 Blood type: A Height: 5'11" Weight: 165 lbs.
Likes: Seigen, root vegetables
Dislikes: Women and children (not including Mayura and Yuzuru), raisins

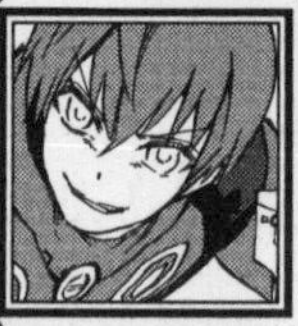

Keiji Ikaruga (25 years old)

Birthday: December 10 Blood type: B Height: 6'1" Weight: 168 lbs.
Likes: Girls ♡
Dislikes: Dirty old men

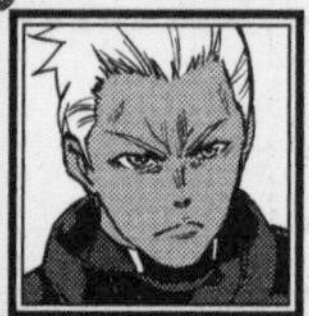

Gunki Ioroi (25 years old)

Birthday: September 21 Blood type: A Height: 6'9" Weight: 220 lbs.
Likes: Family, his mother's fish dishes
Dislikes: Womanizers, cheese

#43: Dreams and Aspirations

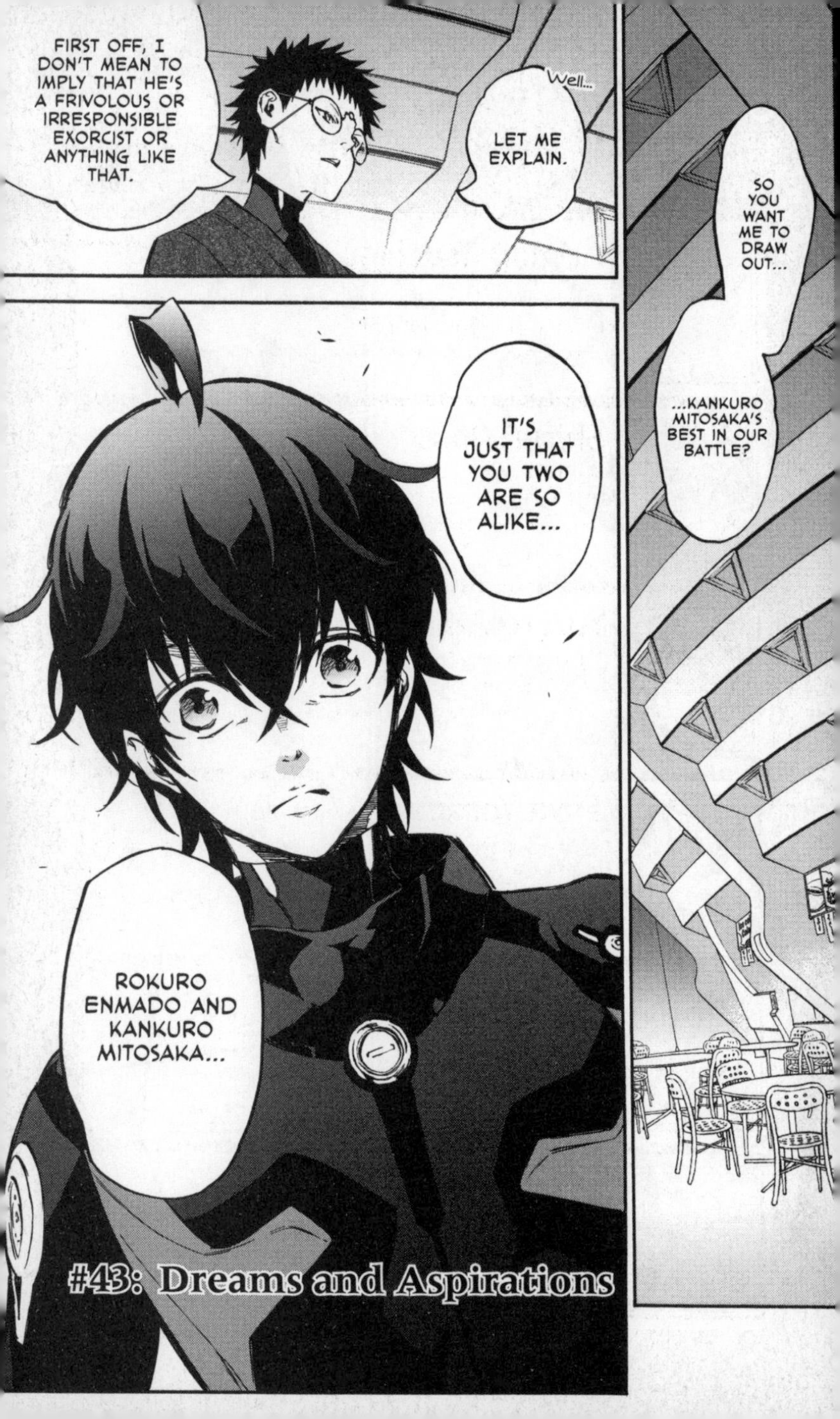
SO YOU WANT ME TO DRAW OUT...
...KANKURO MITOSAKA'S BEST IN OUR BATTLE?
Well...
LET ME EXPLAIN.
FIRST OFF, I DON'T MEAN TO IMPLY THAT HE'S A FRIVOLOUS OR IRRESPONSIBLE EXORCIST OR ANYTHING LIKE THAT.
IT'S JUST THAT YOU TWO ARE SO ALIKE...
ROKURO ENMADO AND KANKURO MITOSAKA...

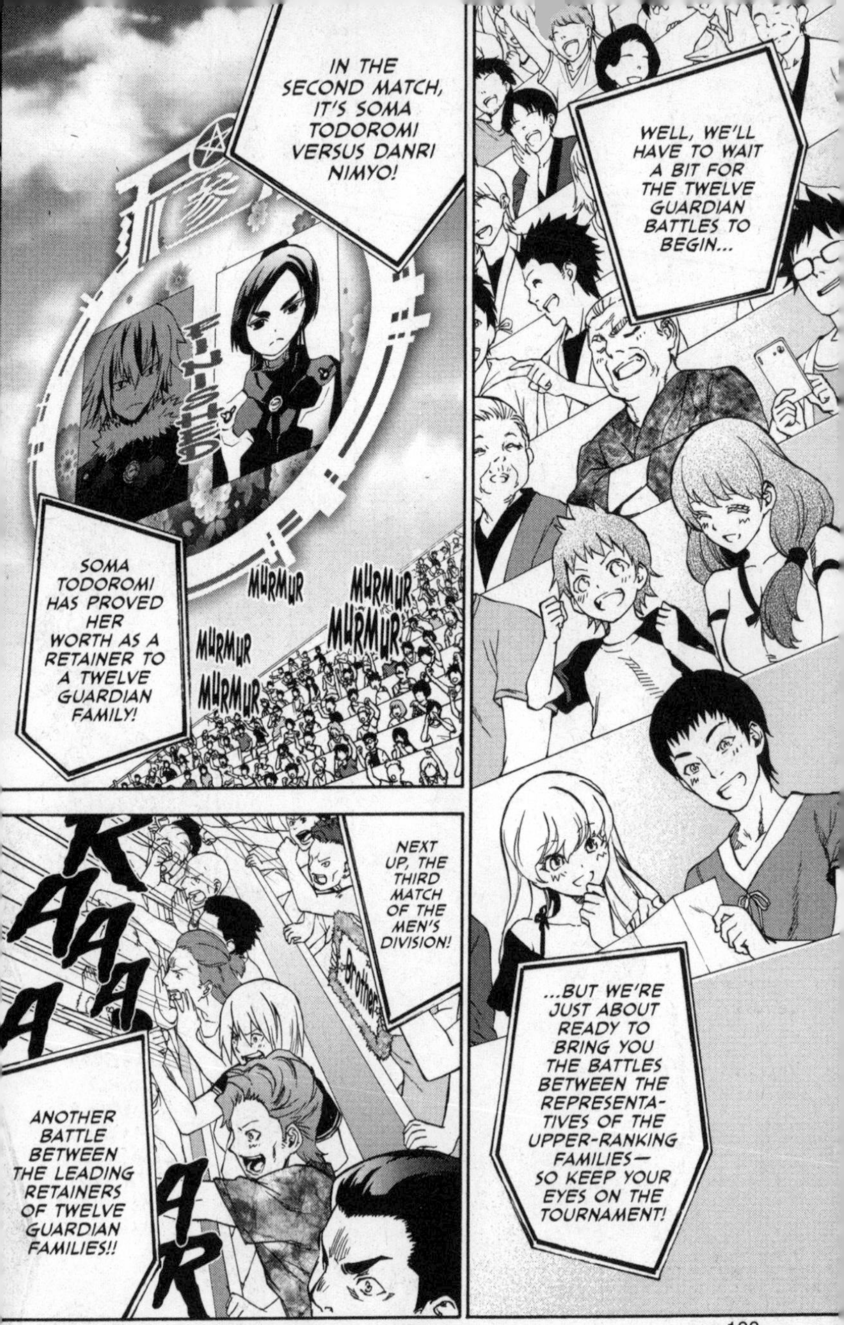
WELL, WE'LL HAVE TO WAIT A BIT FOR THE TWELVE GUARDIAN BATTLES TO BEGIN...
...BUT WE'RE JUST ABOUT READY TO BRING YOU THE BATTLES BETWEEN THE REPRESENTA-TIVES OF THE UPPER-RANKING FAMILIES— SO KEEP YOUR EYES ON THE TOURNAMENT!
IN THE SECOND MATCH, IT'S SOMA TODOROMI VERSUS DANRI NIMYO!
FINISHED
SOMA TODOROMI HAS PROVED HER WORTH AS A RETAINER TO A TWELVE GUARDIAN FAMILY!
MURMUR
MURMUR
MURMUR
MURMUR
MURMUR
NEXT UP, THE THIRD MATCH OF THE MEN'S DIVISION!
Brother
KAAAAAAR
ANOTHER BATTLE BETWEEN THE LEADING RETAINERS OF TWELVE GUARDIAN FAMILIES!!

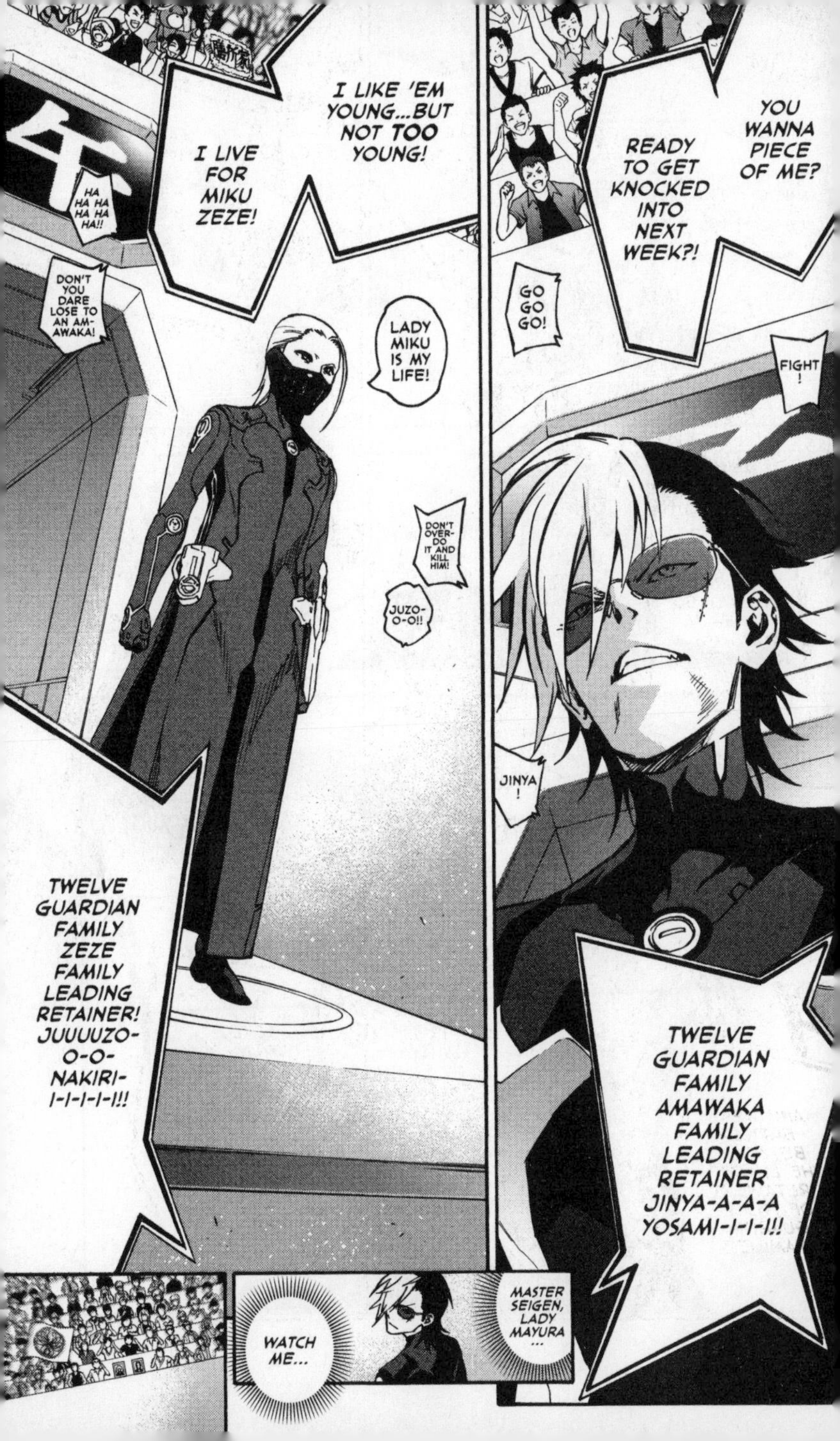
YOU WANNA PIECE OF ME?
READY TO GET KNOCKED INTO NEXT WEEK?!
GO GO GO!
FIGHT!
JINYA!
TWELVE GUARDIAN FAMILY AMAWAKA FAMILY LEADING RETAINER JINYA-A-A-A YOSAMI-I-I-I!!
I LIKE 'EM YOUNG...BUT NOT TOO YOUNG!
I LIVE FOR MIKU ZEZE!
HA HA HA HA HA HA!!
LADY MIKU IS MY LIFE!
DON'T YOU DARE LOSE TO AN AMAWAKA!
DON'T OVER-DO IT AND KILL HIM!
JUZO-O-O!!
TWELVE GUARDIAN FAMILY ZEZE FAMILY LEADING RETAINER! JUUUUZO-O-O-NAKIRI-I-I-I-I-I!!
MASTER SEIGEN, LADY MAYURA ...
WATCH ME...

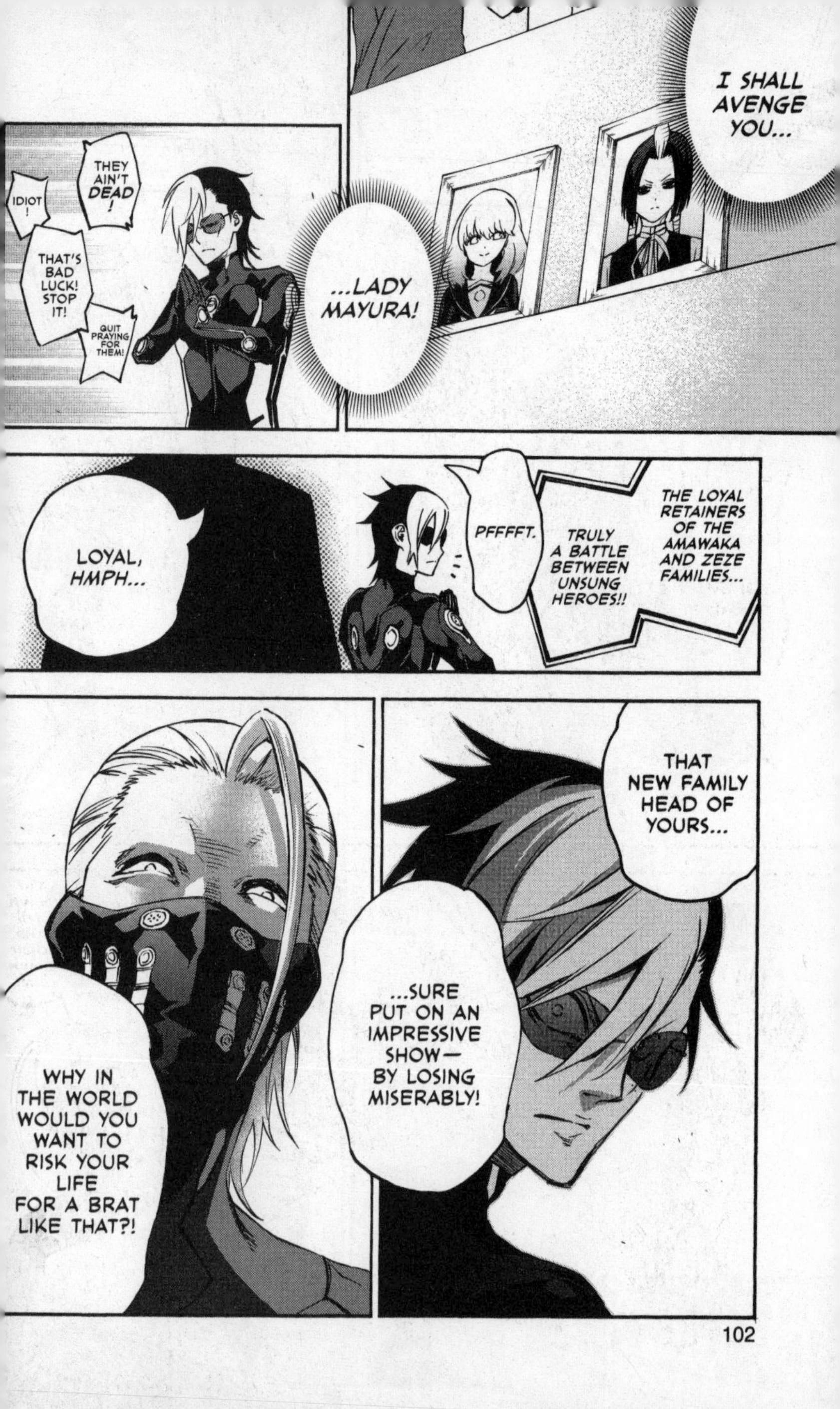

I SHALL AVENGE YOU...
...LADY MAYURA!
THEY AIN'T DEAD!
IDIOT!
THAT'S BAD LUCK! STOP IT!
QUIT PRAYING FOR THEM!
THE LOYAL RETAINERS OF THE AMAWAKA AND ZEZE FAMILIES...
TRULY A BATTLE BETWEEN UNSUNG HEROES!!
PFFFFT.
LOYAL, HMPH...
THAT NEW FAMILY HEAD OF YOURS...
...SURE PUT ON AN IMPRESSIVE SHOW—BY LOSING MISERABLY!
WHY IN THE WORLD WOULD YOU WANT TO RISK YOUR LIFE FOR A BRAT LIKE THAT?!

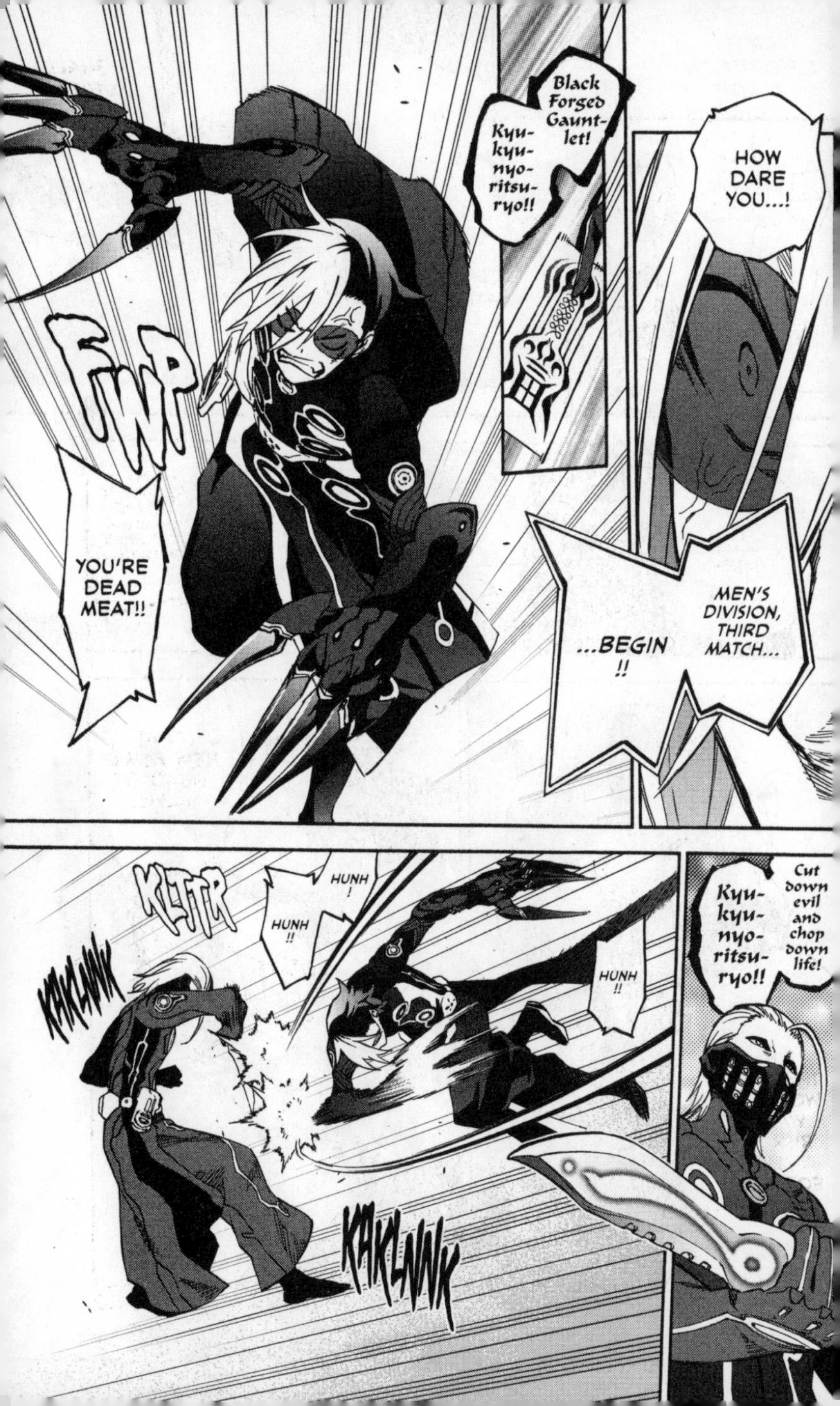
HOW DARE YOU...!
Black Forged Gauntlet!
Kyu-kyu-nyo-ritsu-ryo!!
MEN'S DIVISION, THIRD MATCH...
...BEGIN!!
YOU'RE DEAD MEAT!!
FWP
Cut down evil and chop down life!
Kyu-kyu-nyo-ritsu-ryo!!
HUNH!
KLTTR
HUNH!!
HUNH!!
KAKLNNK
KAKLNNK

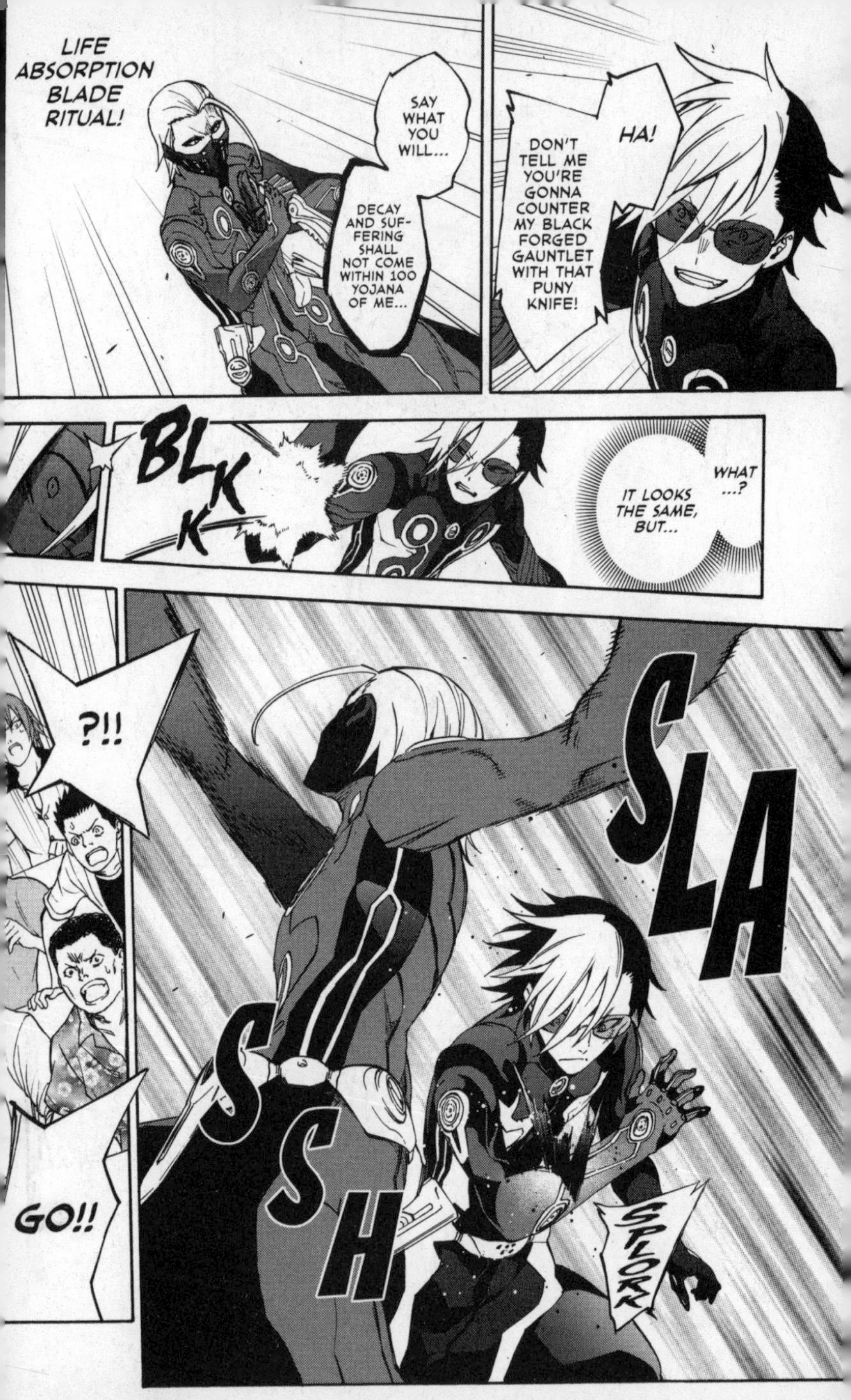
HA!
DON'T TELL ME YOU'RE GONNA COUNTER MY BLACK FORGED GAUNTLET WITH THAT PUNY KNIFE!
SAY WHAT YOU WILL...
DECAY AND SUFFERING SHALL NOT COME WITHIN 100 YOJANA OF ME...
LIFE ABSORPTION BLADE RITUAL!
WHAT ...?
IT LOOKS THE SAME, BUT...
BLKK
SLA
SSH
SPLOKK
?!!
GO!!

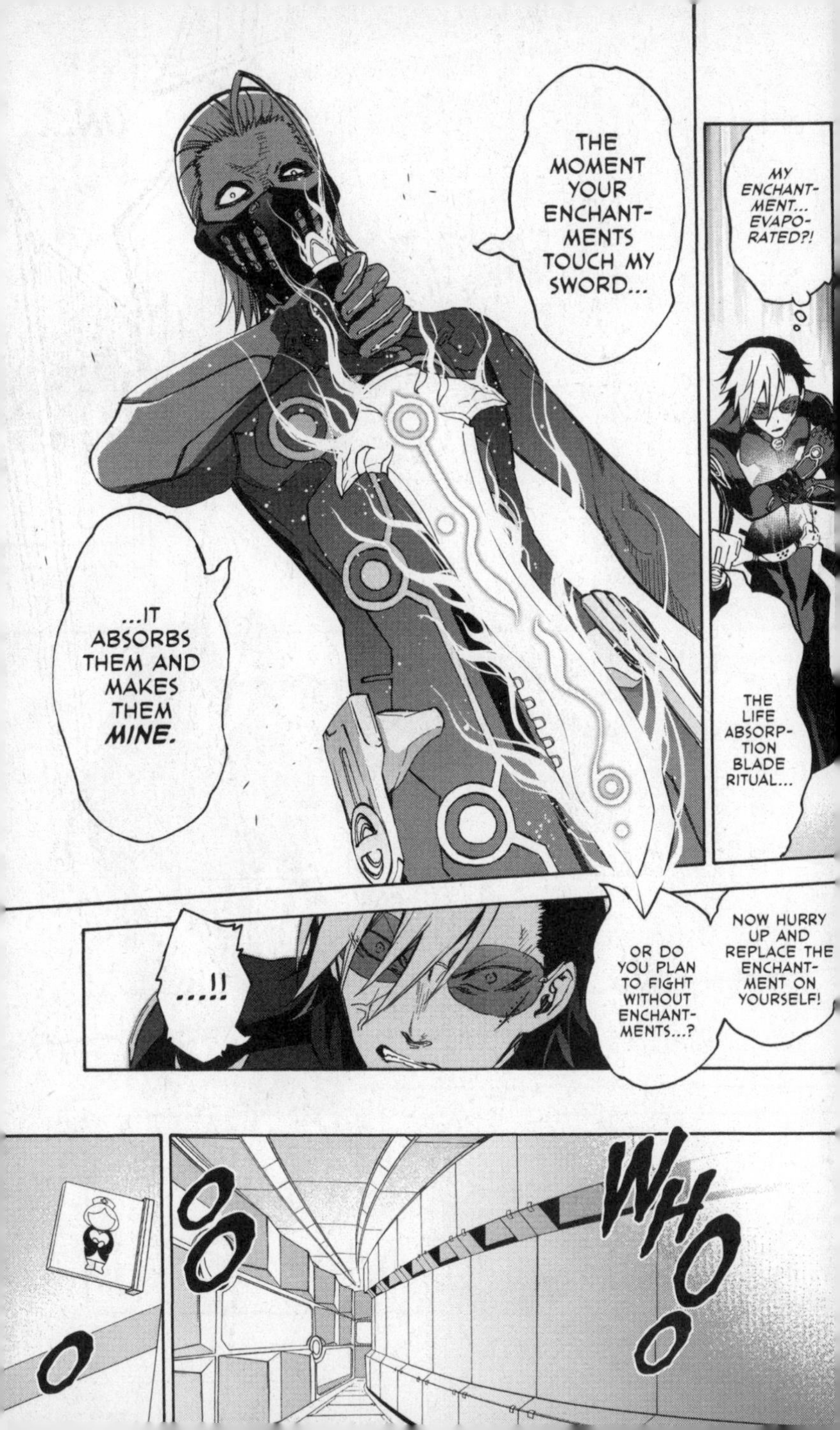
MY ENCHANTMENT... EVAPORATED?!
THE LIFE ABSORPTION BLADE RITUAL...
THE MOMENT YOUR ENCHANTMENTS TOUCH MY SWORD...
...IT ABSORBS THEM AND MAKES THEM *MINE.*
NOW HURRY UP AND REPLACE THE ENCHANTMENT ON YOURSELF!
OR DO YOU PLAN TO FIGHT WITHOUT ENCHANTMENTS...?
...!!
WHOOO
OOO

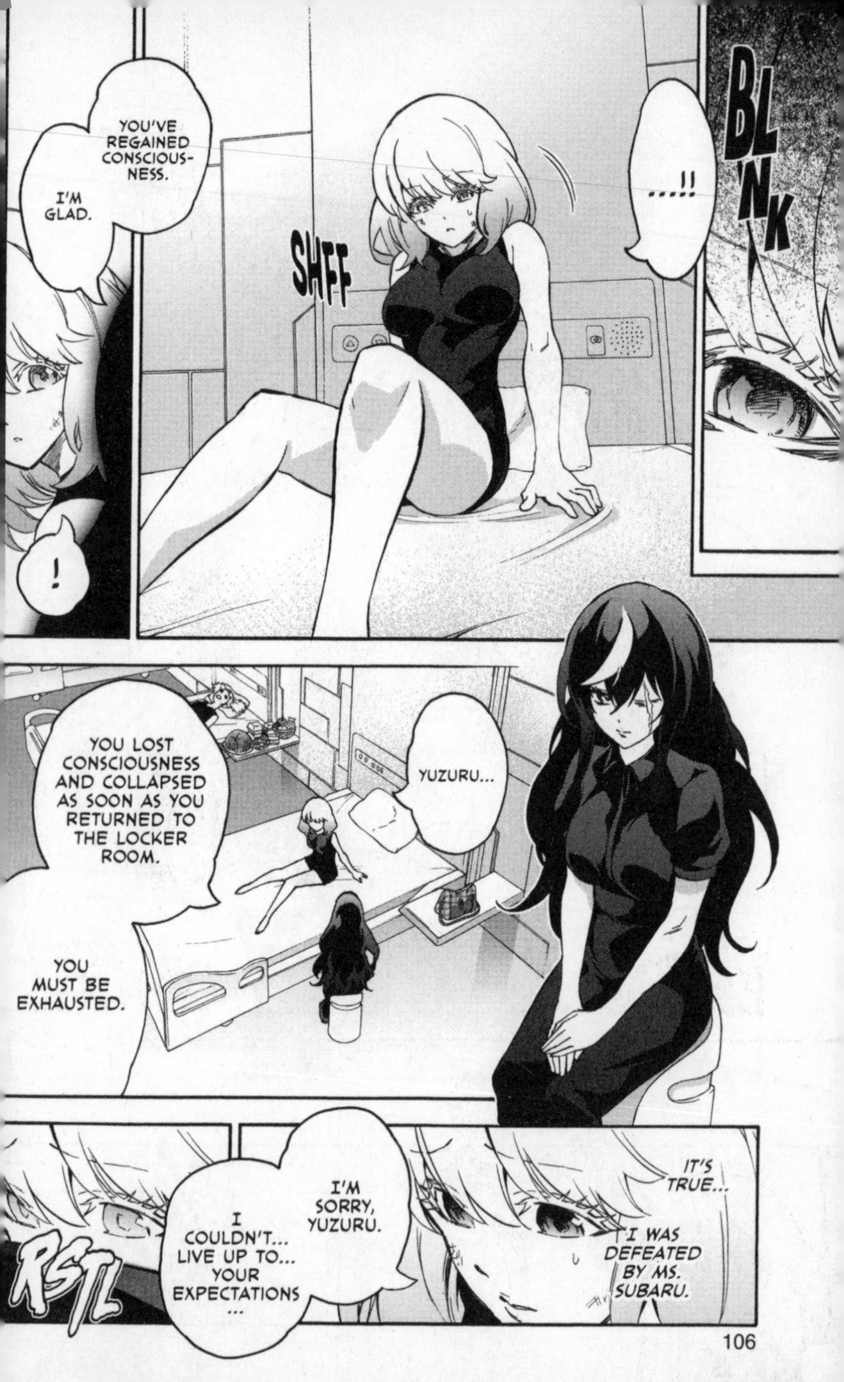
BLINK
...!!
SHFF
YOU'VE REGAINED CONSCIOUSNESS.
I'M GLAD.
!
YUZURU...
YOU LOST CONSCIOUSNESS AND COLLAPSED AS SOON AS YOU RETURNED TO THE LOCKER ROOM.
YOU MUST BE EXHAUSTED.
IT'S TRUE...
I WAS DEFEATED BY MS. SUBARU.
I'M SORRY, YUZURU.
I COULDN'T... LIVE UP TO... YOUR EXPECTATIONS ...
RSTL

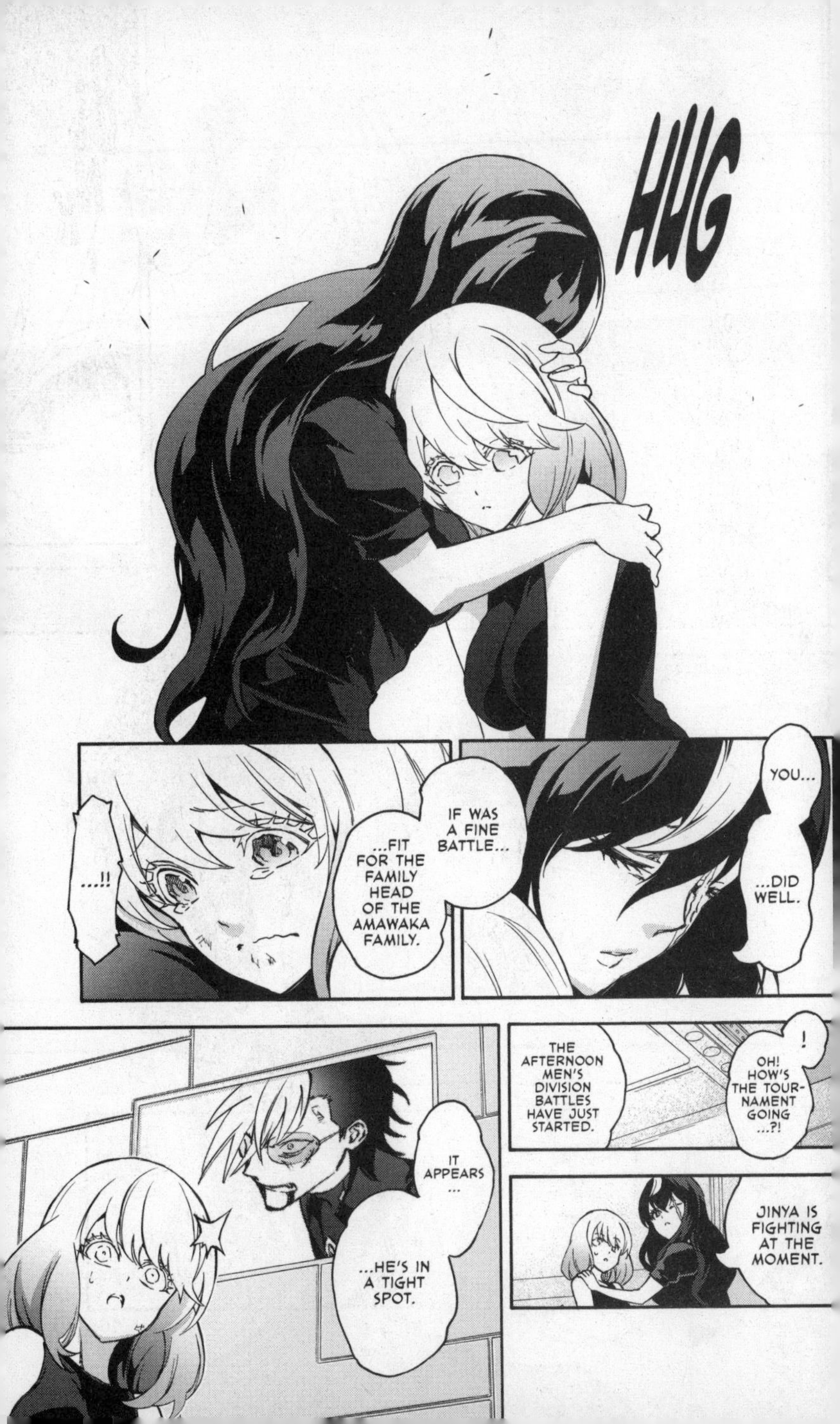
HUG
YOU...
...DID WELL.
IF WAS A FINE BATTLE...
...FIT FOR THE FAMILY HEAD OF THE AMAWAKA FAMILY.
...!!
!
OH! HOW'S THE TOUR-NAMENT GOING ...?!
THE AFTERNOON MEN'S DIVISION BATTLES HAVE JUST STARTED.
JINYA IS FIGHTING AT THE MOMENT.
IT APPEARS ...
...HE'S IN A TIGHT SPOT.

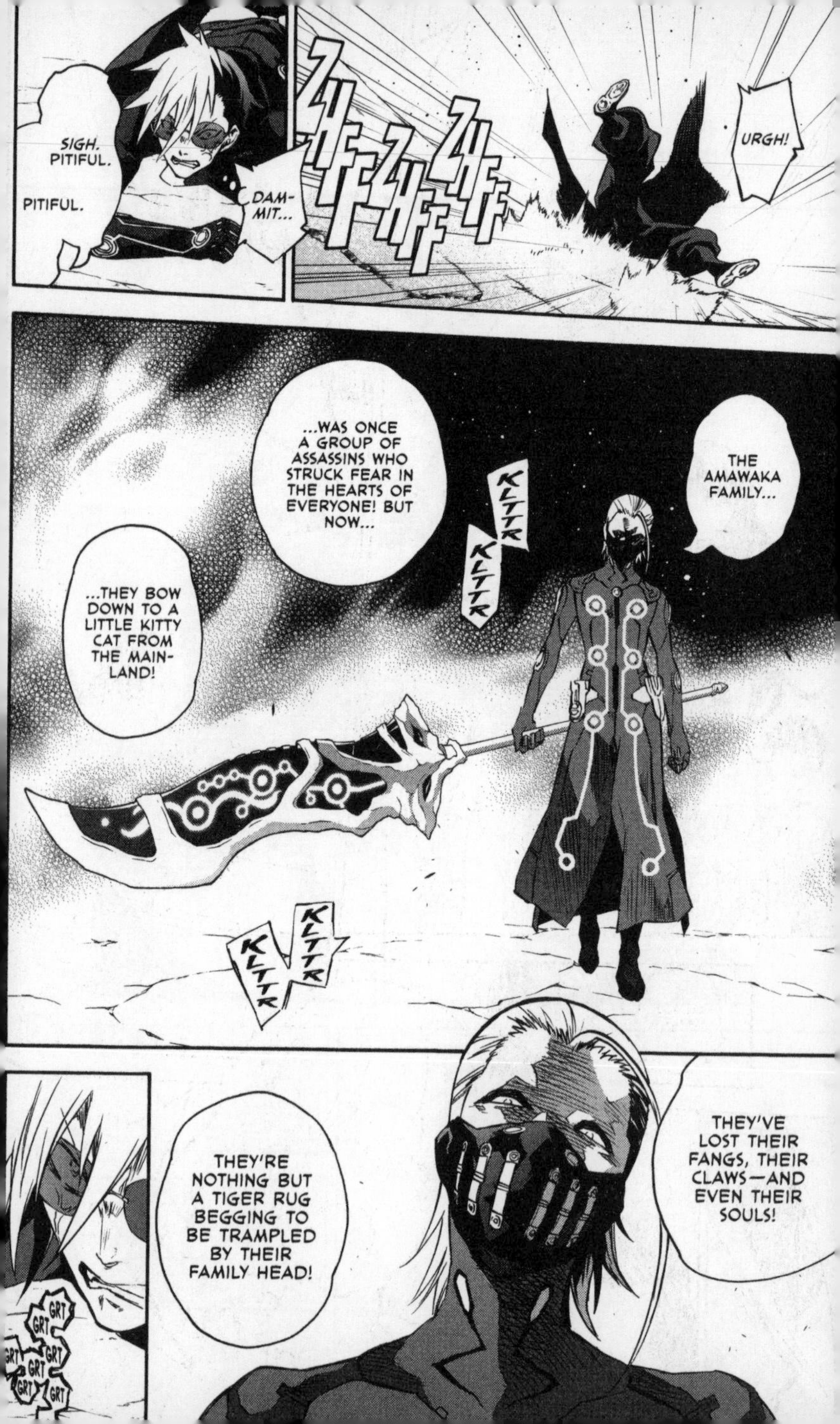
URGH!
ZHFF ZHFF ZHFF
DAM-MIT...
SIGH. PITIFUL.
PITIFUL.
THE AMAWAKA FAMILY...
KLTTR KLTTR
...WAS ONCE A GROUP OF ASSASSINS WHO STRUCK FEAR IN THE HEARTS OF EVERYONE! BUT NOW...
...THEY BOW DOWN TO A LITTLE KITTY CAT FROM THE MAIN-LAND!
KLTTR KLTTR
THEY'VE LOST THEIR FANGS, THEIR CLAWS—AND EVEN THEIR SOULS!
THEY'RE NOTHING BUT A TIGER RUG BEGGING TO BE TRAMPLED BY THEIR FAMILY HEAD!
GRT GRT GRT GRT GRT GRT GRT GRT

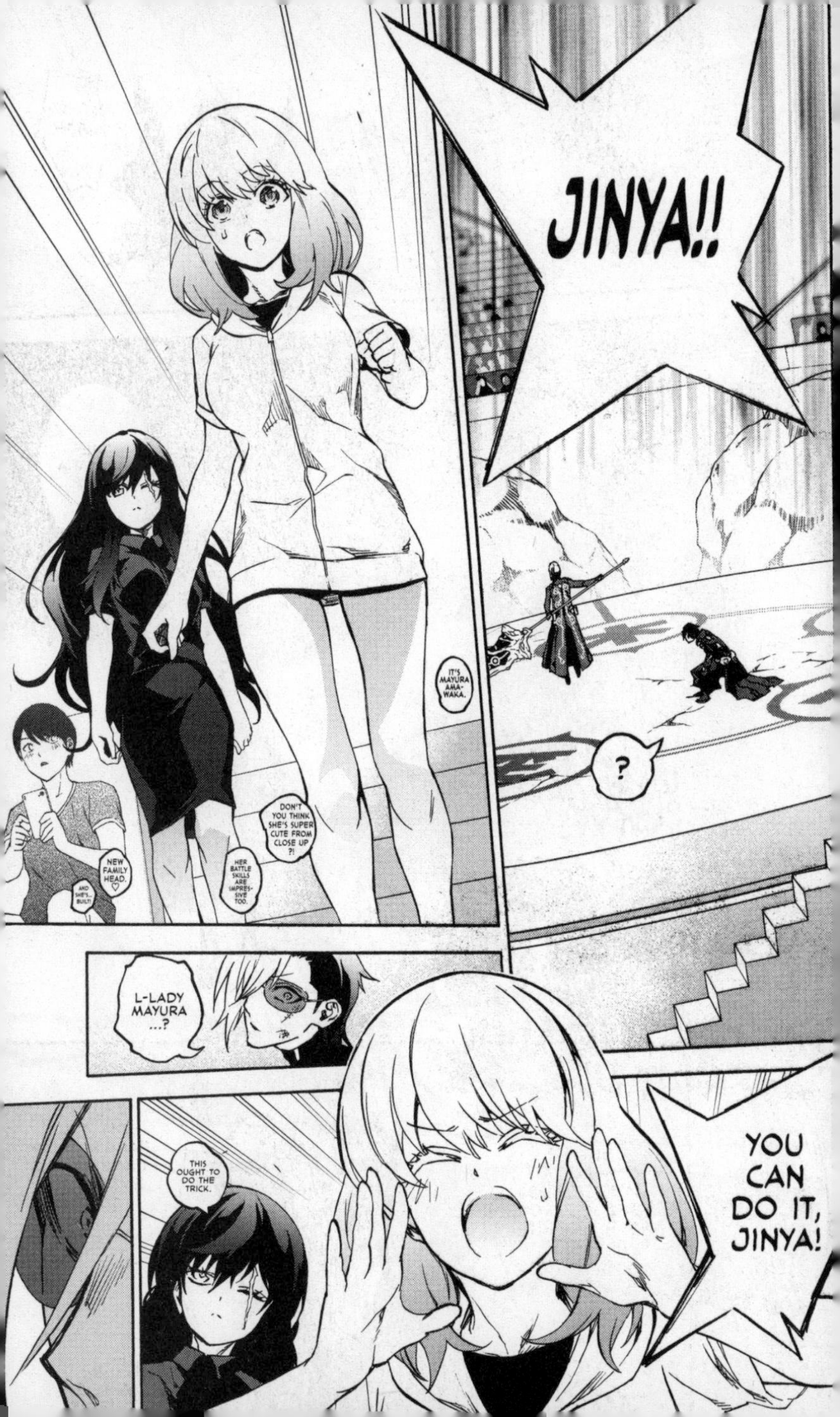
JINYA!!
?
IT'S MAYURA AMAWAKA.
DON'T YOU THINK SHE'S SUPER CUTE FROM CLOSE UP ?!
HER BATTLE SKILLS ARE IMPRESSIVE TOO.
NEW FAMILY HEAD. ♡
AND SHE'S... BUILT!
YOU CAN DO IT, JINYA!
L-LADY MAYURA ...?
THIS OUGHT TO DO THE TRICK.

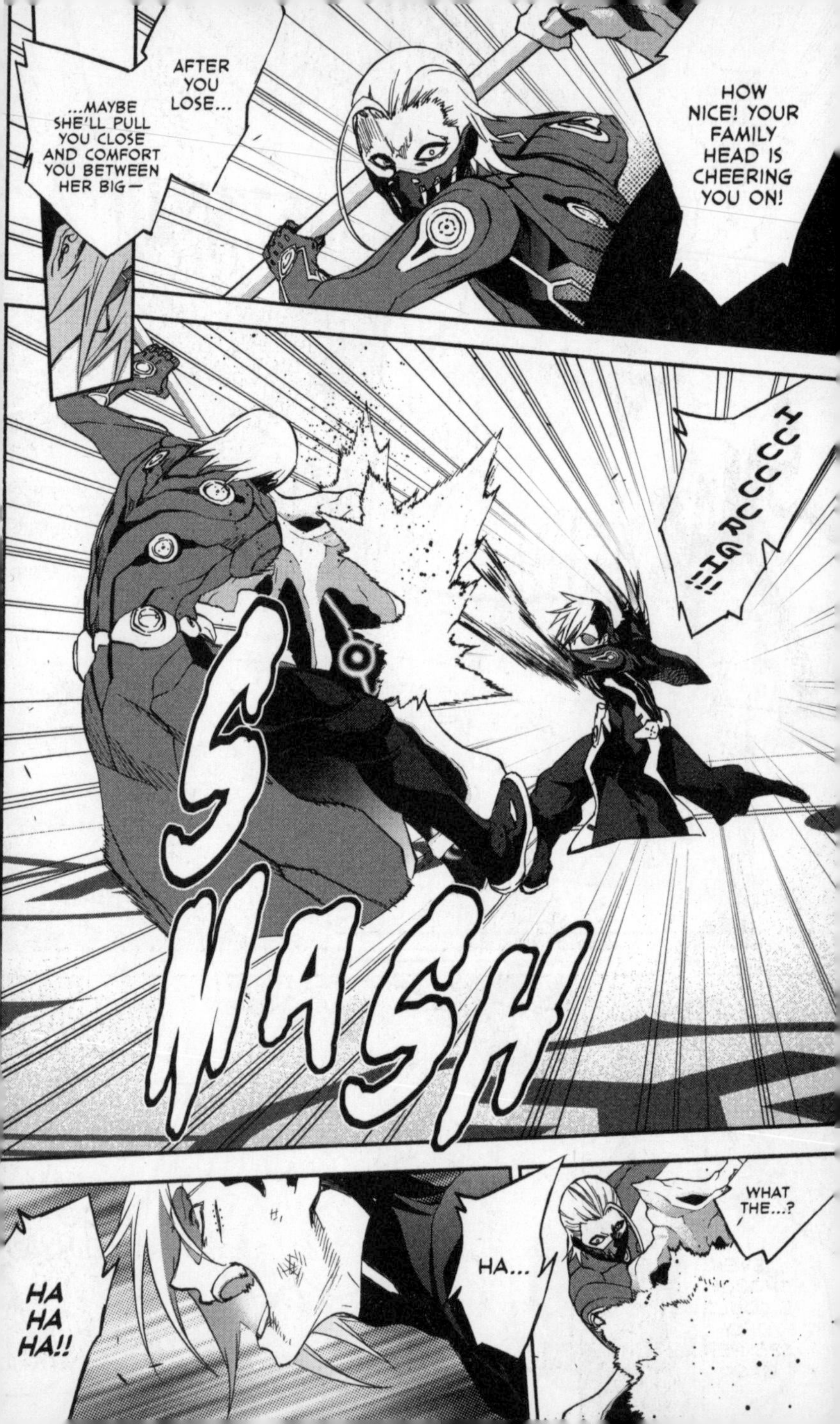
HOW NICE! YOUR FAMILY HEAD IS CHEERING YOU ON!
AFTER YOU LOSE...
...MAYBE SHE'LL PULL YOU CLOSE AND COMFORT YOU BETWEEN HER BIG—
HUUUURGH!!!
SMASH
WHAT THE...?
HA...
HA HA HA!!

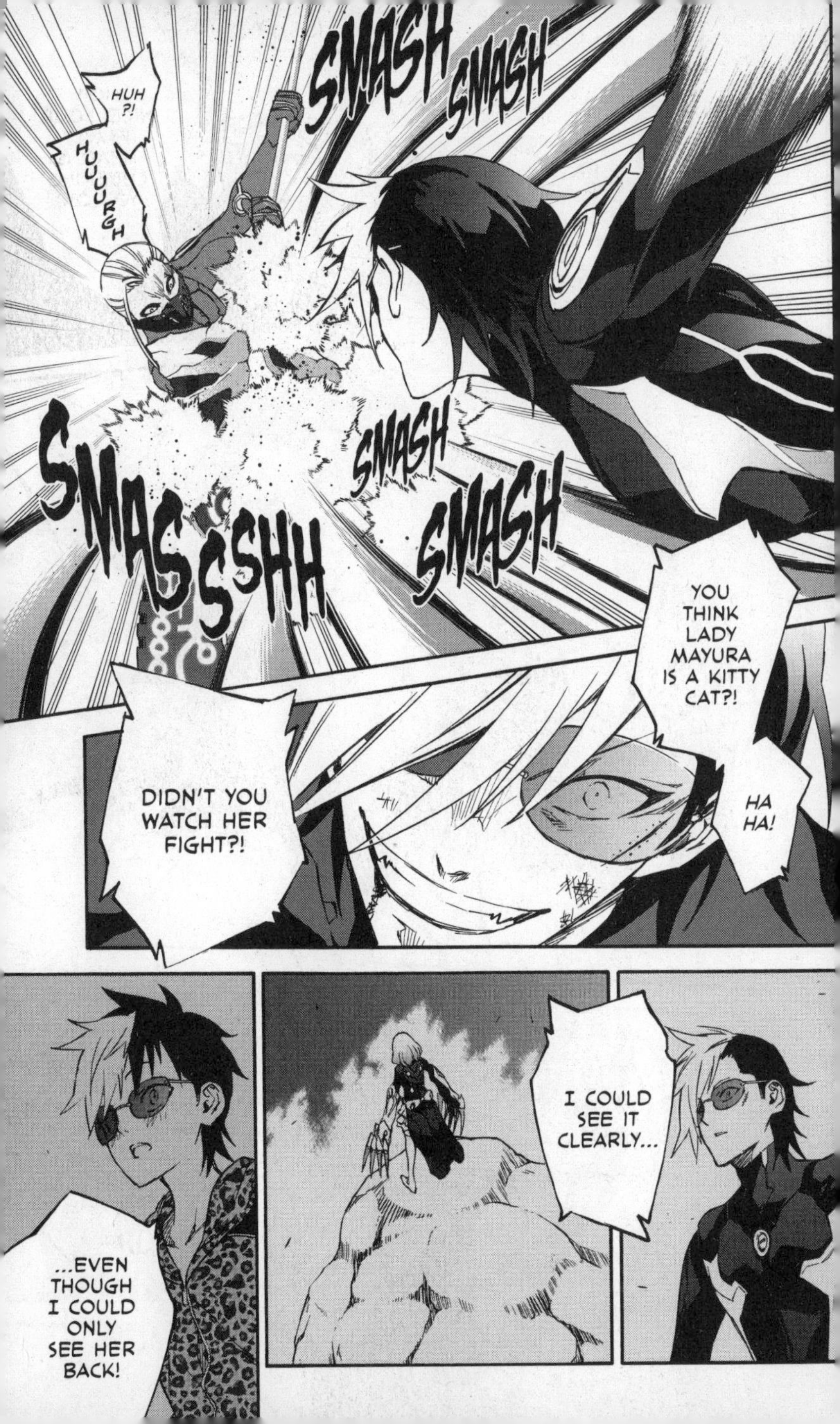
SMASH
SMASH
HUH ?!
HUUURGH
SMASH
SMASH
SMASSSHH
YOU THINK LADY MAYURA IS A KITTY CAT?!
HA HA!
DIDN'T YOU WATCH HER FIGHT?!
I COULD SEE IT CLEARLY...
...EVEN THOUGH I COULD ONLY SEE HER BACK!

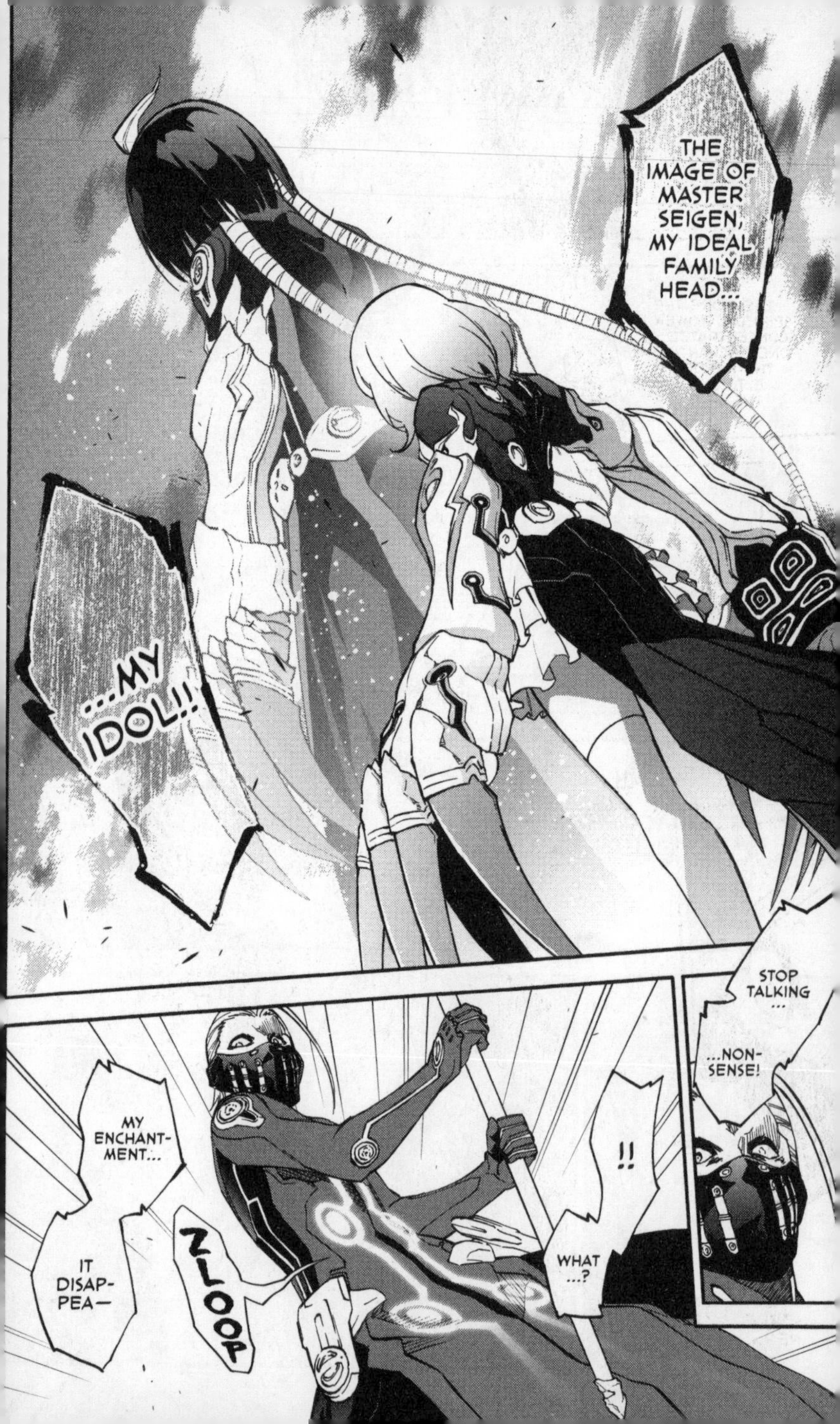
THE IMAGE OF MASTER SEIGEN, MY IDEAL FAMILY HEAD...
...MY IDOL!!
STOP TALKING ...
...NON-SENSE!
!!
MY ENCHANT-MENT...
WHAT ...?
ZLOOP
IT DISAP-PEA—

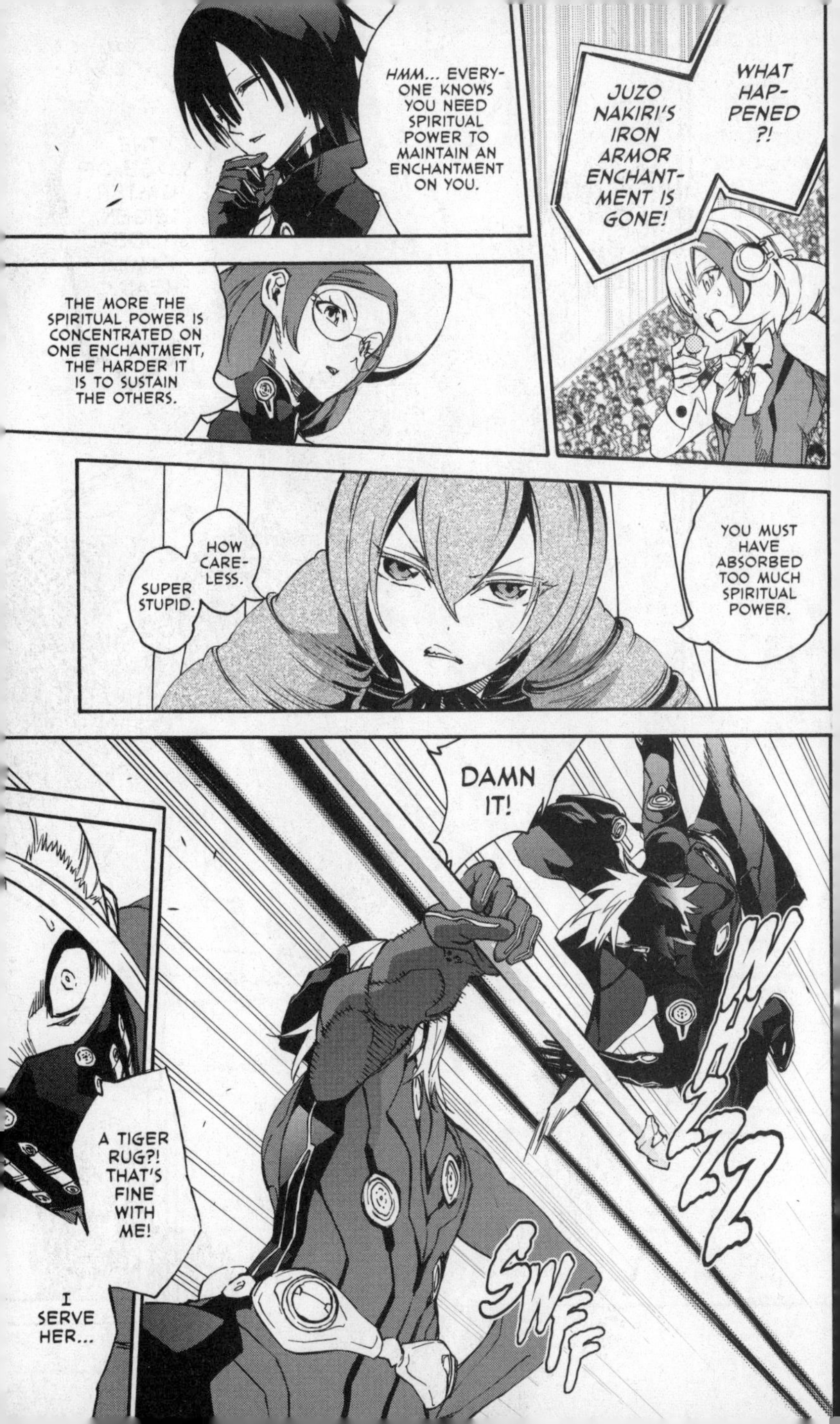
WHAT HAP-PENED?!
JUZO NAKIRI'S IRON ARMOR ENCHANT-MENT IS GONE!
HMM... EVERY-ONE KNOWS YOU NEED SPIRITUAL POWER TO MAINTAIN AN ENCHANTMENT ON YOU.
THE MORE THE SPIRITUAL POWER IS CONCENTRATED ON ONE ENCHANTMENT, THE HARDER IT IS TO SUSTAIN THE OTHERS.
YOU MUST HAVE ABSORBED TOO MUCH SPIRITUAL POWER.
HOW CARE-LESS.
SUPER STUPID.
DAMN IT!
A TIGER RUG?! THAT'S FINE WITH ME!
I SERVE HER...

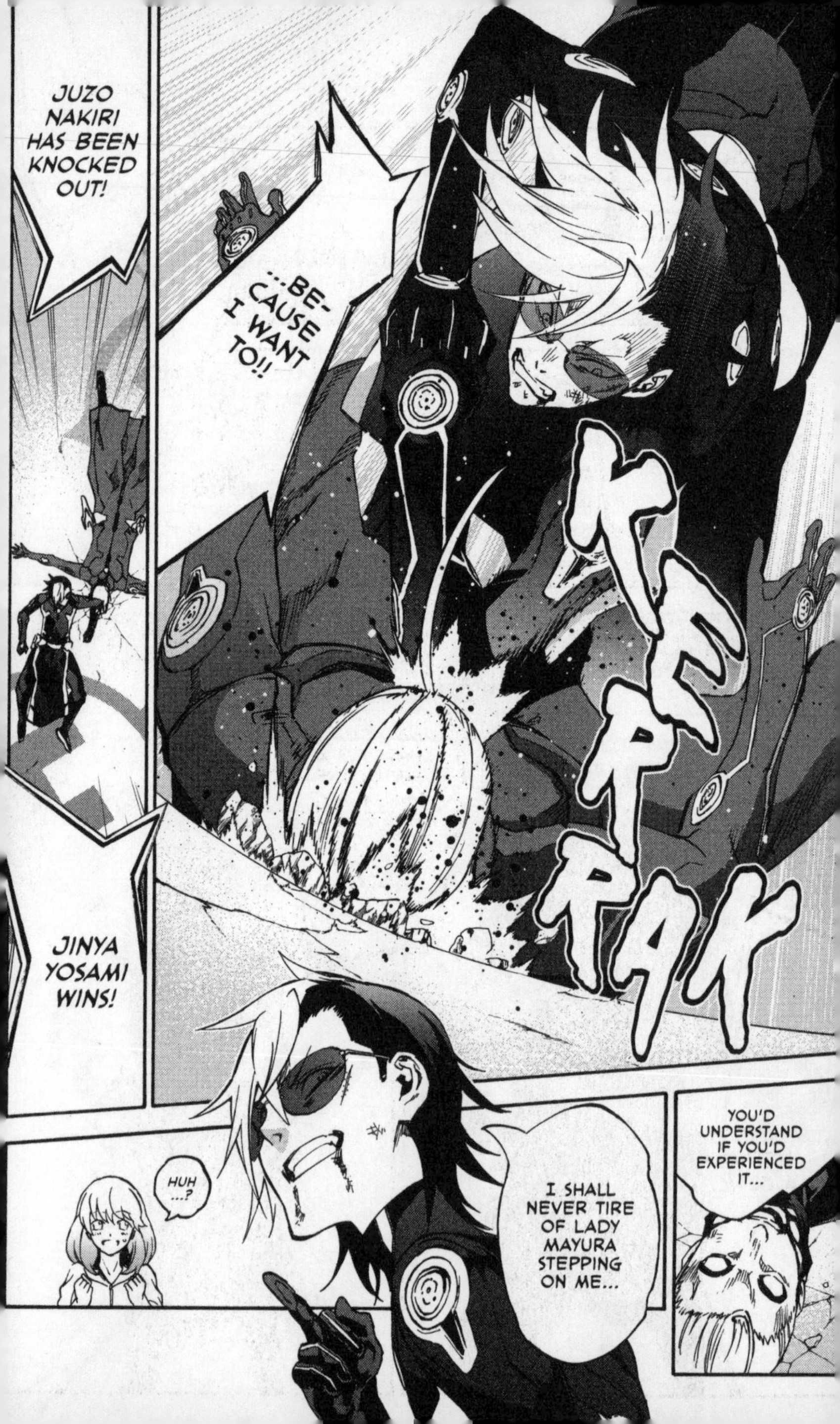

...BE-CAUSE I WANT TO!!
KERRAK
JUZO NAKIRI HAS BEEN KNOCKED OUT!
JINYA YOSAMI WINS!
YOU'D UNDERSTAND IF YOU'D EXPERIENCED IT...
I SHALL NEVER TIRE OF LADY MAYURA STEPPING ON ME...
HUH ...?

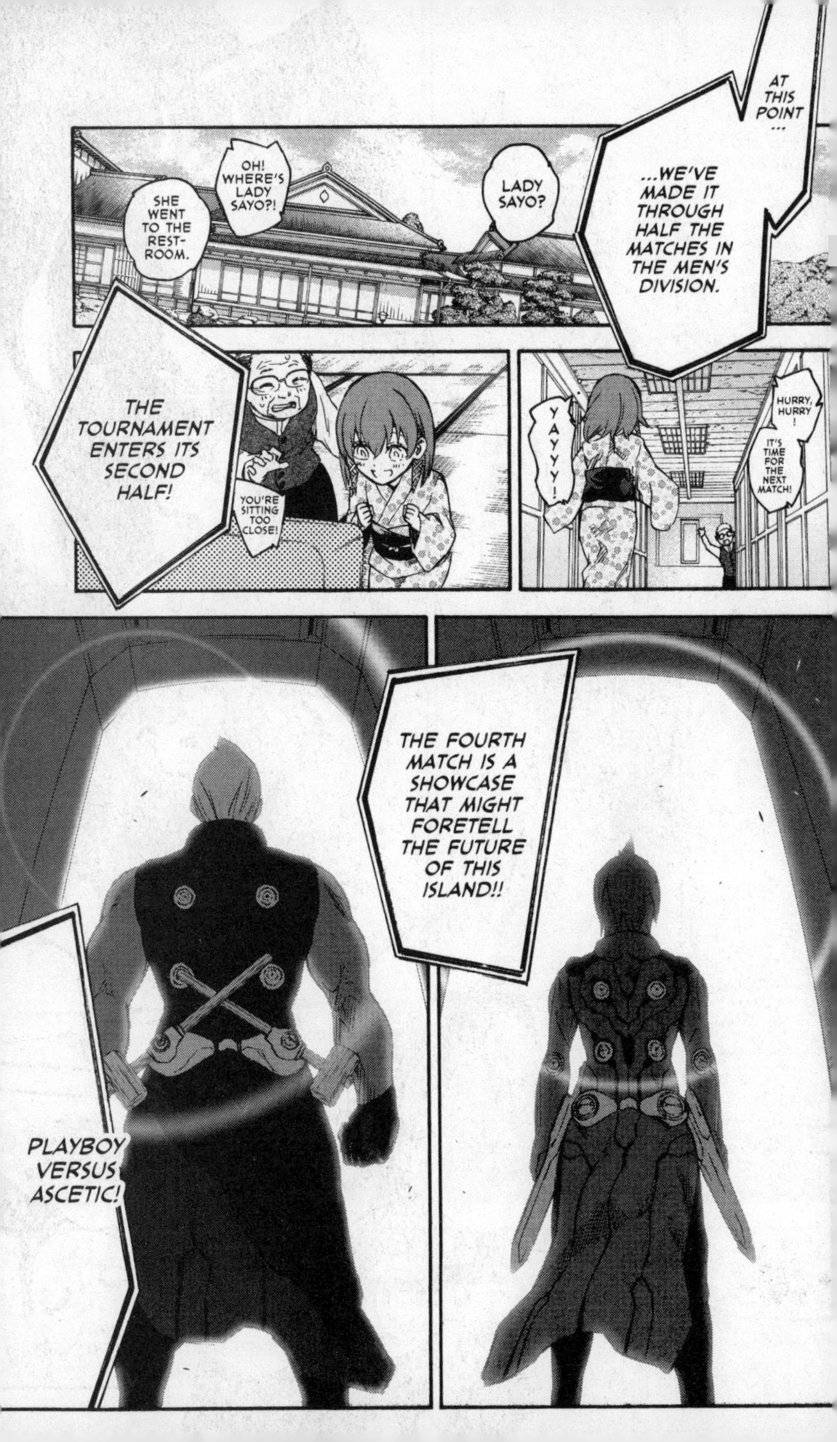
AT THIS POINT...
...WE'VE MADE IT THROUGH HALF THE MATCHES IN THE MEN'S DIVISION.
LADY SAYO?
OH! WHERE'S LADY SAYO?!
SHE WENT TO THE REST-ROOM.
HURRY, HURRY!
IT'S TIME FOR THE NEXT MATCH!
YAYYY!
THE TOURNAMENT ENTERS ITS SECOND HALF!
YOU'RE SITTING TOO CLOSE!
THE FOURTH MATCH IS A SHOWCASE THAT MIGHT FORETELL THE FUTURE OF THIS ISLAND!!
PLAYBOY VERSUS ASCETIC!

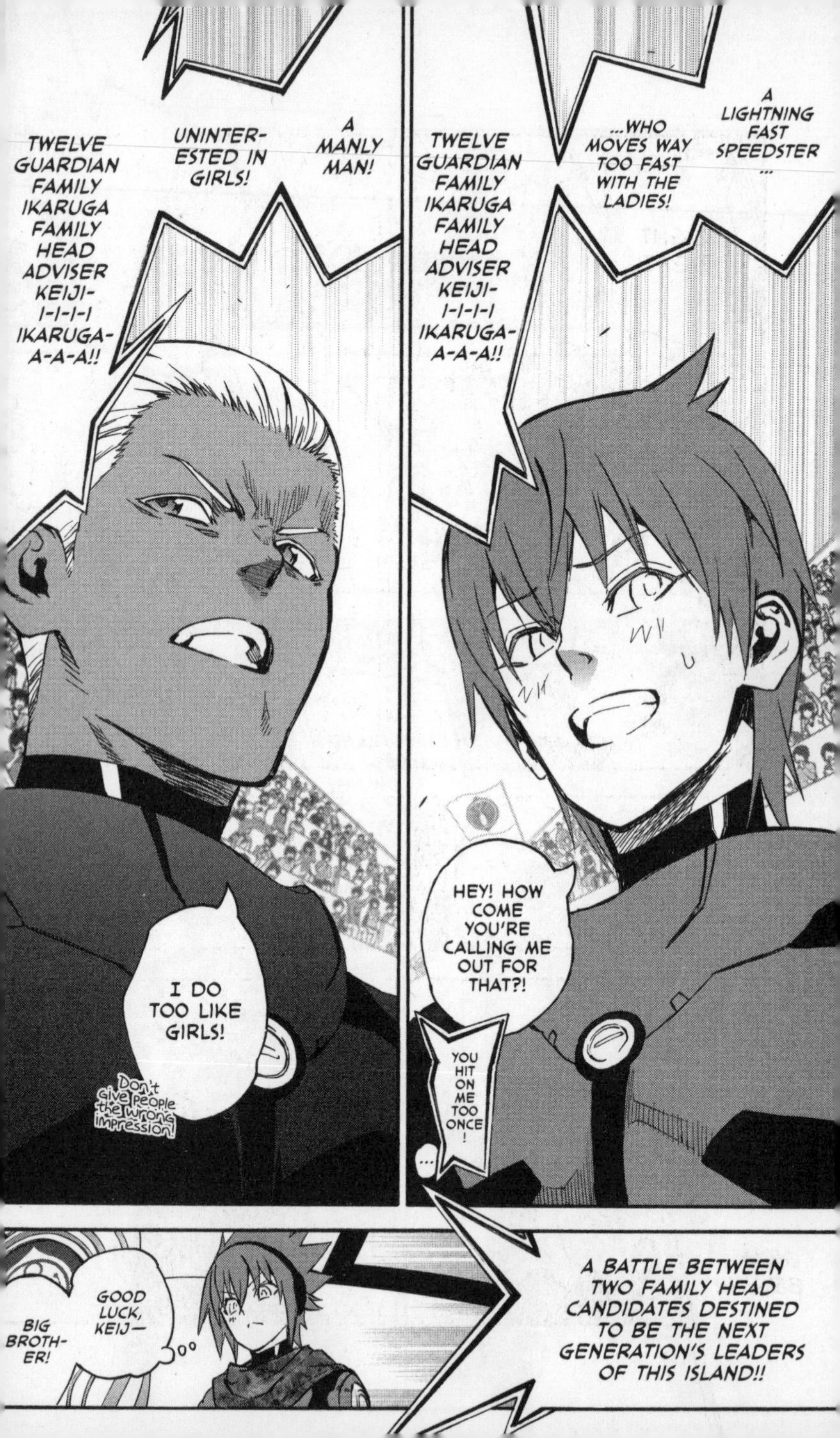
A LIGHTNING FAST SPEEDSTER...
...WHO MOVES WAY TOO FAST WITH THE LADIES!
TWELVE GUARDIAN FAMILY IKARUGA FAMILY HEAD ADVISER KEIJI-I-I-I-I IKARUGA-A-A-A!!
HEY! HOW COME YOU'RE CALLING ME OUT FOR THAT?!
YOU HIT ON ME TOO ONCE!
...
A MANLY MAN!
UNINTER-ESTED IN GIRLS!
TWELVE GUARDIAN FAMILY IKARUGA FAMILY HEAD ADVISER KEIJI-I-I-I-I IKARUGA-A-A-A!!
I DO TOO LIKE GIRLS!
Don't give people the wrong impression!
A BATTLE BETWEEN TWO FAMILY HEAD CANDIDATES DESTINED TO BE THE NEXT GENERATION'S LEADERS OF THIS ISLAND!!
GOOD LUCK, KEIJ—
BIG BROTHER!

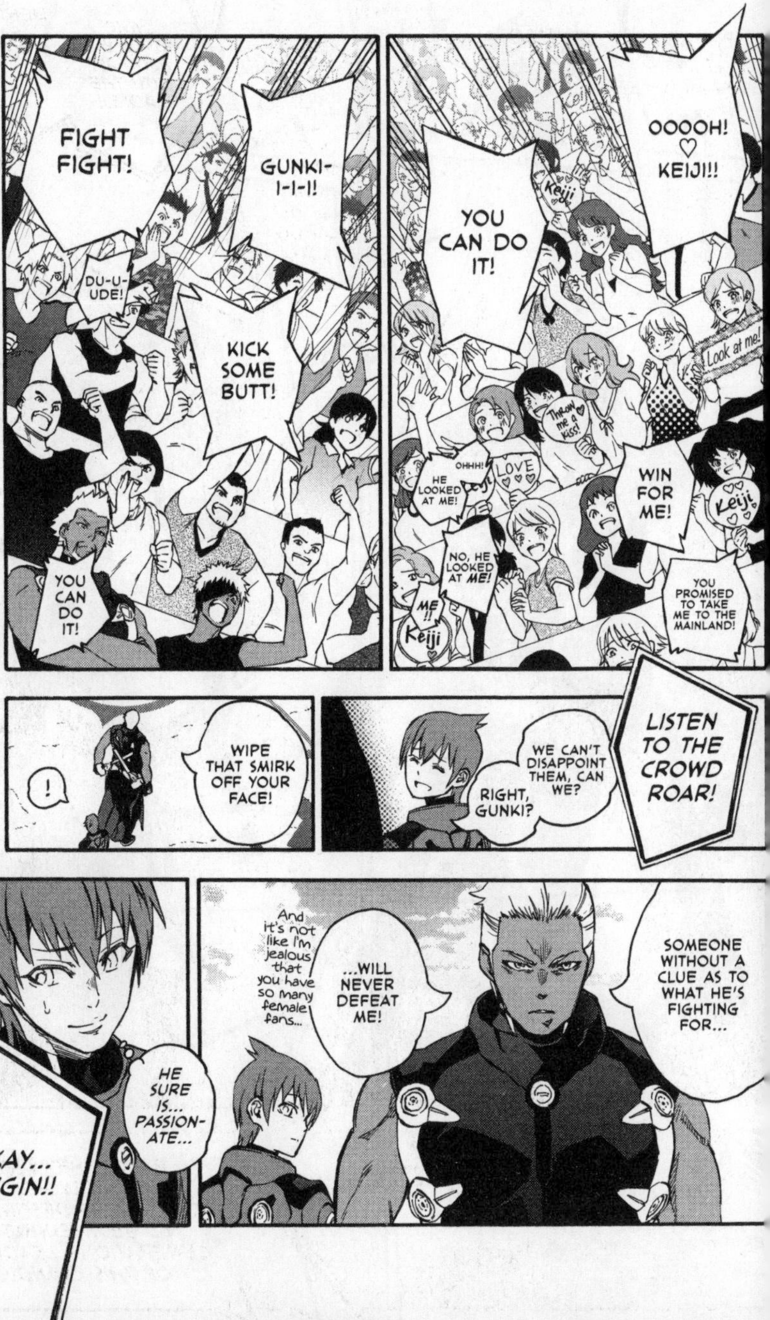
OOOOH! ♡ KEIJI!!
YOU CAN DO IT!
Keiji
Look at me!
Throw me a kiss!
LOVE
WIN FOR ME!
Keiji
OHHH! HE LOOKED AT ME!
NO, HE LOOKED AT ME!
ME!! Keiji
YOU PROMISED TO TAKE ME TO THE MAINLAND!
GUNKI-I-I-I!
FIGHT FIGHT!
KICK SOME BUTT!
DU-U-UDE!
YOU CAN DO IT!
LISTEN TO THE CROWD ROAR!
WE CAN'T DISAPPOINT THEM, CAN WE?
RIGHT, GUNKI?
WIPE THAT SMIRK OFF YOUR FACE!
!
SOMEONE WITHOUT A CLUE AS TO WHAT HE'S FIGHTING FOR...
...WILL NEVER DEFEAT ME!
And it's not like I'm jealous that you have so many female fans...
HE SURE IS... PASSION-ATE...
OKAY... BEGIN!!

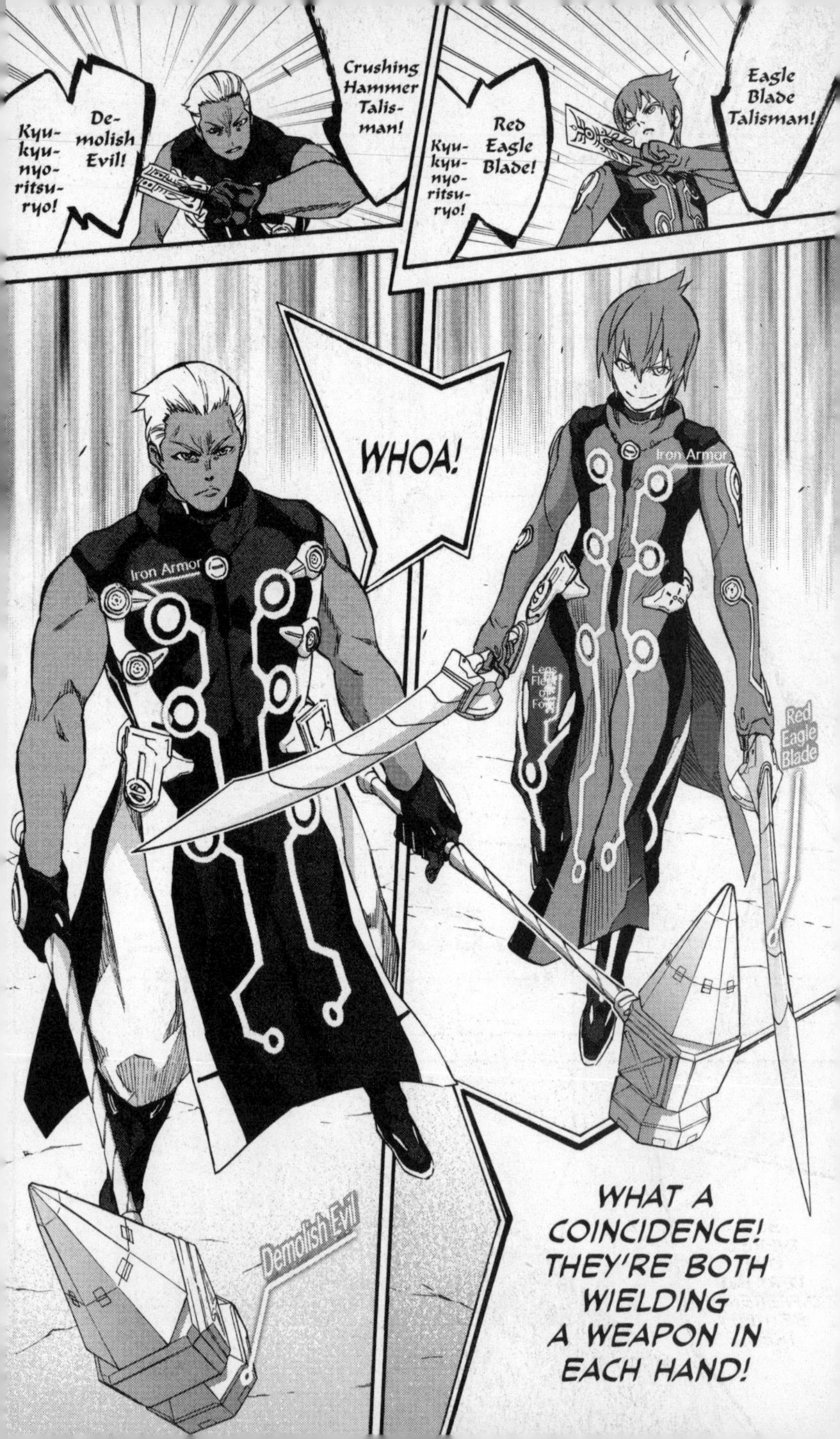

Eagle Blade Talisman!
Red Eagle Blade!
Kyu-kyu-nyo-ritsu-ryo!
Crushing Hammer Talis-man!
Demolish Evil!
Kyu-kyu-nyo-ritsu-ryo!
Iron Armor
WHOA!
Iron Armor
Red Eagle Blade
Demolish Evil
WHAT A COINCIDENCE! THEY'RE BOTH WIELDING A WEAPON IN EACH HAND!

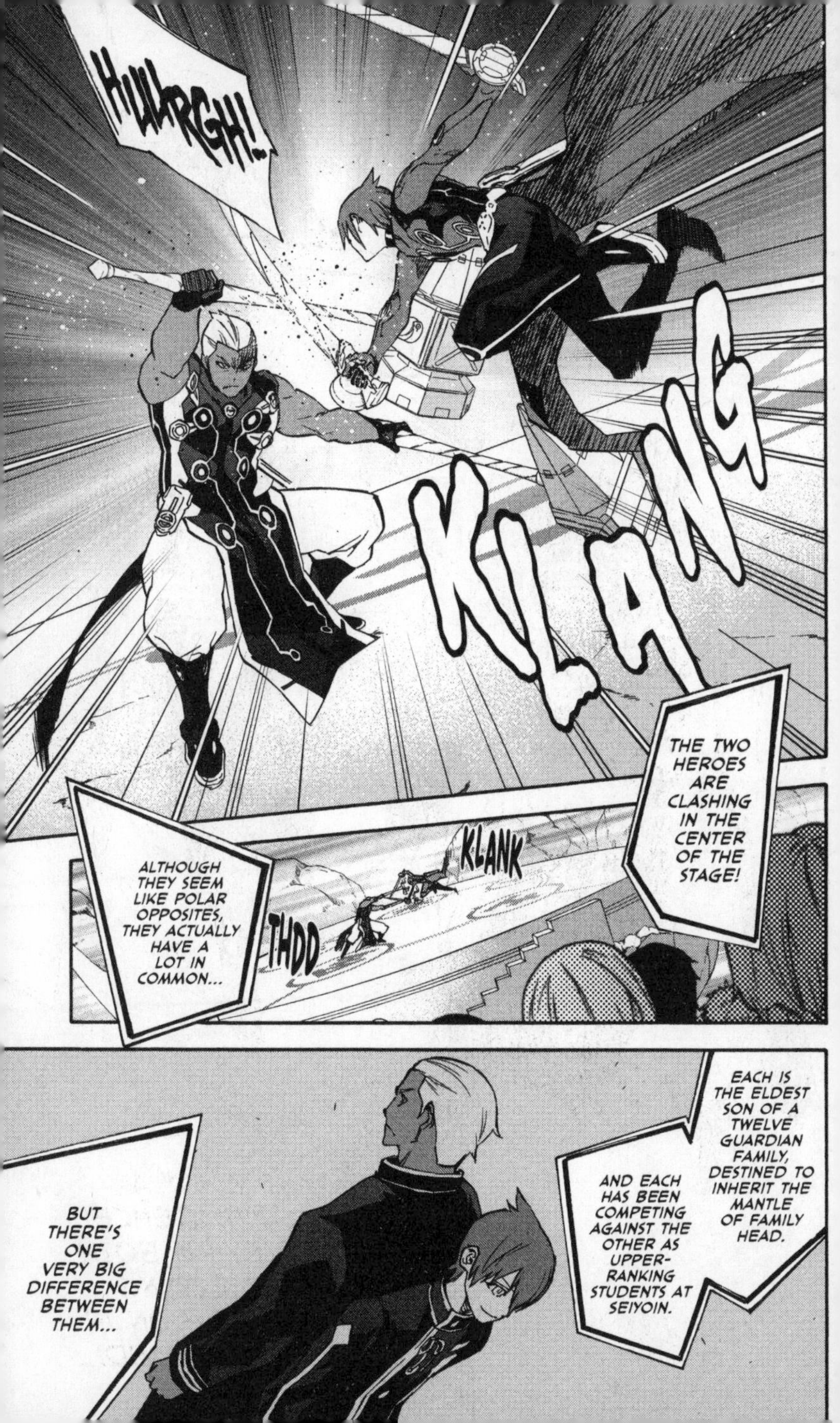
HUURGH!
KLANG
THE TWO HEROES ARE CLASHING IN THE CENTER OF THE STAGE!
KLANK
THDD
ALTHOUGH THEY SEEM LIKE POLAR OPPOSITES, THEY ACTUALLY HAVE A LOT IN COMMON...
EACH IS THE ELDEST SON OF A TWELVE GUARDIAN FAMILY, DESTINED TO INHERIT THE MANTLE OF FAMILY HEAD.
AND EACH HAS BEEN COMPETING AGAINST THE OTHER AS UPPER-RANKING STUDENTS AT SEIYOIN.
BUT THERE'S ONE VERY BIG DIFFERENCE BETWEEN THEM...

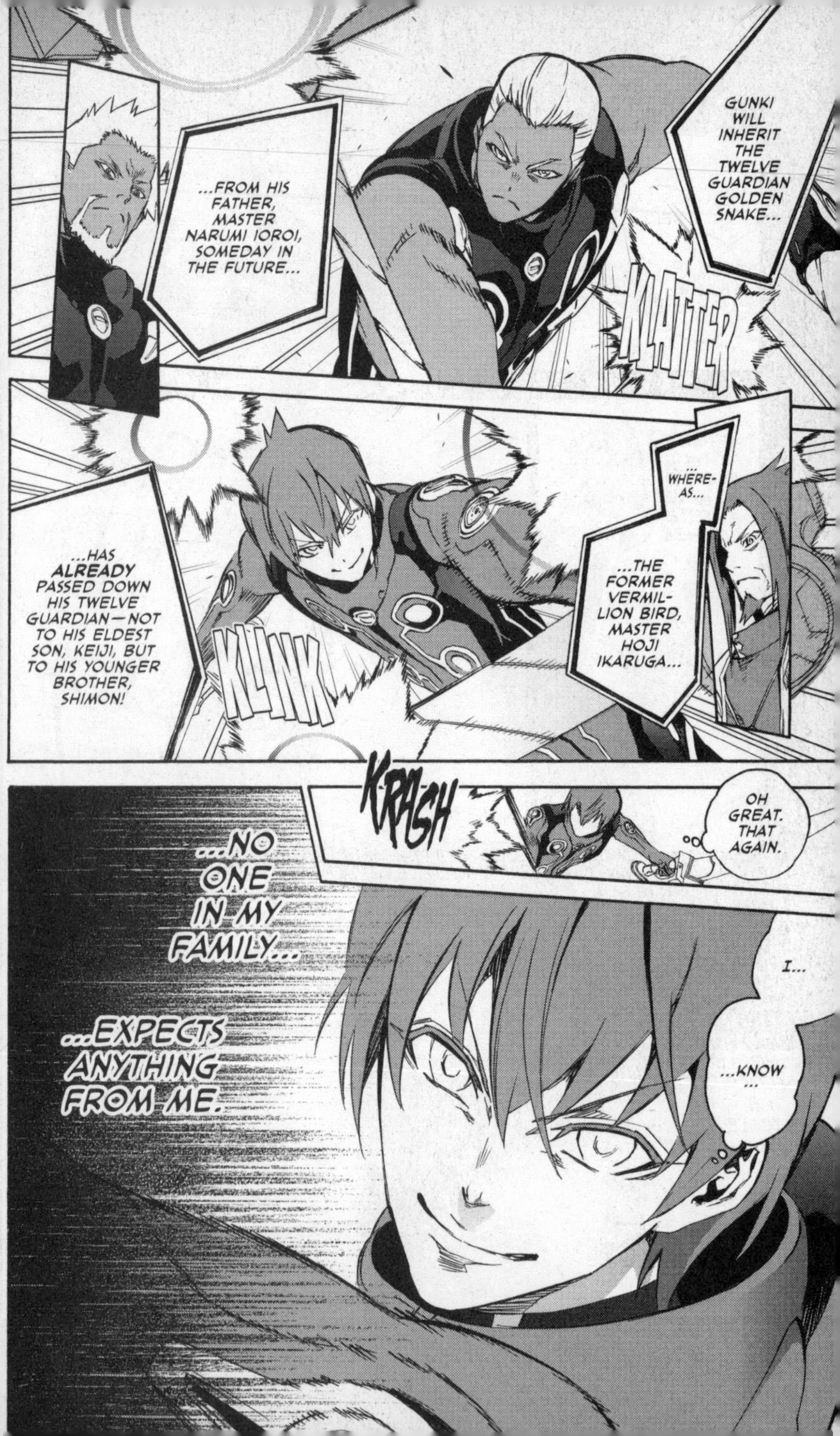
GUNKI WILL INHERIT THE TWELVE GUARDIAN GOLDEN SNAKE...
...FROM HIS FATHER, MASTER NARUMI IOROI, SOMEDAY IN THE FUTURE...
KLATTER
...WHERE-AS...
...THE FORMER VERMIL-LION BIRD, MASTER HOJI IKARUGA...
...HAS **ALREADY** PASSED DOWN HIS TWELVE GUARDIAN—NOT TO HIS ELDEST SON, KEIJI, BUT TO HIS YOUNGER BROTHER, SHIMON!
KLINK
OH GREAT. THAT AGAIN.
KRASH
I...
...KNOW...
...NO ONE IN MY FAMILY...
...EXPECTS ANYTHING FROM ME.

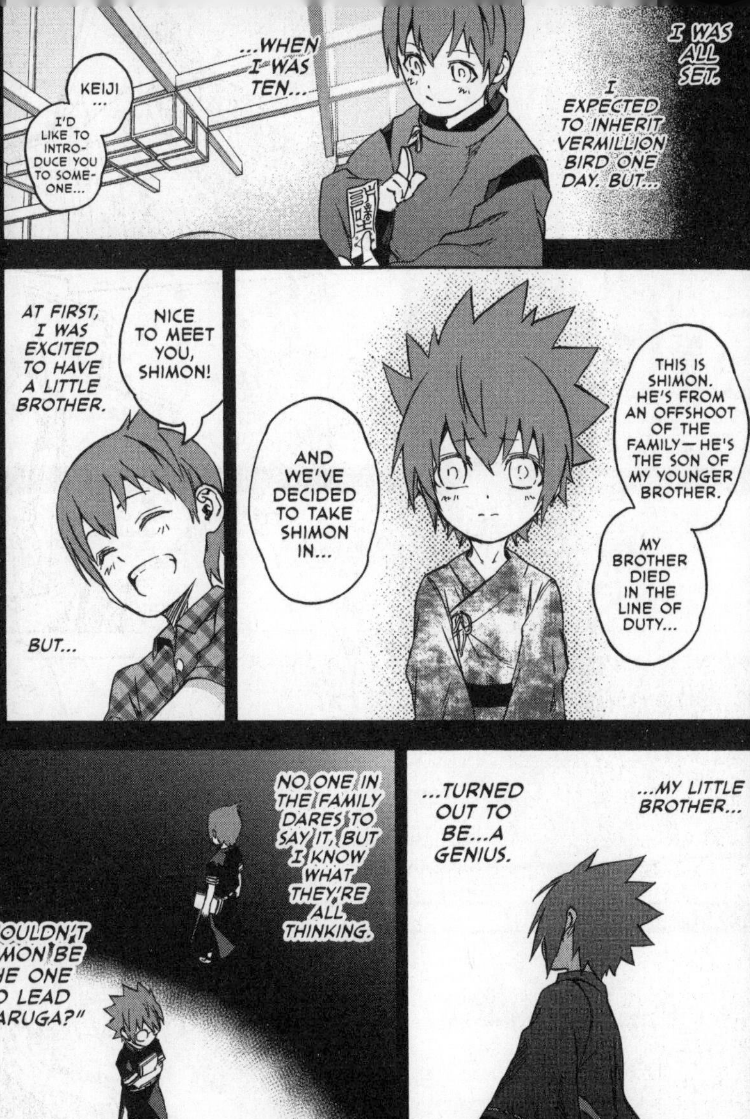
I WAS ALL SET.
I EXPECTED TO INHERIT VERMILLION BIRD ONE DAY. BUT...
...WHEN I WAS TEN...
KEIJI...
I'D LIKE TO INTRODUCE YOU TO SOMEONE...
THIS IS SHIMON. HE'S FROM AN OFFSHOOT OF THE FAMILY—HE'S THE SON OF MY YOUNGER BROTHER.
MY BROTHER DIED IN THE LINE OF DUTY...
AND WE'VE DECIDED TO TAKE SHIMON IN...
NICE TO MEET YOU, SHIMON!
AT FIRST, I WAS EXCITED TO HAVE A LITTLE BROTHER.
BUT...
...MY LITTLE BROTHER...
...TURNED OUT TO BE...A GENIUS.
NO ONE IN THE FAMILY DARES TO SAY IT, BUT I KNOW WHAT THEY'RE ALL THINKING.
"SHOULDN'T SHIMON BE THE ONE TO LEAD IKARUGA?"

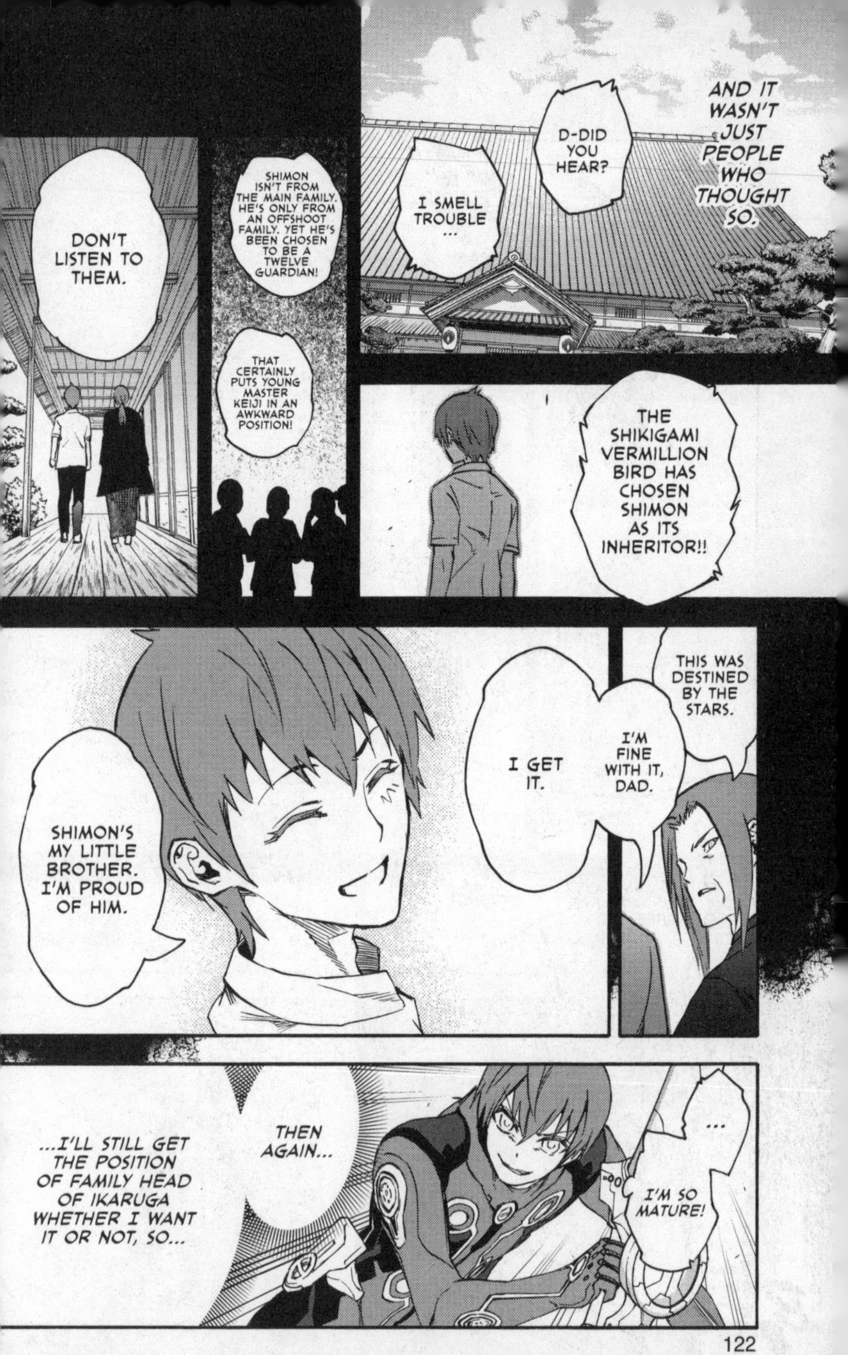
AND IT WASN'T JUST PEOPLE WHO THOUGHT SO.
D-DID YOU HEAR?
I SMELL TROUBLE ...
THE SHIKIGAMI VERMILLION BIRD HAS CHOSEN SHIMON AS ITS INHERITOR!!
SHIMON ISN'T FROM THE MAIN FAMILY. HE'S ONLY FROM AN OFFSHOOT FAMILY. YET HE'S BEEN CHOSEN TO BE A TWELVE GUARDIAN!
THAT CERTAINLY PUTS YOUNG MASTER KEIJI IN AN AWKWARD POSITION!
DON'T LISTEN TO THEM.
THIS WAS DESTINED BY THE STARS.
I'M FINE WITH IT, DAD.
I GET IT.
SHIMON'S MY LITTLE BROTHER. I'M PROUD OF HIM.
...
I'M SO MATURE!
THEN AGAIN...
...I'LL STILL GET THE POSITION OF FAMILY HEAD OF IKARUGA WHETHER I WANT IT OR NOT, SO...

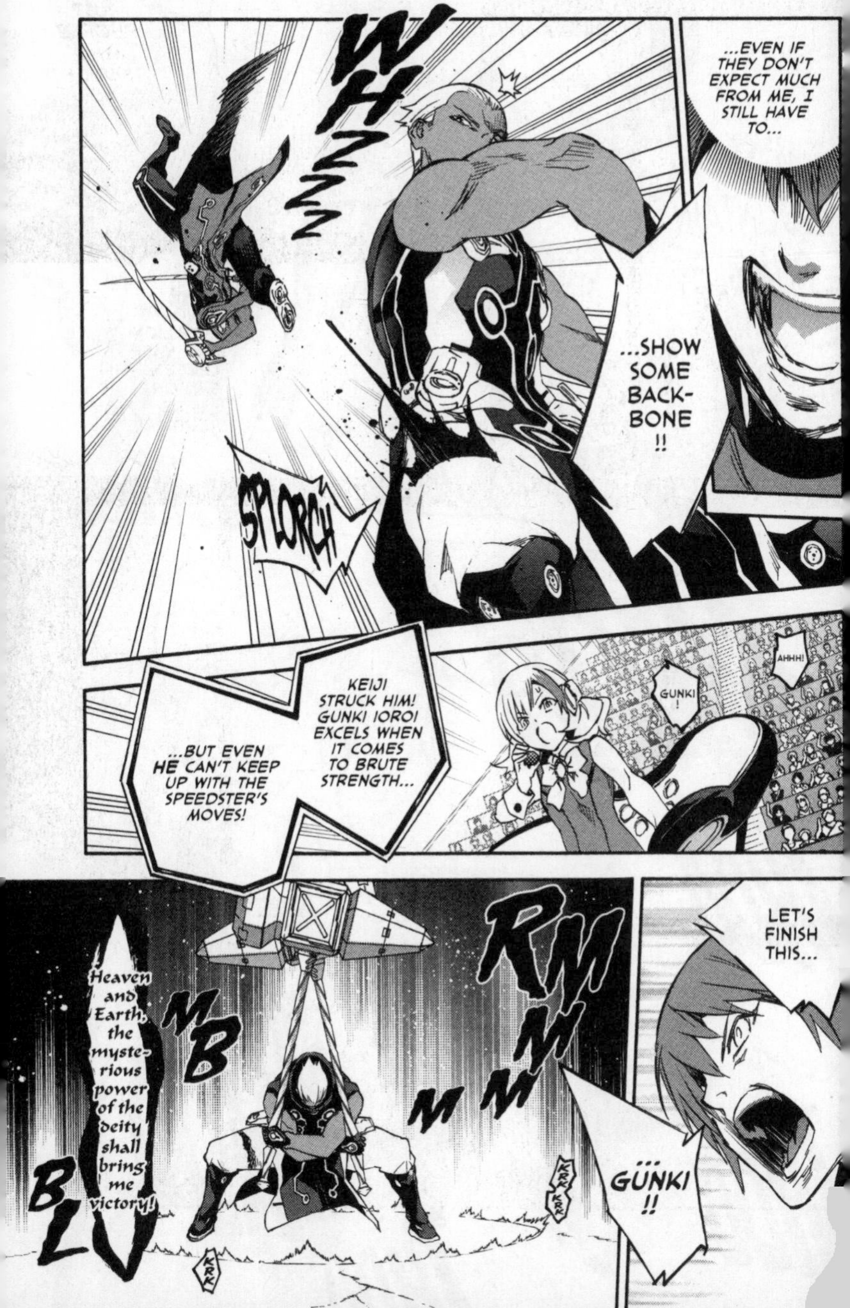
...EVEN IF THEY DON'T EXPECT MUCH FROM ME, I STILL HAVE TO...
...SHOW SOME BACK-BONE !!
WHZZZZ
SPLORCH
AHHH!
GUNKI !
KEIJI STRUCK HIM! GUNKI IOROI EXCELS WHEN IT COMES TO BRUTE STRENGTH...
...BUT EVEN HE CAN'T KEEP UP WITH THE SPEEDSTER'S MOVES!
LET'S FINISH THIS...
GÜNKI !!
KRK KRK
RMMMM
MB
Heaven and Earth, the myste-rious power of the deity shall bring me victory!
BL
KRK

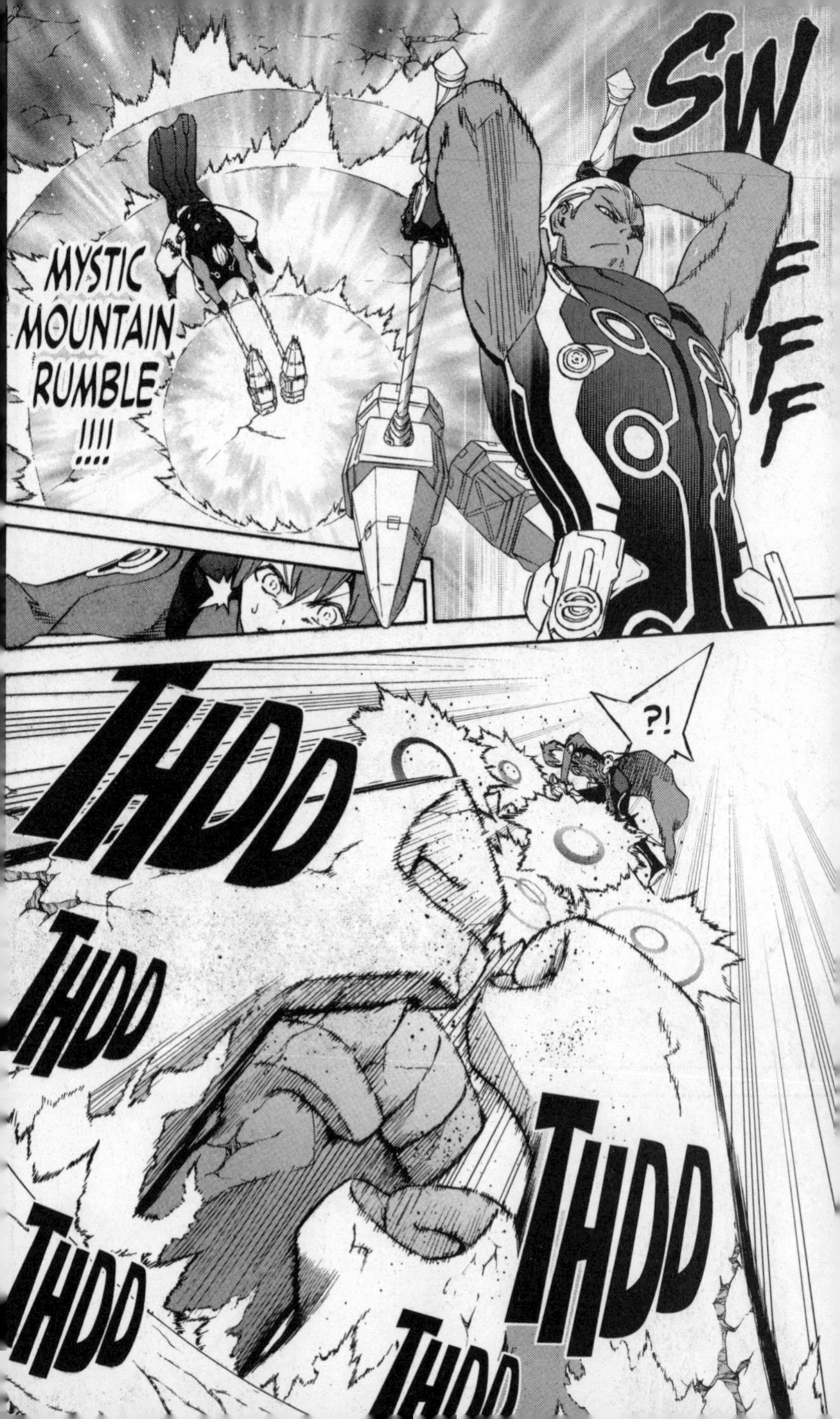
SWFFF
MYSTIC MOUNTAIN RUMBLE!!!!
?!
THDD
THDD
THDD
THDD
THDD

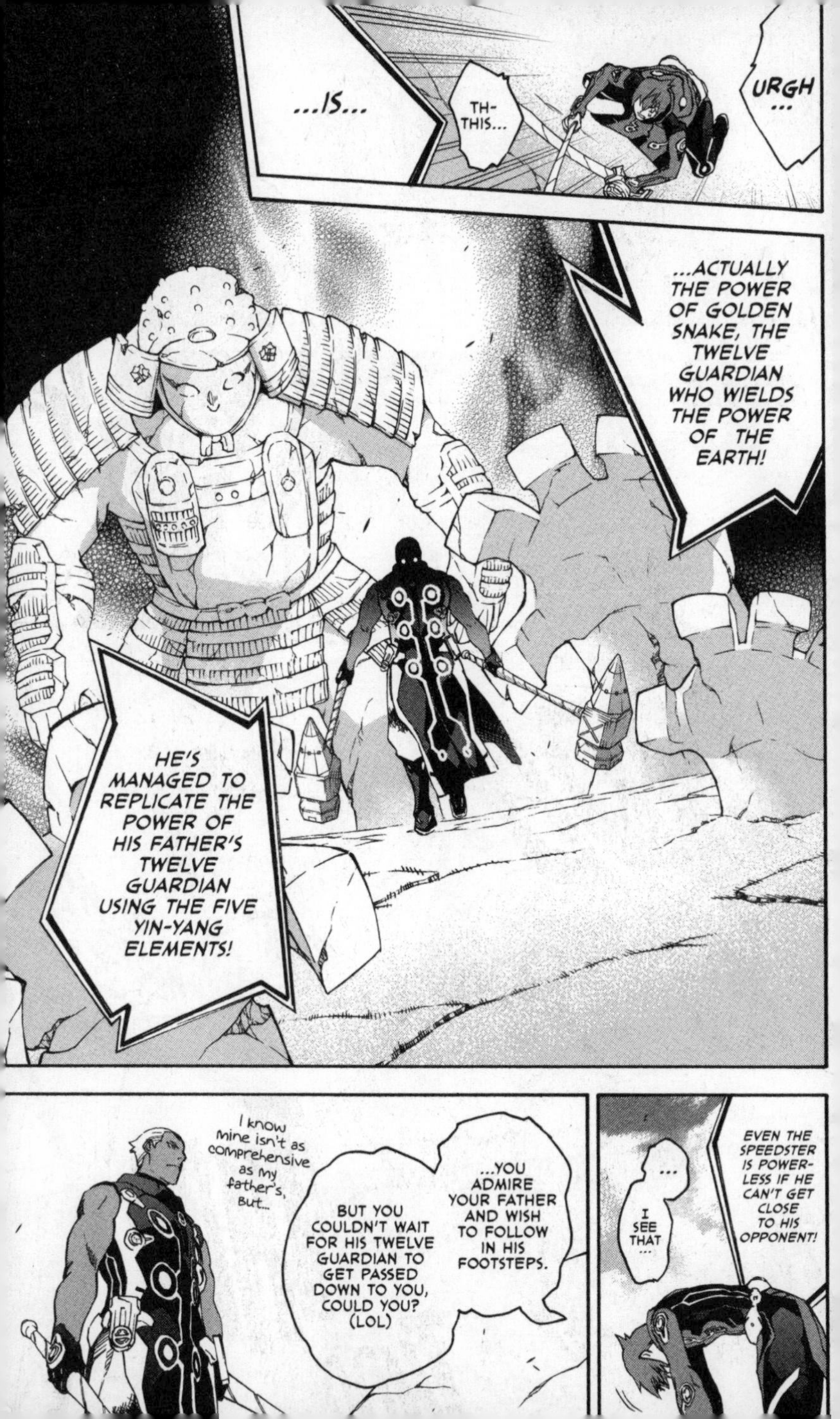
URGH ...
TH- THIS...
...IS...
...ACTUALLY THE POWER OF GOLDEN SNAKE, THE TWELVE GUARDIAN WHO WIELDS THE POWER OF THE EARTH!
HE'S MANAGED TO REPLICATE THE POWER OF HIS FATHER'S TWELVE GUARDIAN USING THE FIVE YIN-YANG ELEMENTS!
EVEN THE SPEEDSTER IS POWER-LESS IF HE CAN'T GET CLOSE TO HIS OPPONENT!
...
I SEE THAT ...
...YOU ADMIRE YOUR FATHER AND WISH TO FOLLOW IN HIS FOOTSTEPS.
BUT YOU COULDN'T WAIT FOR HIS TWELVE GUARDIAN TO GET PASSED DOWN TO YOU, COULD YOU? (LOL)
I know mine isn't as comprehensive as my father's, but...

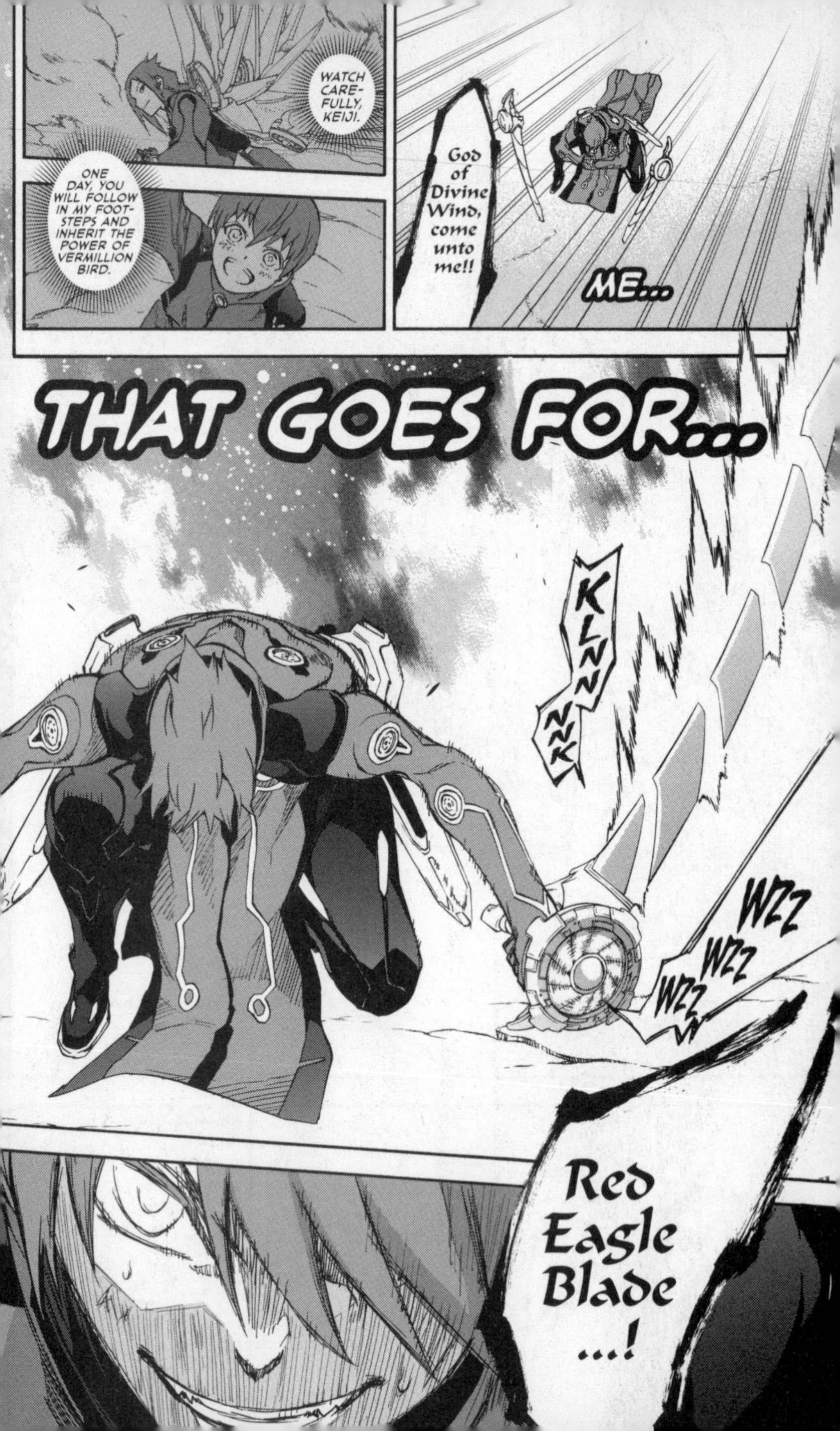
God of Divine Wind, come unto me!!
ME...
WATCH CARE-FULLY, KEIJI.
ONE DAY, YOU WILL FOLLOW IN MY FOOT-STEPS AND INHERIT THE POWER OF VERMILLION BIRD.
THAT GOES FOR...
KLNNNNK
WZZ
WZZ
WZZ
Red Eagle Blade ...!

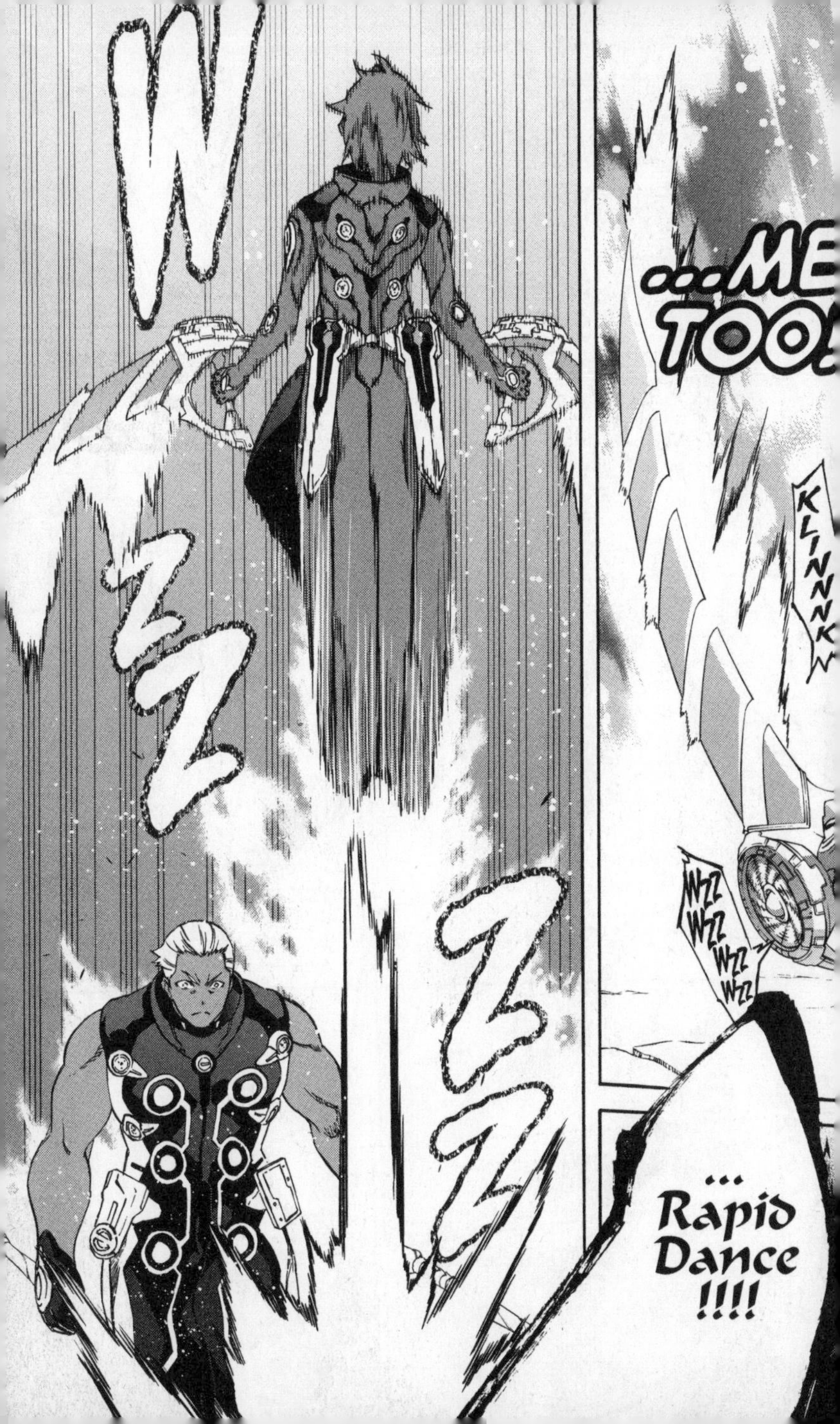

...ME TOO!
KLINNNK
WZZ WZZ WZZ WZZ
... Rapid Dance !!!!
W
ZZ
ZZZ

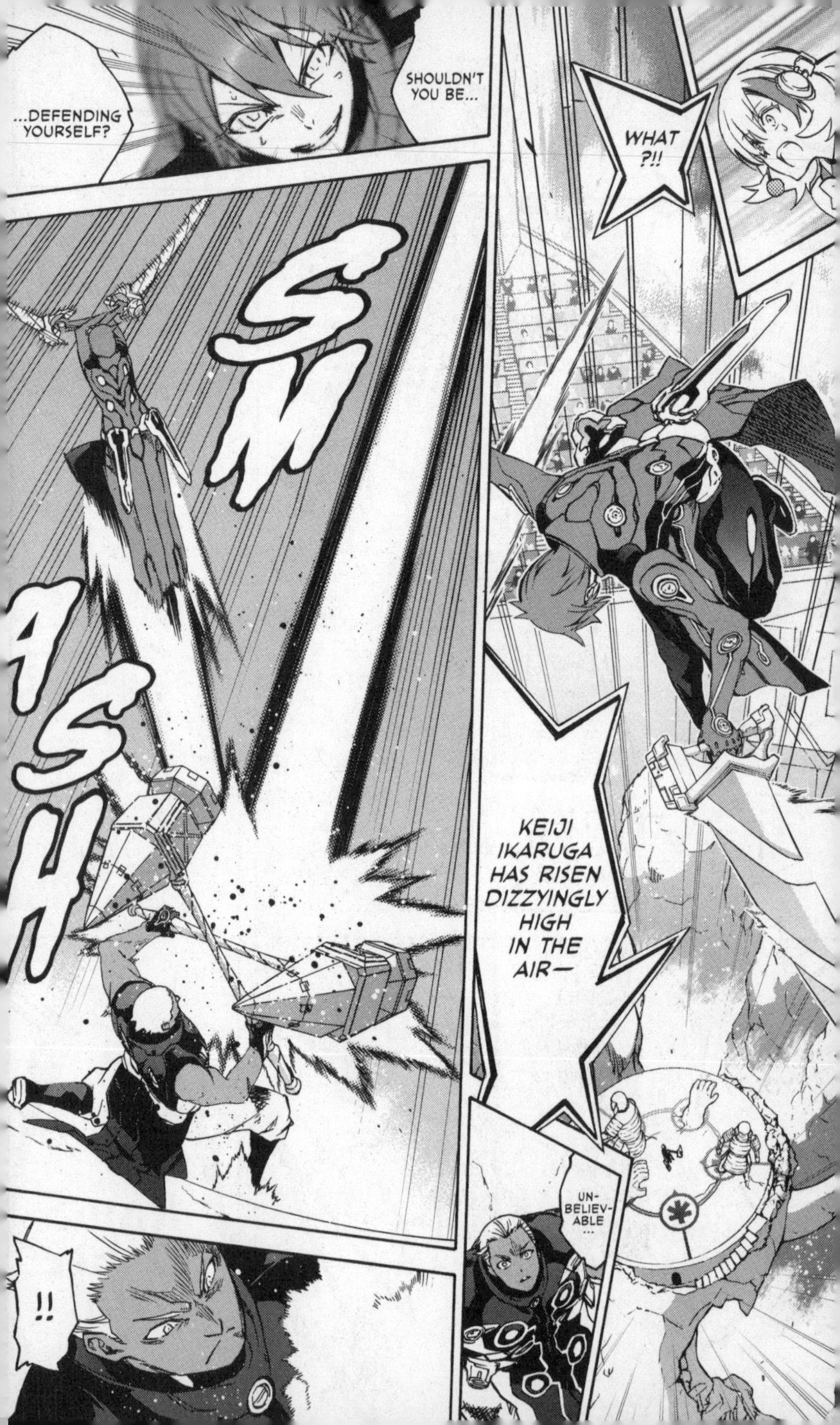
WHAT ?!!
SHOULDN'T YOU BE...
...DEFENDING YOURSELF?
KEIJI IKARUGA HAS RISEN DIZZYINGLY HIGH IN THE AIR—
SMASH
UN-BELIEV-ABLE...
!!

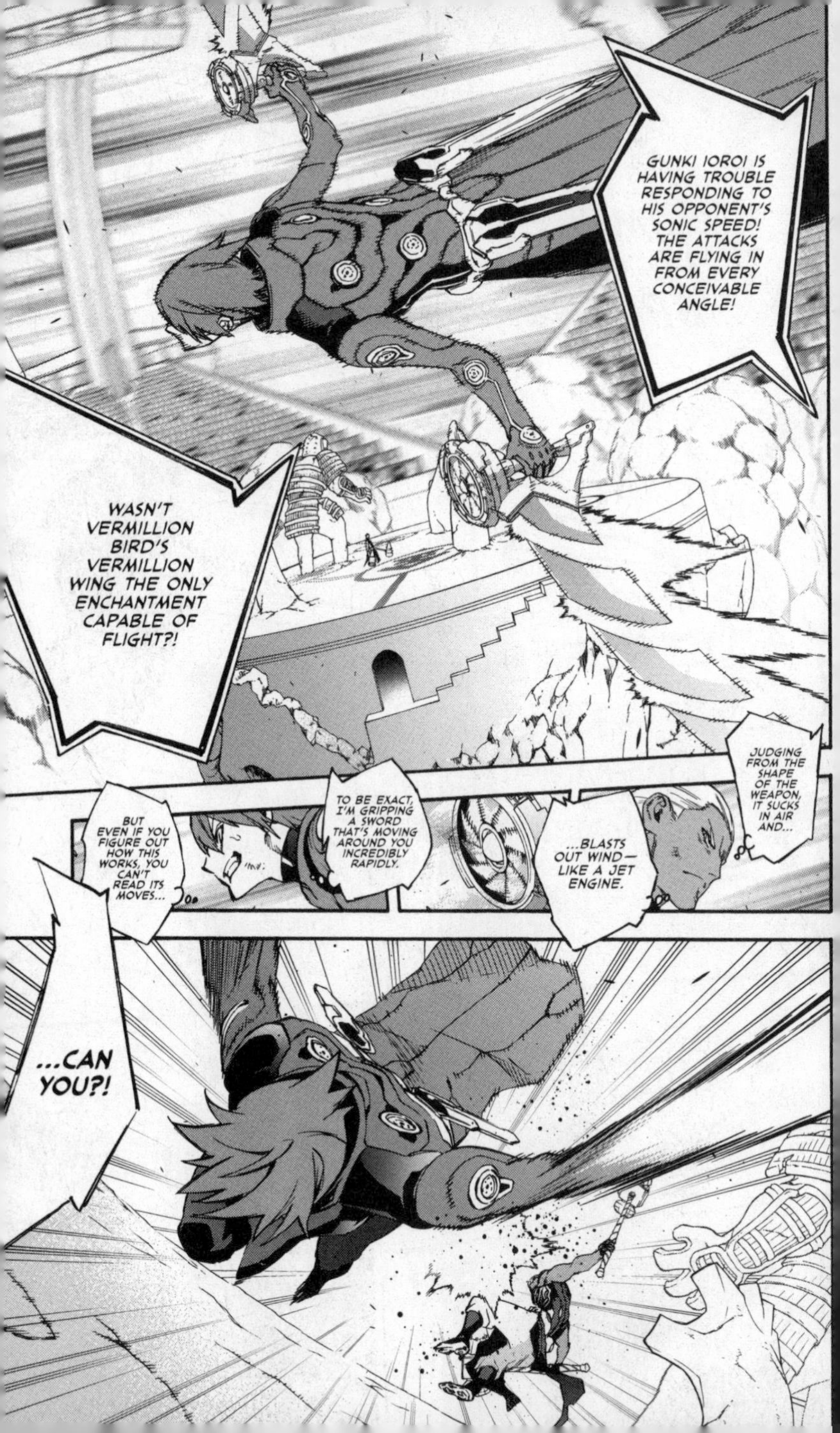
GUNKI IOROI IS HAVING TROUBLE RESPONDING TO HIS OPPONENT'S SONIC SPEED! THE ATTACKS ARE FLYING IN FROM EVERY CONCEIVABLE ANGLE!
WASN'T VERMILLION BIRD'S VERMILLION WING THE ONLY ENCHANTMENT CAPABLE OF FLIGHT?!
JUDGING FROM THE SHAPE OF THE WEAPON, IT SUCKS IN AIR AND...
...BLASTS OUT WIND— LIKE A JET ENGINE.
TO BE EXACT, I'M GRIPPING A SWORD THAT'S MOVING AROUND YOU INCREDIBLY RAPIDLY.
BUT EVEN IF YOU FIGURE OUT HOW THIS WORKS, YOU CAN'T READ ITS MOVES...
...CAN YOU?!

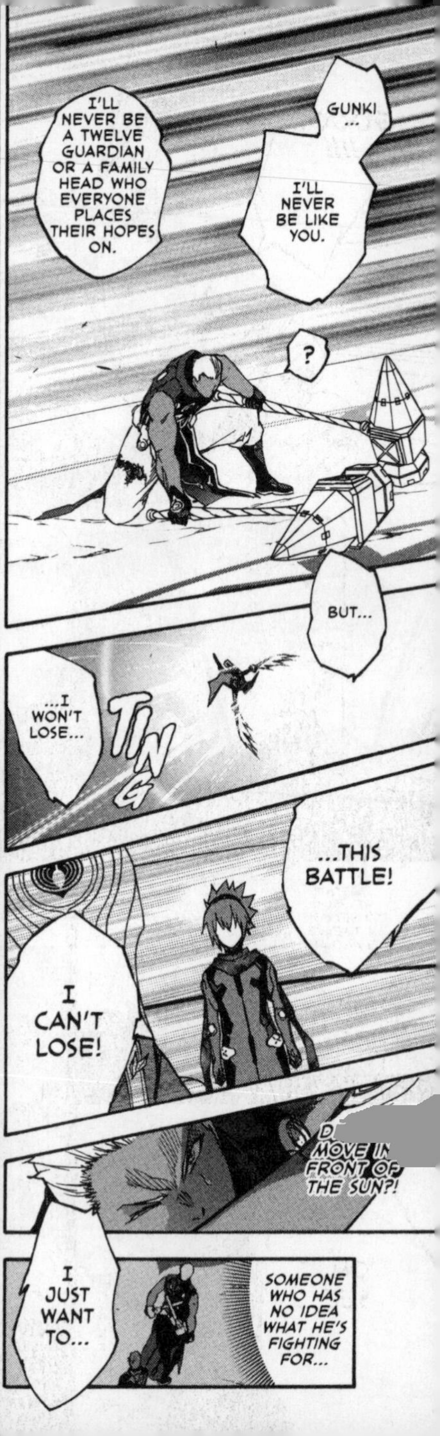
GUNKI...
I'LL NEVER BE LIKE YOU.
I'LL NEVER BE A TWELVE GUARDIAN OR A FAMILY HEAD WHO EVERYONE PLACES THEIR HOPES ON.
?
BUT...
...I WON'T LOSE...
TING
...THIS BATTLE!
I CAN'T LOSE!
D MOVE IN FRONT OF THE SUN?!
SOMEONE WHO HAS NO IDEA WHAT HE'S FIGHTING FOR...
I JUST WANT TO...
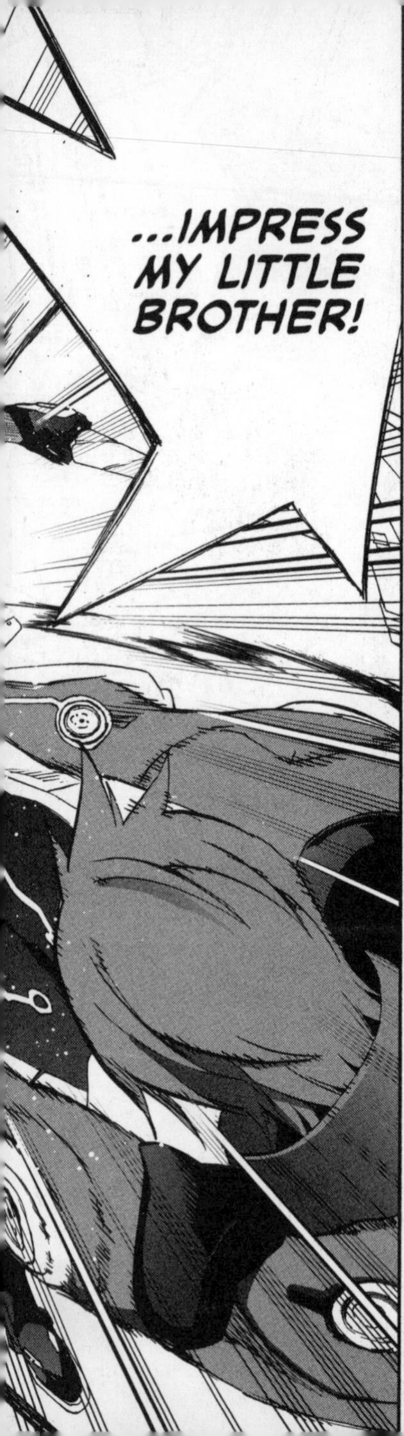
...IMPRESS MY LITTLE BROTHER!

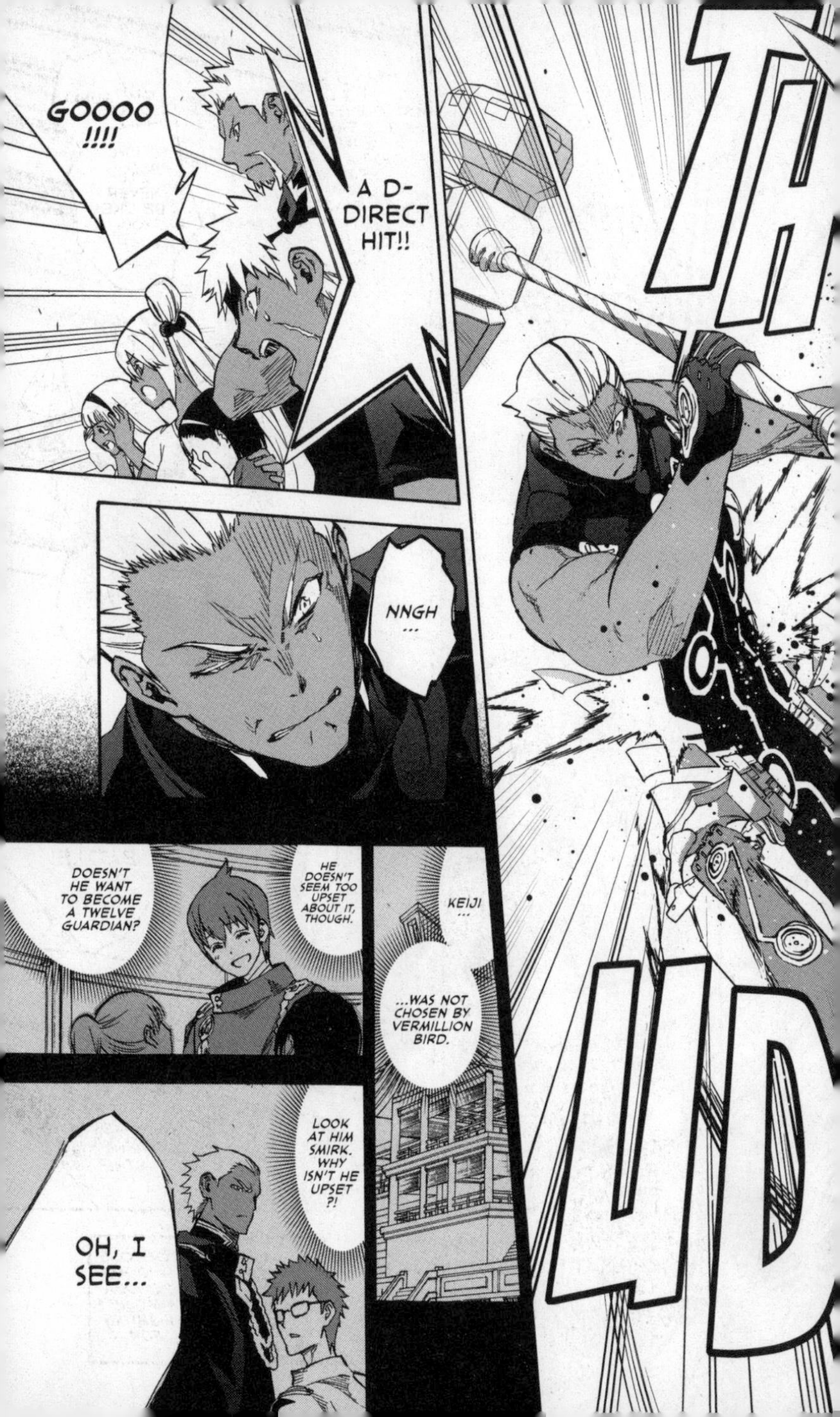
TH
UD
A D-DIRECT HIT!!
GOOOO!!!!
NNGH...
KEIJI...
...WAS NOT CHOSEN BY VERMILLION BIRD.
HE DOESN'T SEEM TOO UPSET ABOUT IT, THOUGH.
DOESN'T HE WANT TO BECOME A TWELVE GUARDIAN?
LOOK AT HIM SMIRK. WHY ISN'T HE UPSET?!
OH, I SEE...

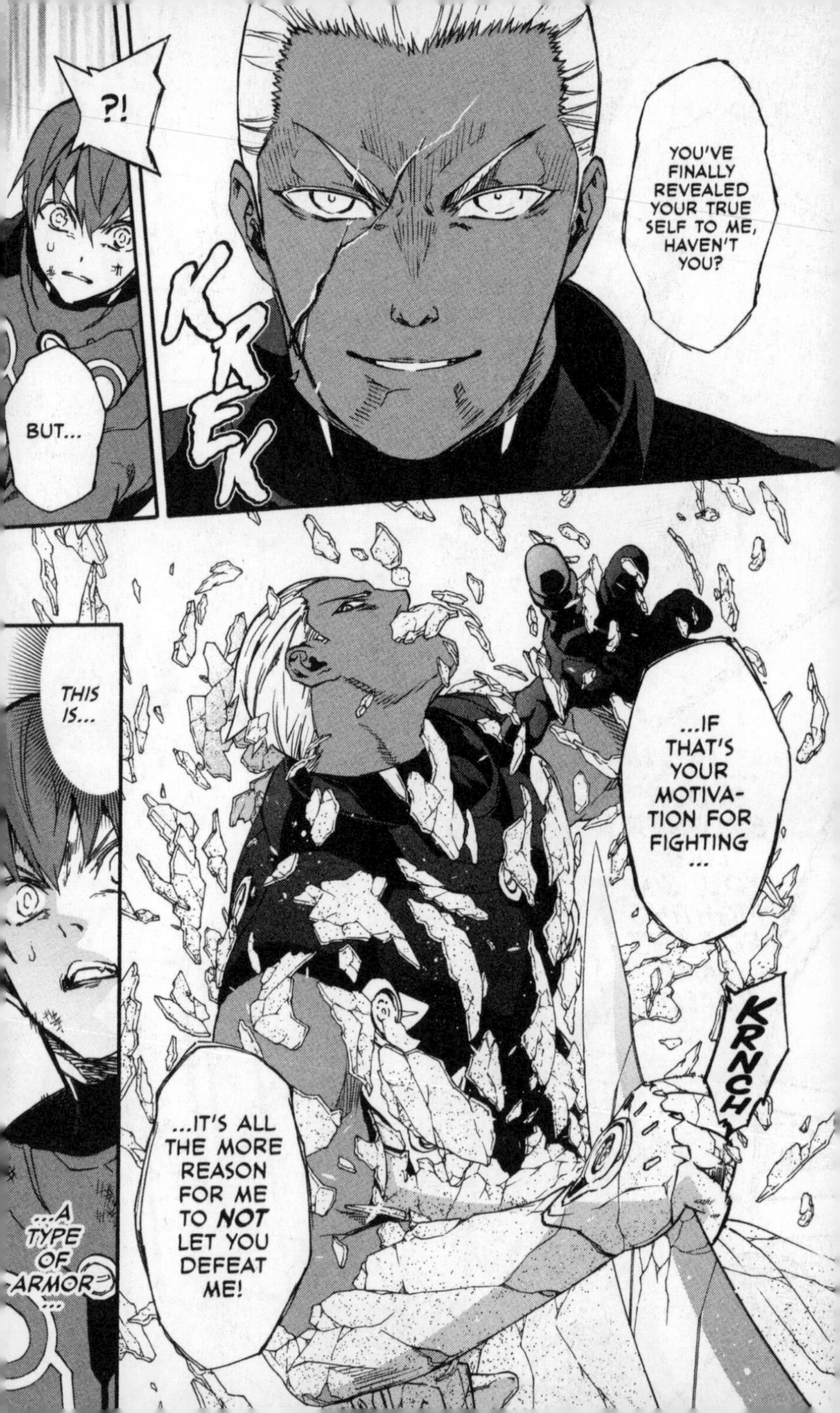
YOU'VE FINALLY REVEALED YOUR TRUE SELF TO ME, HAVEN'T YOU?
KREK
?!
BUT...
...IF THAT'S YOUR MOTIVATION FOR FIGHTING ...
KRNCH
...IT'S ALL THE MORE REASON FOR ME TO NOT LET YOU DEFEAT ME!
THIS IS...
...A TYPE OF ARMOR...

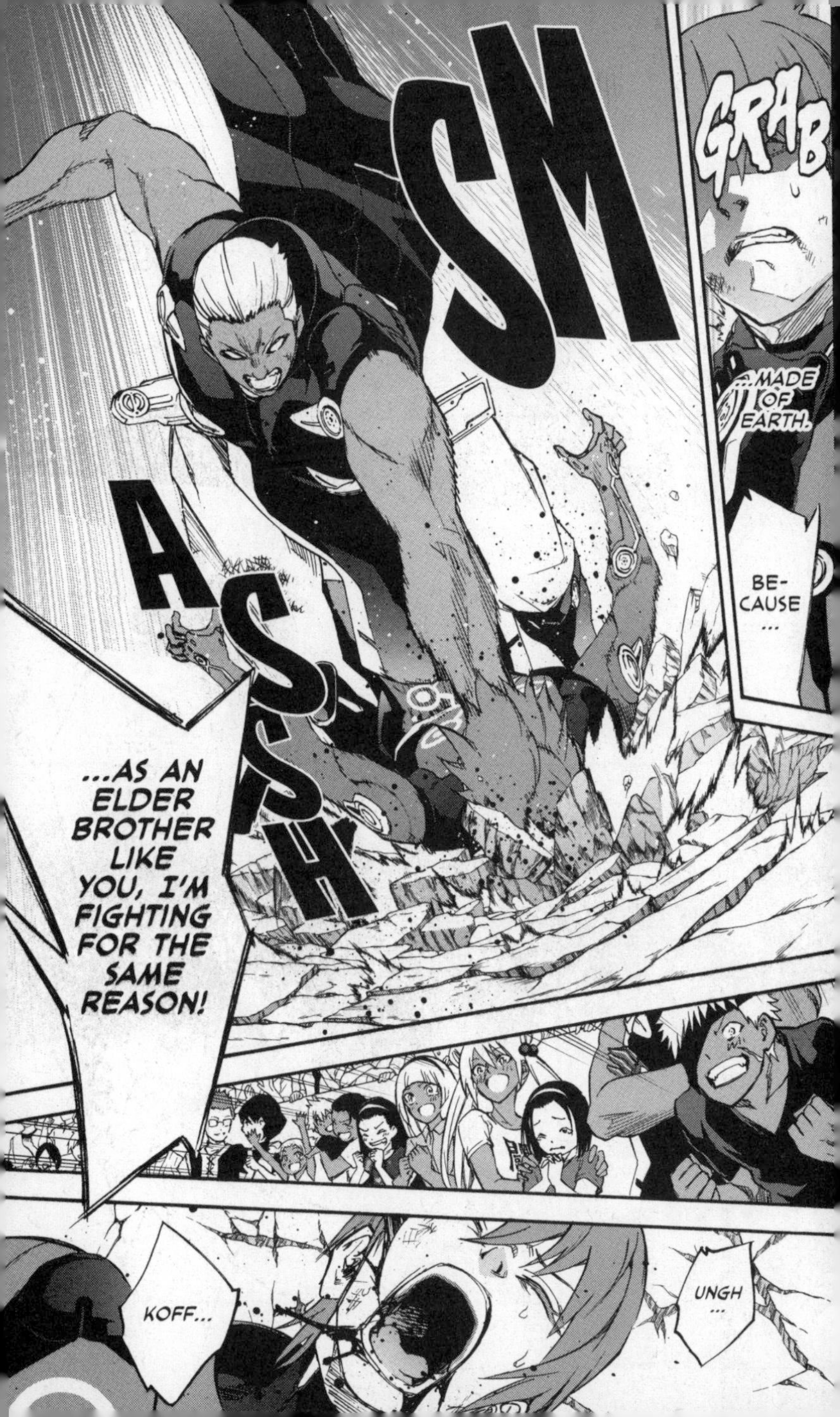
GRAB
...MADE OF EARTH.
BE-CAUSE ...
SMASH
...AS AN ELDER BROTHER LIKE YOU, I'M FIGHTING FOR THE SAME REASON!
UNGH ...
KOFF...

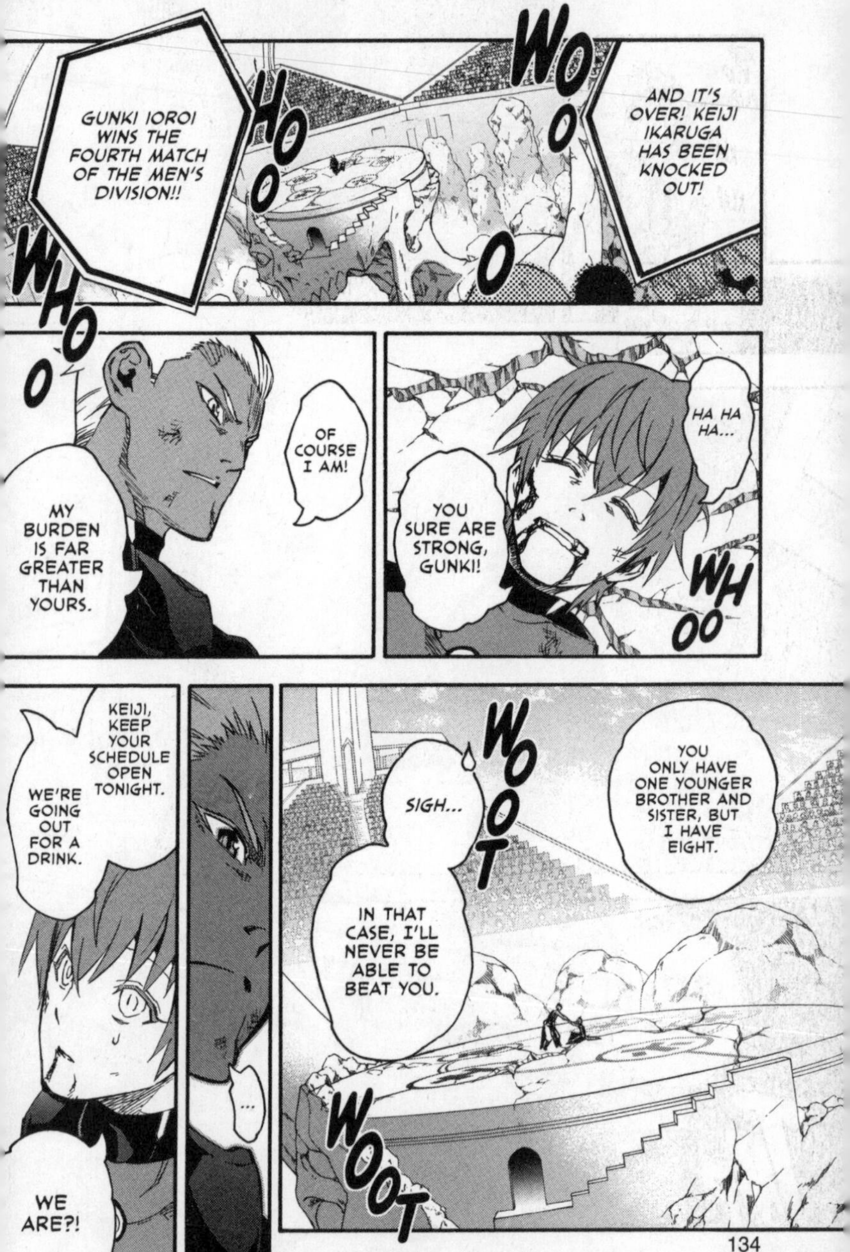
AND IT'S OVER! KEIJI IKARUGA HAS BEEN KNOCKED OUT!
WOOO
HOOO
GUNKI IOROI WINS THE FOURTH MATCH OF THE MEN'S DIVISION!!
WHOOO
HA HA HA...
YOU SURE ARE STRONG, GUNKI!
WHOO
OF COURSE I AM!
MY BURDEN IS FAR GREATER THAN YOURS.
YOU ONLY HAVE ONE YOUNGER BROTHER AND SISTER, BUT I HAVE EIGHT.
WOOOT
SIGH...
IN THAT CASE, I'LL NEVER BE ABLE TO BEAT YOU.
WOOOT
...
KEIJI, KEEP YOUR SCHEDULE OPEN TONIGHT.
WE'RE GOING OUT FOR A DRINK.
WE ARE?!
I'd like to, but...

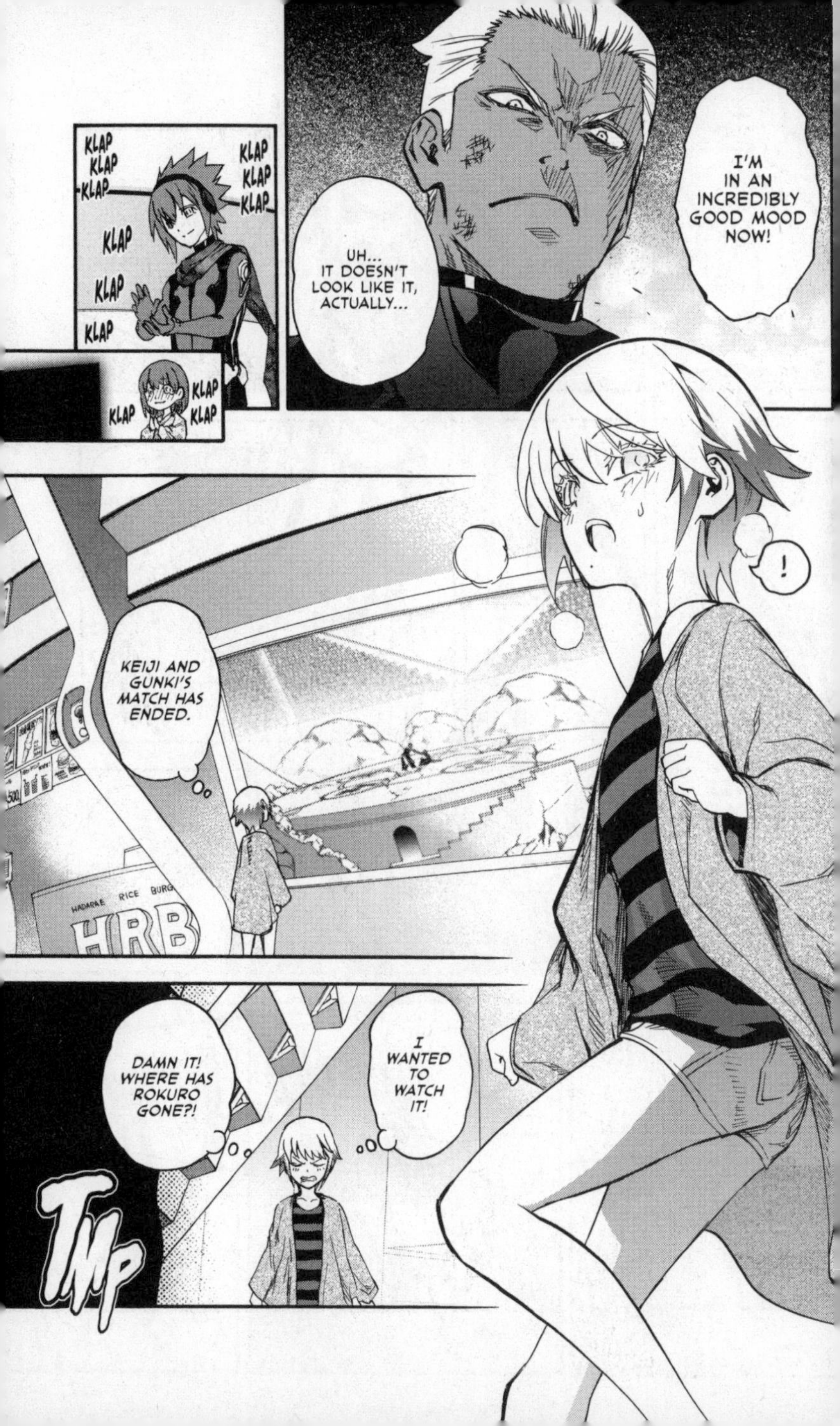
I'M IN AN INCREDIBLY GOOD MOOD NOW!
UH... IT DOESN'T LOOK LIKE IT, ACTUALLY...
KLAP KLAP KLAP
KLAP KLAP KLAP
KLAP
KLAP
KLAP
KLAP KLAP
KLAP
!
KEIJI AND GUNKI'S MATCH HAS ENDED.
HADARAE RICE BURG
HRB
I WANTED TO WATCH IT!
DAMN IT! WHERE HAS ROKURO GONE?!
TMP

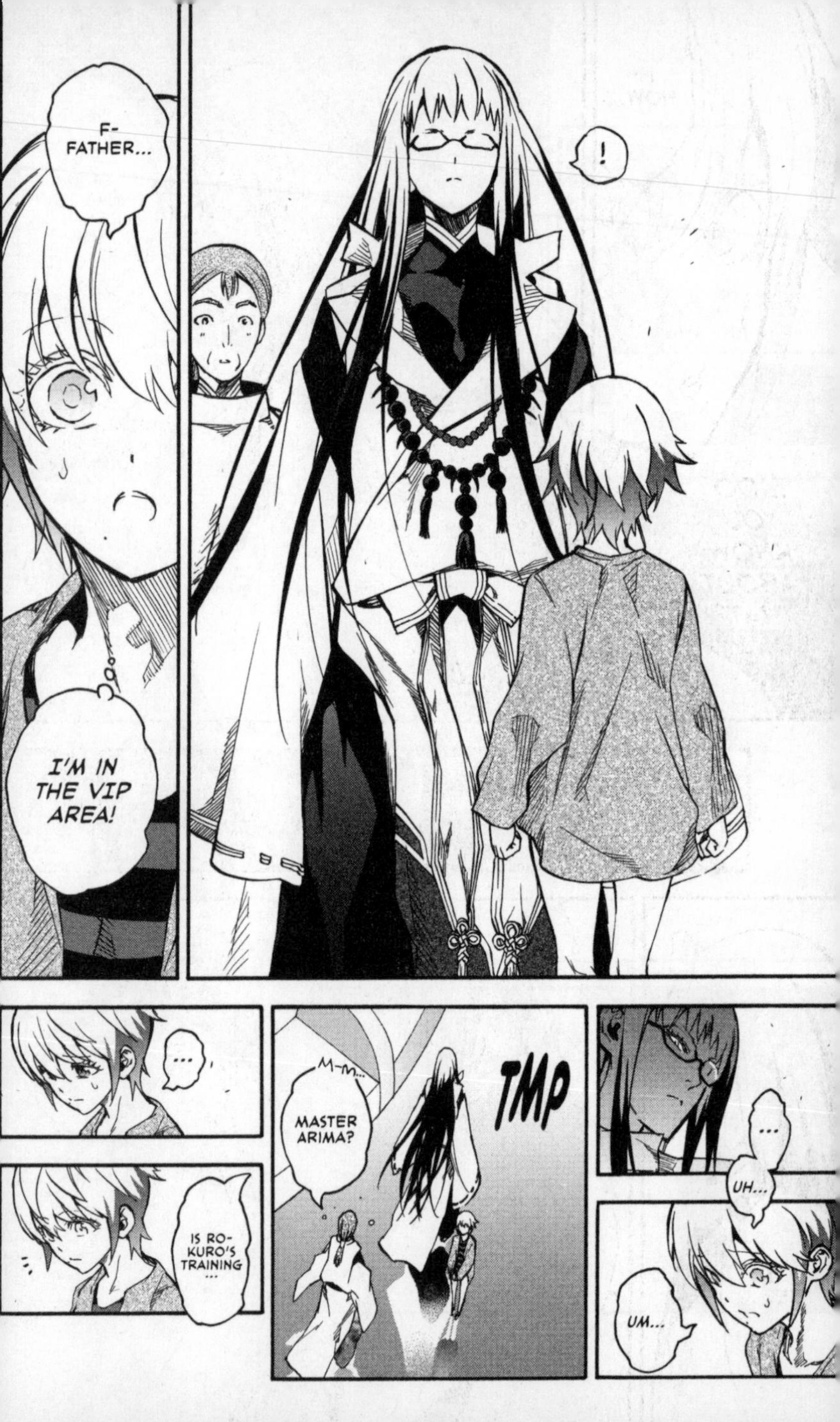
!
F- FATHER...
I'M IN THE VIP AREA!
...
UH...
UM...
TMP
M-M... MASTER ARIMA?
...
IS RO-KURO'S TRAINING ...

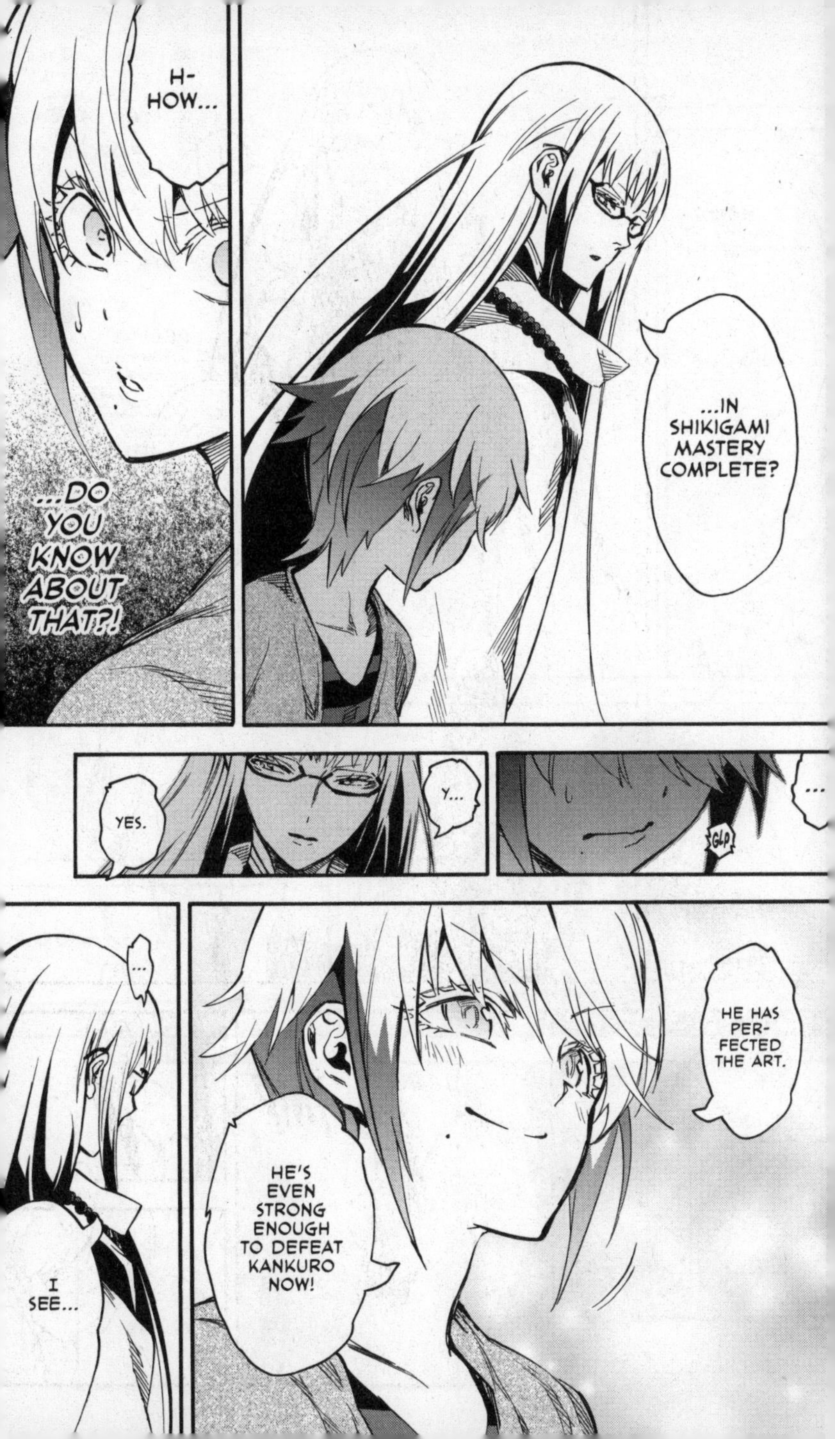
...IN SHIKIGAMI MASTERY COMPLETE?
H- HOW...
...DO YOU KNOW ABOUT THAT?!
...
GLP
Y...
YES.
HE HAS PER- FECTED THE ART.
HE'S EVEN STRONG ENOUGH TO DEFEAT KANKURO NOW!
...
I SEE...

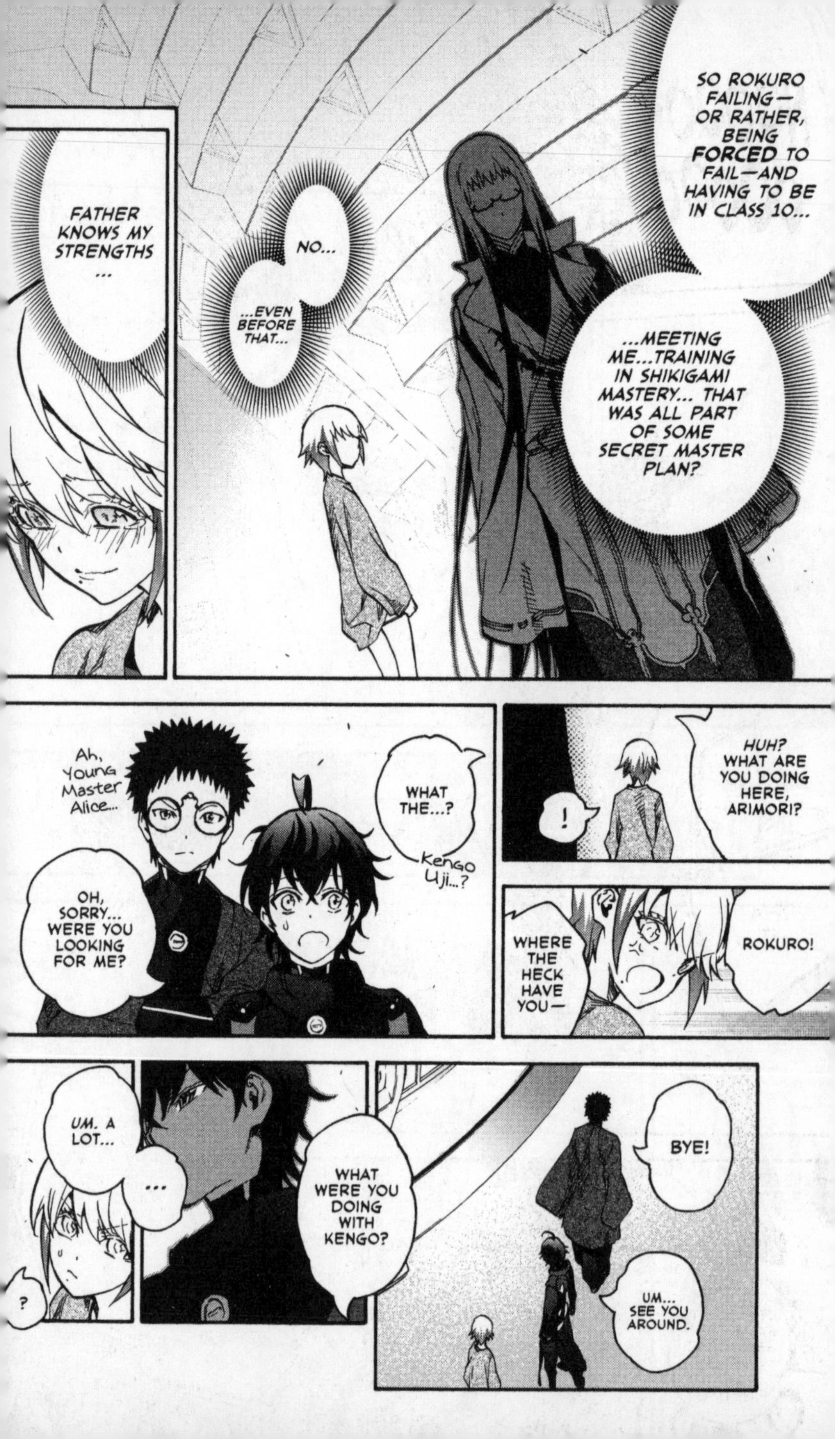
SO ROKURO FAILING— OR RATHER, BEING FORCED TO FAIL—AND HAVING TO BE IN CLASS 10...
...MEETING ME...TRAINING IN SHIKIGAMI MASTERY... THAT WAS ALL PART OF SOME SECRET MASTER PLAN?
NO...
...EVEN BEFORE THAT...
FATHER KNOWS MY STRENGTHS ...
HUH? WHAT ARE YOU DOING HERE, ARIMORI?
!
ROKURO!
WHERE THE HECK HAVE YOU—
WHAT THE...?
Kengo Uji...?
Ah, Young Master Alice...
OH, SORRY... WERE YOU LOOKING FOR ME?
BYE!
UM... SEE YOU AROUND.
WHAT WERE YOU DOING WITH KENGO?
UM. A LOT...
...
?

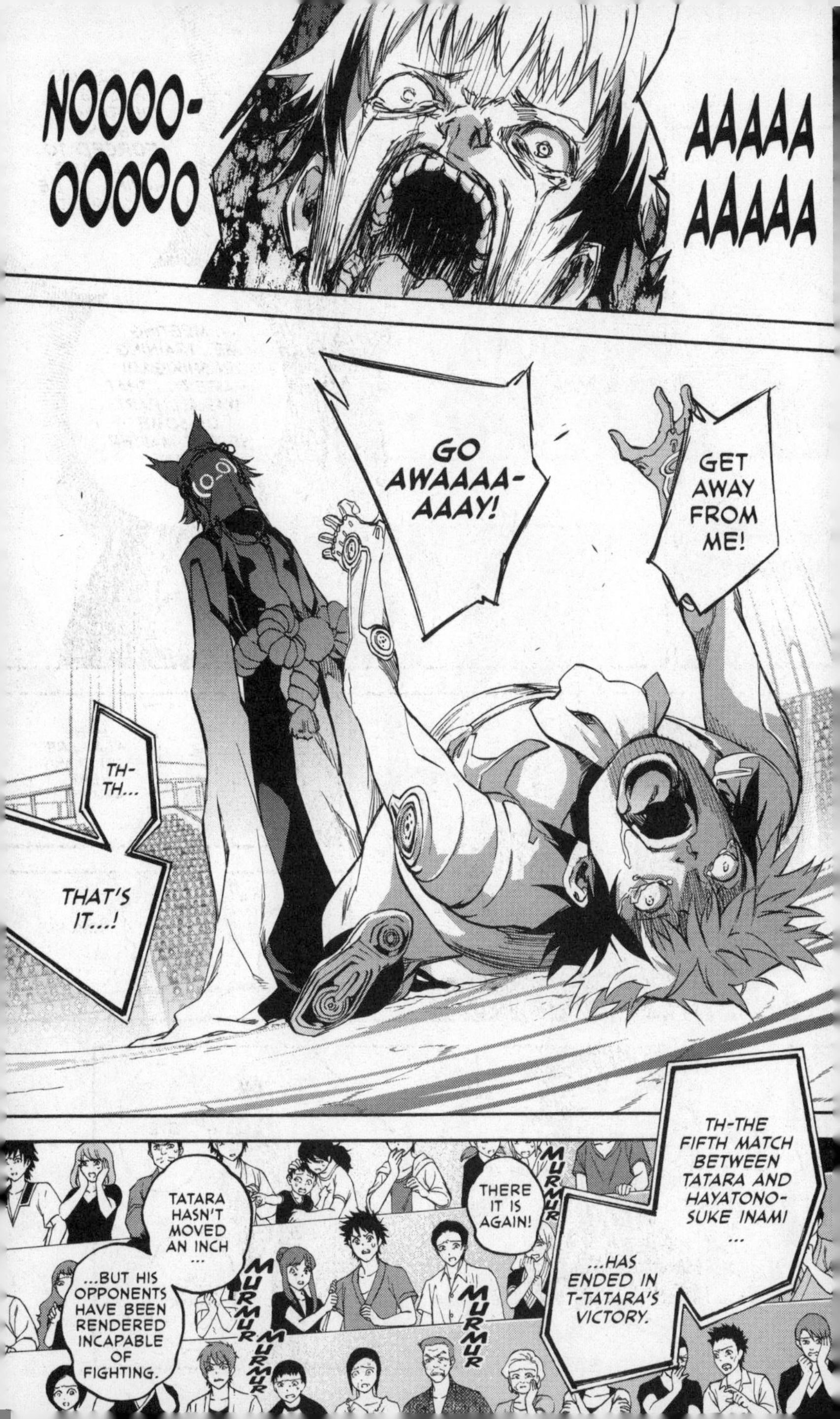
AAAAA AAAAA
NOOOO-OOOOO
GET AWAY FROM ME!
GO AWAAAA-AAAY!
TH-TH...
THAT'S IT...!
TH-THE FIFTH MATCH BETWEEN TATARA AND HAYATONOSUKE INAMI ...
...HAS ENDED IN T-TATARA'S VICTORY.
MURMUR
THERE IT IS AGAIN!
MURMUR
TATARA HASN'T MOVED AN INCH ...
...BUT HIS OPPONENTS HAVE BEEN RENDERED INCAPABLE OF FIGHTING.
MURMUR
MURMUR

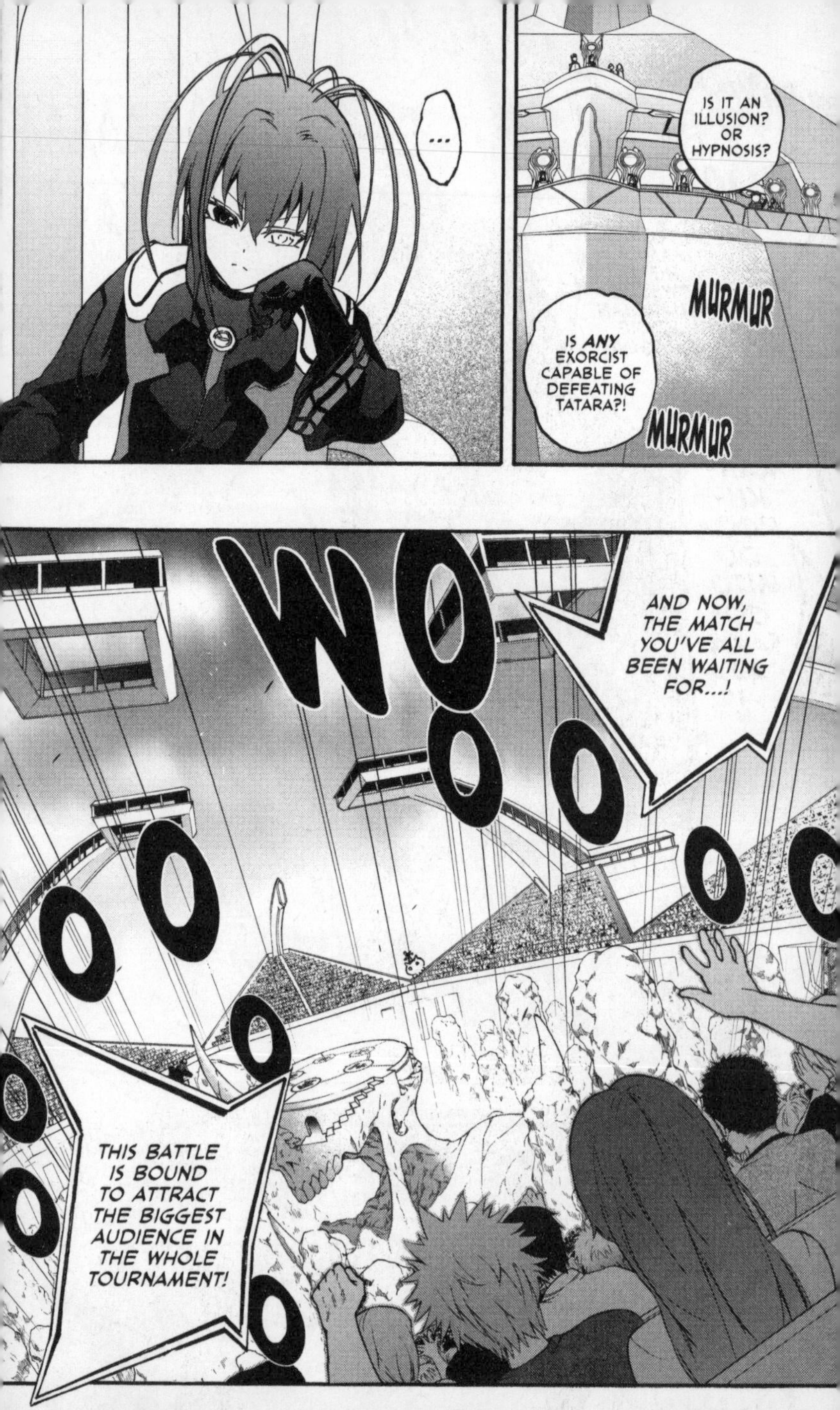
IS IT AN ILLUSION? OR HYPNOSIS?
MURMUR
IS ANY EXORCIST CAPABLE OF DEFEATING TATARA?!
MURMUR
...
WOOOOOOOOOOOO
AND NOW, THE MATCH YOU'VE ALL BEEN WAITING FOR...!
THIS BATTLE IS BOUND TO ATTRACT THE BIGGEST AUDIENCE IN THE WHOLE TOURNAMENT!

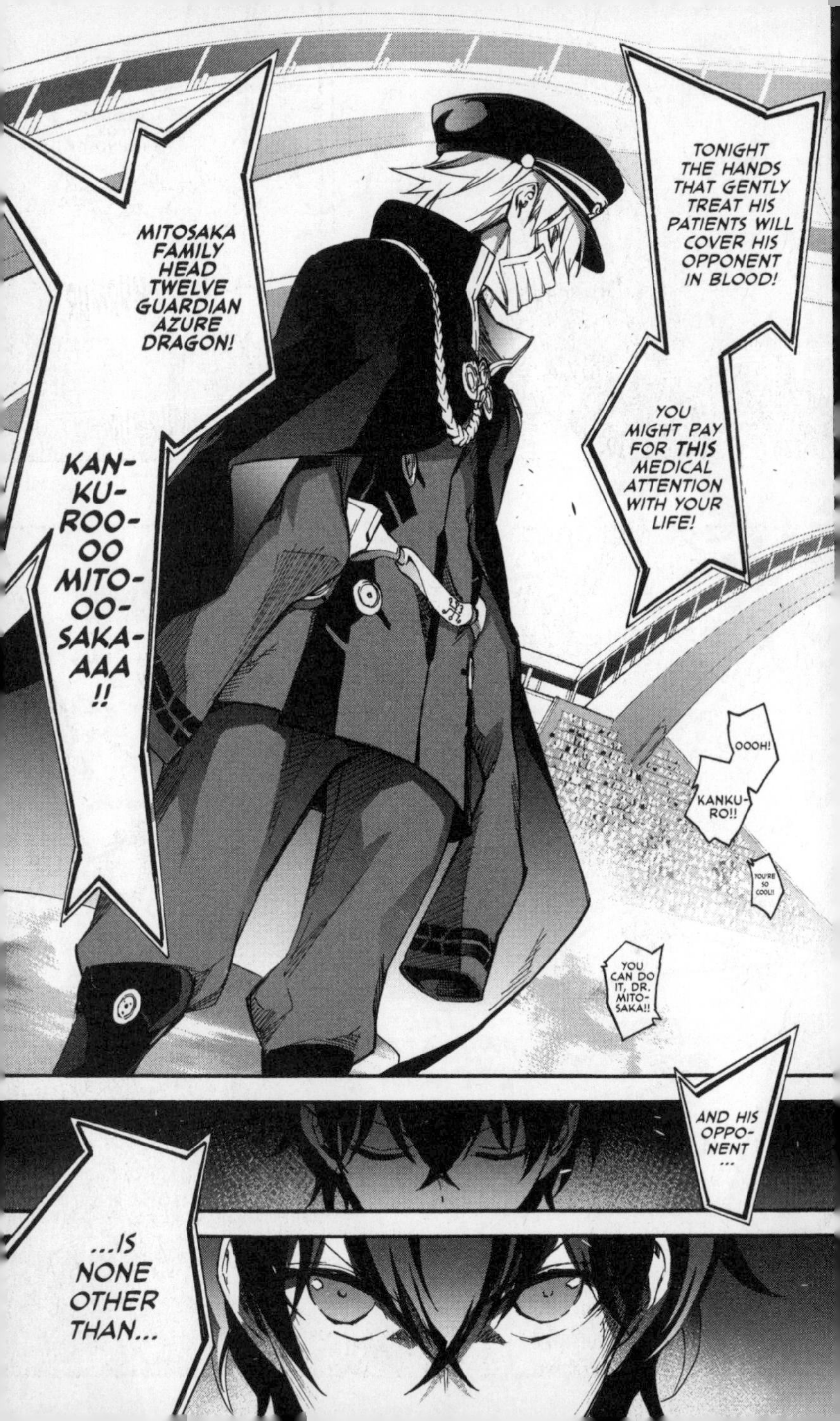
TONIGHT THE HANDS THAT GENTLY TREAT HIS PATIENTS WILL COVER HIS OPPONENT IN BLOOD!
MITOSAKA FAMILY HEAD TWELVE GUARDIAN AZURE DRAGON!
YOU MIGHT PAY FOR THIS MEDICAL ATTENTION WITH YOUR LIFE!
KAN-KU-ROO-OO MITO-OO-SAKA-AAA!!
OOOH!
KANKU-RO!!
YOU'RE SO COOL!!
YOU CAN DO IT, DR. MITO-SAKA!!
AND HIS OPPO-NENT...
...IS NONE OTHER THAN...

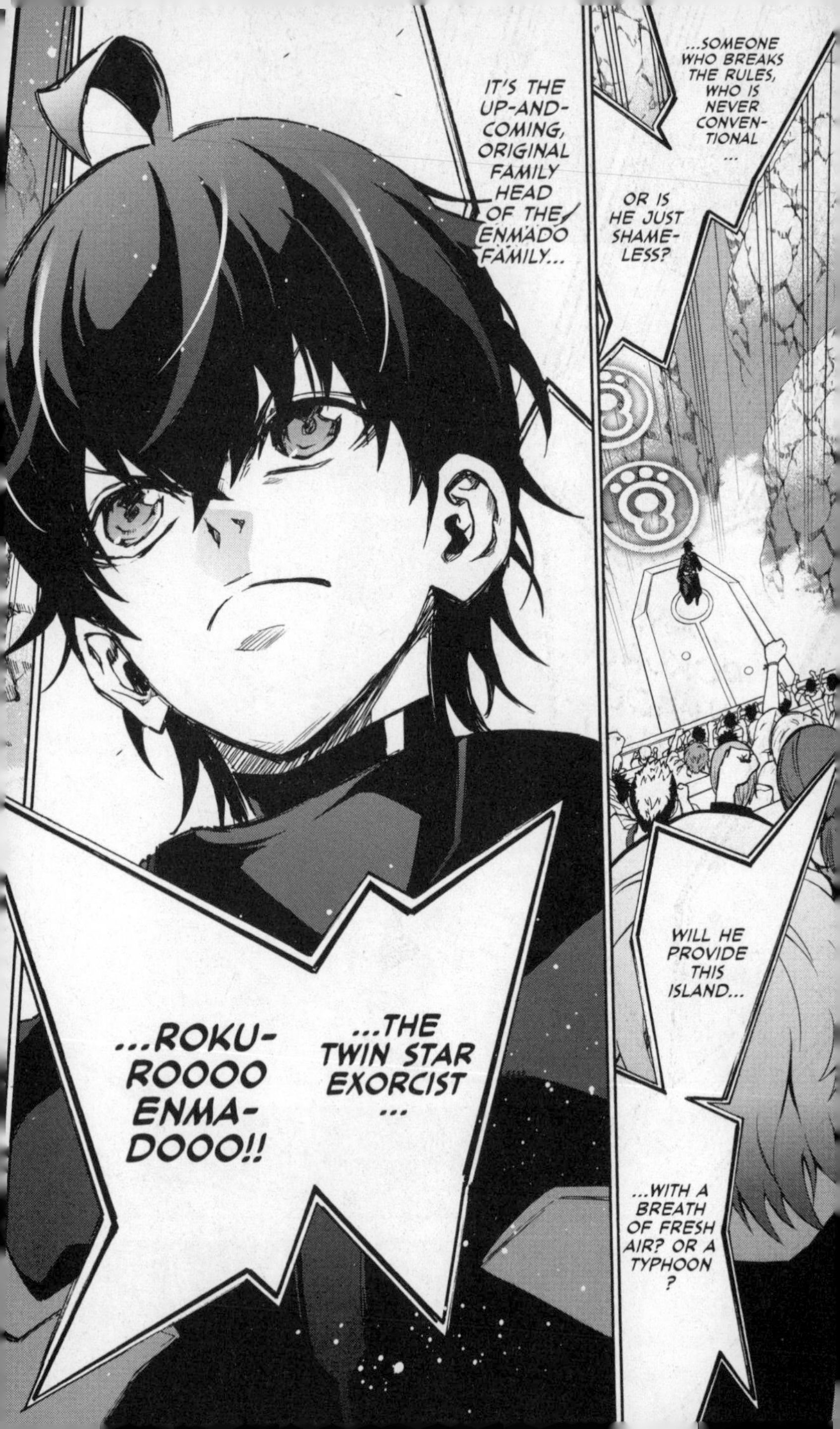
...SOMEONE WHO BREAKS THE RULES, WHO IS NEVER CONVEN-TIONAL...
OR IS HE JUST SHAME-LESS?
WILL HE PROVIDE THIS ISLAND...
...WITH A BREATH OF FRESH AIR? OR A TYPHOON?
IT'S THE UP-AND-COMING, ORIGINAL FAMILY HEAD OF THE ENMADO FAMILY...
...THE TWIN STAR EXORCIST...
...ROKU-ROOOO ENMA-DOOO!!

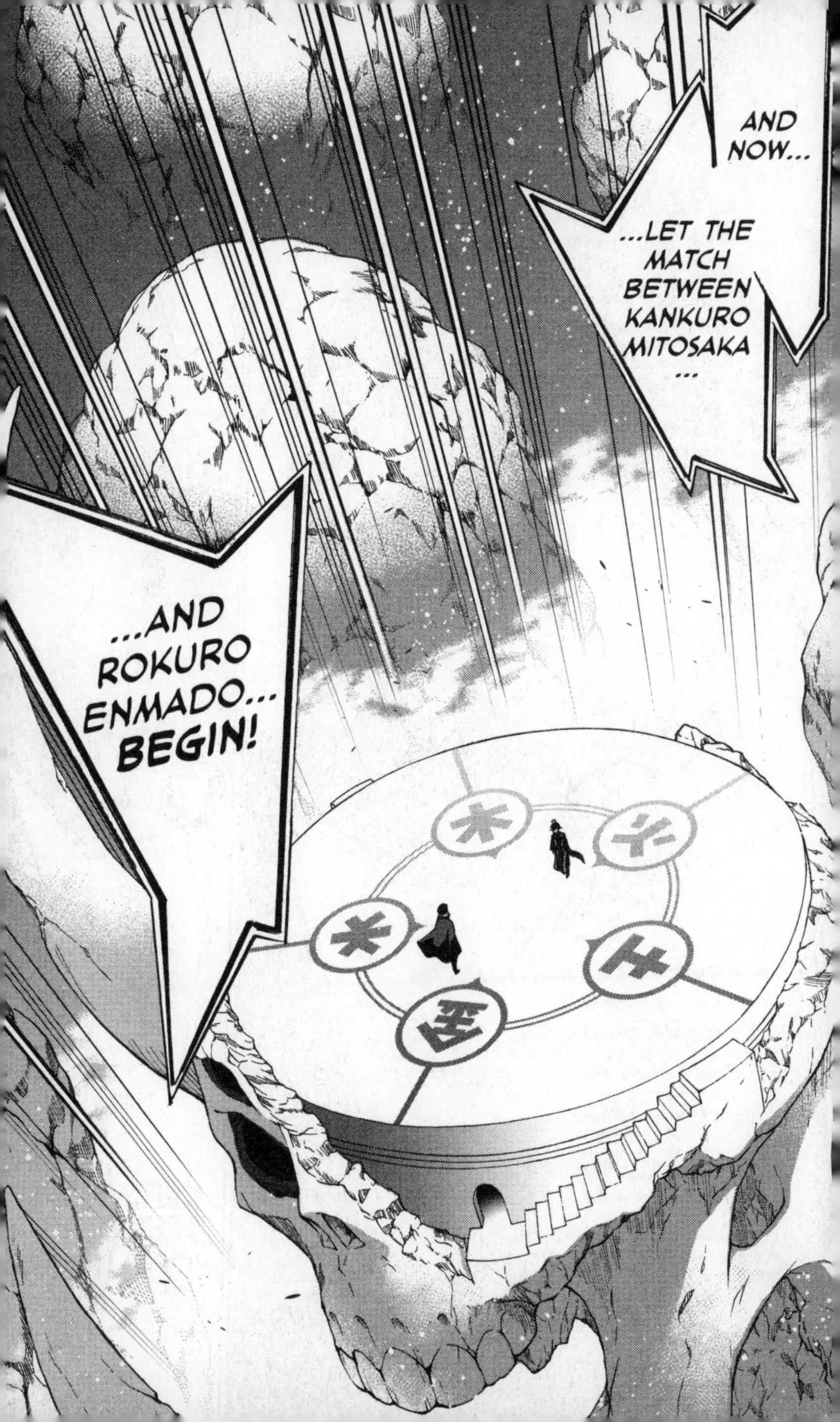
AND NOW...
...LET THE MATCH BETWEEN KANKURO MITOSAKA ...
...AND ROKURO ENMADO... BEGIN!

RENA KOSHI

The young woman entrusted with the tournament's play-by-play announcements. In the beginning, I thought I'd have her do it through dialogue with her little brother, Leo Koshi, but it seemed too complicated, so I limited the dialogue to just Rena in almost all the scenes. Sorry.

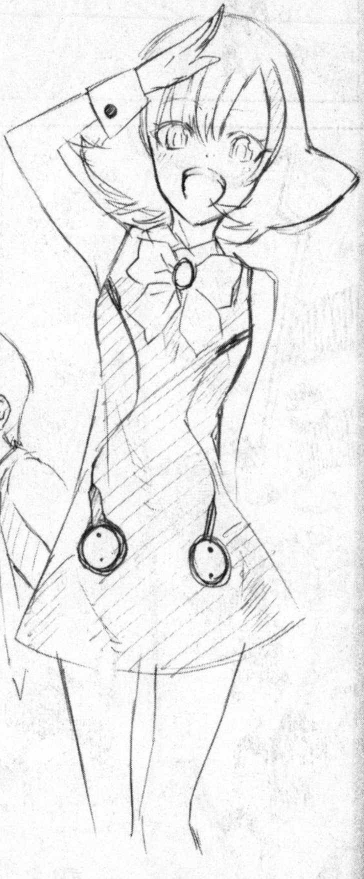

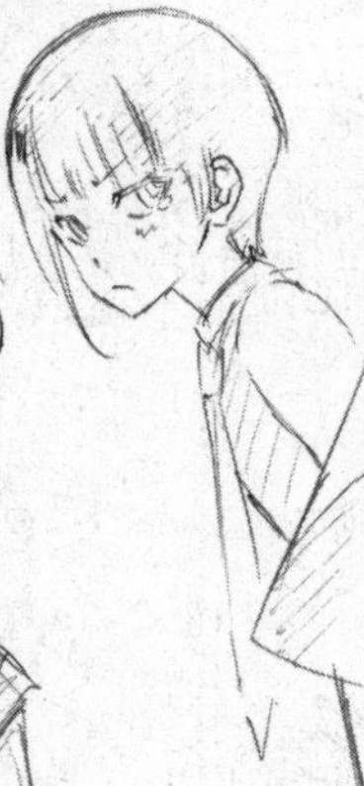

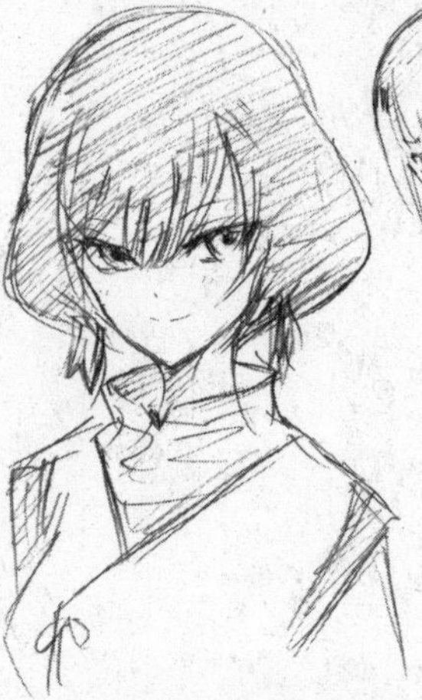

MASUMI KATAGIHARA (IOROI)

The eldest daughter (23) of the Ioroi family. She has already married into the Katagihara family, who are Ioroi family retainers.

MEMBERS OF THE NOSO FAMILY

Their job is to repair the battle stage between matches after it gets torn apart by the fighting. Of the five yin-yang elements, they wield the power of Earth.

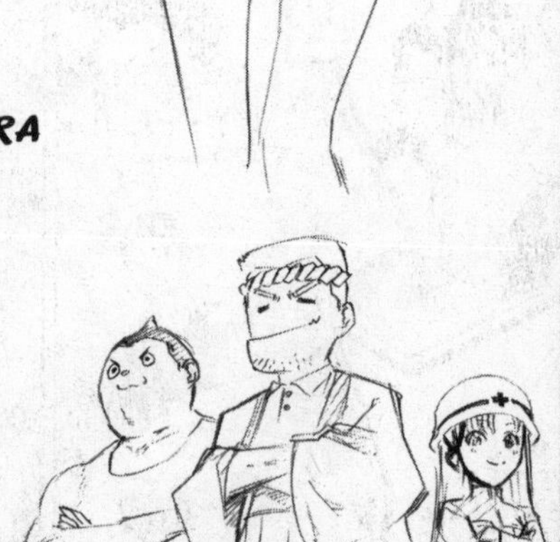

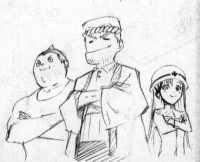

#44

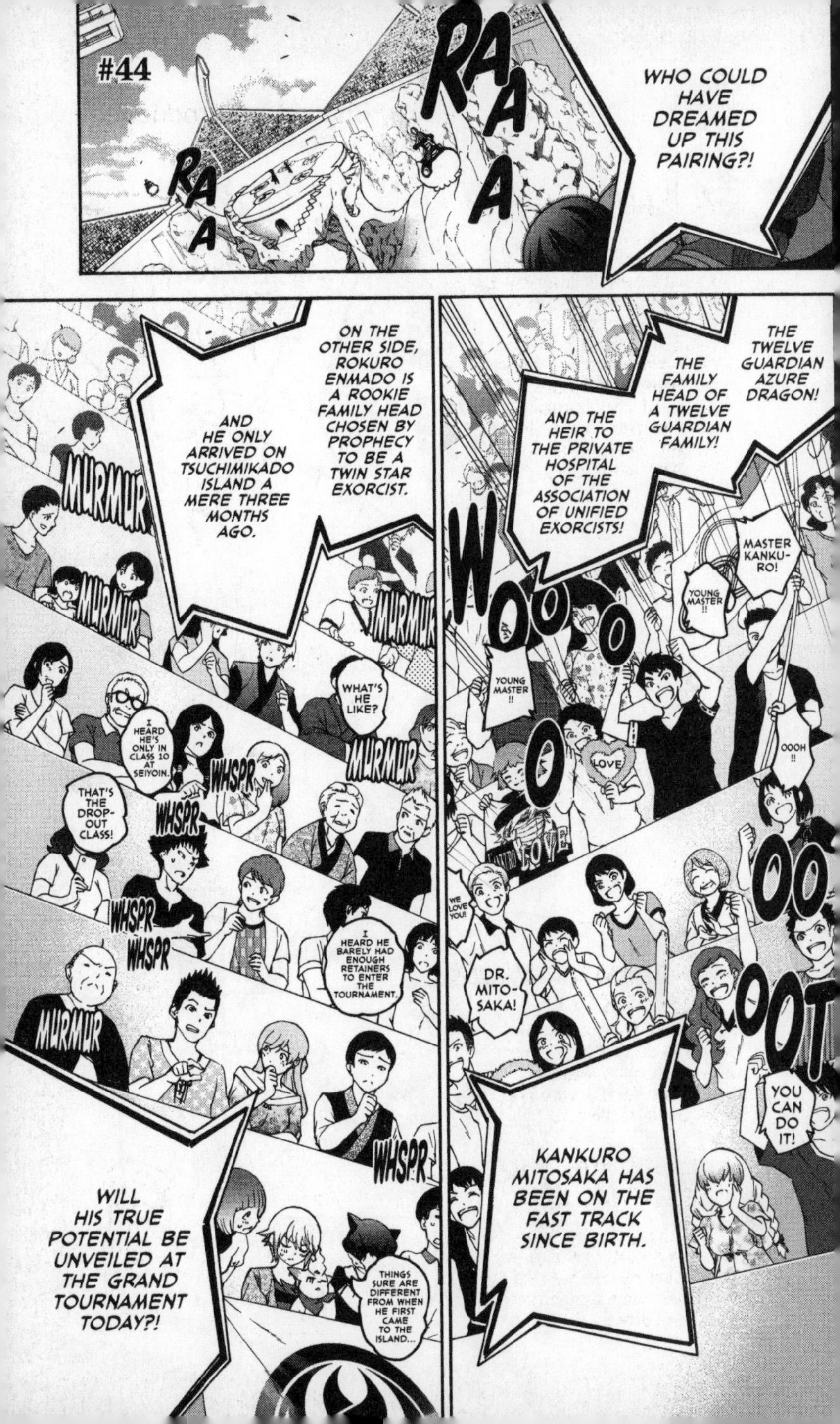
RAAA
WHO COULD HAVE DREAMED UP THIS PAIRING?!
RAA
THE TWELVE GUARDIAN AZURE DRAGON!
THE FAMILY HEAD OF A TWELVE GUARDIAN FAMILY!
AND THE HEIR TO THE PRIVATE HOSPITAL OF THE ASSOCIATION OF UNIFIED EXORCISTS!
WOOOO
MASTER KANKURO!
YOUNG MASTER!!
YOUNG MASTER!!
OOOH!!
LOVE
OOOT
WE LOVE YOU!
DR. MITOSAKA!
YOU CAN DO IT!
KANKURO MITOSAKA HAS BEEN ON THE FAST TRACK SINCE BIRTH.
ON THE OTHER SIDE, ROKURO ENMADO IS A ROOKIE FAMILY HEAD CHOSEN BY PROPHECY TO BE A TWIN STAR EXORCIST.
AND HE ONLY ARRIVED ON TSUCHIMIKADO ISLAND A MERE THREE MONTHS AGO.
MURMUR
MURMUR
MURMUR
WHAT'S HE LIKE?
MURMUR
I HEARD HE'S ONLY IN CLASS 10 AT SEIYOIN.
WHSPR
THAT'S THE DROP-OUT CLASS!
WHSPR
WHSPR WHSPR
I HEARD HE BARELY HAD ENOUGH RETAINERS TO ENTER THE TOURNAMENT.
MURMUR
WHSPR
THINGS SURE ARE DIFFERENT FROM WHEN HE FIRST CAME TO THE ISLAND...
WILL HIS TRUE POTENTIAL BE UNVEILED AT THE GRAND TOURNAMENT TODAY?!

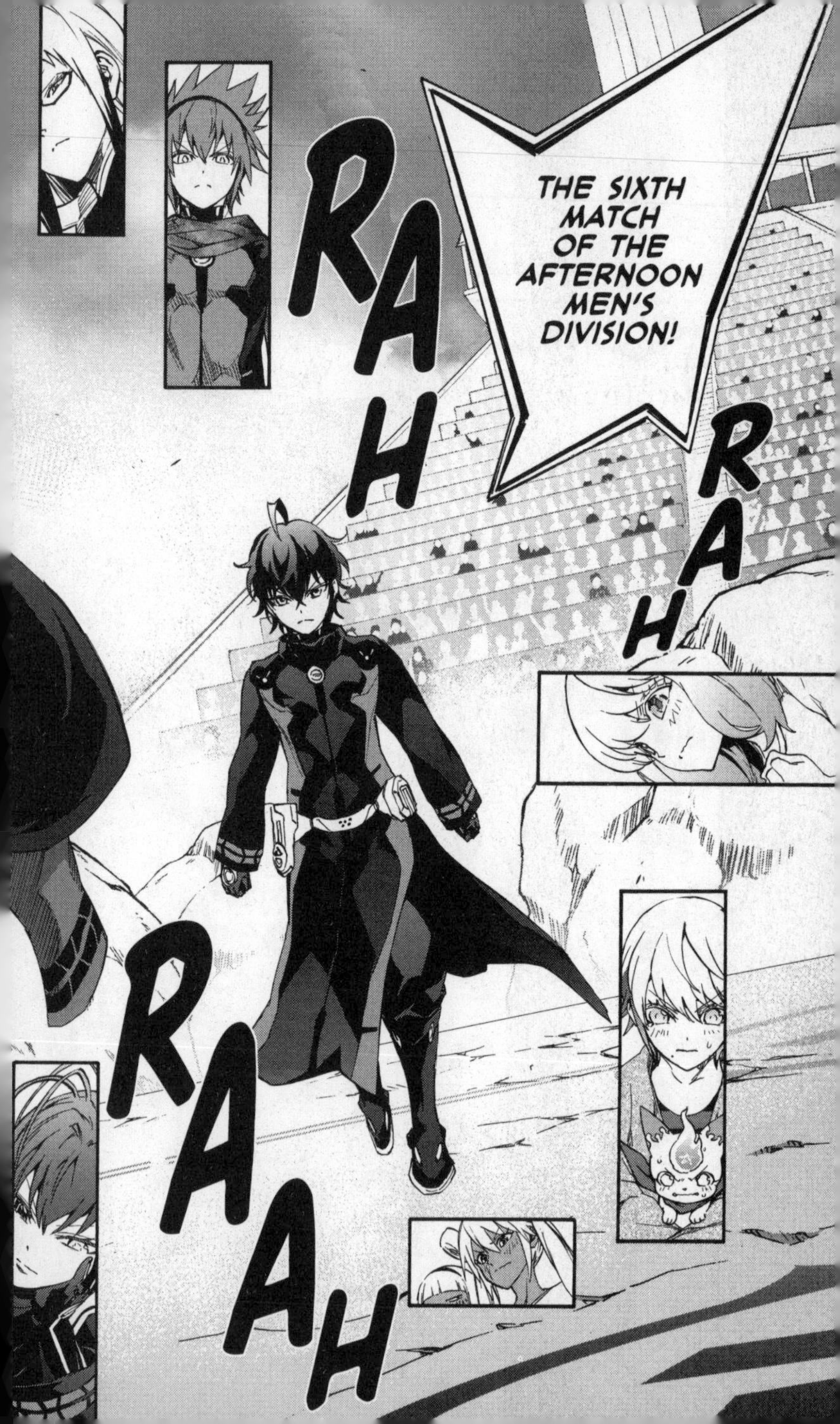
THE SIXTH MATCH OF THE AFTERNOON MEN'S DIVISION!
RAH
RAH
RAAAH

#44: Burning Down Hadarae Castle!

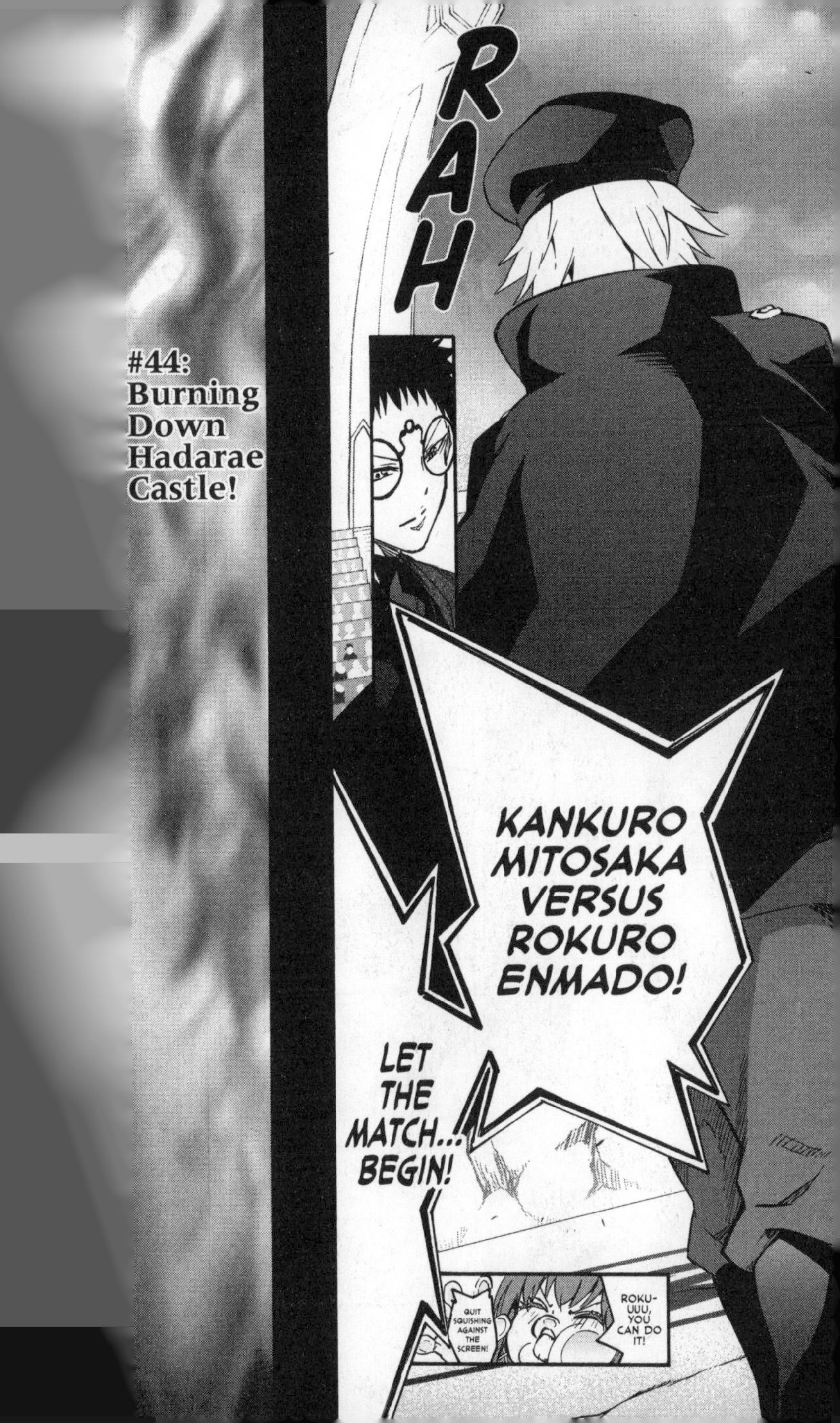
RAH
KANKURO MITOSAKA VERSUS ROKURO ENMADO!
LET THE MATCH... BEGIN!
ROKU-UUU, YOU CAN DO IT!
QUIT SQUISHING AGAINST THE SCREEN!

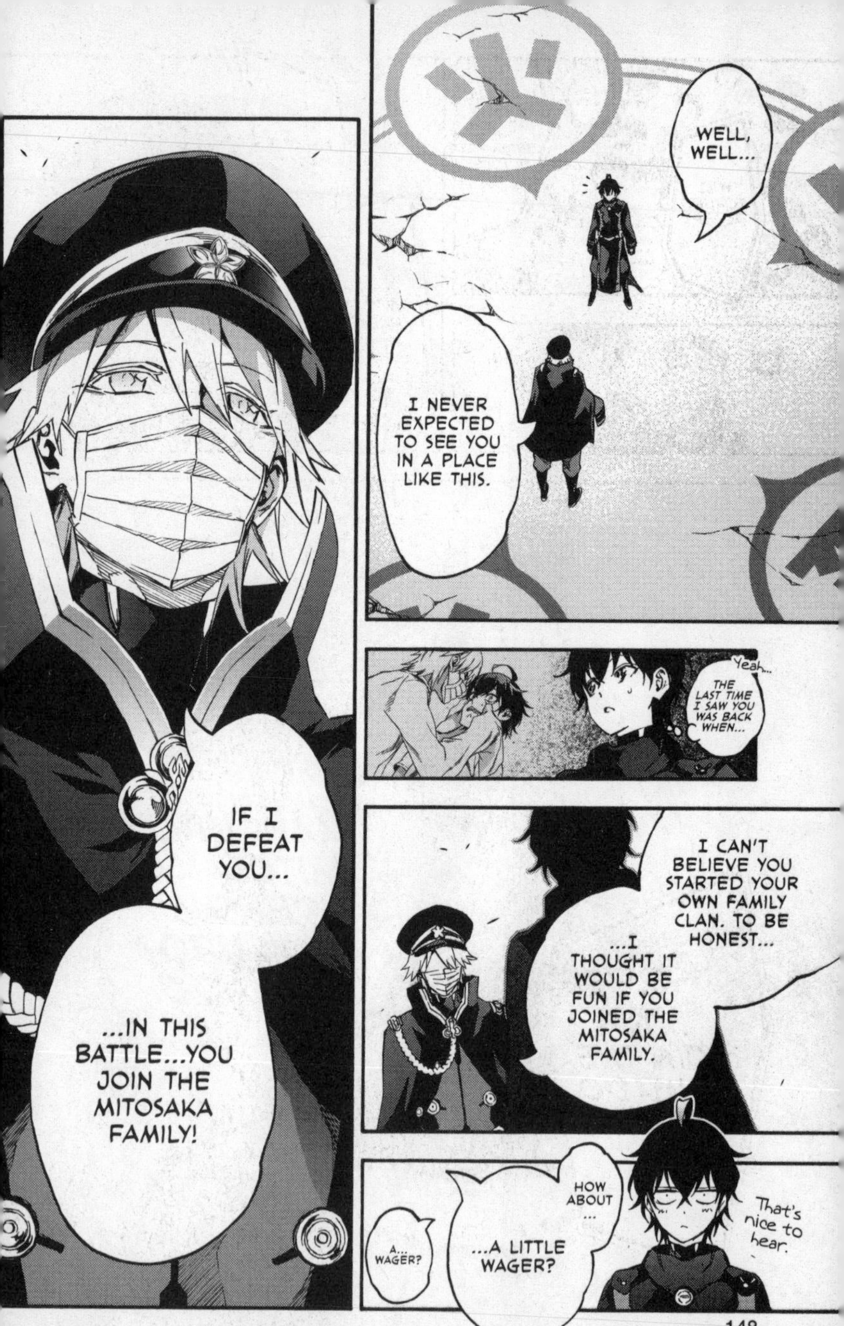
WELL, WELL...
I NEVER EXPECTED TO SEE YOU IN A PLACE LIKE THIS.
Yeah...
THE LAST TIME I SAW YOU WAS BACK WHEN...
I CAN'T BELIEVE YOU STARTED YOUR OWN FAMILY CLAN. TO BE HONEST...
...I THOUGHT IT WOULD BE FUN IF YOU JOINED THE MITOSAKA FAMILY.
That's nice to hear.
HOW ABOUT...
...A LITTLE WAGER?
A... WAGER?
IF I DEFEAT YOU...
...IN THIS BATTLE...YOU JOIN THE MITOSAKA FAMILY!

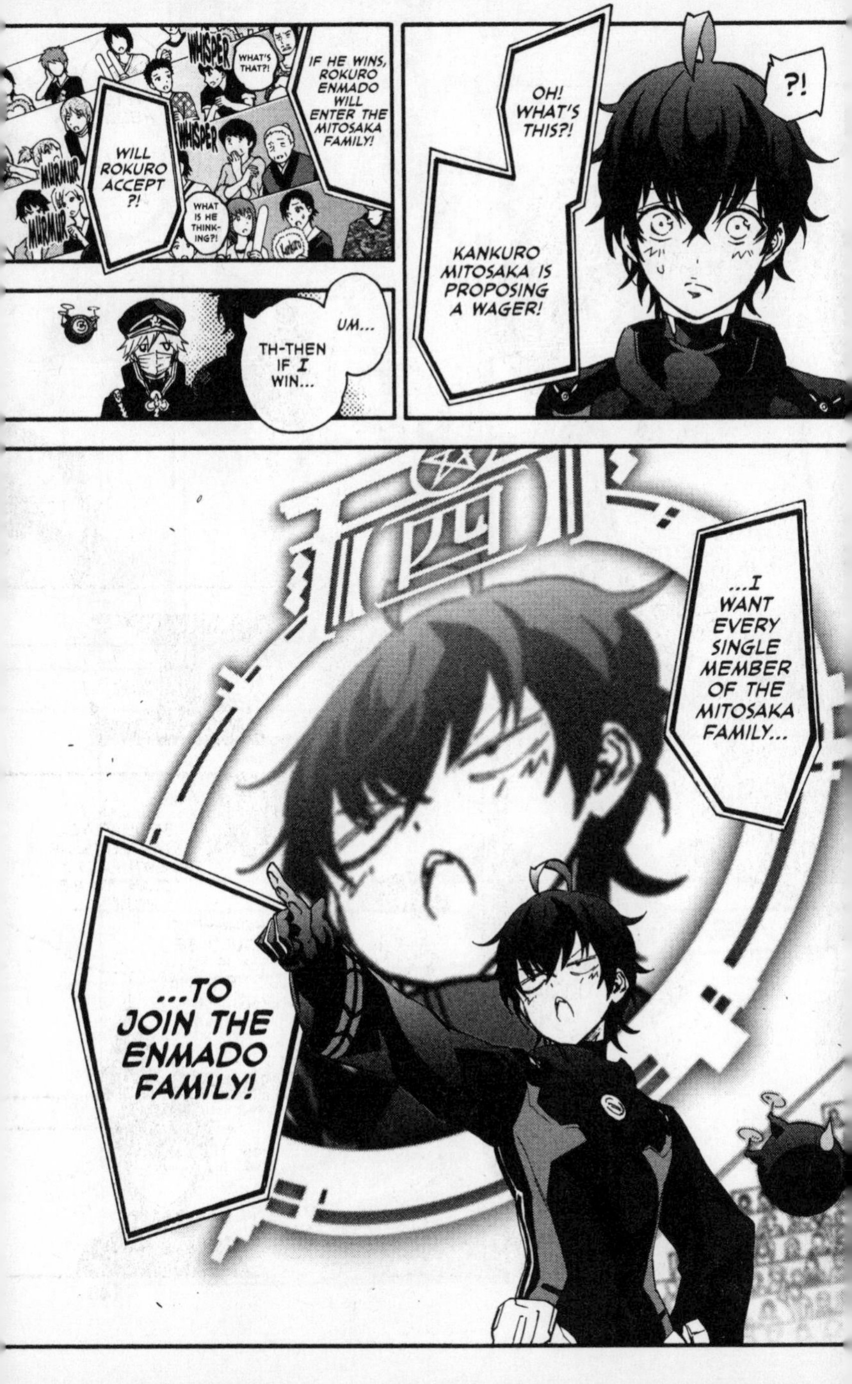
?!
OH! WHAT'S THIS?!
KANKURO MITOSAKA IS PROPOSING A WAGER!
IF HE WINS, ROKURO ENMADO WILL ENTER THE MITOSAKA FAMILY!
WHISPER
WHAT'S THAT?!
WHISPER
WILL ROKURO ACCEPT ?!
WHAT IS HE THINKING?!
MURMUR
MURMUR
UM...
TH-THEN IF *I* WIN...
...*I* WANT EVERY SINGLE MEMBER OF THE MITOSAKA FAMILY...
...TO JOIN THE ENMADO FAMILY!

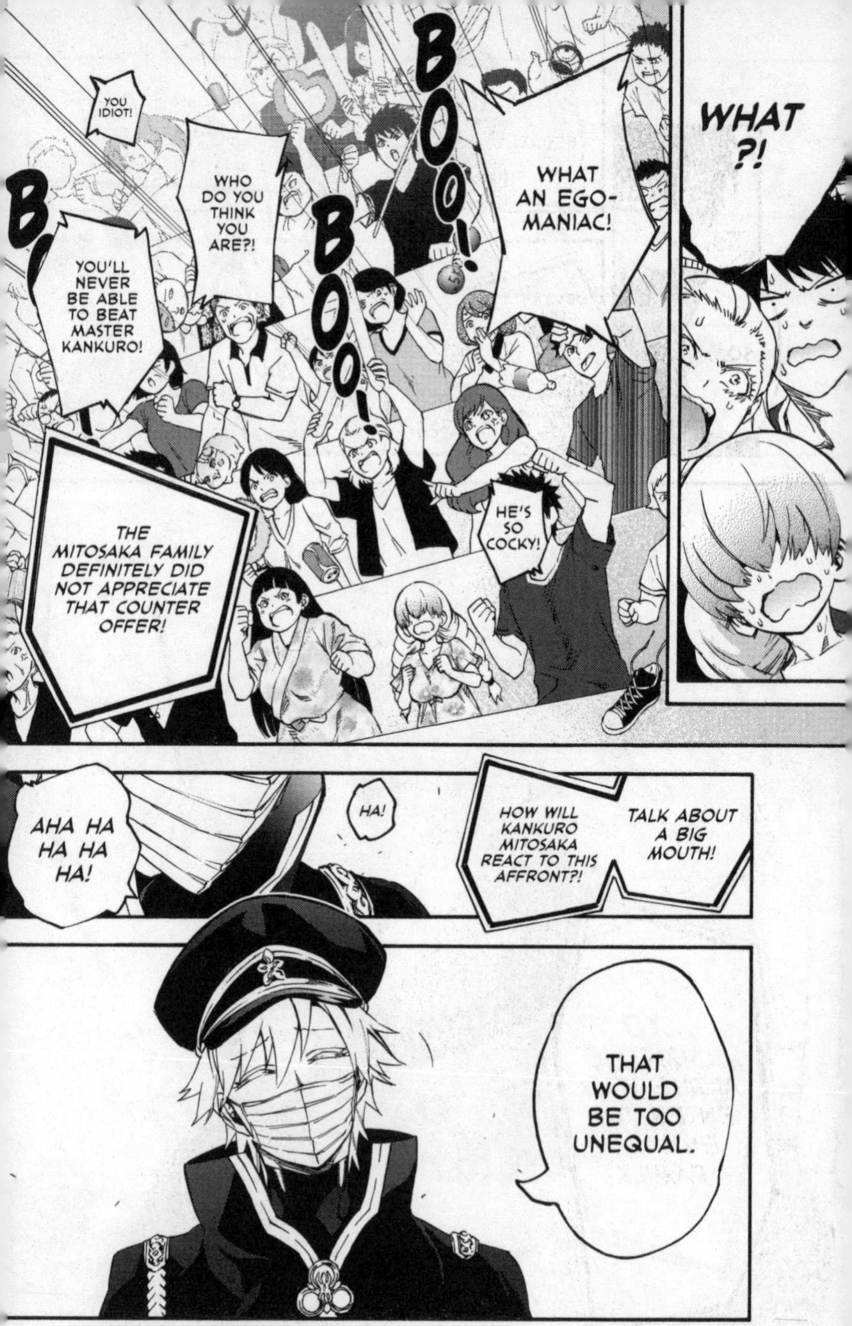
WHAT?!
WHAT AN EGO-MANIAC!
BOO!
BOO!
WHO DO YOU THINK YOU ARE?!
YOU IDIOT!
YOU'LL NEVER BE ABLE TO BEAT MASTER KANKURO!
HE'S SO COCKY!
THE MITOSAKA FAMILY DEFINITELY DID NOT APPRECIATE THAT COUNTER OFFER!
TALK ABOUT A BIG MOUTH!
HOW WILL KANKURO MITOSAKA REACT TO THIS AFFRONT?!
HA!
AHA HA HA HA HA!
THAT WOULD BE TOO UNEQUAL.

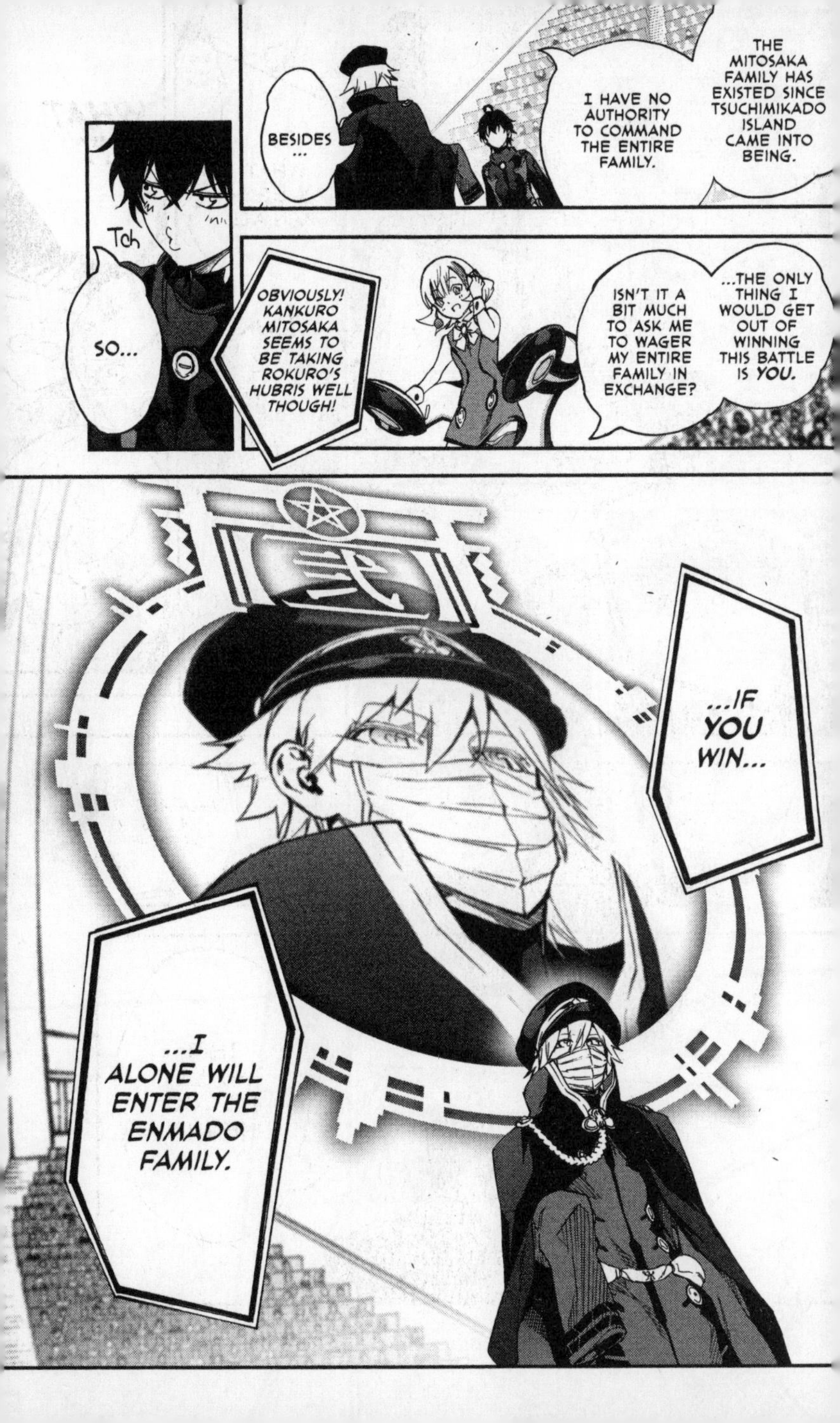

THE MITOSAKA FAMILY HAS EXISTED SINCE TSUCHIMIKADO ISLAND CAME INTO BEING.
I HAVE NO AUTHORITY TO COMMAND THE ENTIRE FAMILY.
BESIDES...
...THE ONLY THING I WOULD GET OUT OF WINNING THIS BATTLE IS *YOU.*
ISN'T IT A BIT MUCH TO ASK ME TO WAGER MY ENTIRE FAMILY IN EXCHANGE?
OBVIOUSLY! KANKURO MITOSAKA SEEMS TO BE TAKING ROKURO'S HUBRIS WELL THOUGH!
Tch
SO...
...IF YOU WIN...
...I ALONE WILL ENTER THE ENMADO FAMILY.

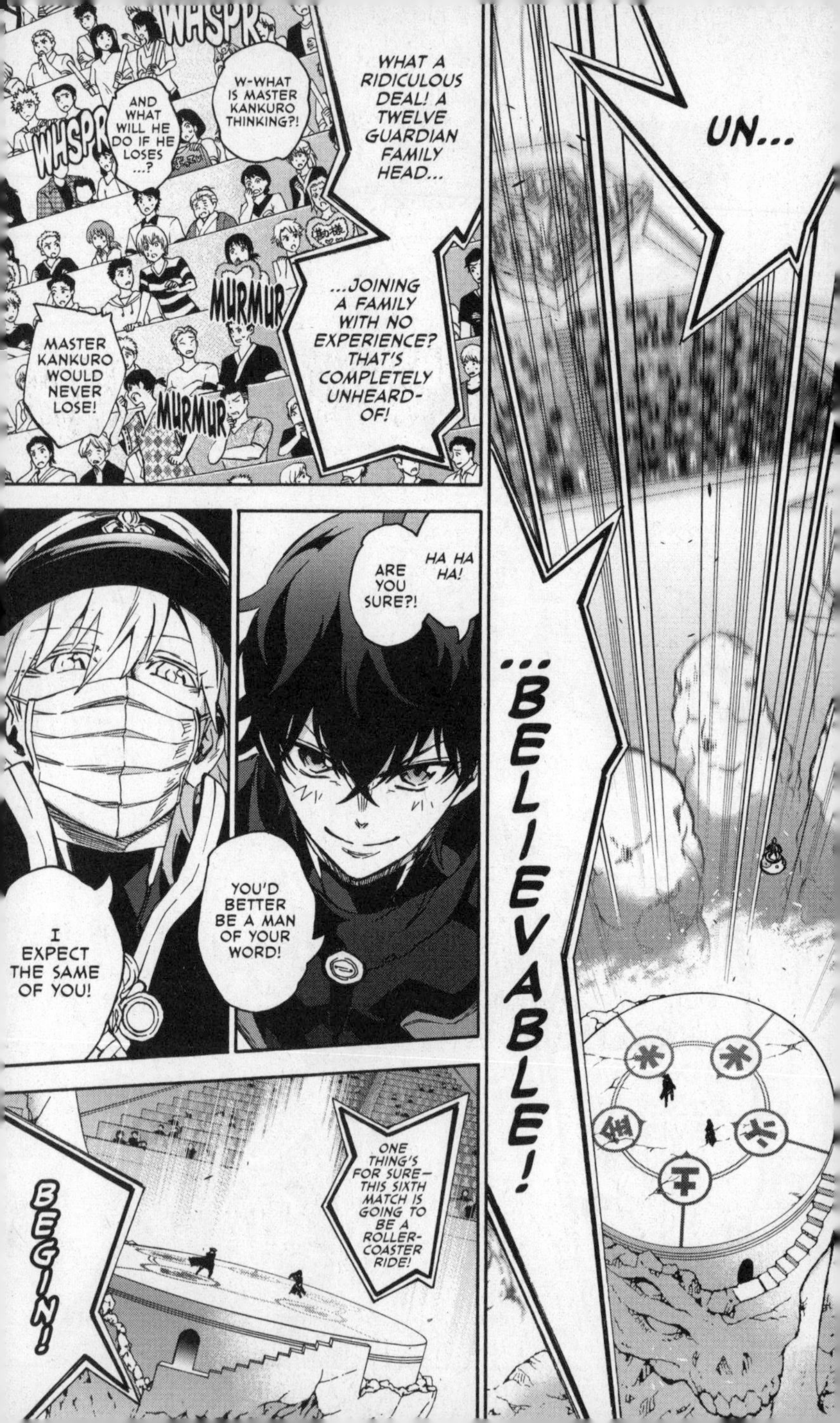
UN...
...BELIEVABLE!
WHAT A RIDICULOUS DEAL! A TWELVE GUARDIAN FAMILY HEAD...
WHSPR
W-WHAT IS MASTER KANKURO THINKING?!
AND WHAT WILL HE DO IF HE LOSES ...?
WHSPR
...JOINING A FAMILY WITH NO EXPERIENCE? THAT'S COMPLETELY UNHEARD-OF!
MURMUR
MASTER KANKURO WOULD NEVER LOSE!
MURMUR
HA HA HA!
ARE YOU SURE?!
YOU'D BETTER BE A MAN OF YOUR WORD!
I EXPECT THE SAME OF YOU!
ONE THING'S FOR SURE— THIS SIXTH MATCH IS GOING TO BE A ROLLER-COASTER RIDE!
BEGIN!

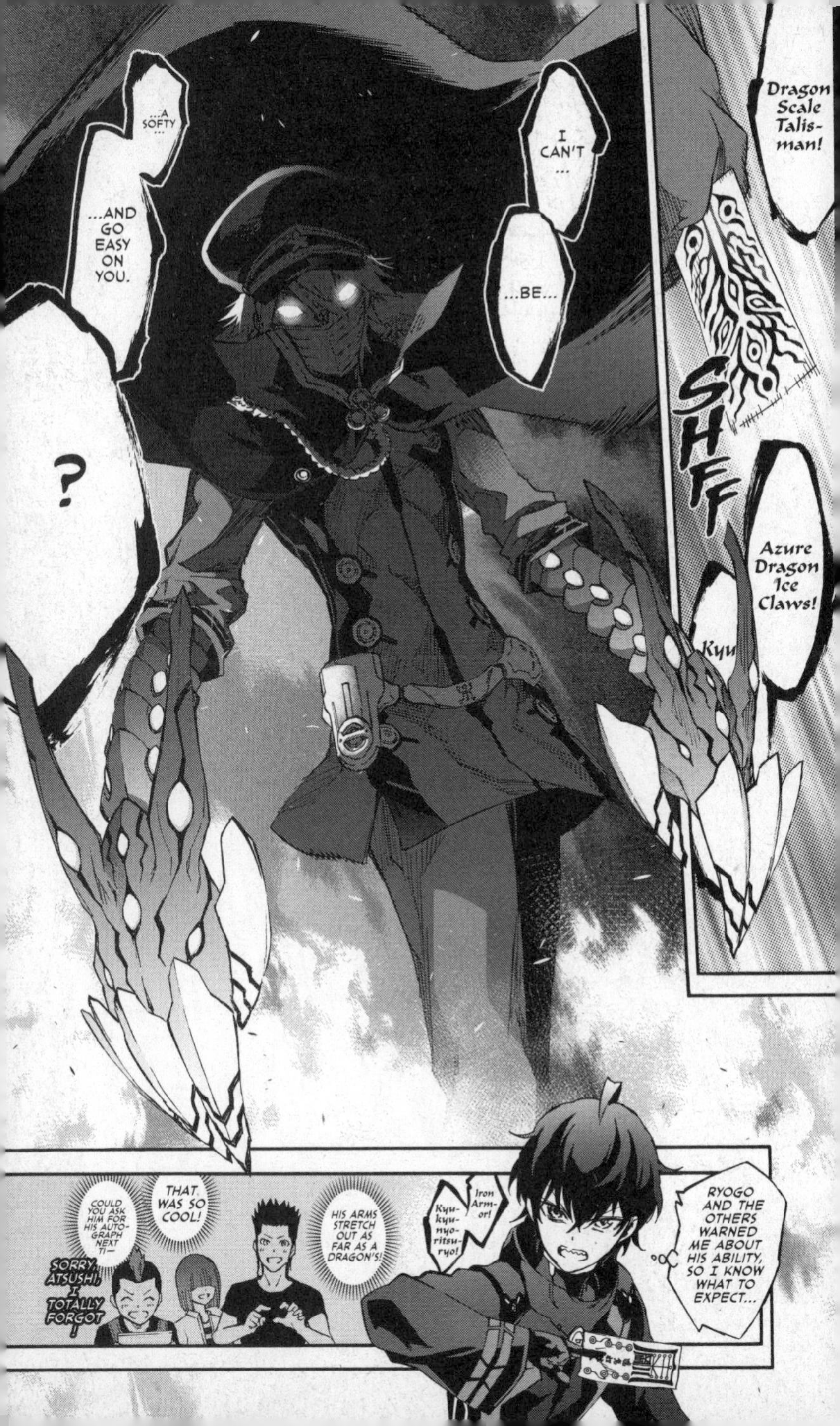
Dragon Scale Talis-man!
SHFF
Azure Dragon Ice Claws!
Kyu
I CAN'T ...
...BE...
...A SOFTY ...
...AND GO EASY ON YOU.
?
RYOGO AND THE OTHERS WARNED ME ABOUT HIS ABILITY, SO I KNOW WHAT TO EXPECT...
Iron Arm-or!
Kyu-kyu-nyo-ritsu-ryo!
HIS ARMS STRETCH OUT AS FAR AS A DRAGON'S!
THAT WAS SO COOL!
COULD YOU ASK HIM FOR HIS AUTO-GRAPH NEXT TI—
SORRY, ATSUSHI, I TOTALLY FORGOT!

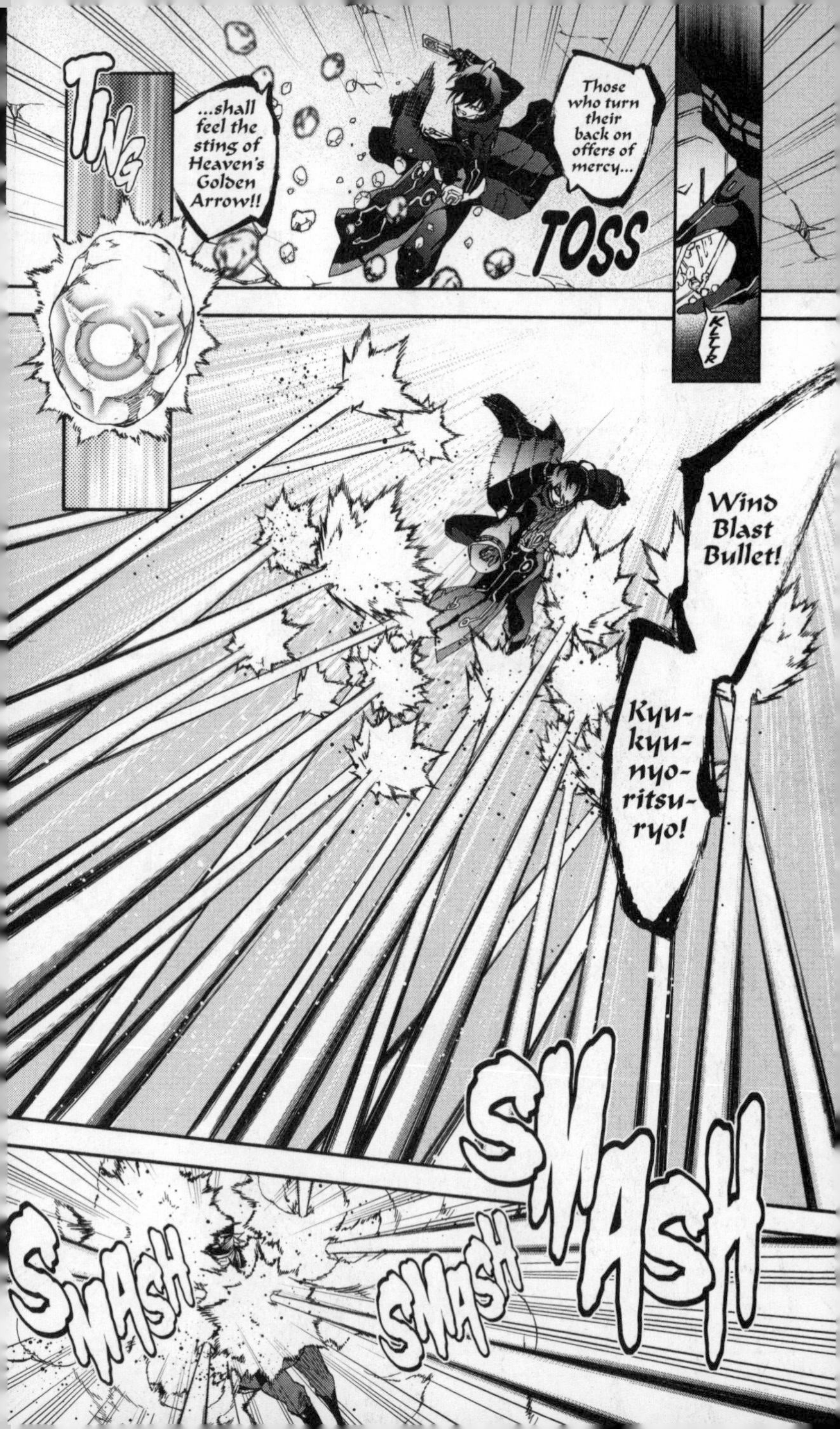
KLIK
Those who turn their back on offers of mercy...
TOSS
...shall feel the sting of Heaven's Golden Arrow!!
TING
Wind Blast Bullet!
Kyu-kyu-nyo-ritsu-ryo!
SMASH
SMASH
SMASH

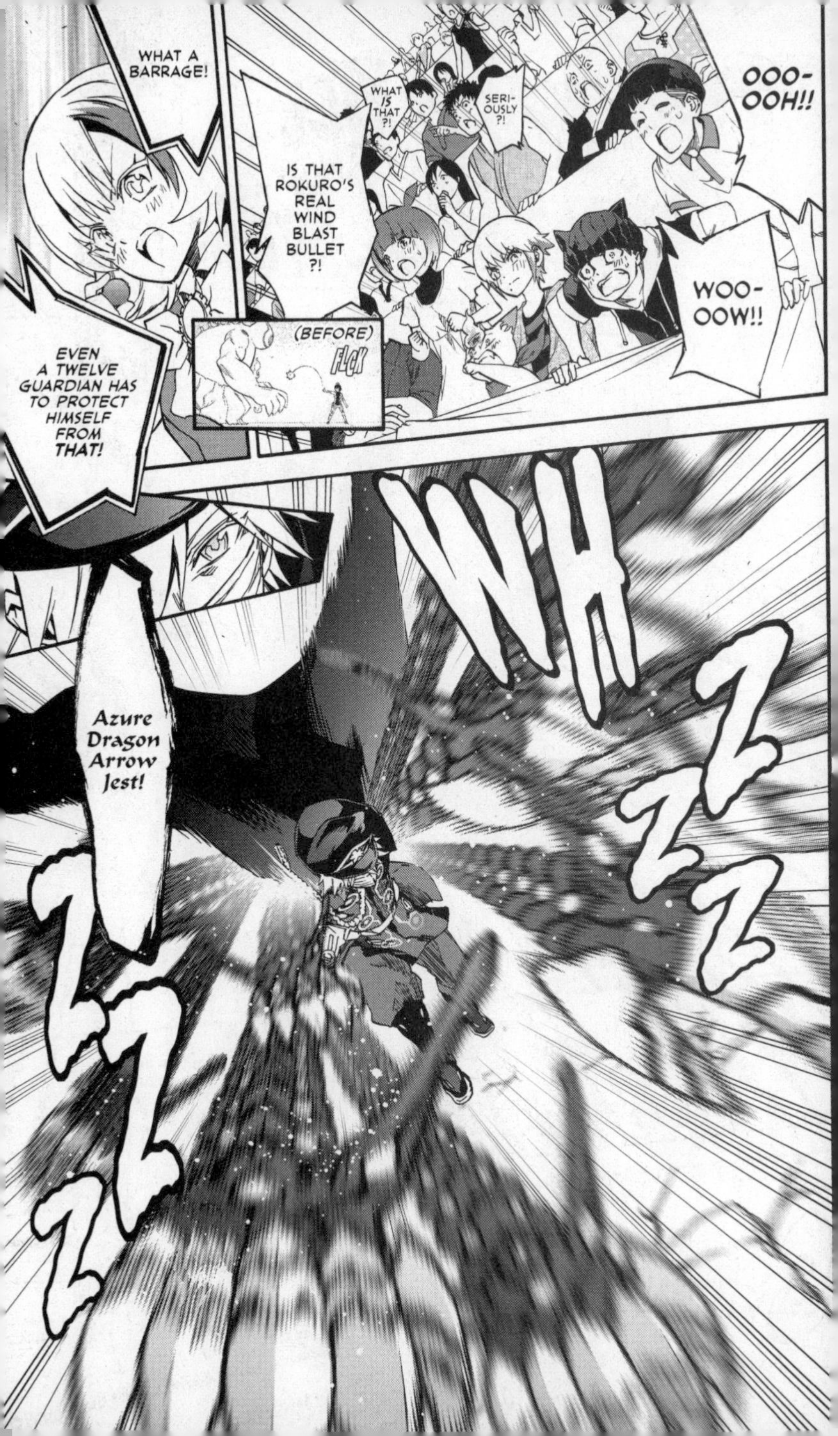
OOO-OOH!!
SERIOUSLY?!
WHAT IS THAT?!
IS THAT ROKURO'S REAL WIND BLAST BULLET?!
WOO-OOW!!
(BEFORE)
FLICK
WHAT A BARRAGE!
EVEN A TWELVE GUARDIAN HAS TO PROTECT HIMSELF FROM THAT!
WHZZZ
Azure Dragon Arrow Jest!
ZZZ

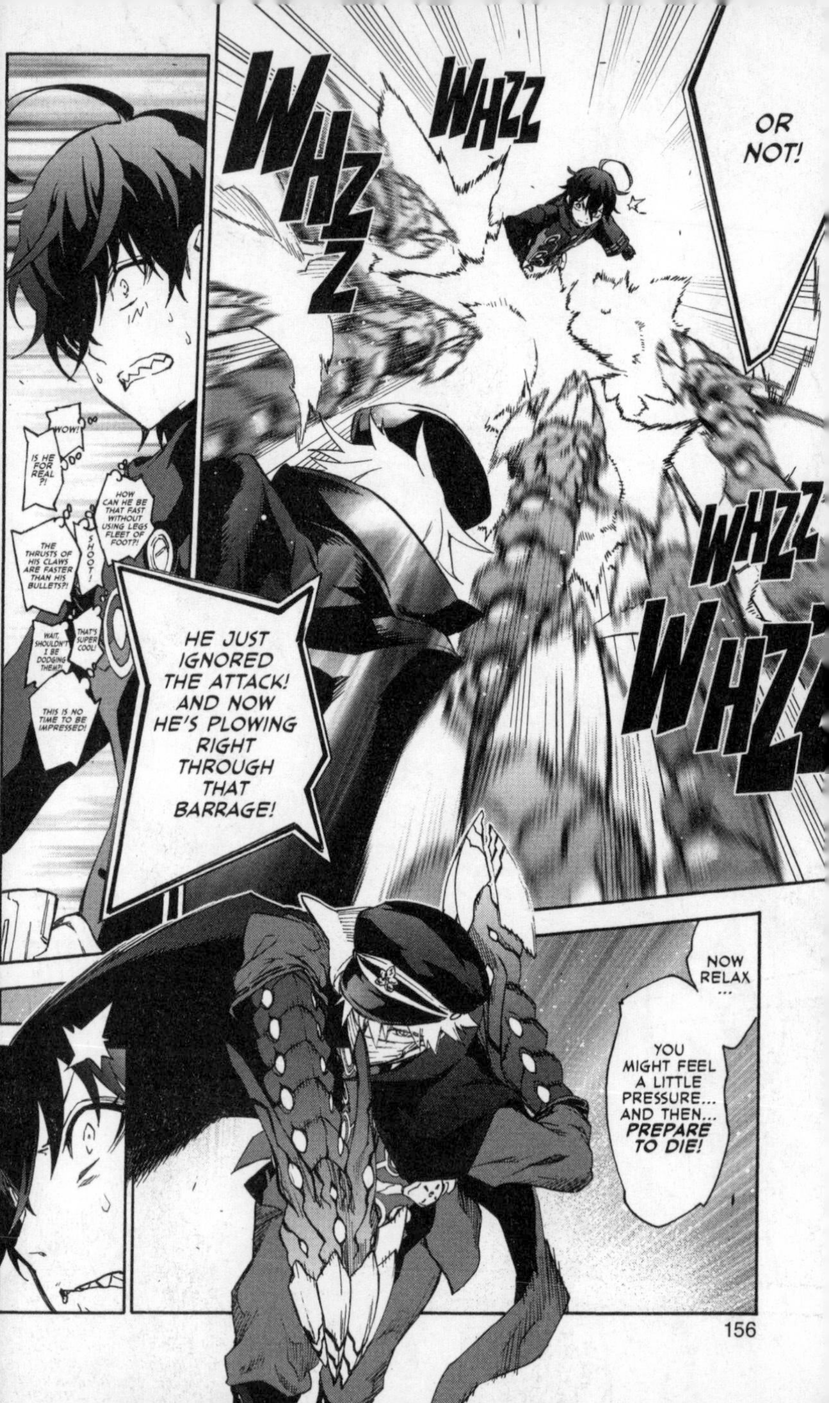
WHZZ
OR NOT!
WHZZ
WHZZZ
WHZZ
HE JUST IGNORED THE ATTACK! AND NOW HE'S PLOWING RIGHT THROUGH THAT BARRAGE!
HOW CAN HE BE THAT FAST WITHOUT USING LEGS FLEET OF FOOT?!
WOW!
IS HE FOR REAL?!
SHOOT!
THE THRUSTS OF HIS CLAWS ARE FASTER THAN HIS BULLETS?!
THAT'S SUPER COOL!
WAIT, SHOULDN'T I BE DODGING THEM?!
THIS IS NO TIME TO BE IMPRESSED!
NOW RELAX...
YOU MIGHT FEEL A LITTLE PRESSURE... AND THEN... PREPARE TO DIE!

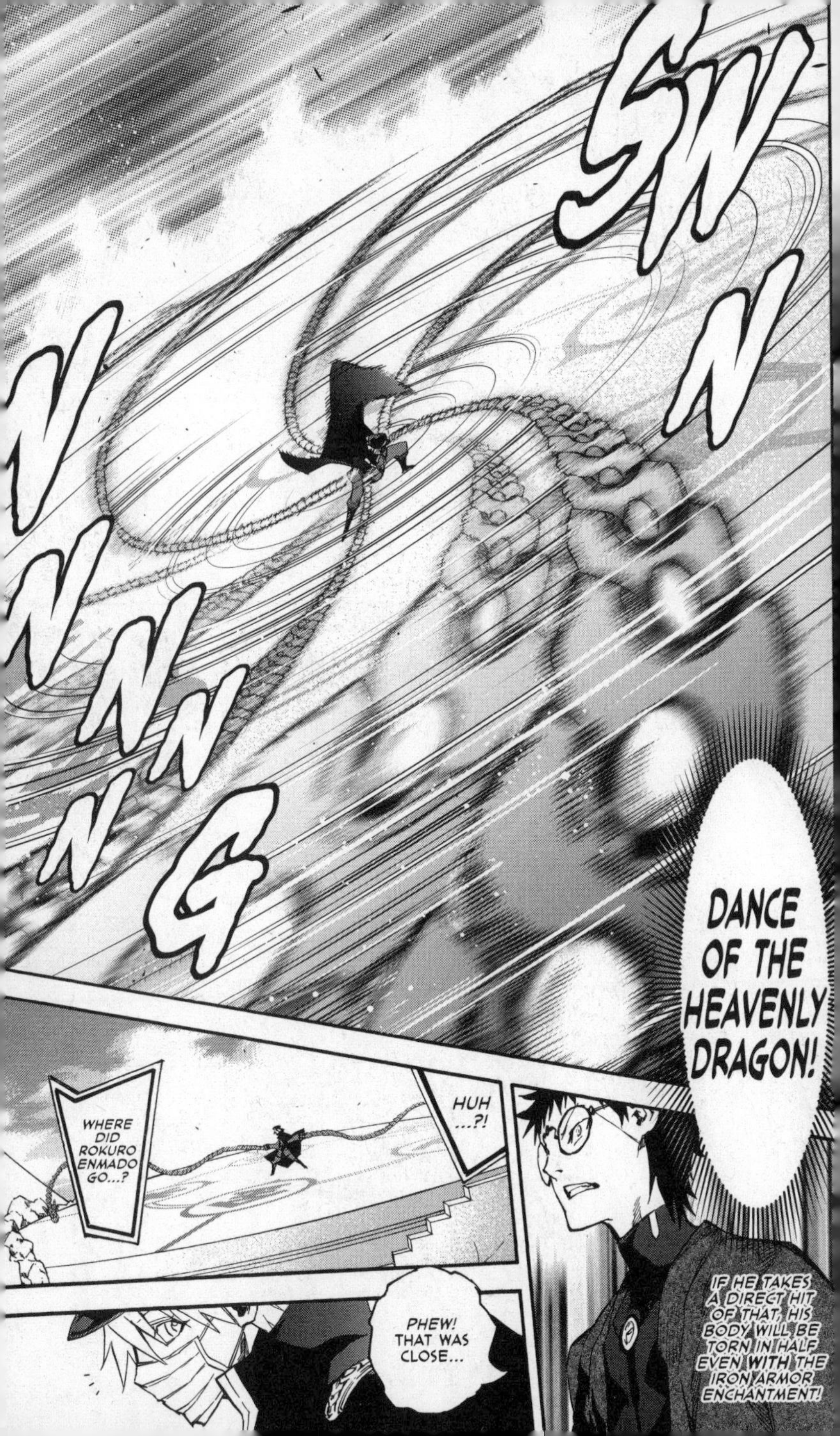
SWNNNNNNG
DANCE OF THE HEAVENLY DRAGON!
IF HE TAKES A DIRECT HIT OF THAT, HIS BODY WILL BE TORN IN HALF EVEN WITH THE IRON ARMOR ENCHANTMENT!
HUH ...?!
WHERE DID ROKURO ENMADO GO...?
PHEW! THAT WAS CLOSE...

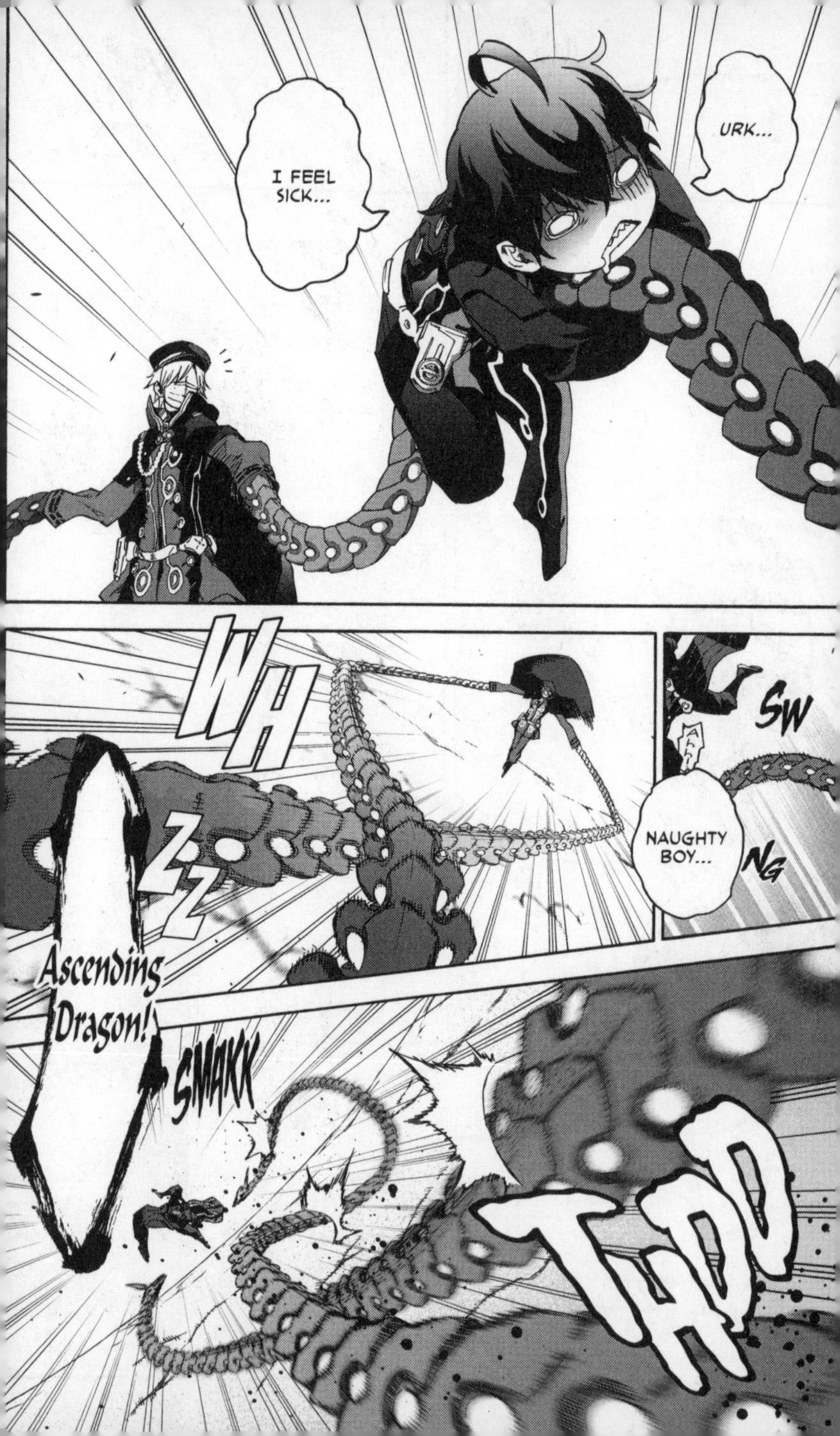
URK...
I FEEL SICK...
SW
Ahh!
NAUGHTY BOY...
NG
WH
ZZ
Ascending Dragon!
SMAKK

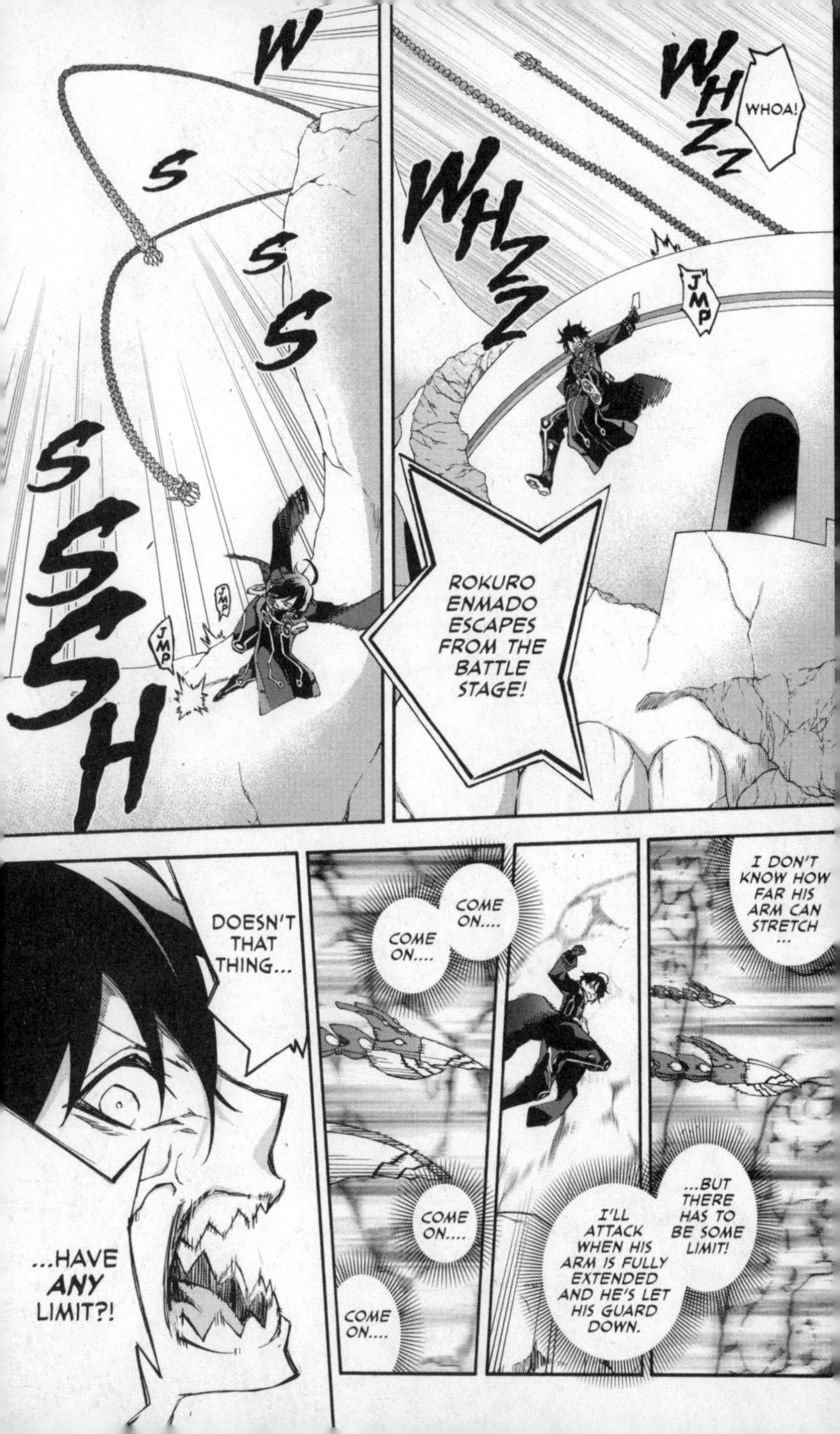
WHZZZ
WHOA!
WHZZ
JMP
ROKURO ENMADO ESCAPES FROM THE BATTLE STAGE!
W
S
S
S
S
SSSH
JMP
JMP
I DON'T KNOW HOW FAR HIS ARM CAN STRETCH ...
...BUT THERE HAS TO BE SOME LIMIT!
I'LL ATTACK WHEN HIS ARM IS FULLY EXTENDED AND HE'S LET HIS GUARD DOWN.
COME ON....
COME ON....
COME ON....
COME ON....
DOESN'T THAT THING...
...HAVE ANY LIMIT?!

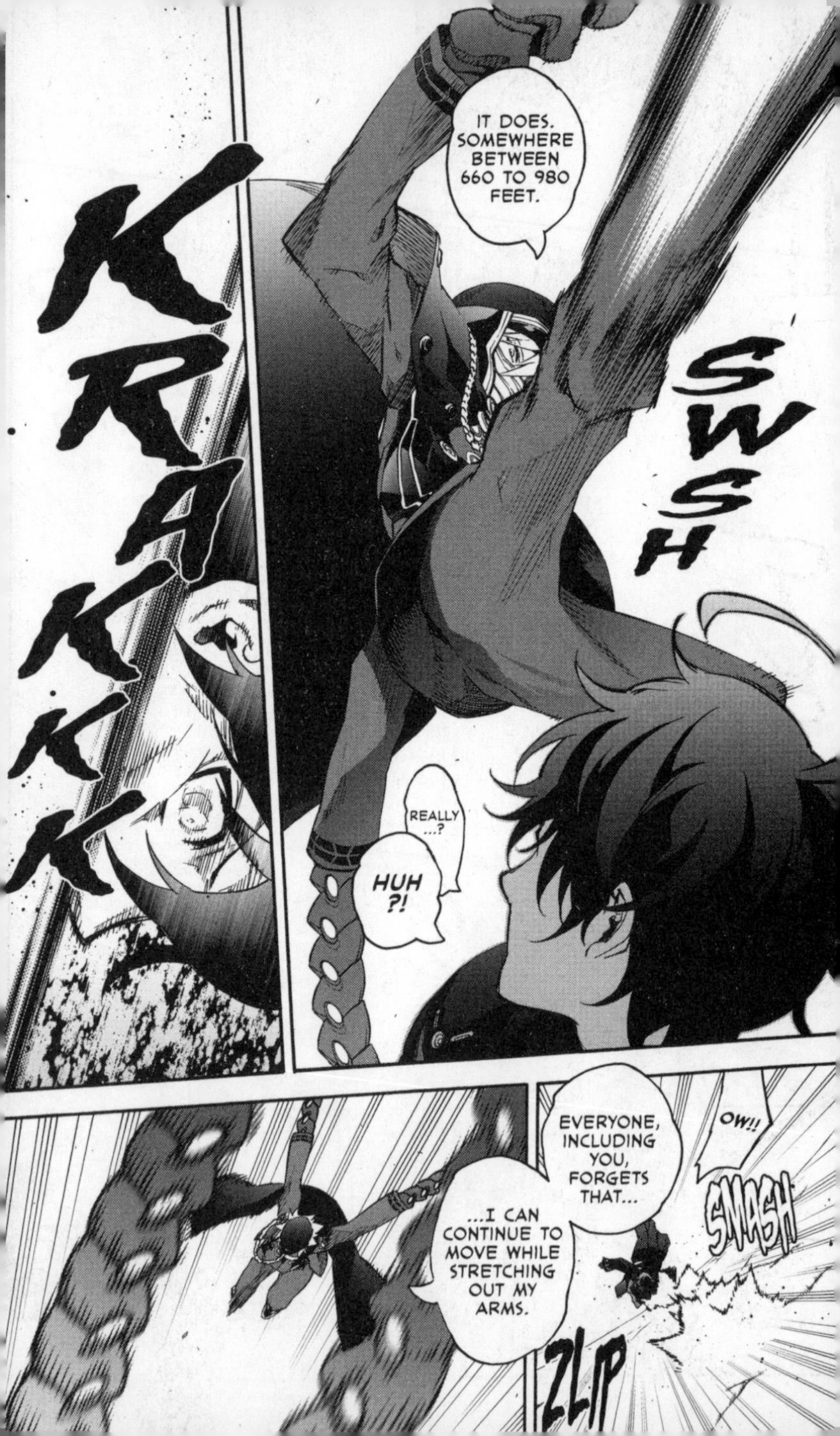
IT DOES. SOMEWHERE BETWEEN 660 TO 980 FEET.
SWSH
REALLY ...?
HUH ?!
KRAKKK
OW!!
SMASH
EVERYONE, INCLUDING YOU, FORGETS THAT...
...I CAN CONTINUE TO MOVE WHILE STRETCHING OUT MY ARMS.
ZLIP

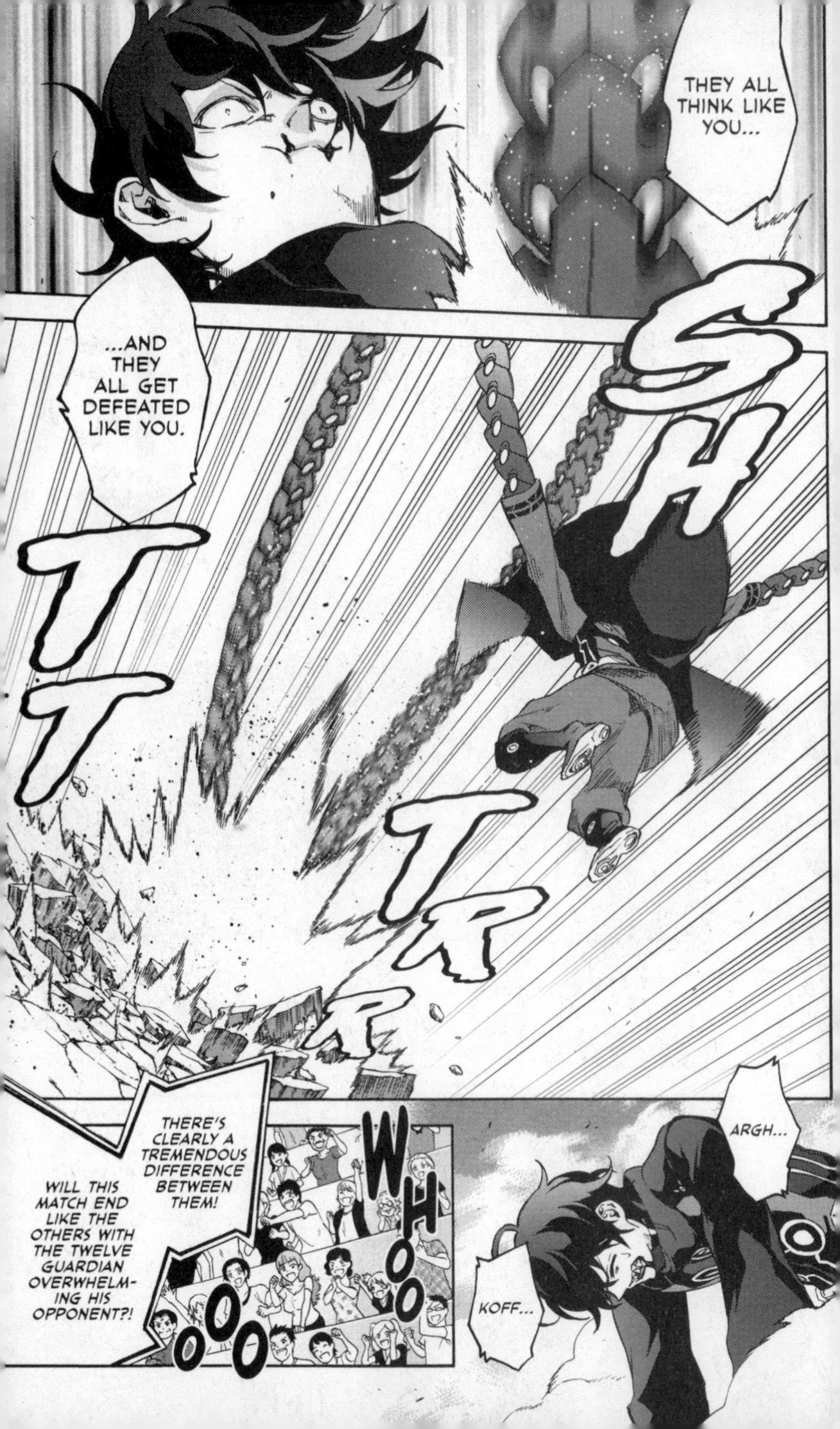

THEY ALL THINK LIKE YOU...
...AND THEY ALL GET DEFEATED LIKE YOU.
SHTTRR
ARGH...
KOFF...
WHOOOOO
THERE'S CLEARLY A TREMENDOUS DIFFERENCE BETWEEN THEM!
WILL THIS MATCH END LIKE THE OTHERS WITH THE TWELVE GUARDIAN OVERWHELMING HIS OPPONENT?!

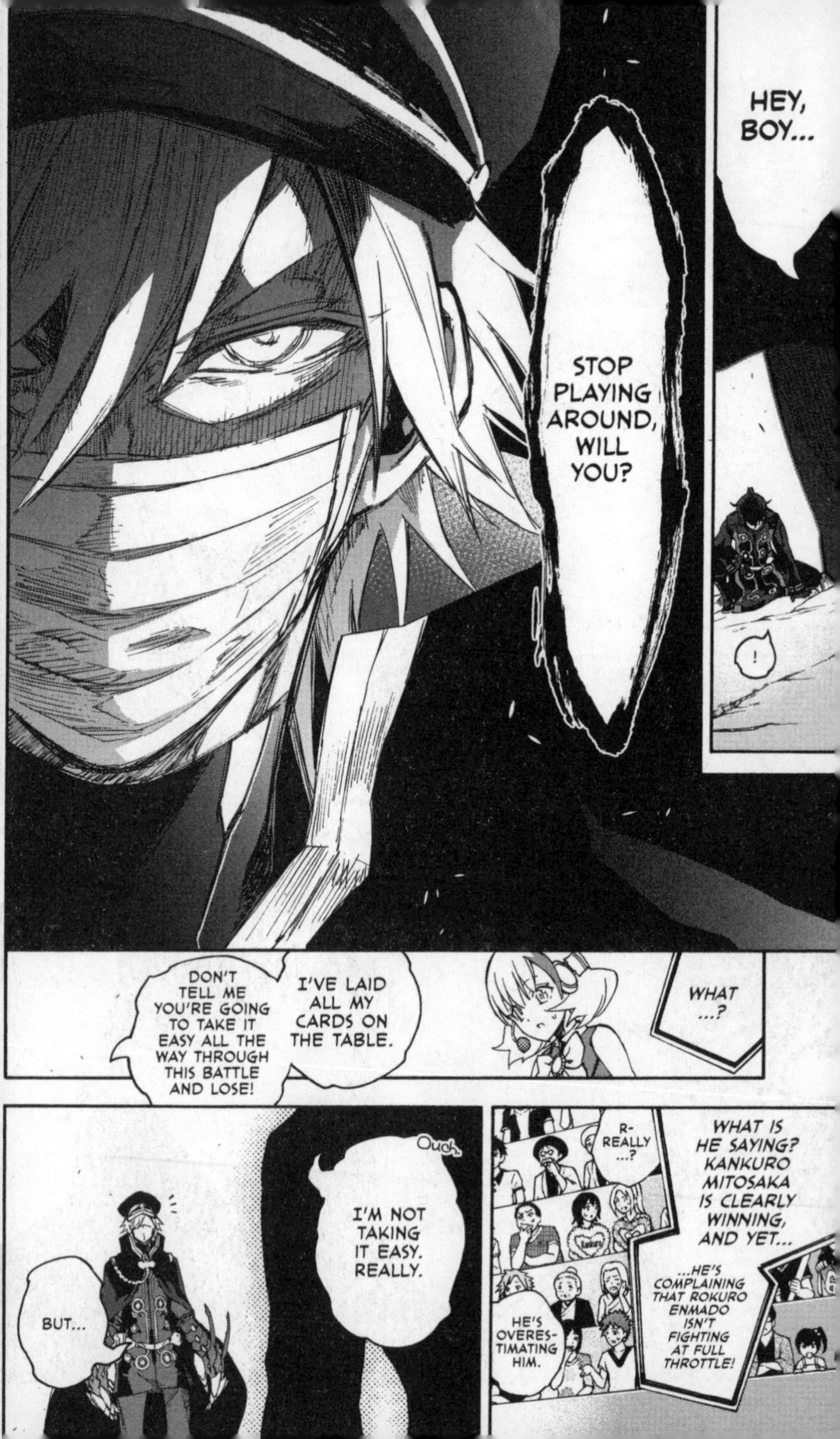

HEY, BOY...
!
STOP PLAYING AROUND, WILL YOU?
WHAT ...?
I'VE LAID ALL MY CARDS ON THE TABLE.
DON'T TELL ME YOU'RE GOING TO TAKE IT EASY ALL THE WAY THROUGH THIS BATTLE AND LOSE!
WHAT IS HE SAYING? KANKURO MITOSAKA IS CLEARLY WINNING, AND YET...
R-REALLY ...?
...HE'S COMPLAINING THAT ROKURO ENMADO ISN'T FIGHTING AT FULL THROTTLE!
HE'S OVERES-TIMATING HIM.
Ouch
I'M NOT TAKING IT EASY. REALLY.
BUT...

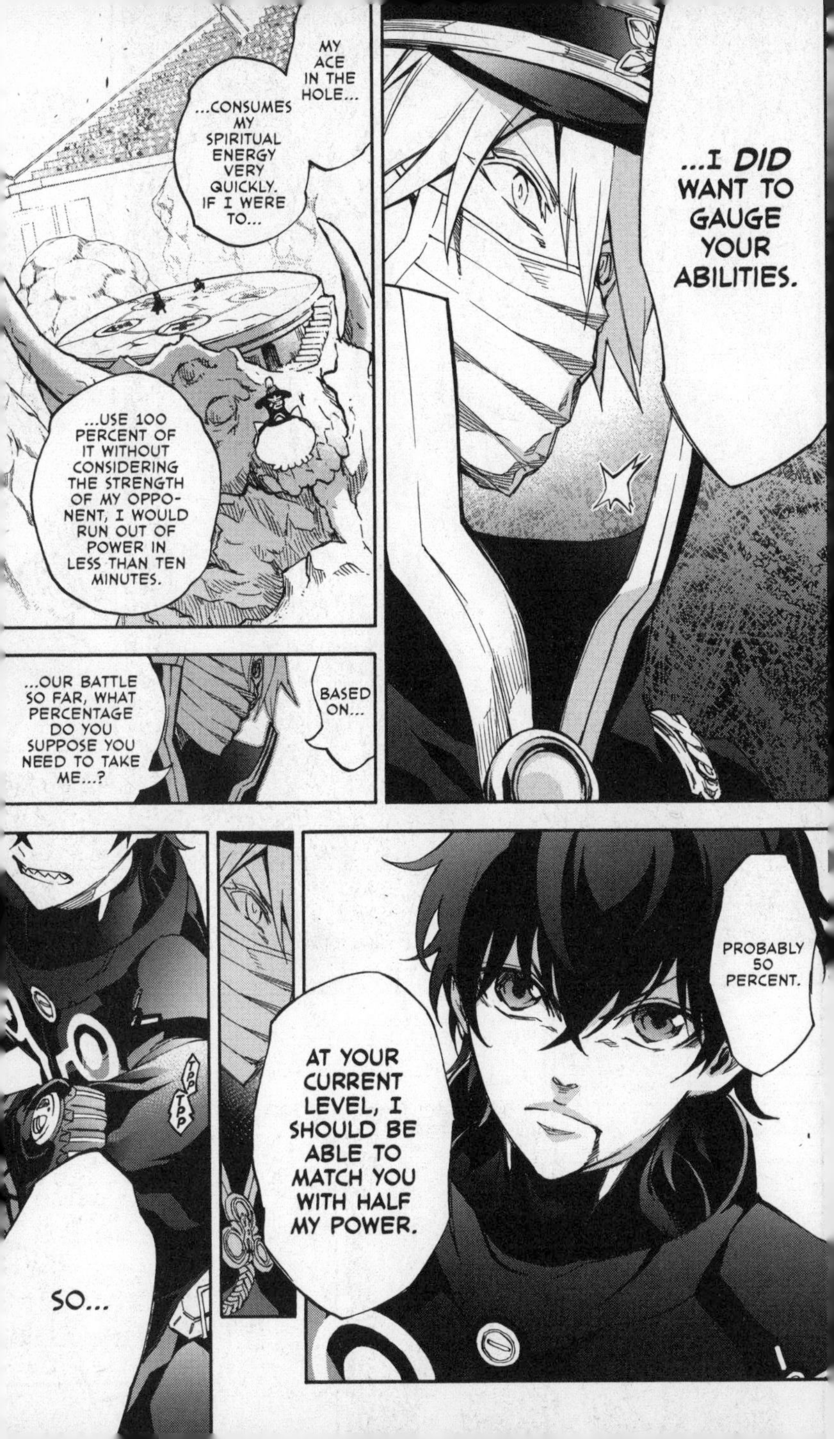
...I DID WANT TO GAUGE YOUR ABILITIES.
MY ACE IN THE HOLE...
...CONSUMES MY SPIRITUAL ENERGY VERY QUICKLY. IF I WERE TO...
...USE 100 PERCENT OF IT WITHOUT CONSIDERING THE STRENGTH OF MY OPPO-NENT, I WOULD RUN OUT OF POWER IN LESS THAN TEN MINUTES.
BASED ON...
...OUR BATTLE SO FAR, WHAT PERCENTAGE DO YOU SUPPOSE YOU NEED TO TAKE ME...?
PROBABLY 50 PERCENT.
AT YOUR CURRENT LEVEL, I SHOULD BE ABLE TO MATCH YOU WITH HALF MY POWER.
TPP TPP
SO...

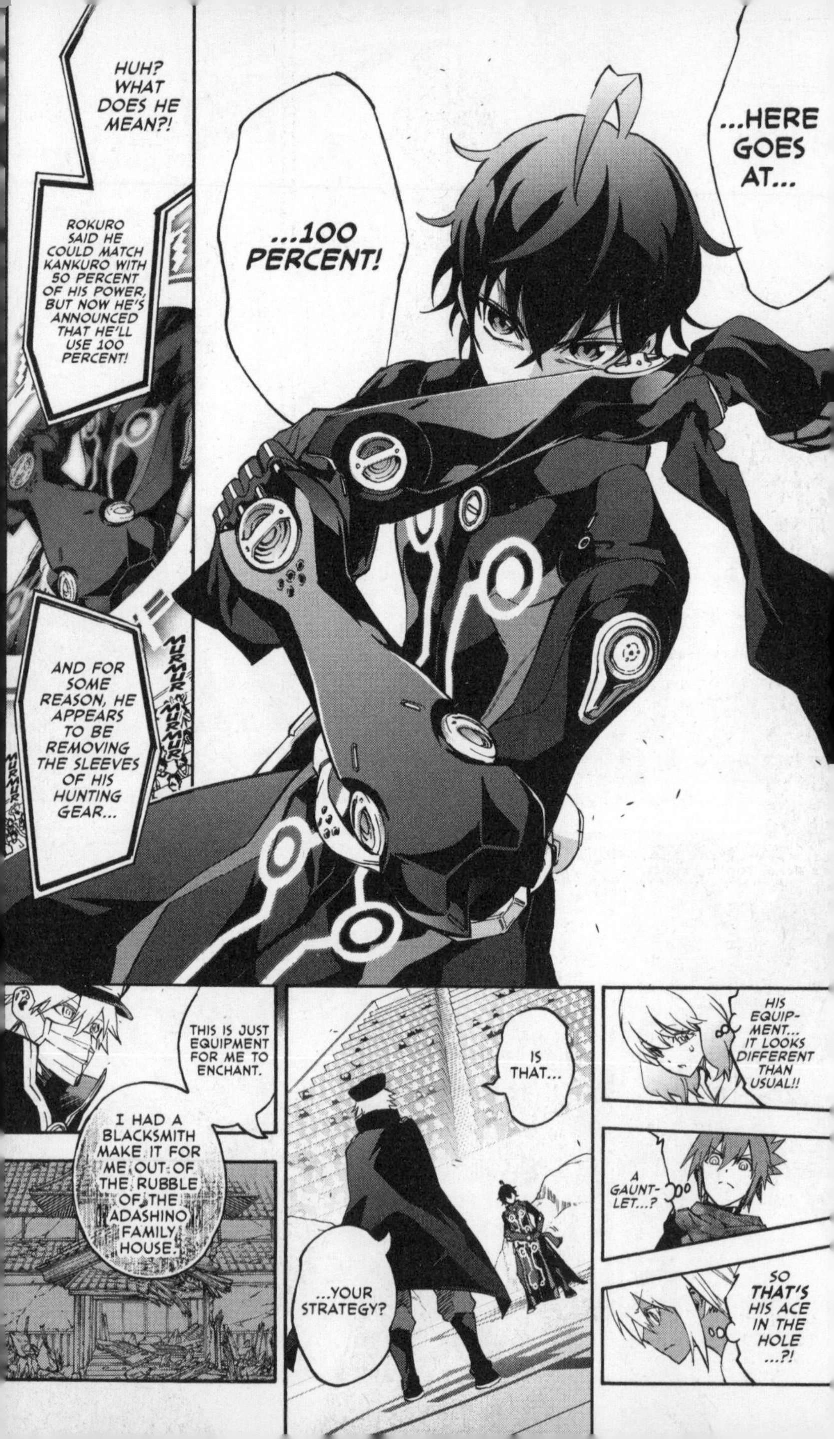
...HERE GOES AT...
...100 PERCENT!
HUH? WHAT DOES HE MEAN?!
ROKURO SAID HE COULD MATCH KANKURO WITH 50 PERCENT OF HIS POWER, BUT NOW HE'S ANNOUNCED THAT HE'LL USE 100 PERCENT!
MURMUR
MURMUR
MURMUR
AND FOR SOME REASON, HE APPEARS TO BE REMOVING THE SLEEVES OF HIS HUNTING GEAR...
HIS EQUIPMENT... IT LOOKS DIFFERENT THAN USUAL!!
A GAUNTLET...?
SO *THAT'S* HIS ACE IN THE HOLE...?!
IS THAT...
...YOUR STRATEGY?
THIS IS JUST EQUIPMENT FOR ME TO ENCHANT.
I HAD A BLACKSMITH MAKE IT FOR ME OUT OF THE RUBBLE OF THE ADASHINO FAMILY HOUSE.

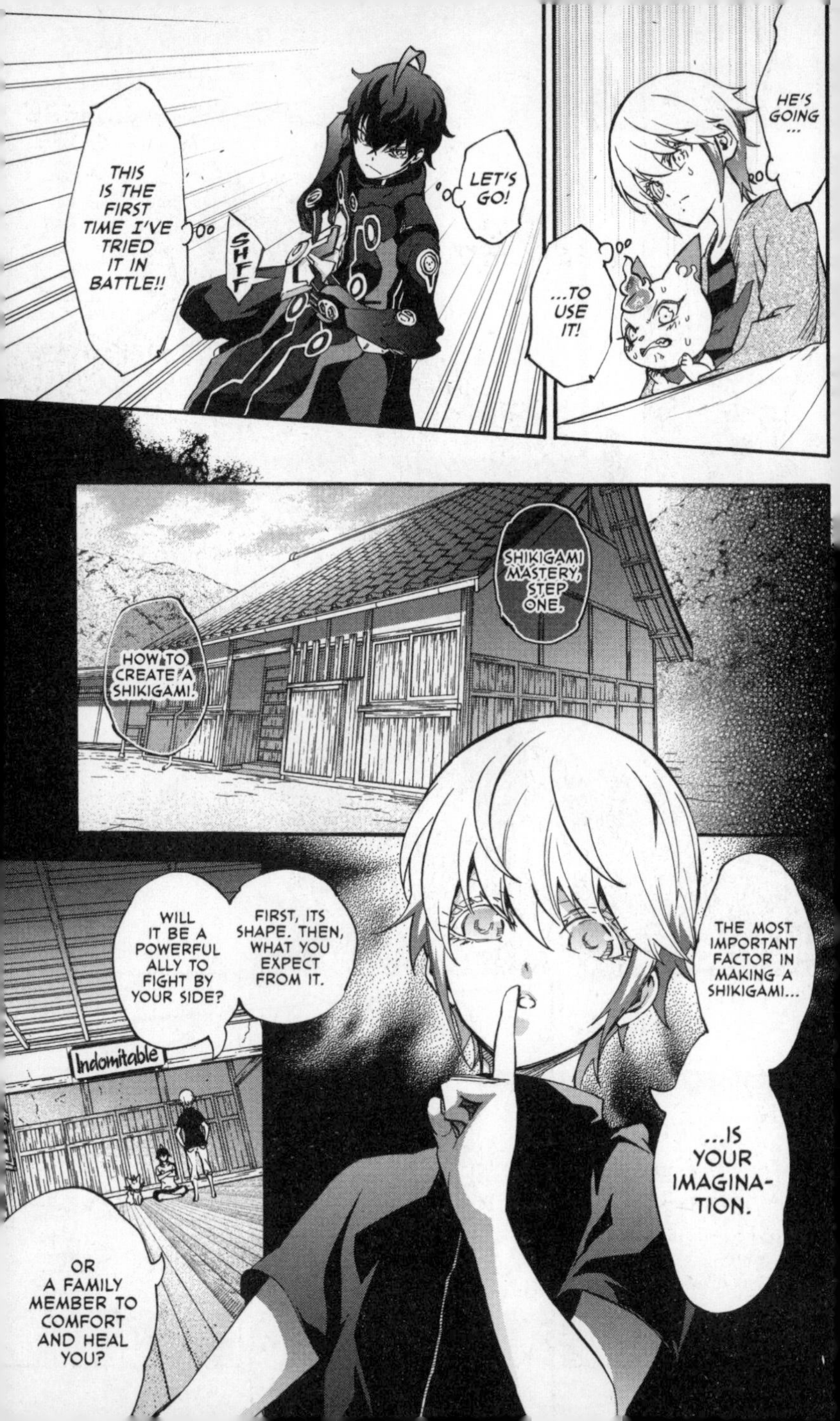
HE'S GOING ...
RO
...TO USE IT!
LET'S GO!
SHFF
THIS IS THE FIRST TIME I'VE TRIED IT IN BATTLE!!
SHIKIGAMI MASTERY, STEP ONE.
HOW TO CREATE A SHIKIGAMI.
THE MOST IMPORTANT FACTOR IN MAKING A SHIKIGAMI...
...IS YOUR IMAGINATION.
FIRST, ITS SHAPE. THEN, WHAT YOU EXPECT FROM IT.
WILL IT BE A POWERFUL ALLY TO FIGHT BY YOUR SIDE?
Indomitable
OR A FAMILY MEMBER TO COMFORT AND HEAL YOU?

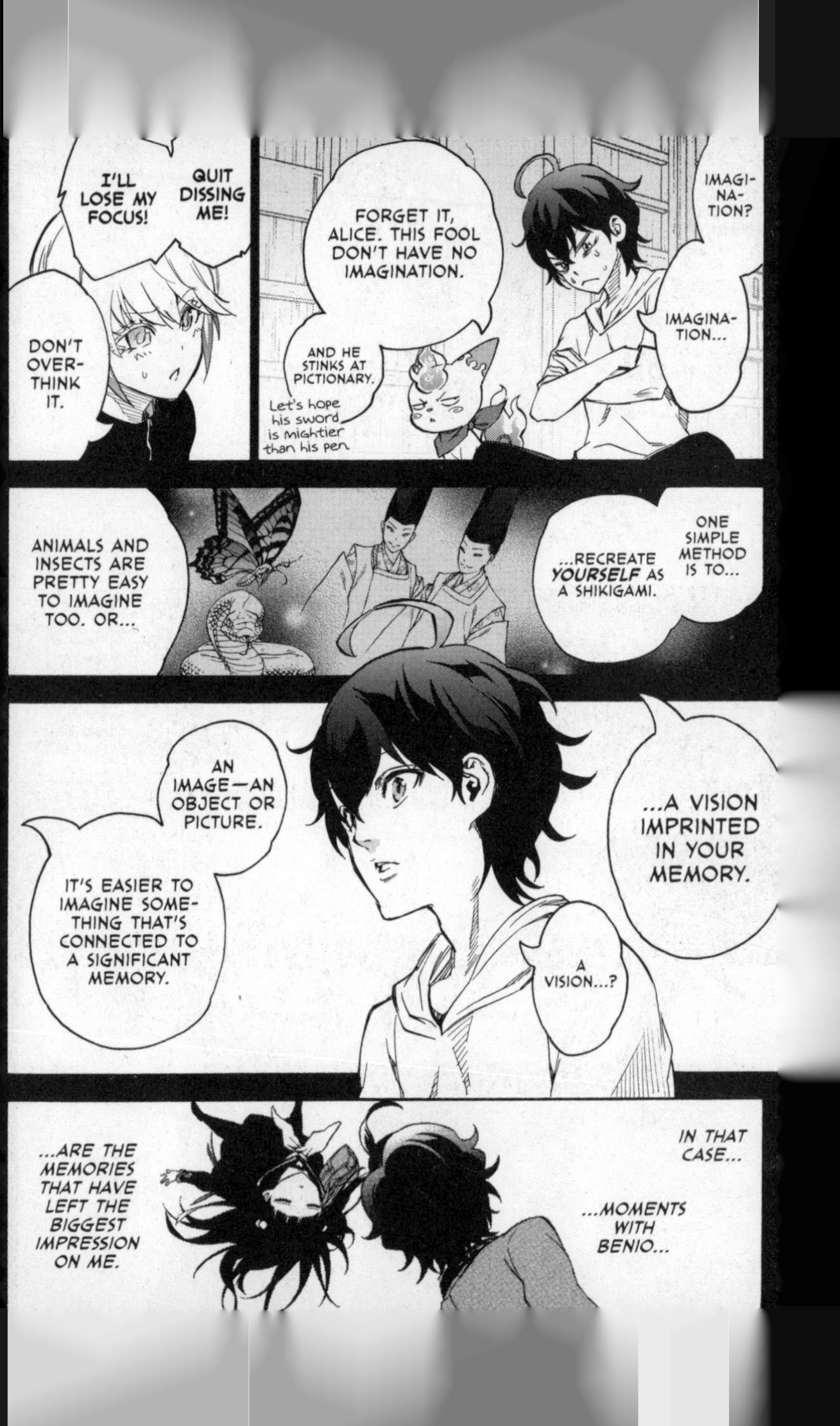
IMAGI-NA-TION?
IMAGINA-TION...
FORGET IT, ALICE. THIS FOOL DON'T HAVE NO IMAGINATION.
AND HE STINKS AT PICTIONARY.
Let's hope his sword is mightier than his pen.
QUIT DISSING ME!
I'LL LOSE MY FOCUS!
DON'T OVER-THINK IT.
ONE SIMPLE METHOD IS TO...
...RECREATE *YOURSELF* AS A SHIKIGAMI.
ANIMALS AND INSECTS ARE PRETTY EASY TO IMAGINE TOO. OR...
...A VISION IMPRINTED IN YOUR MEMORY.
A VISION...?
AN IMAGE—AN OBJECT OR PICTURE.
IT'S EASIER TO IMAGINE SOME-THING THAT'S CONNECTED TO A SIGNIFICANT MEMORY.
IN THAT CASE...
...MOMENTS WITH BENIO...
...ARE THE MEMORIES THAT HAVE LEFT THE BIGGEST IMPRESSION ON ME.

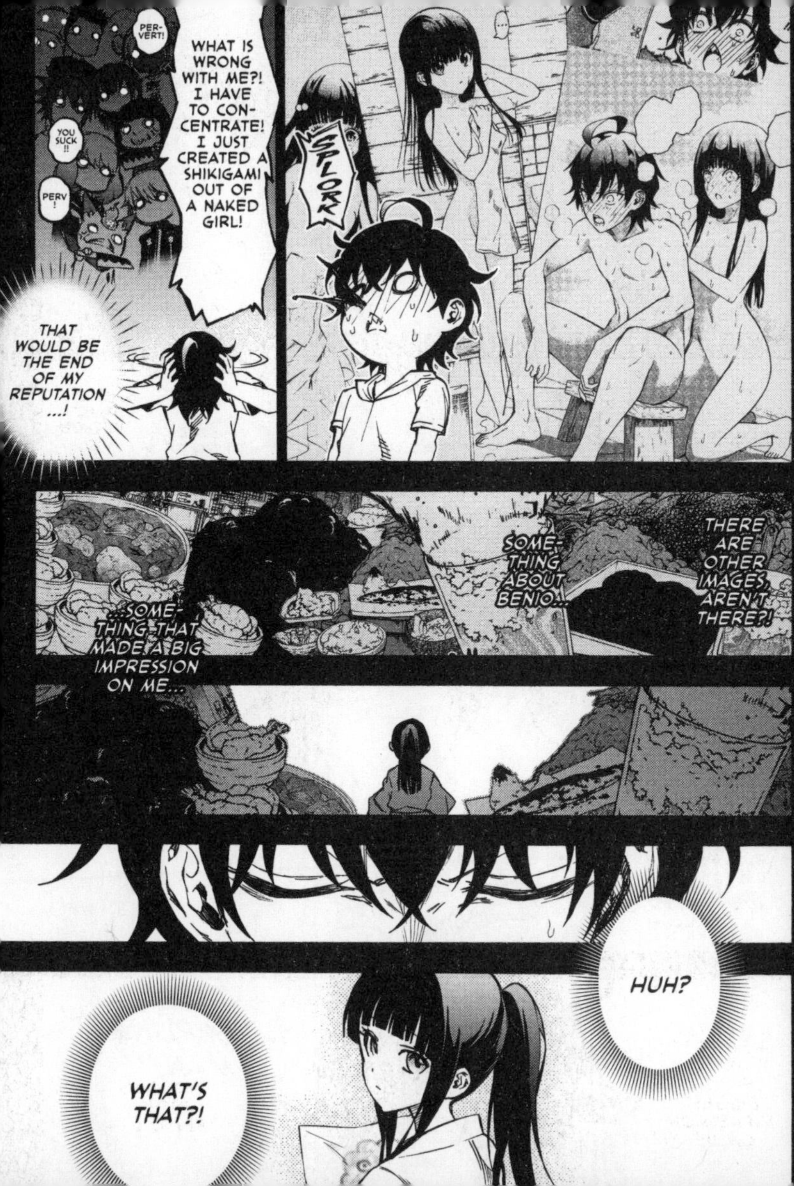
SPLORK
WHAT IS WRONG WITH ME?! I HAVE TO CONCENTRATE! I JUST CREATED A SHIKIGAMI OUT OF A NAKED GIRL!
PER-VERT!
YOU SUCK!!
PERV!
THAT WOULD BE THE END OF MY REPUTATION...!
THERE ARE OTHER IMAGES, AREN'T THERE?!
SOME-THING ABOUT BENIO...
...SOME-THING THAT MADE A BIG IMPRESSION ON ME...
HUH?
WHAT'S THAT?!

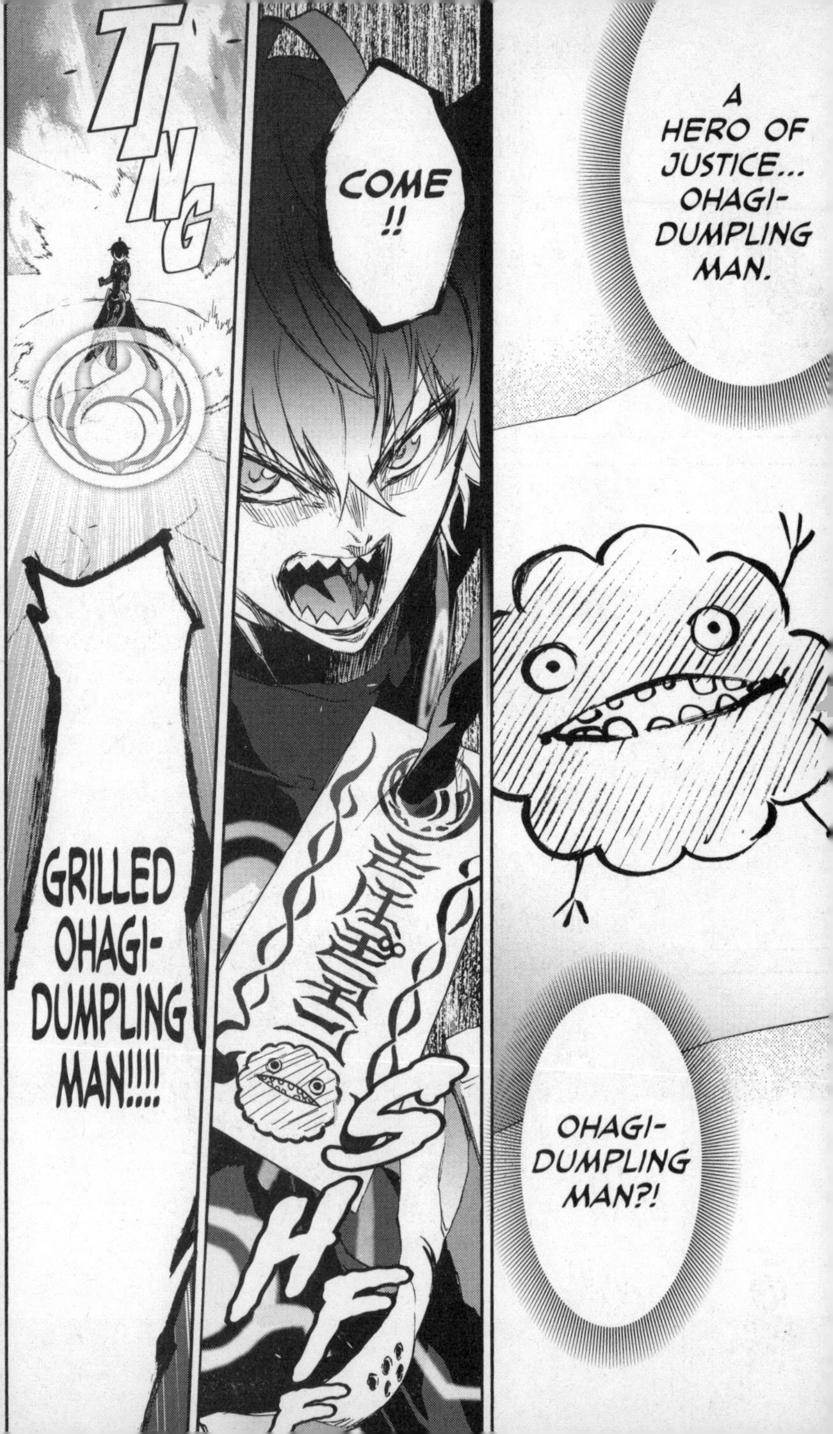
A HERO OF JUSTICE... OHAGI-DUMPLING MAN.
OHAGI-DUMPLING MAN?!
COME !!
SHF
TING
GRILLED OHAGI-DUMPLING MAN!!!!

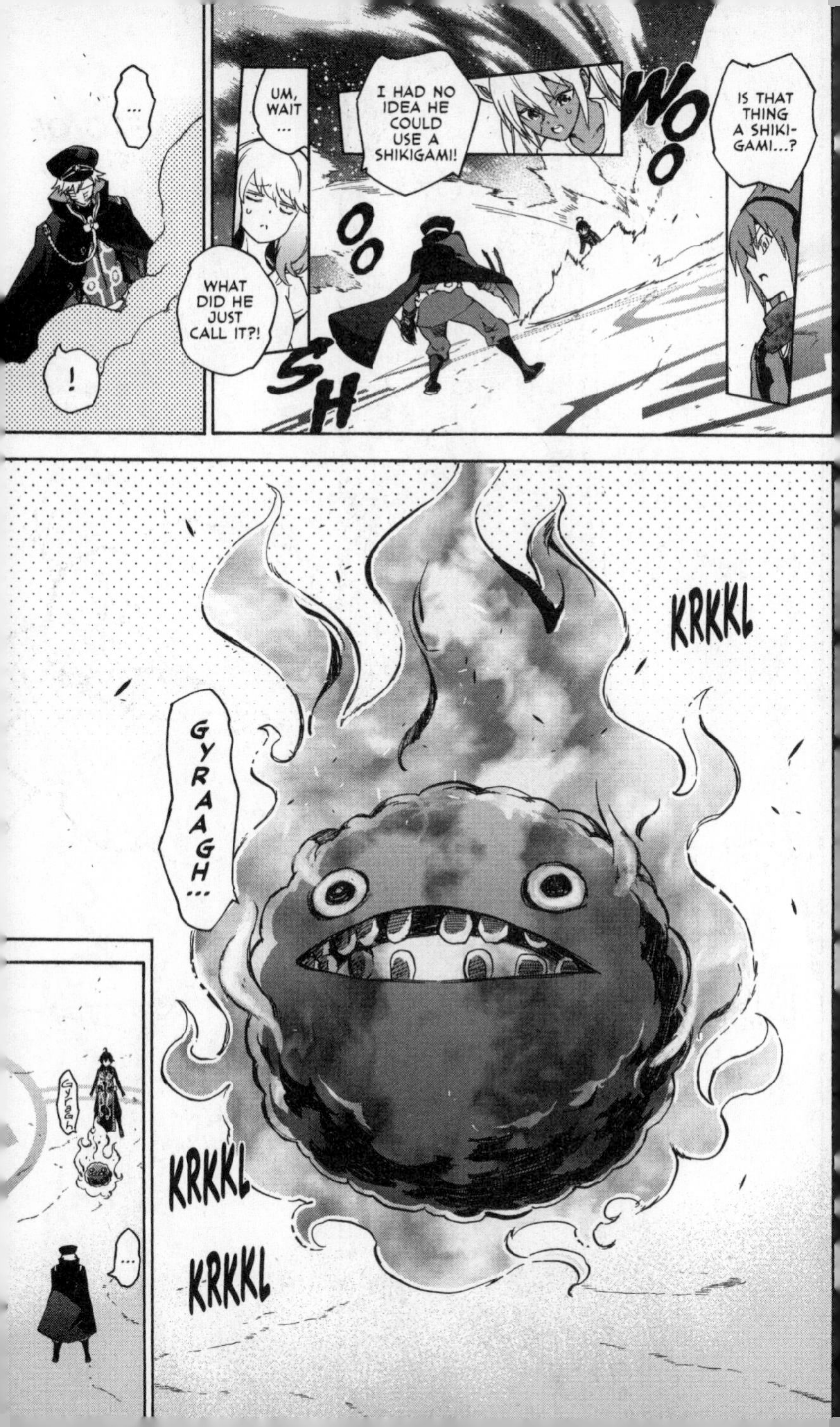
IS THAT THING A SHIKIGAMI...?
WOOOO
I HAD NO IDEA HE COULD USE A SHIKIGAMI!
UM, WAIT ...
WHAT DID HE JUST CALL IT?!
SH
...
!
KRKKL
GYRAAGH...
KRKKL
KRKKL
Gyragh
...

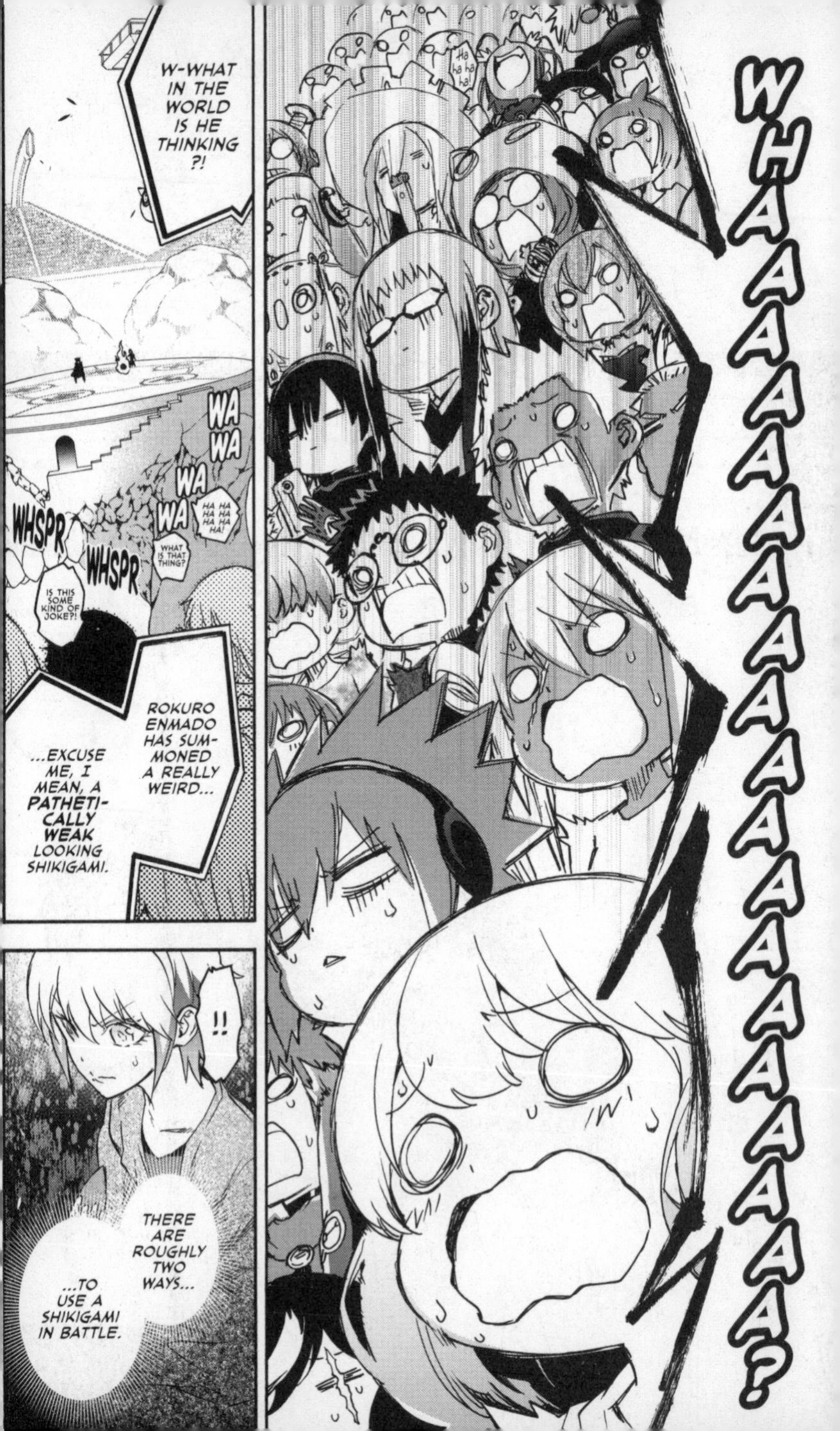

Ha ha ha ha!
WHAAAAAAAAAAAAAAAAA?
W-WHAT IN THE WORLD IS HE THINKING?!
WA WA
WA WA
HA HA HA HA HA HA!
WHAT IS THAT THING?
WHSPR
WHSPR
IS THIS SOME KIND OF JOKE?!
ROKURO ENMADO HAS SUM-MONED A REALLY WEIRD...
...EXCUSE ME, I MEAN, A PATHETI-CALLY WEAK LOOKING SHIKIGAMI.
!!
THERE ARE ROUGHLY TWO WAYS...
...TO USE A SHIKIGAMI IN BATTLE.

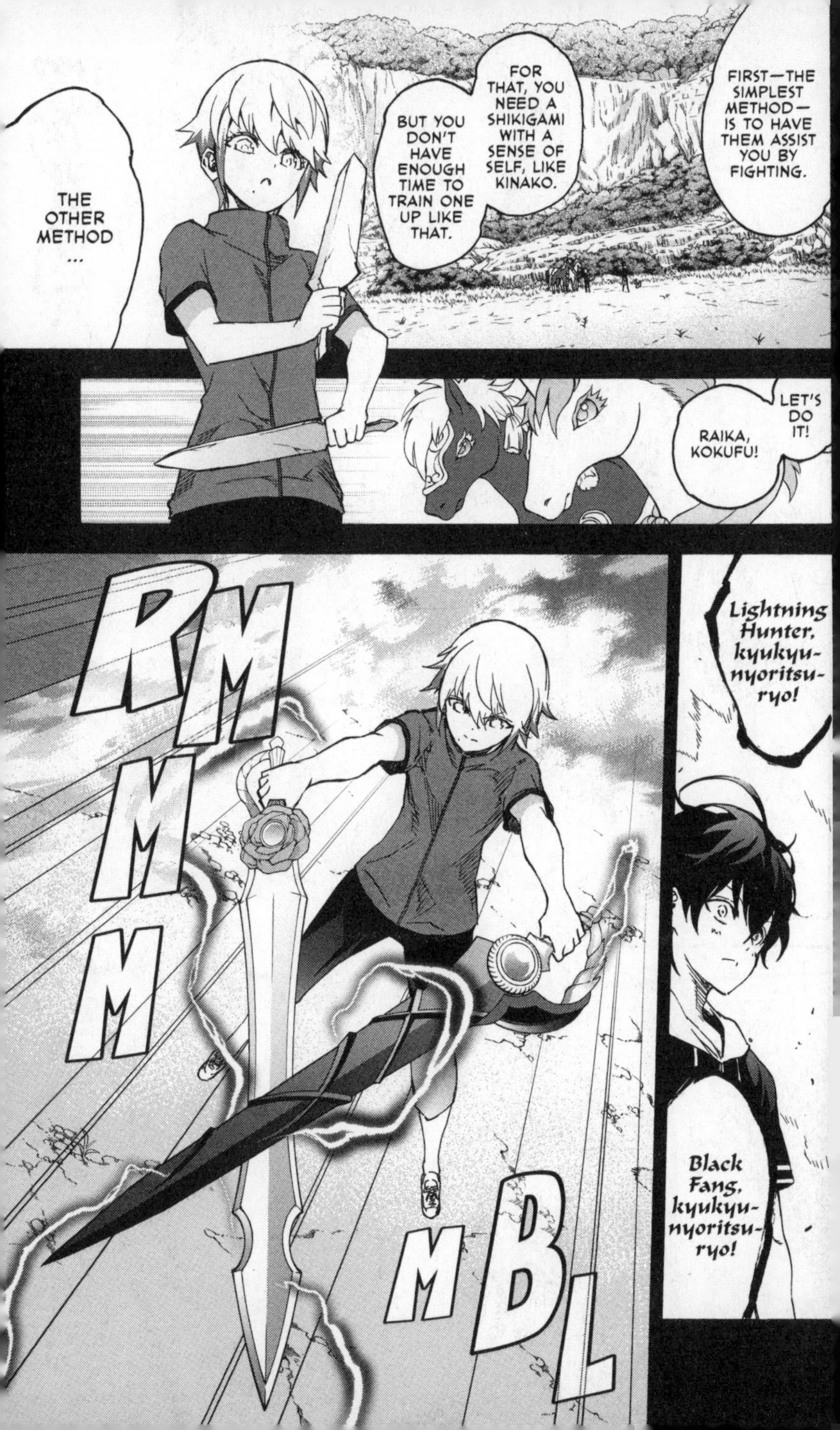

FIRST—THE SIMPLEST METHOD—IS TO HAVE THEM ASSIST YOU BY FIGHTING.
FOR THAT, YOU NEED A SHIKIGAMI WITH A SENSE OF SELF, LIKE KINAKO.
BUT YOU DON'T HAVE ENOUGH TIME TO TRAIN ONE UP LIKE THAT.
THE OTHER METHOD ...
LET'S DO IT!
RAIKA, KOKUFU!
Lightning Hunter, kyukyu-nyoritsu-ryo!
Black Fang, kyukyu-nyoritsu-ryo!
RMMMM
MBL

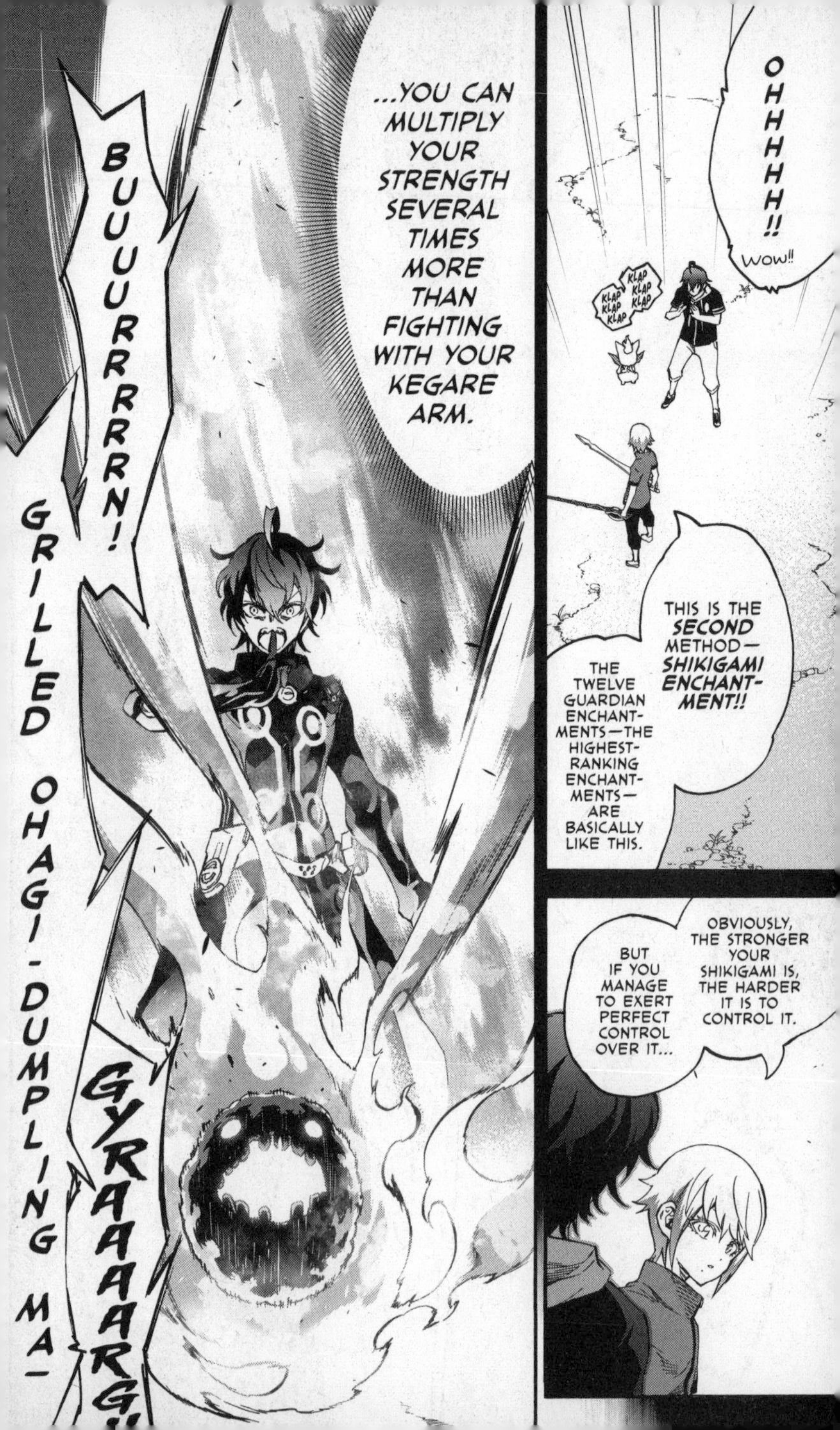
OHHHHH!!
WOW!!
KLAP KLAP KLAP KLAP KLAP KLAP KLAP
THIS IS THE SECOND METHOD—SHIKIGAMI ENCHANTMENT!!
THE TWELVE GUARDIAN ENCHANTMENTS—THE HIGHEST-RANKING ENCHANTMENTS—ARE BASICALLY LIKE THIS.
OBVIOUSLY, THE STRONGER YOUR SHIKIGAMI IS, THE HARDER IT IS TO CONTROL IT.
BUT IF YOU MANAGE TO EXERT PERFECT CONTROL OVER IT...
...YOU CAN MULTIPLY YOUR STRENGTH SEVERAL TIMES MORE THAN FIGHTING WITH YOUR KEGARE ARM.
BUUUURRRRRN!
GRILLED OHAGI-DUMPLING MA-
GYRAAAAARG!!

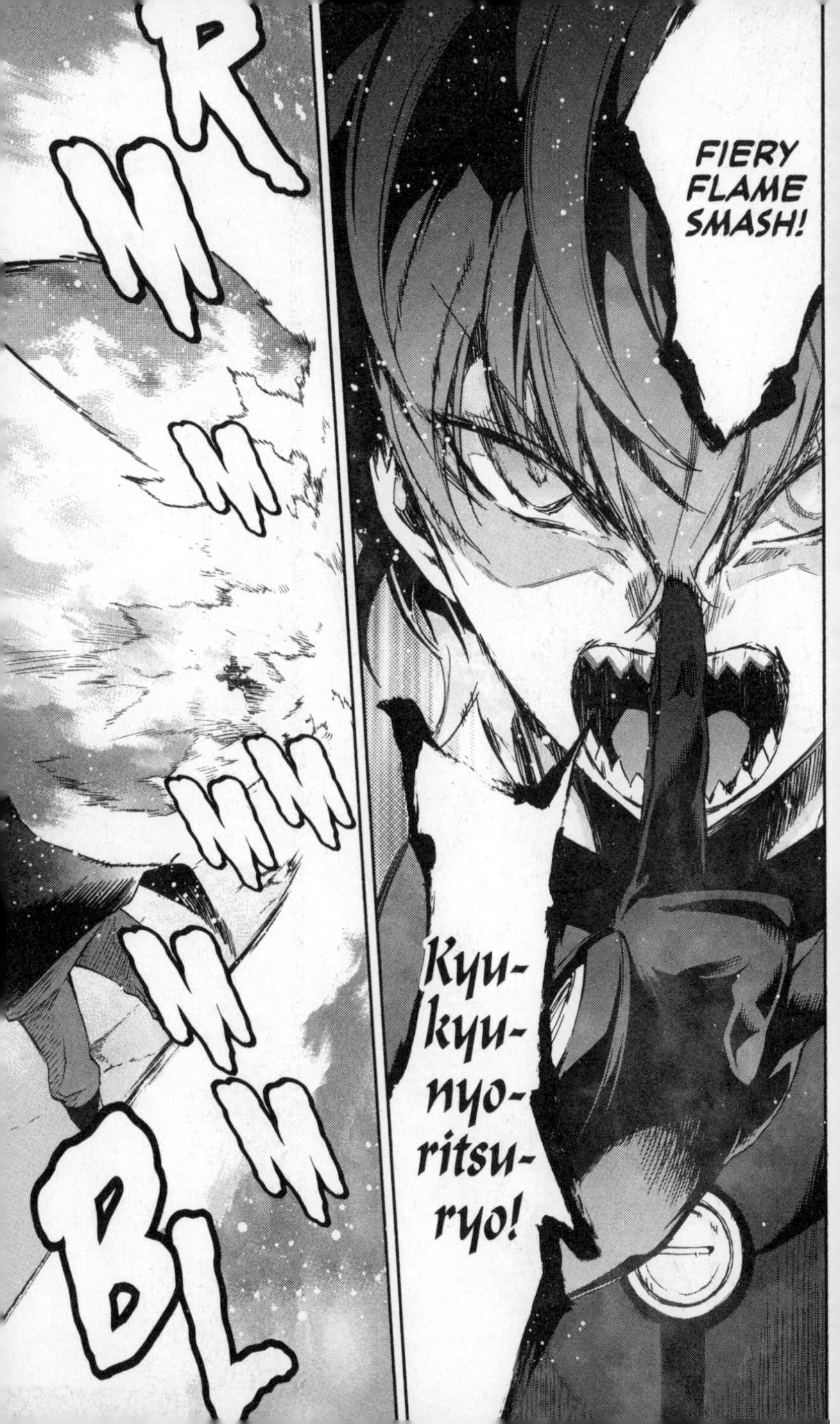
FIERY FLAME SMASH!
Kyu-kyu-nyo-ritsu-ryo!

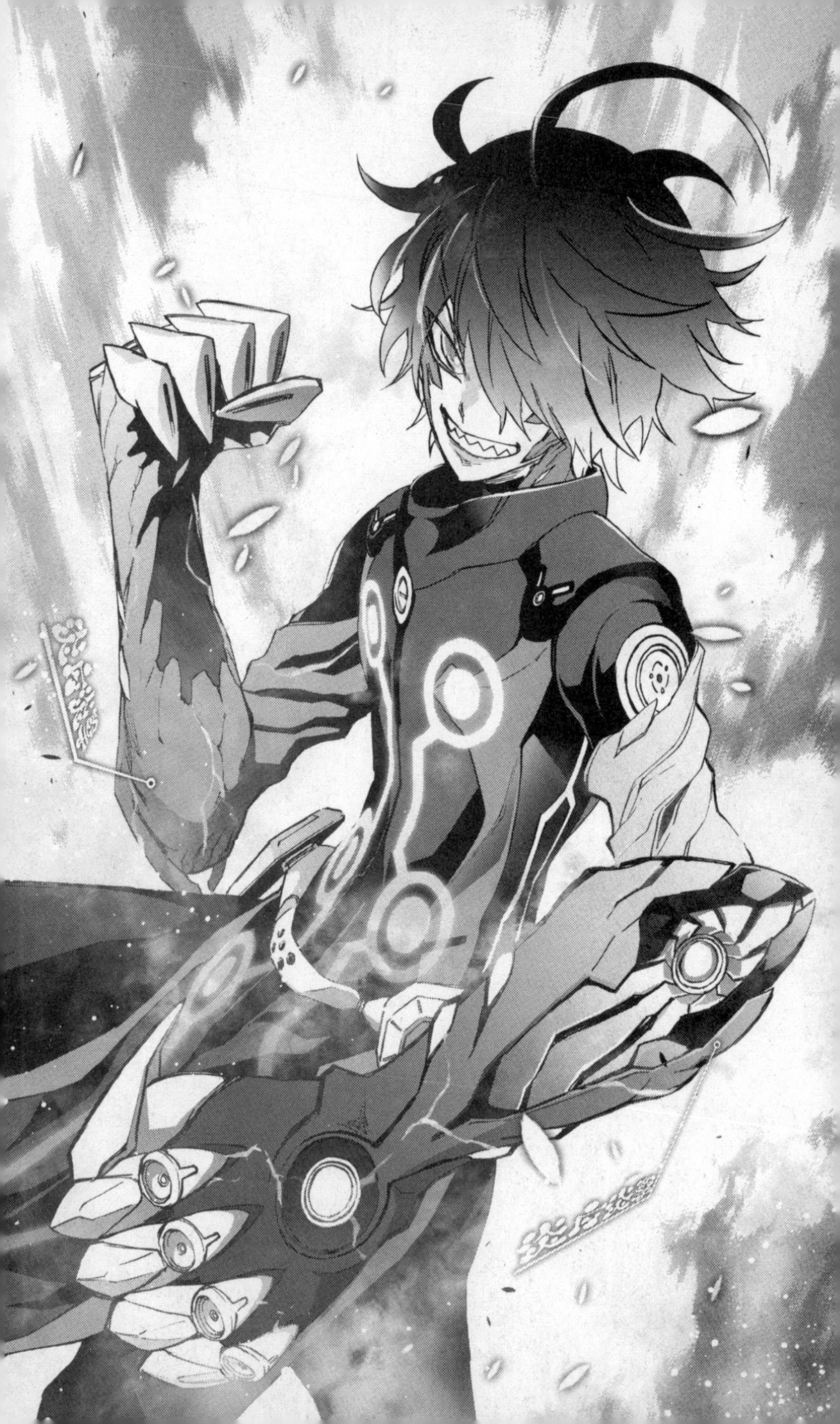

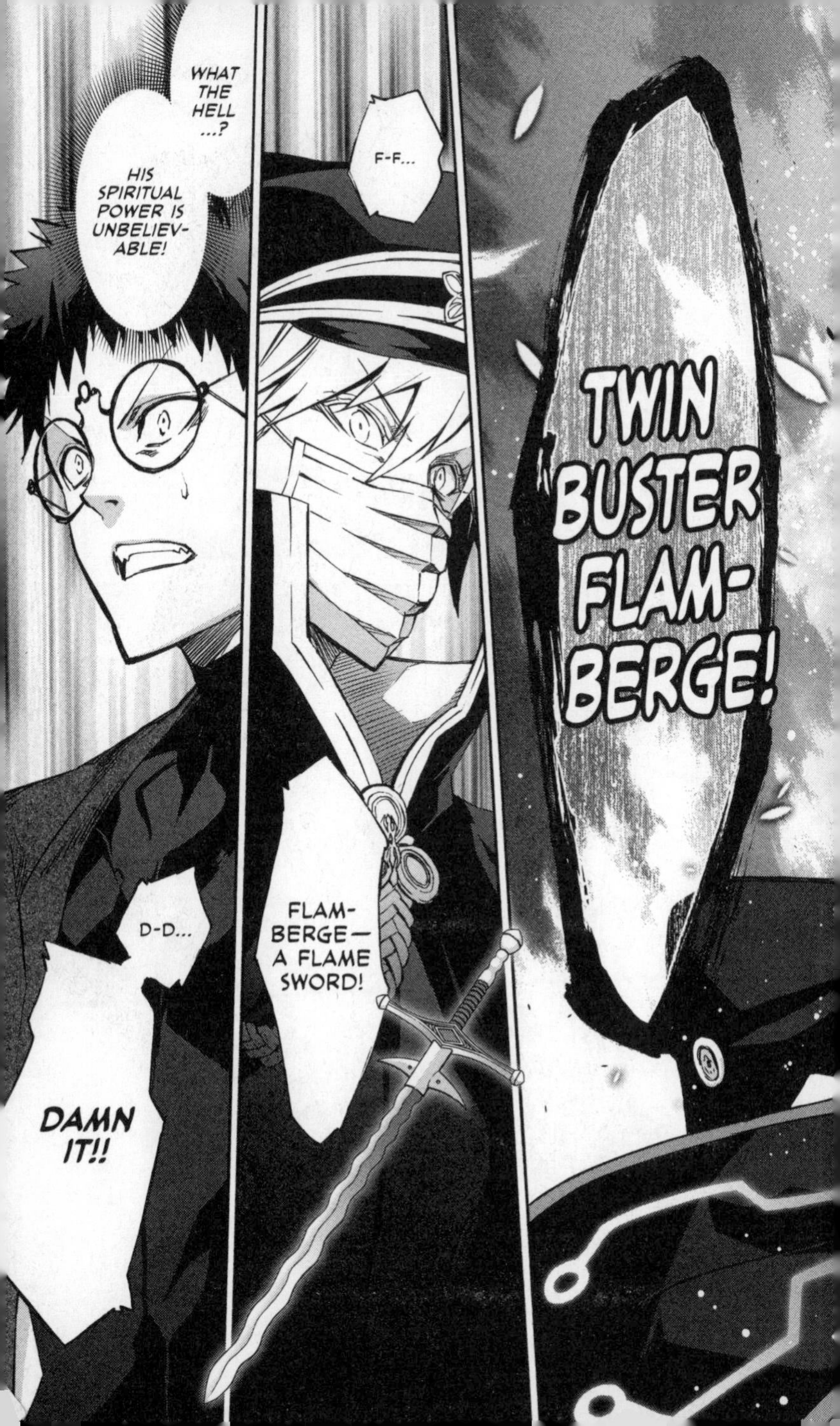
TWIN BUSTER FLAM-BERGE!
F-F...
FLAM-BERGE— A FLAME SWORD!
WHAT THE HELL ...? HIS SPIRITUAL POWER IS UNBELIEV-ABLE!
D-D...
DAMN IT!!

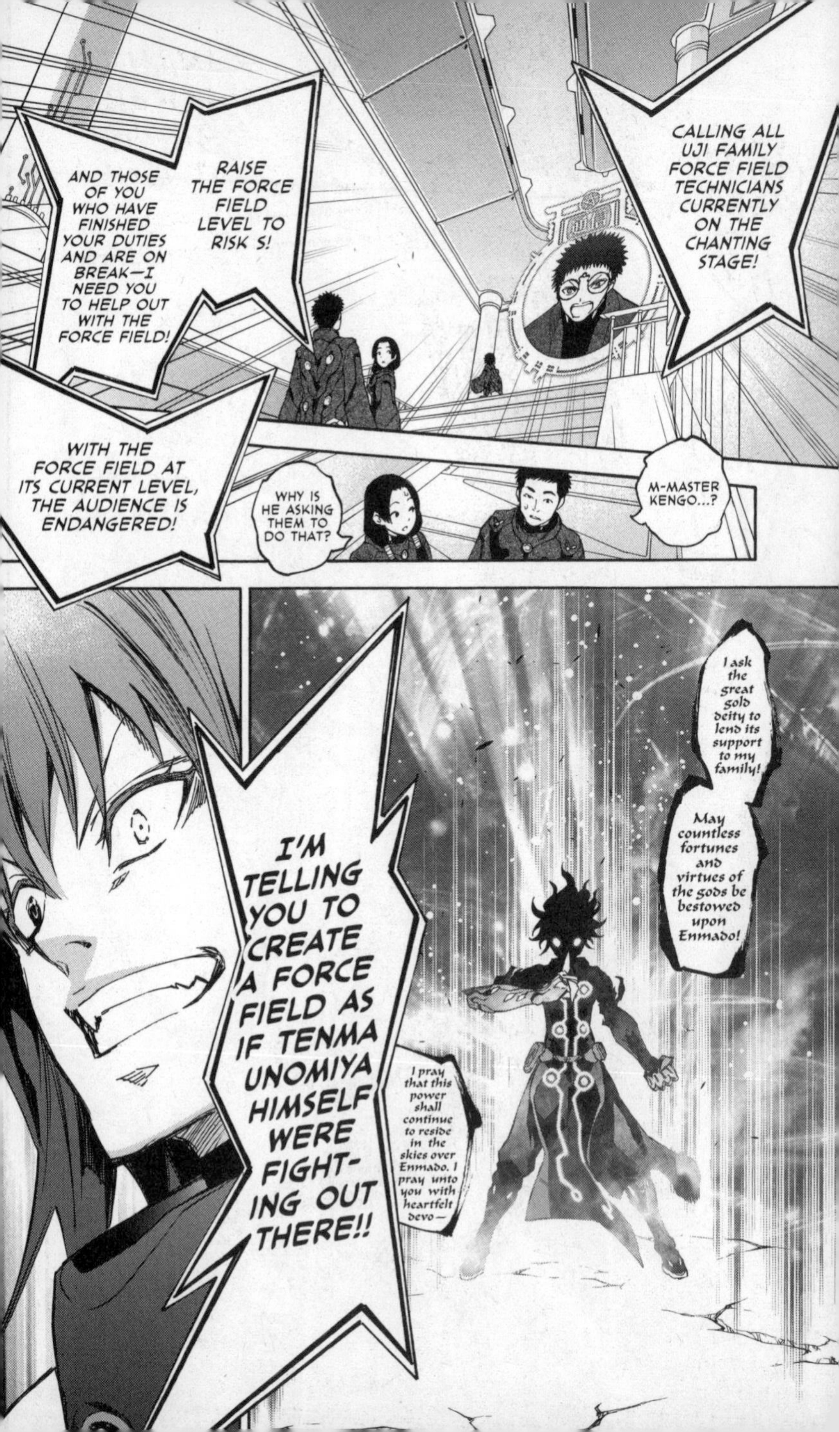
CALLING ALL UJI FAMILY FORCE FIELD TECHNICIANS CURRENTLY ON THE CHANTING STAGE!
RAISE THE FORCE FIELD LEVEL TO RISK 5!
AND THOSE OF YOU WHO HAVE FINISHED YOUR DUTIES AND ARE ON BREAK—I NEED YOU TO HELP OUT WITH THE FORCE FIELD!
WITH THE FORCE FIELD AT ITS CURRENT LEVEL, THE AUDIENCE IS ENDANGERED!
M-MASTER KENGO...?
WHY IS HE ASKING THEM TO DO THAT?
I ask the great gold deity to lend its support to my family!
May countless fortunes and virtues of the gods be bestowed upon Enmado!
I pray that this power shall continue to reside in the skies over Enmado. I pray unto you with heartfelt devo—
I'M TELLING YOU TO CREATE A FORCE FIELD AS IF TENMA UNOMIYA HIMSELF WERE FIGHT-ING OUT THERE!!

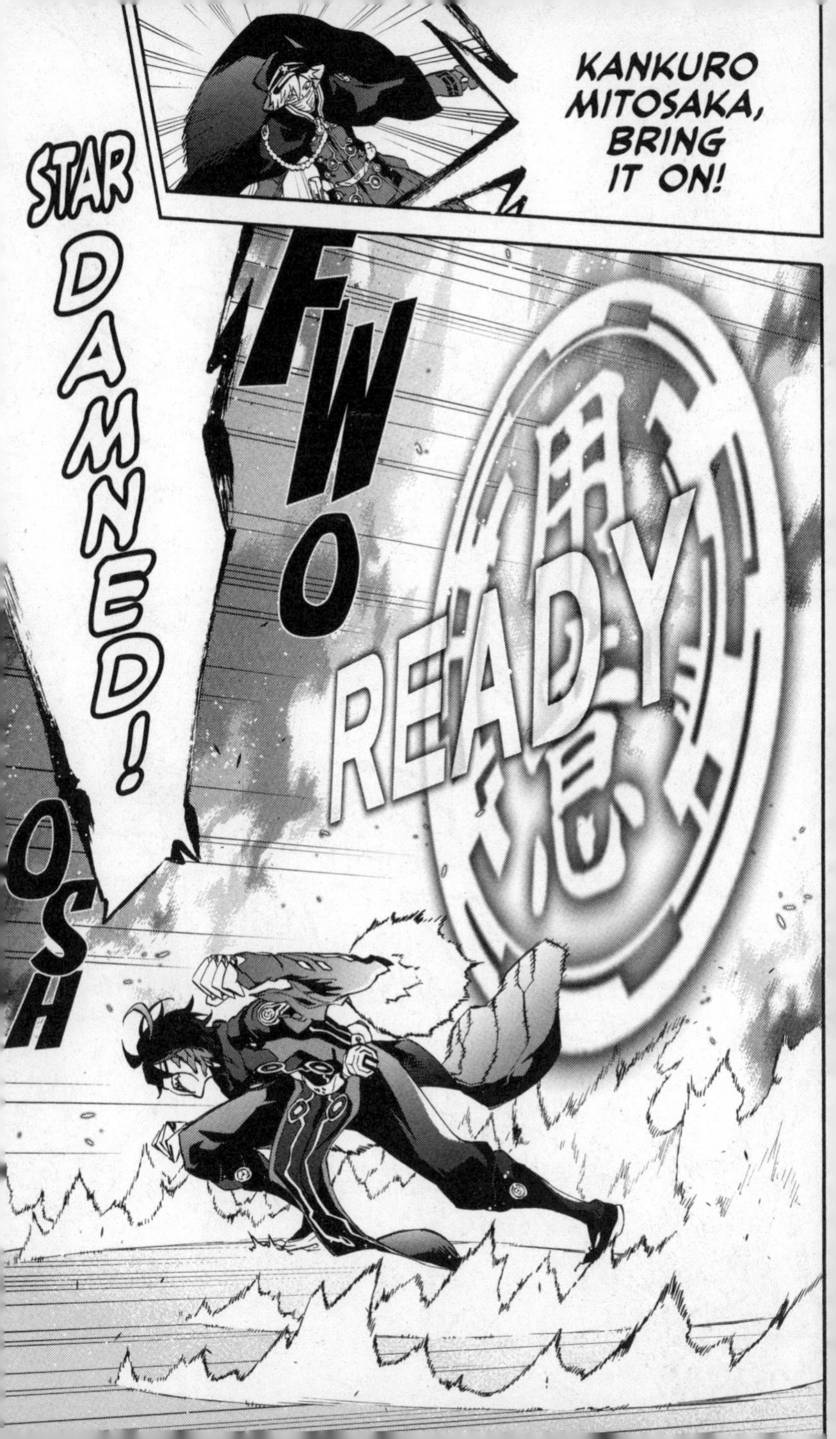
KANKURO MITOSAKA, BRING IT ON!
STAR DAMNED!
FWOOSH
READY

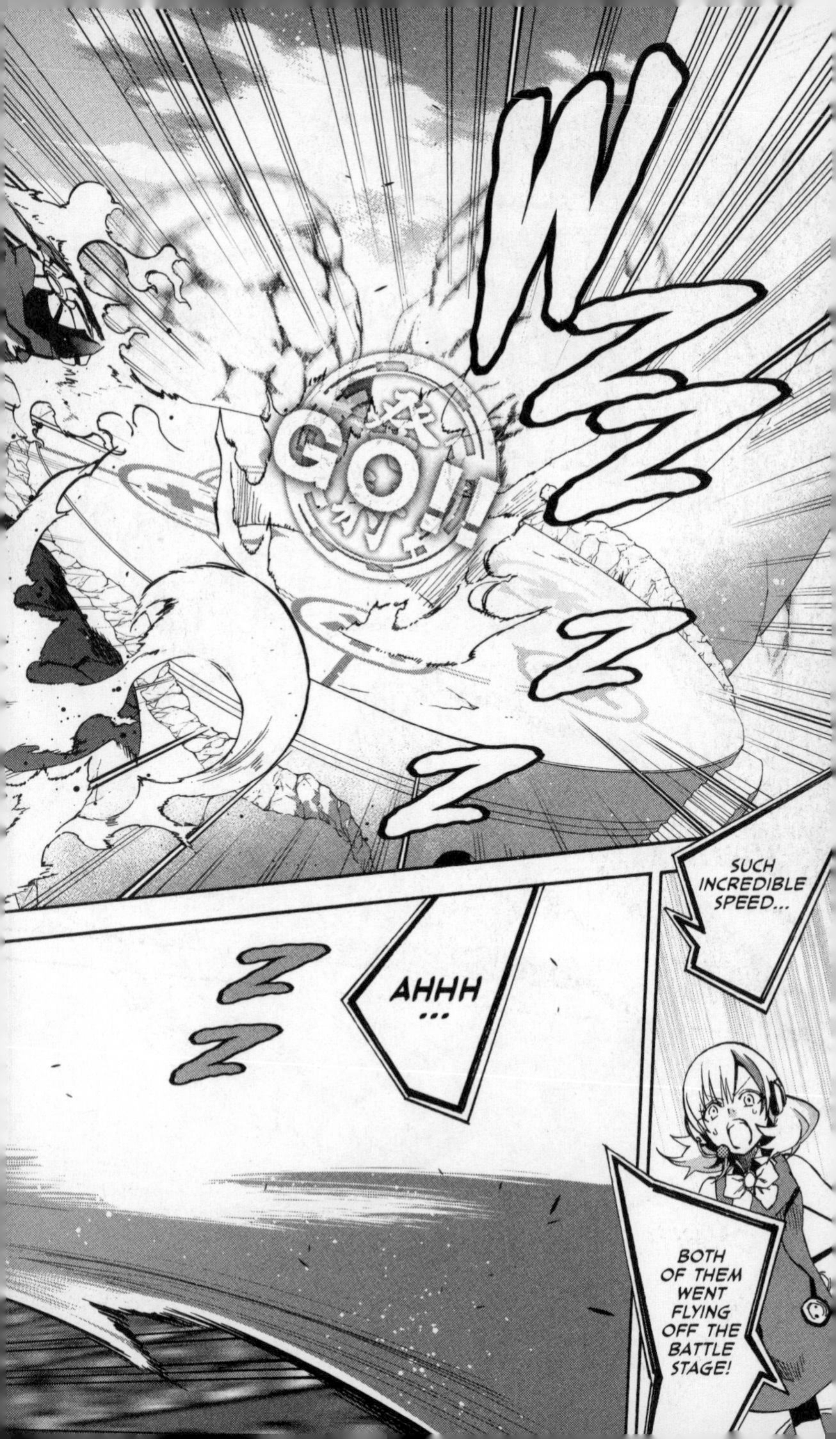
SUCH INCREDIBLE SPEED...
AHHH...
BOTH OF THEM WENT FLYING OFF THE BATTLE STAGE!

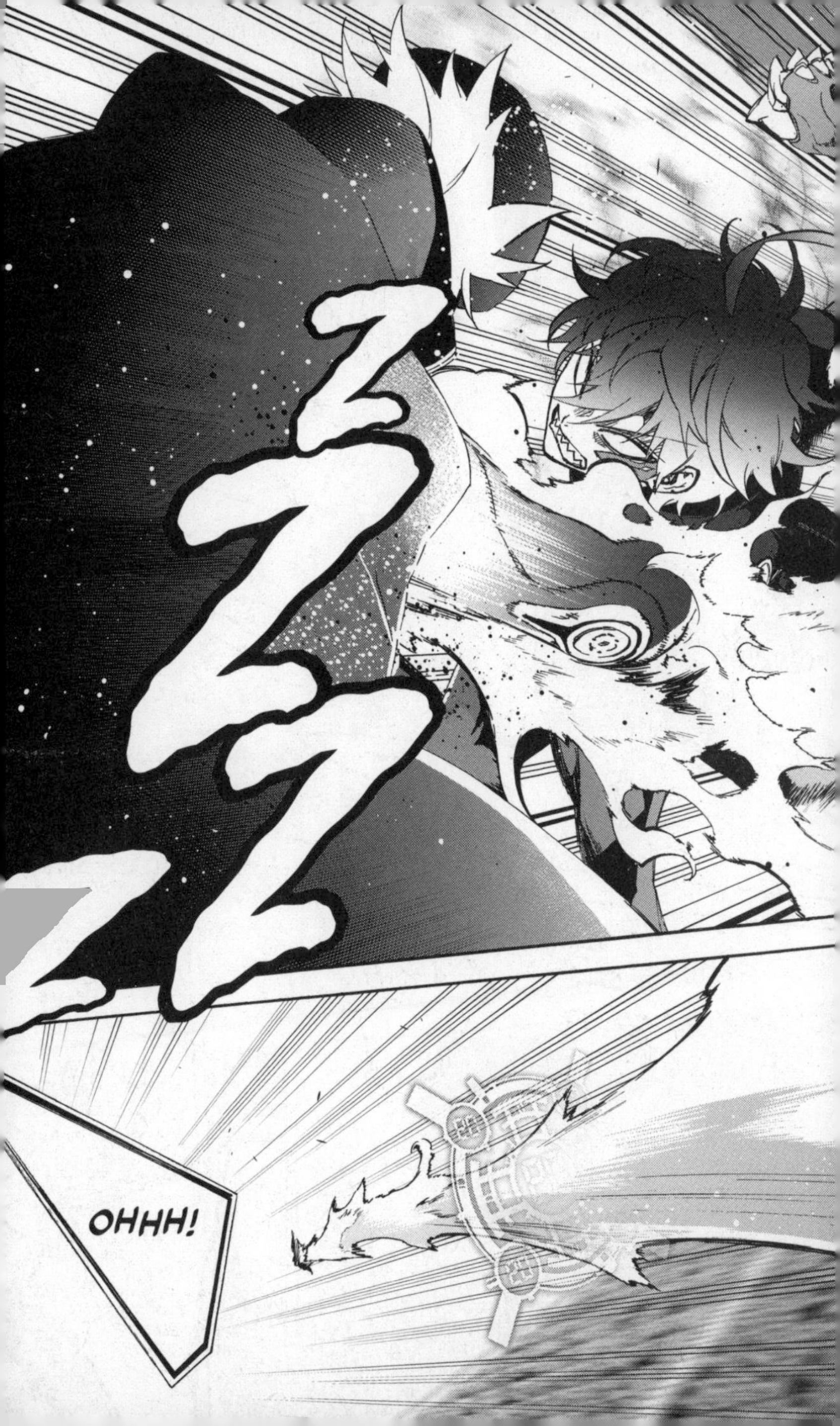
OHHH!

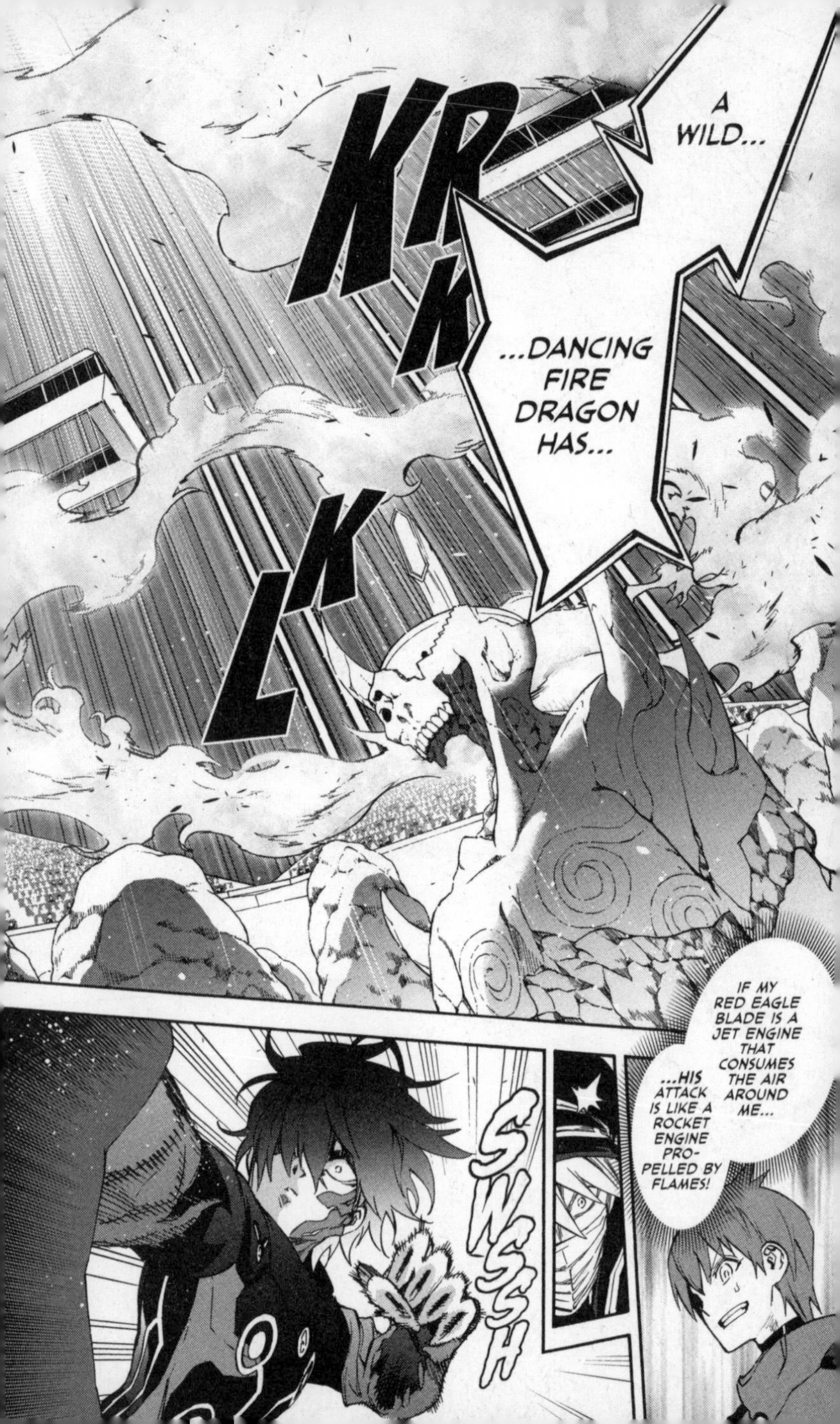
A WILD...
...DANCING FIRE DRAGON HAS...
KRK
KLK
IF MY RED EAGLE BLADE IS A JET ENGINE THAT CONSUMES THE AIR AROUND ME...
...HIS ATTACK IS LIKE A ROCKET ENGINE PRO-PELLED BY FLAMES!
SWSSH

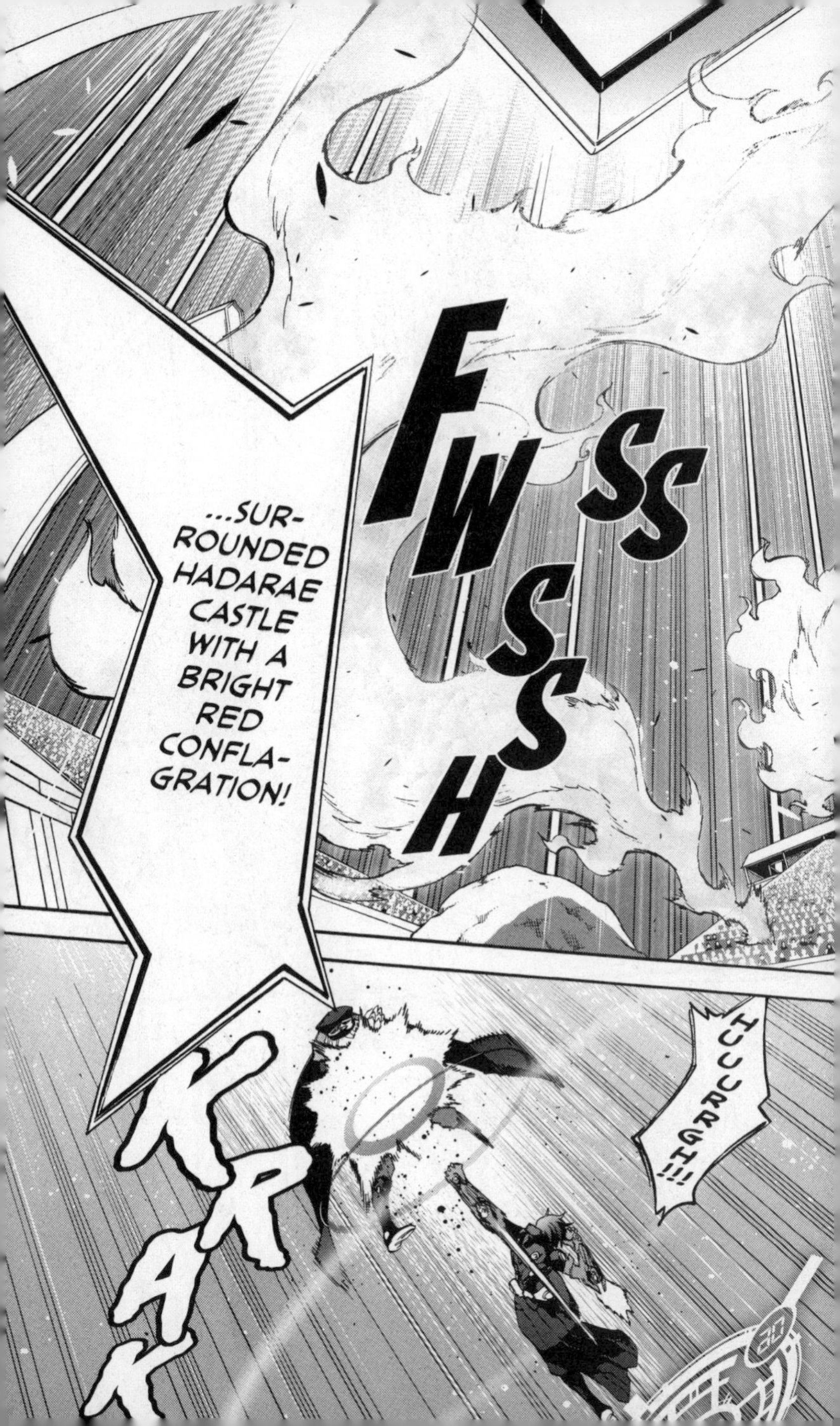
FWSSSSH
...SUR-ROUNDED HADARAE CASTLE WITH A BRIGHT RED CONFLA-GRATION!
HUURRGH!!!
KRAK

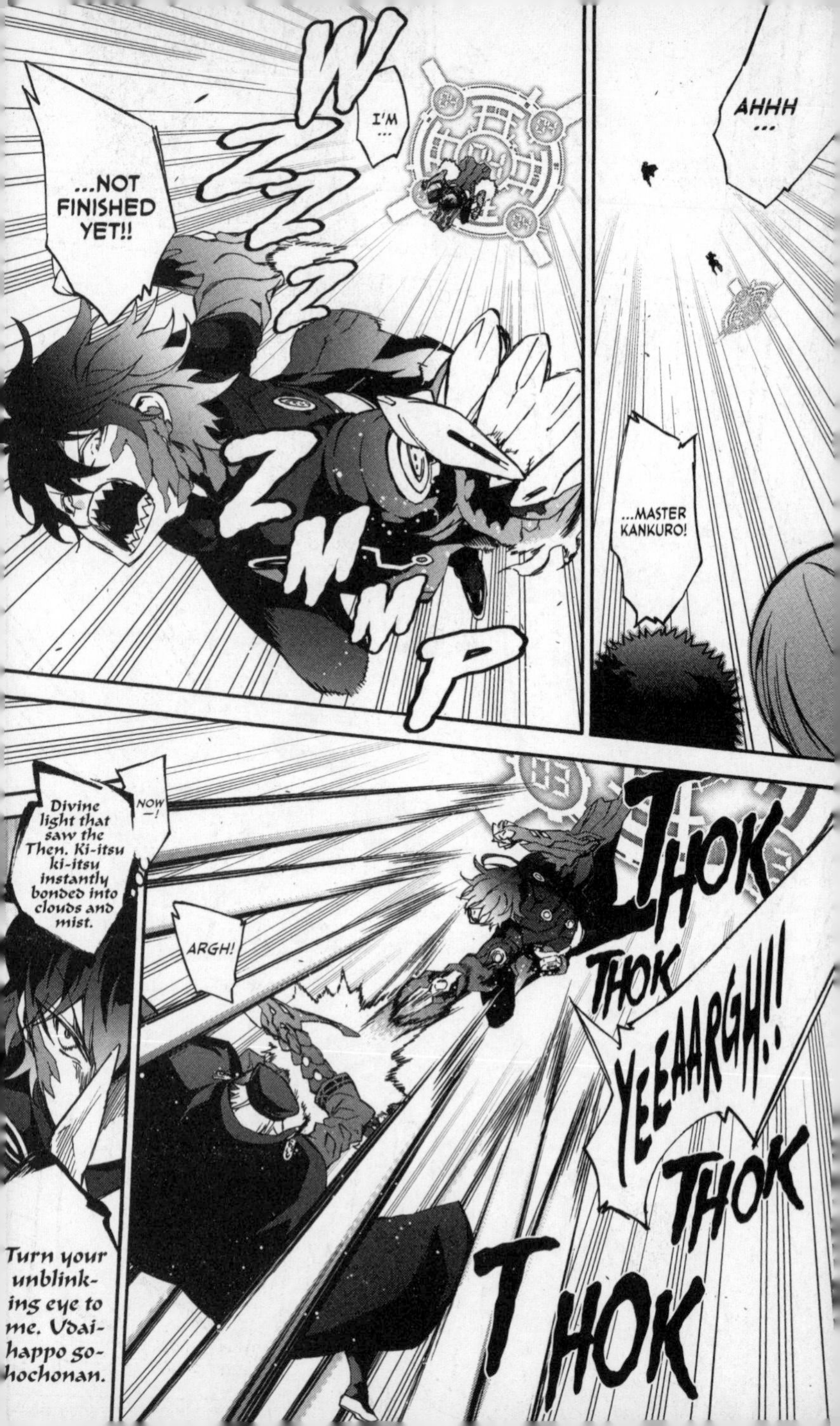
AHHH ...
...MASTER KANKURO!
I'M ...
...NOT FINISHED YET!!
THOK
THOK
YEEAARGH!!
THOK
THOK
NOW—!
Divine light that saw the Then. Ki-itsu ki-itsu instantly bonded into clouds and mist.
ARGH!
Turn your unblinking eye to me. Udai-happo go-hochonan.

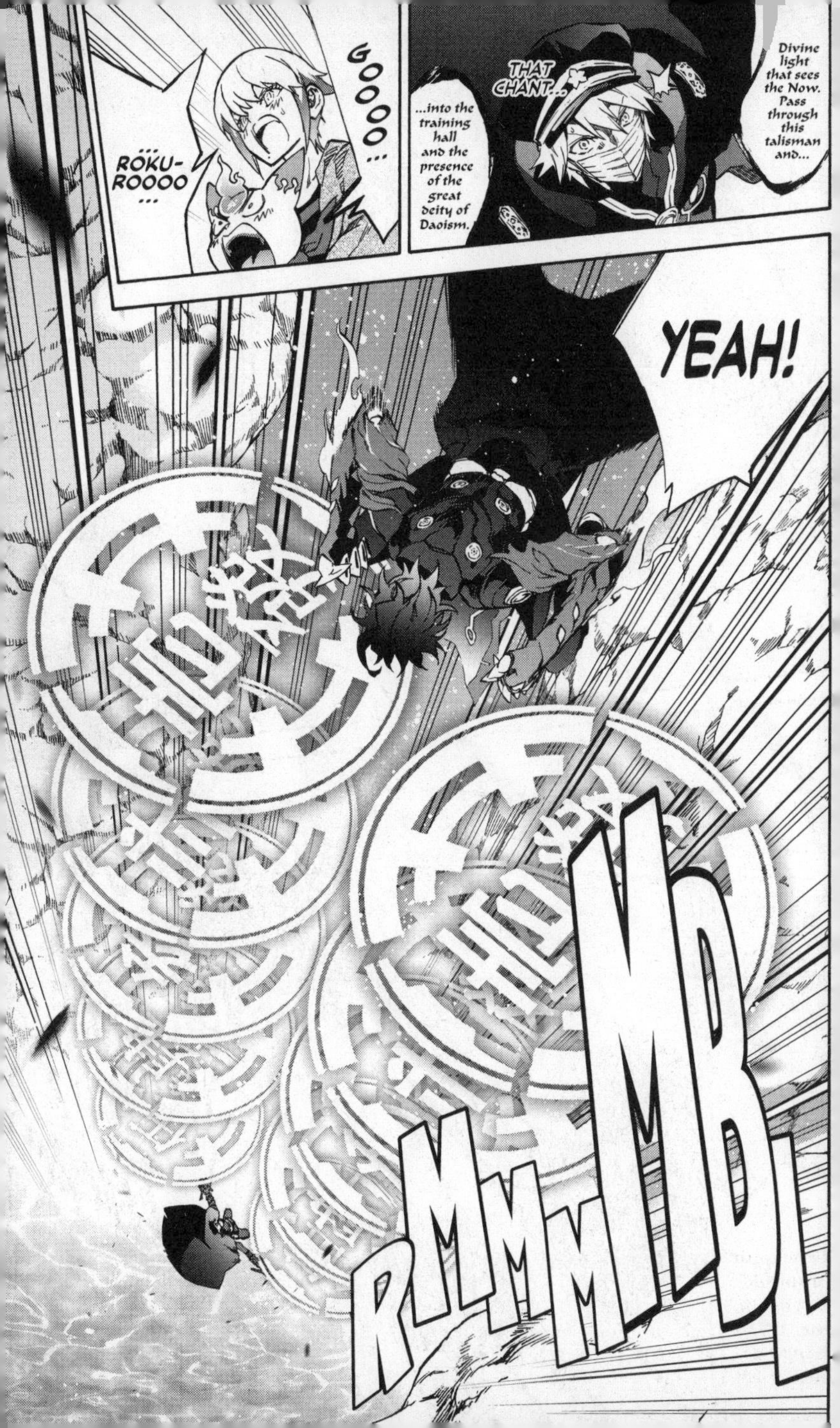
Divine light that sees the Now. Pass through this talisman and...
THAT CHANT...
...into the training hall and the presence of the great deity of Daoism.
GOOOOO...
...RÖKU-ROOOO...
YEAH!
RMMMMMBL

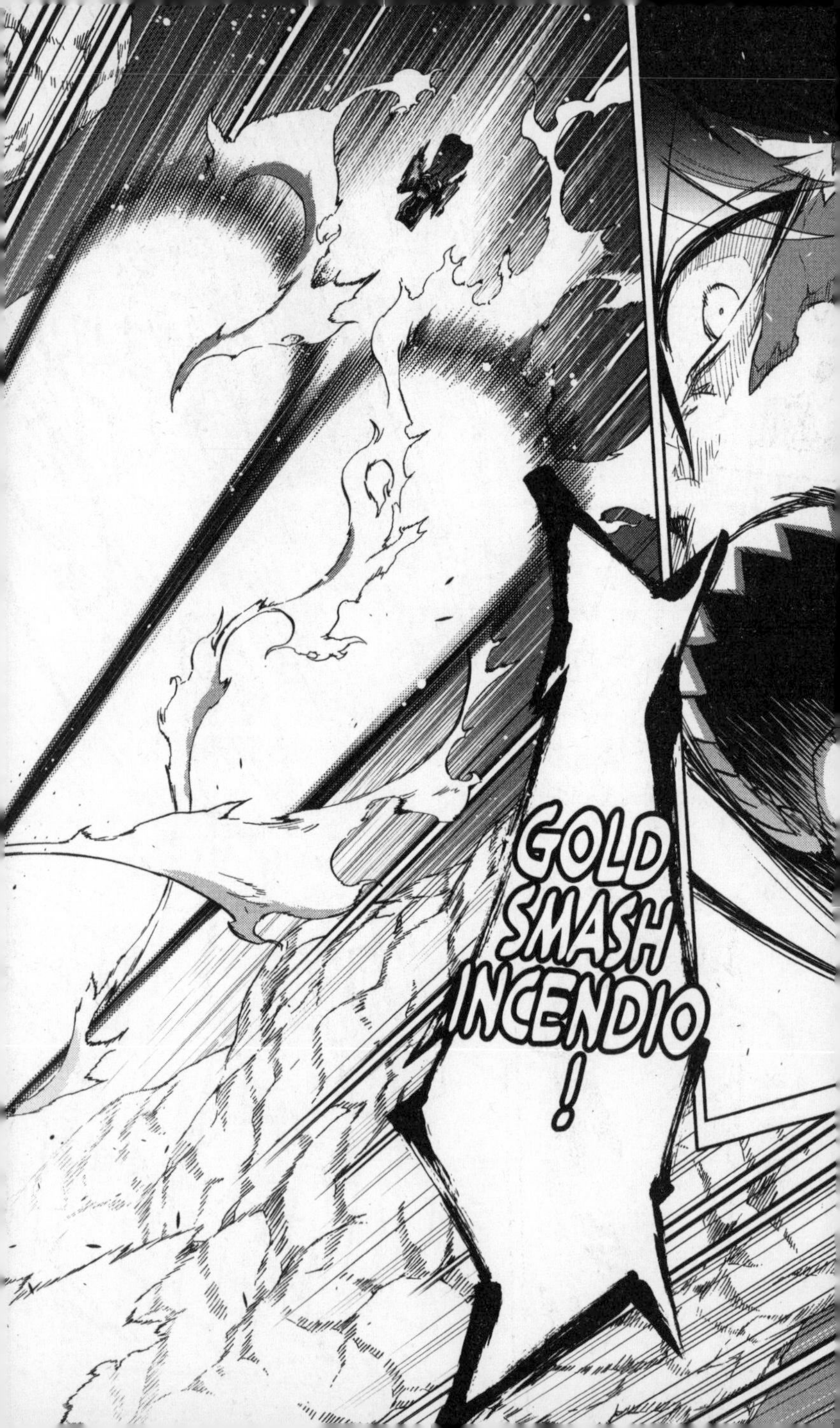
GOLD SMASH INCENDIO!

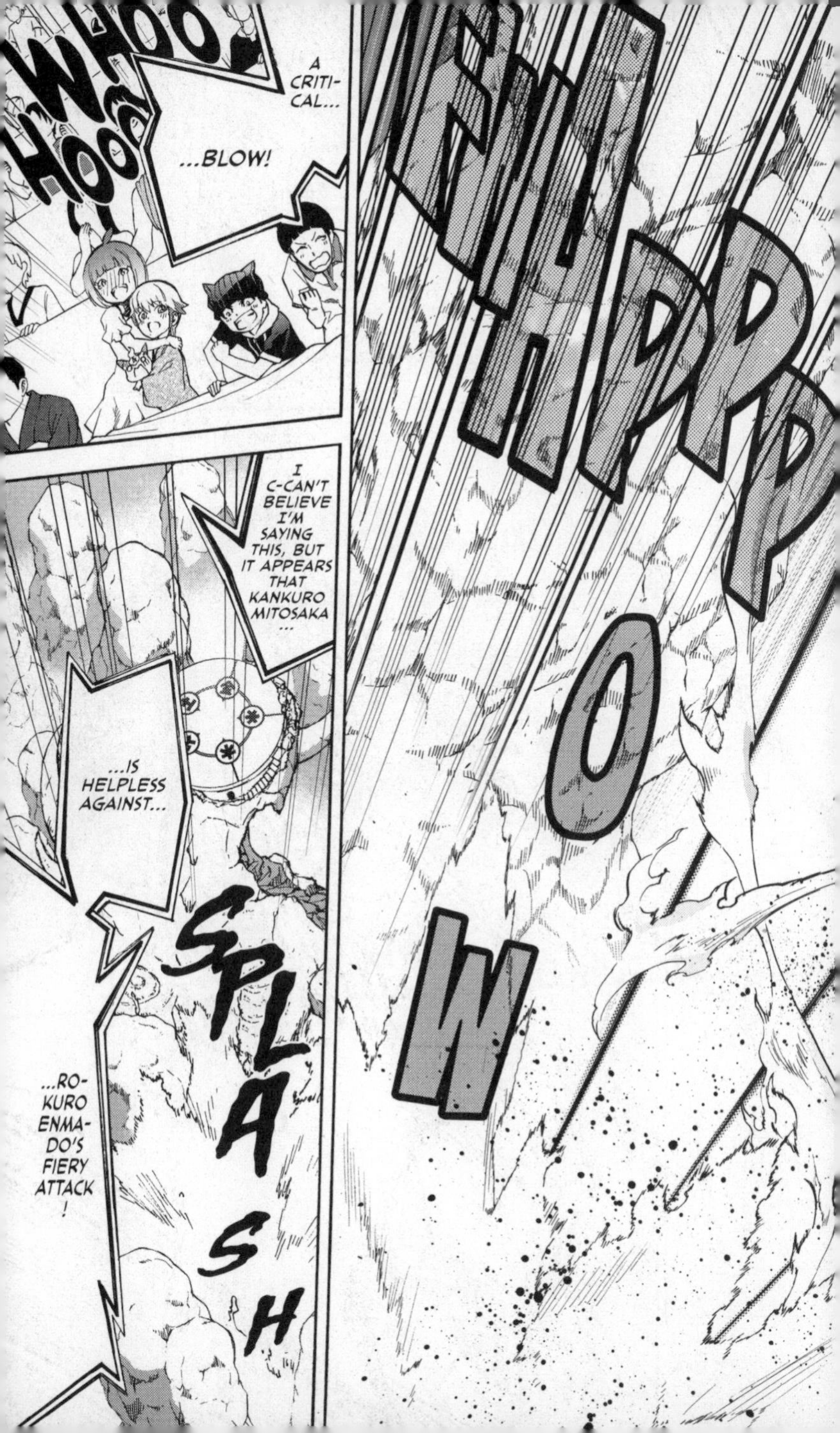
A CRITICAL...
...BLOW!
WHOO HOO!
I C-CAN'T BELIEVE I'M SAYING THIS, BUT IT APPEARS THAT KANKURO MITOSAKA...
...IS HELPLESS AGAINST...
SPLASH
...ROKURO ENMADO'S FIERY ATTACK!

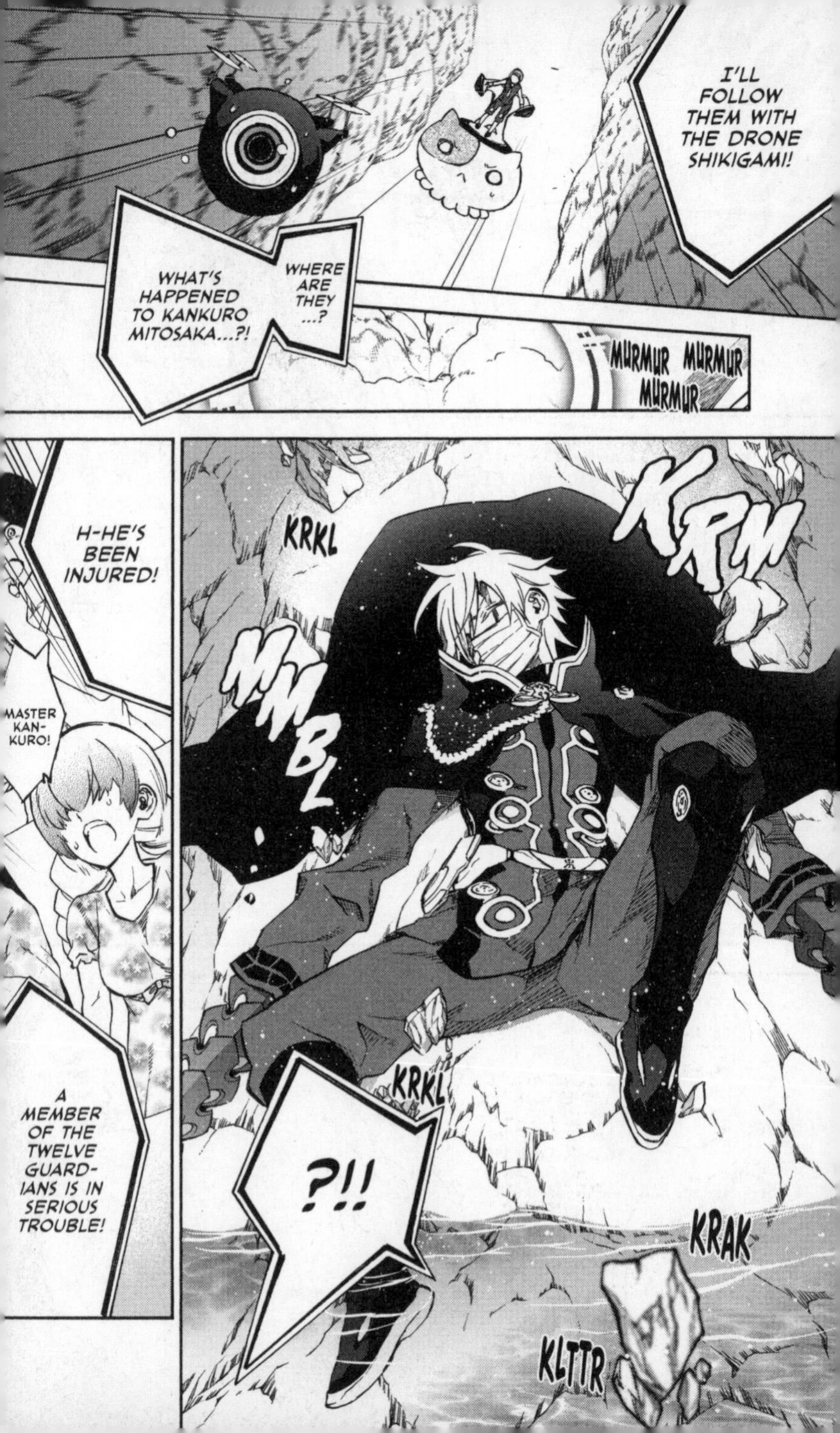
I'LL FOLLOW THEM WITH THE DRONE SHIKIGAMI!
MURMUR MURMUR MURMUR
WHERE ARE THEY ...?
WHAT'S HAPPENED TO KANKURO MITOSAKA...?!
KRPM
KRKL
MMBL
KRKL
?!!
KRAK
KLTTR
H-HE'S BEEN INJURED!
MASTER KAN-KURO!
A MEMBER OF THE TWELVE GUARD-IANS IS IN SERIOUS TROUBLE!

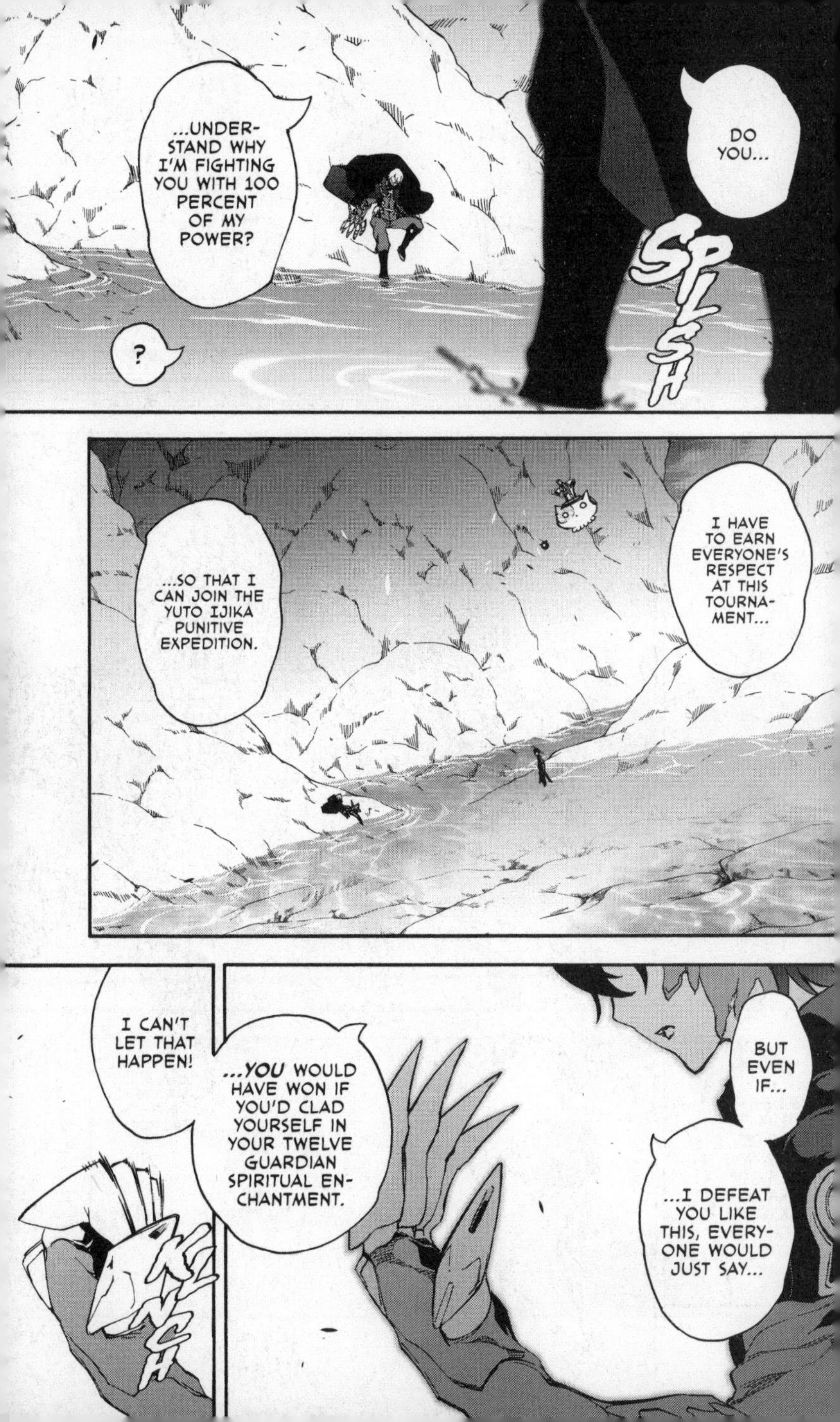
DO YOU...
SPLSH
...UNDERSTAND WHY I'M FIGHTING YOU WITH 100 PERCENT OF MY POWER?
?
I HAVE TO EARN EVERYONE'S RESPECT AT THIS TOURNAMENT...
...SO THAT I CAN JOIN THE YUTO IJIKA PUNITIVE EXPEDITION.
BUT EVEN IF...
...I DEFEAT YOU LIKE THIS, EVERYONE WOULD JUST SAY...
...*YOU* WOULD HAVE WON IF YOU'D CLAD YOURSELF IN YOUR TWELVE GUARDIAN SPIRITUAL ENCHANTMENT.
I CAN'T LET THAT HAPPEN!

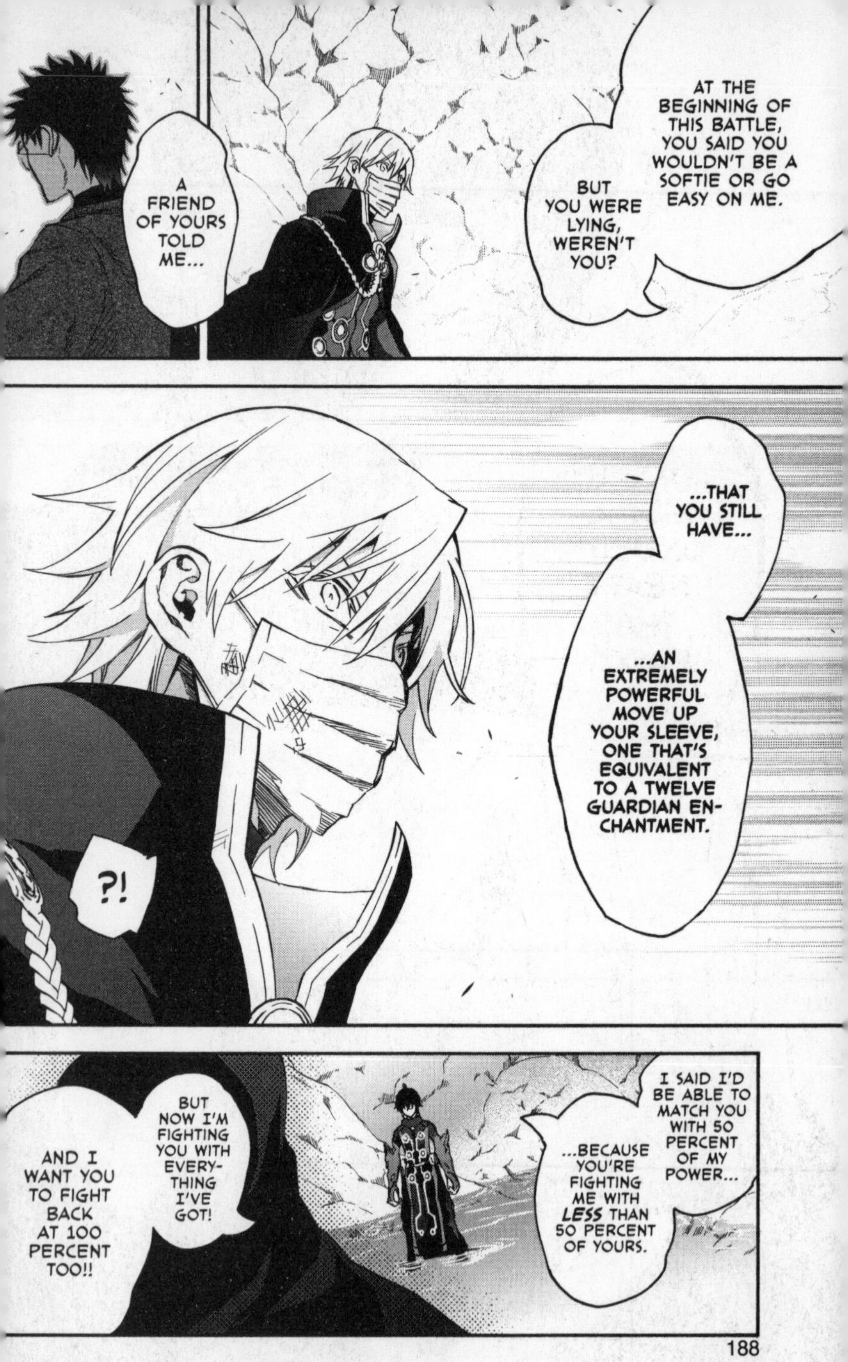
AT THE BEGINNING OF THIS BATTLE, YOU SAID YOU WOULDN'T BE A SOFTIE OR GO EASY ON ME.
BUT YOU WERE LYING, WEREN'T YOU?
A FRIEND OF YOURS TOLD ME...
...THAT YOU STILL HAVE...
...AN EXTREMELY POWERFUL MOVE UP YOUR SLEEVE, ONE THAT'S EQUIVALENT TO A TWELVE GUARDIAN EN-CHANTMENT.
?!
I SAID I'D BE ABLE TO MATCH YOU WITH 50 PERCENT OF MY POWER...
...BECAUSE YOU'RE FIGHTING ME WITH *LESS* THAN 50 PERCENT OF YOURS.
BUT NOW I'M FIGHTING YOU WITH EVERY-THING I'VE GOT!
AND I WANT YOU TO FIGHT BACK AT 100 PERCENT TOO!!

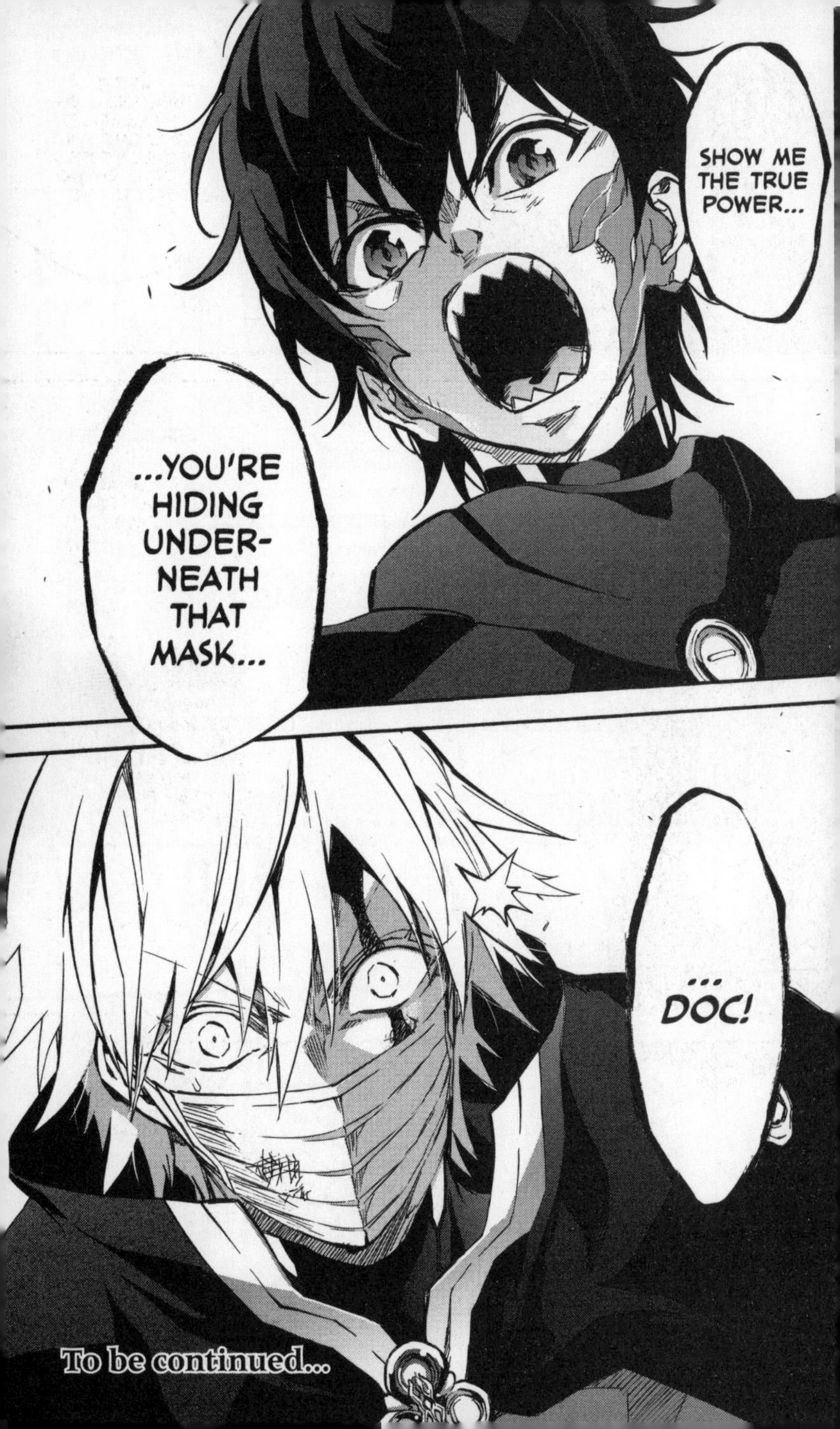
SHOW ME THE TRUE POWER...
...YOU'RE HIDING UNDER-NEATH THAT MASK...
...DOC!
To be continued...

Q Q nyoritsuryo!

Question Corner

Q How many headphones does Shimon have? (From Kuroshio Popcorn)

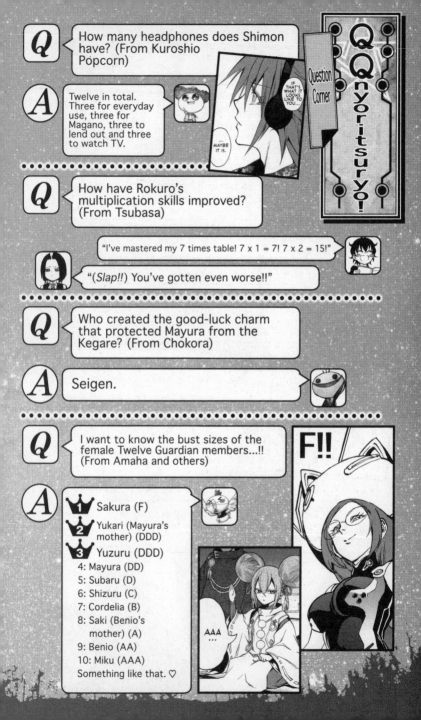

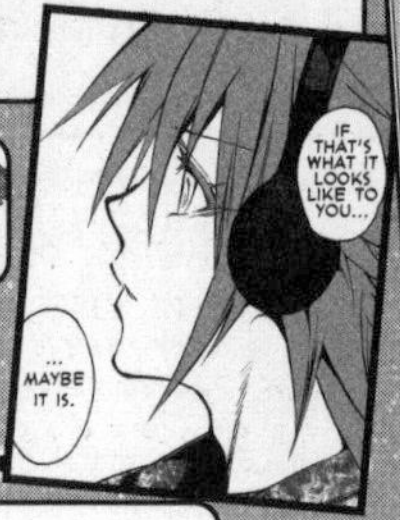
IF THAT'S WHAT IT LOOKS LIKE TO YOU...
...MAYBE IT IS.

A Twelve in total. Three for everyday use, three for Magano, three to lend out and three to watch TV.

Q How have Rokuro's multiplication skills improved? (From Tsubasa)

"I've mastered my 7 times table! 7 x 1 = 7! 7 x 2 = 15!"

"(*Slap!!*) You've gotten even worse!!"

Q Who created the good-luck charm that protected Mayura from the Kegare? (From Chokora)

A Seigen.

Q I want to know the bust sizes of the female Twelve Guardian members...!! (From Amaha and others)

A

1. Sakura (F)
2. Yukari (Mayura's mother) (DDD)
3. Yuzuru (DDD)

4: Mayura (DD)
5: Subaru (D)
6: Shizuru (C)
7: Cordelia (B)
8: Saki (Benio's mother) (A)
9: Benio (AA)
10: Miku (AAA)

Something like that. ♡

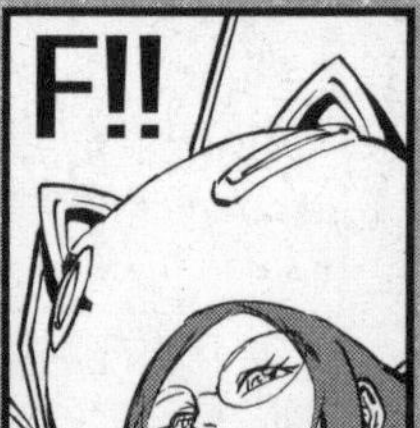
F!!

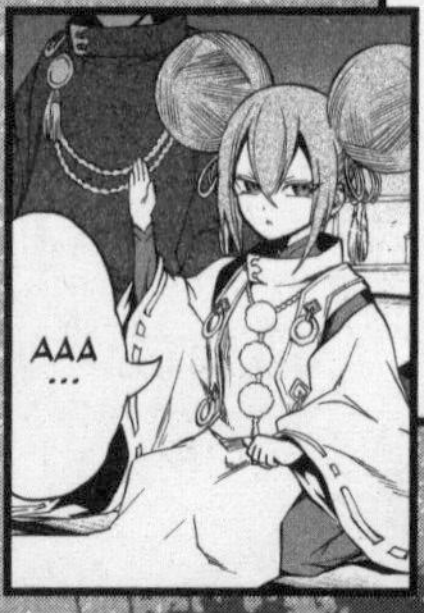
AAA...

Q When did Arata Inanaki become an otaku? (From Maki)

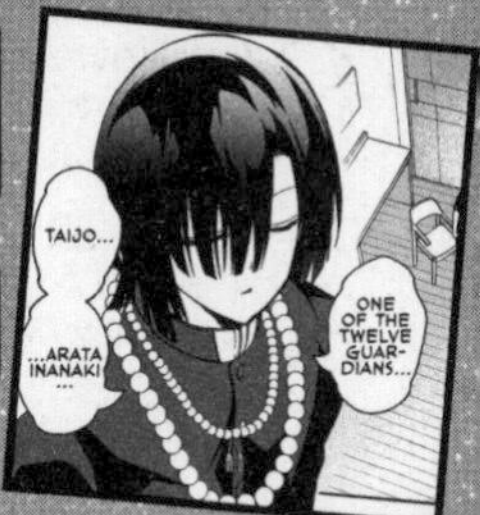
TAIJO...
ONE OF THE TWELVE GUARDIANS...
...ARATA INANAKI...

A When he was 14 years old. It all started when he accompanied Arima's father, the former Chief Exorcist, to the mainland with Arima.

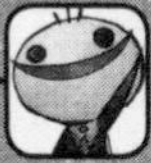

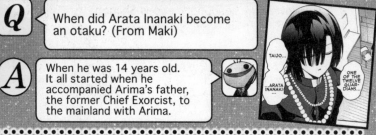

Q Do Basara catch the flu and other illnesses like people? (From Shiren Mama)

A They don't as long as they are Kegare or Basara.

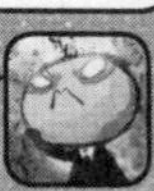

Q How many Force Field technicians from the Uji Family are there in each group? And how long is their shift before they switch out with the next group? Do the Force Field technicians go to Magano to exorcise Kegare? (From Ryosei)

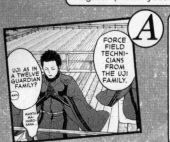

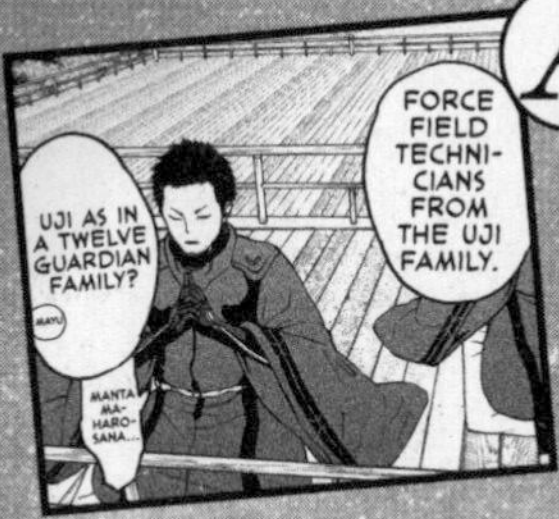
FORCE FIELD TECHNICIANS FROM THE UJI FAMILY.
UJI AS IN A TWELVE GUARDIAN FAMILY?
MAYU
MANTA MA-HARO-SANA...

A There are roughly 60 elite exorcists who work four days a week (two days of an early shift and two days of a late shift). Six groups of three are stationed at the platform. Two groups chant for an hour to keep the force field up, and then they rest for two hours. They go through basic combat training, but force field technicians rarely enter Magano. Experts stick to what they do best.

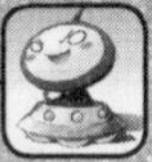

Q I personally would love to find out the nicknames Tenma has given to the Twelve Guardian members. (From Lily)

- Arima ➜ Pervy Specs
- Seigen ➜ Bear Dude
- Narumi ➜ Macho Man
- Tatara ➜ Emoticon Man
- Cordelia ➜ Mecha Girl
- Sakura ➜ Knockers
- Rokuro ➜ Shrimp
- Benio ➜ Pancake Girl
- Shizuru ➜ Macho Girl
- Shimon ➜ Bird Boy
- Arata ➜ Otaku
- Subaru ➜ Madam
- Kankuro ➜ Doc
- Kengo ➜ Miser
- Miku ➜ Loliyo
- Mayura ➜ Boob Girl
- Alice ➜ Junior

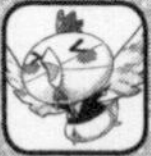

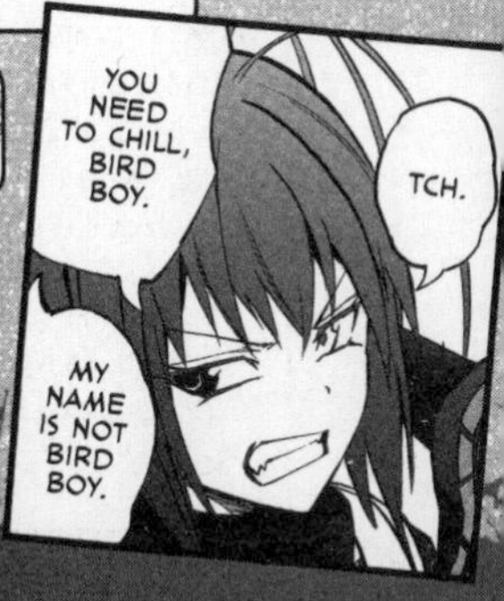
TCH.
YOU NEED TO CHILL, BIRD BOY.
MY NAME IS NOT BIRD BOY.

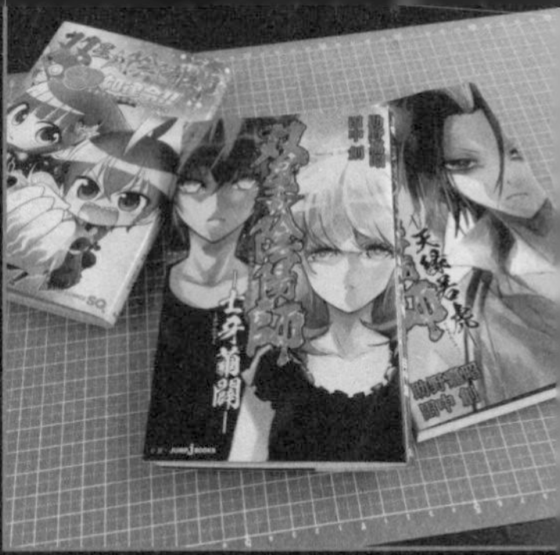

I'd like to introduce three spin-off w
that expand the world of *Twin Star* even
the novels *Heavenly Bond of the White Tig*
The Fang Honing of Shimon and Mayura,
the four-panel comic *SD Nyoritsuryo*! Th
all official spin-offs created through in-
meetings with the authors.

The novels include stories about Mayura
up until the tournament and the backstor
Amawaka family. You won't have any t
following the manga without reading th
if you do, you'll get to know the characte
and will like them even more...proba

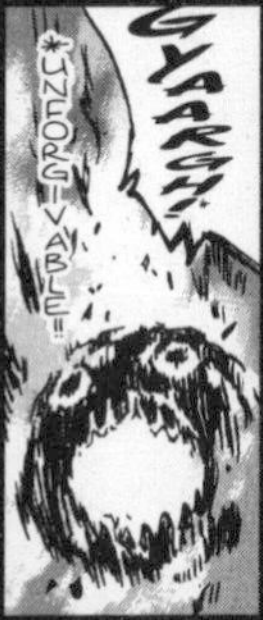
GYAARGH!
*UNFORGIVABLE!!

YOSHIAKI SUKENO was born July 23, 1981, in Wak
He graduated from Kyoto Seika University, where he s
In 2006, he won the Tezuka Award for Best Newcomer
Artist. In 2008, he began his previous work, the super
Binbougami ga!, which was adapted into the anime *Good L*

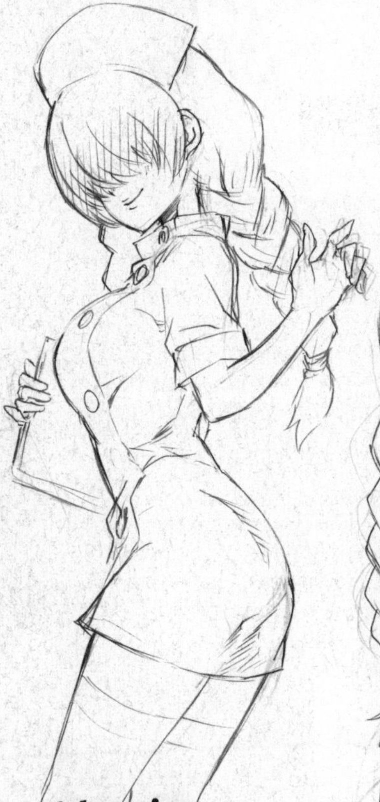

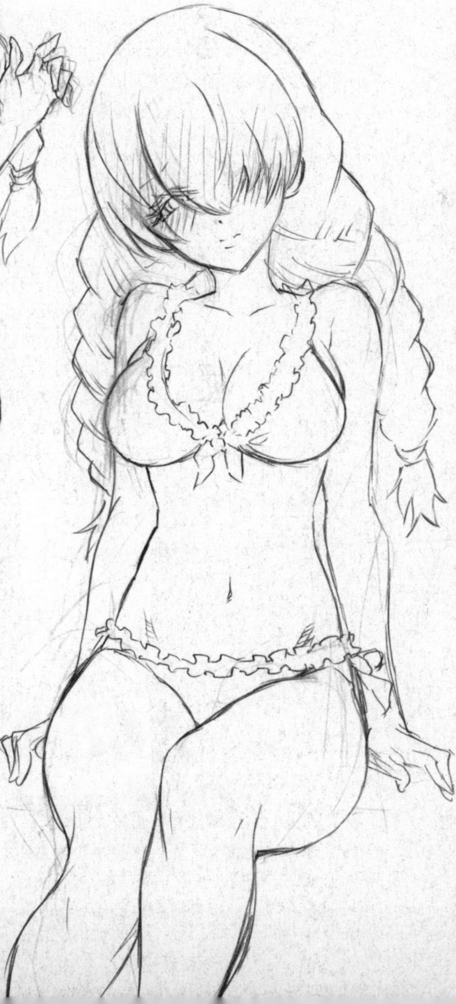

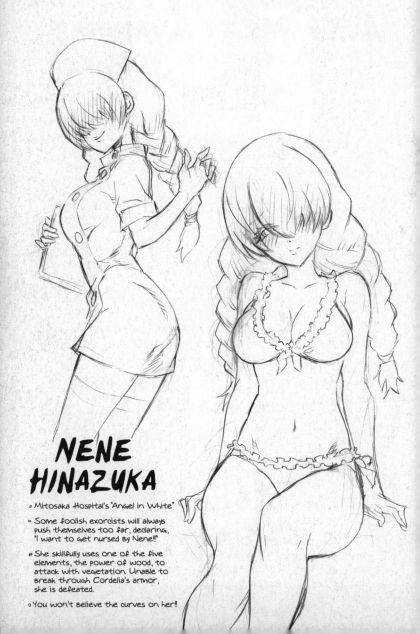

NENE HINAZUKA

- Mitosaka Hospital's "Angel in White"
- Some foolish exorcists will always push themselves too far, declaring, "I want to get nursed by Nene!!"
- She skillfully uses one of the five elements, the power of wood, to attack with vegetation. Unable to break through Cordelia's armor, she is defeated.
- You won't believe the curves on her!!

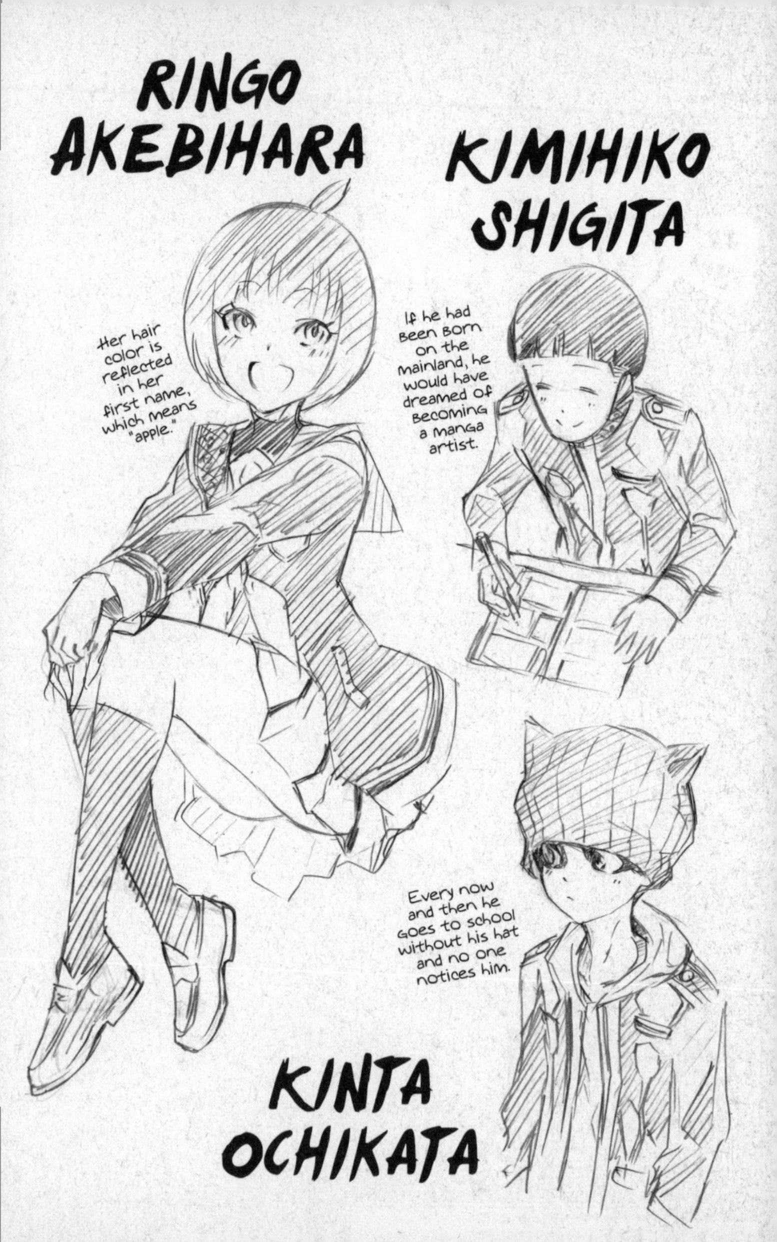
RINGO AKEBIHARA
Her hair color is reflected in her first name, which means "apple."
KIMIHIKO SHIGITA
If he had been born on the mainland, he would have dreamed of becoming a manga artist.
Every now and then he goes to school without his hat and no one notices him.
KINTA OCHIKATA

Twin Star Exorcists
ONMYOJI

12

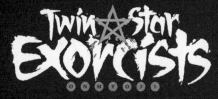

—SHONEN JUMP Manga Edition—

STORY & ART Yoshiaki Sukeno

TRANSLATION Tetsuichiro Miyaki
ENGLISH ADAPTATION Bryant Turnage
TOUCH-UP ART & LETTERING Stephen Dutro
DESIGN Shawn Carrico
EDITOR Annette Roman

Printed in Canada

Published by VIZ Media, LLC
P.O. Box 77010
San Francisco, CA 94107

10 9 8 7 6 5 4 3 2 1
First printing, May 2018

www.viz.com

PARENTAL ADVISORY
TWIN STAR EXORCISTS is rated T for Teen and is recommended for ages 13 and up. This volume contains fantasy violence.
ratings.viz.com

www.shonenjump.com

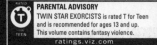

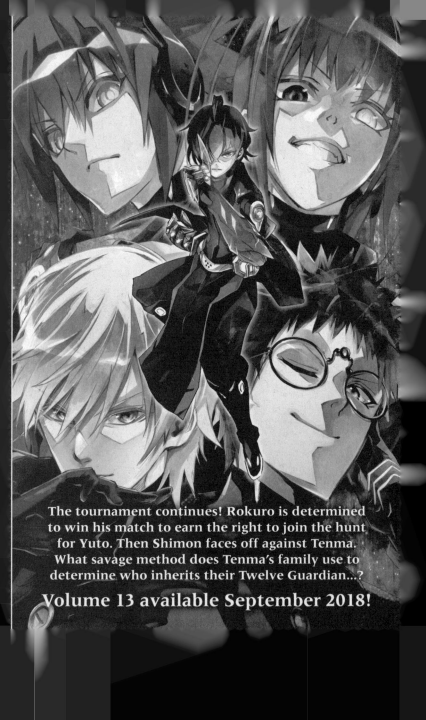

The tournament continues! Rokuro is determined
to win his match to earn the right to join the hunt
for Yuto. Then Shimon faces off against Tenma.
What savage method does Tenma's family use to
determine who inherits their Twelve Guardian...?

Volume 13 available September 2018!

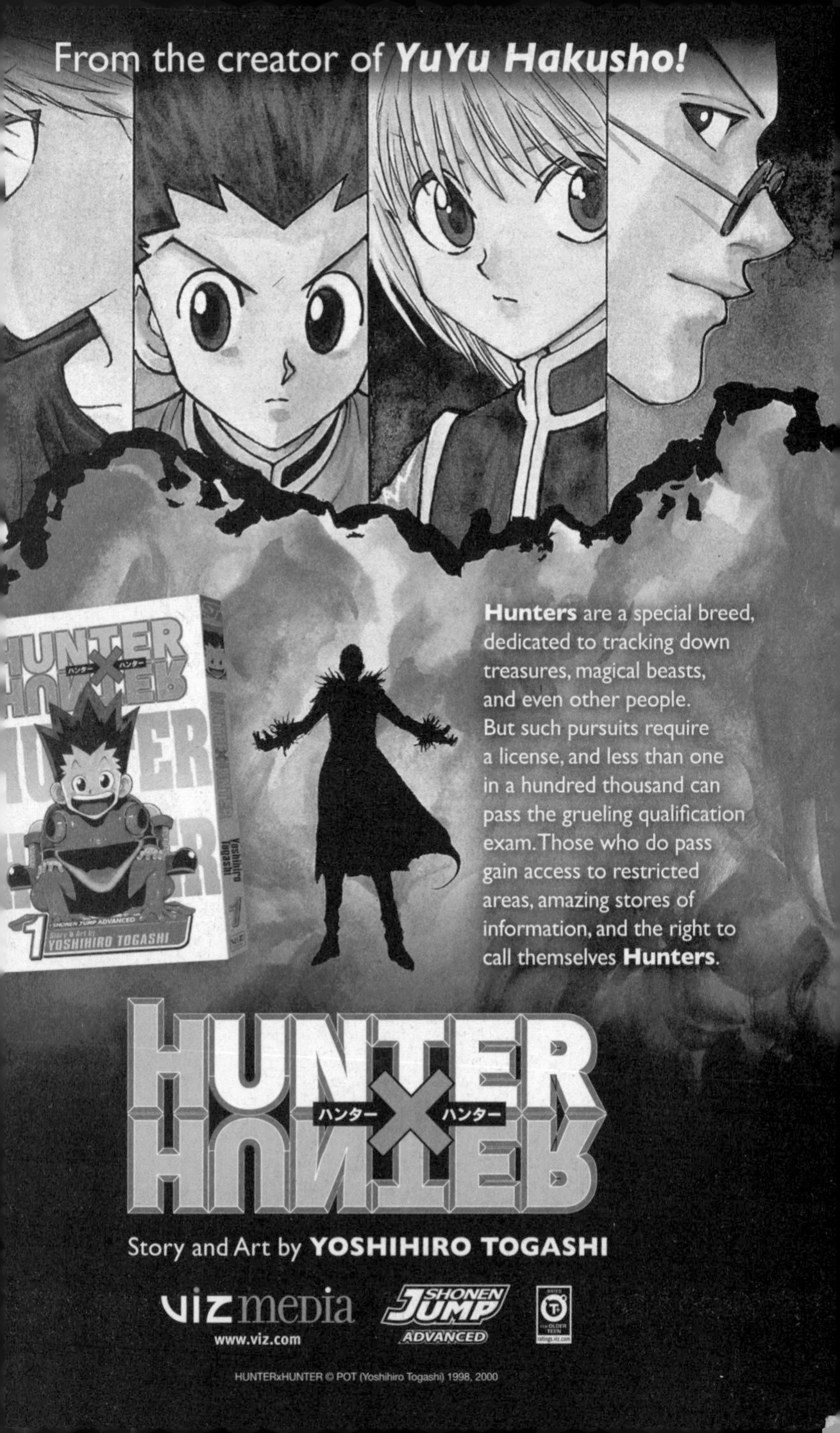
From the creator of YuYu Hakusho!
HUNTER × HUNTER
ハンター ハンター
1
YOSHIHIRO TOGASHI
Hunters are a special breed, dedicated to tracking down treasures, magical beasts, and even other people. But such pursuits require a license, and less than one in a hundred thousand can pass the grueling qualification exam. Those who do pass gain access to restricted areas, amazing stores of information, and the right to call themselves Hunters.
HUNTER × HUNTER
ハンター ハンター
Story and Art by YOSHIHIRO TOGASHI
viz media
www.viz.com
SHONEN JUMP ADVANCED
HUNTERxHUNTER © POT (Yoshihiro Togashi) 1998, 2000

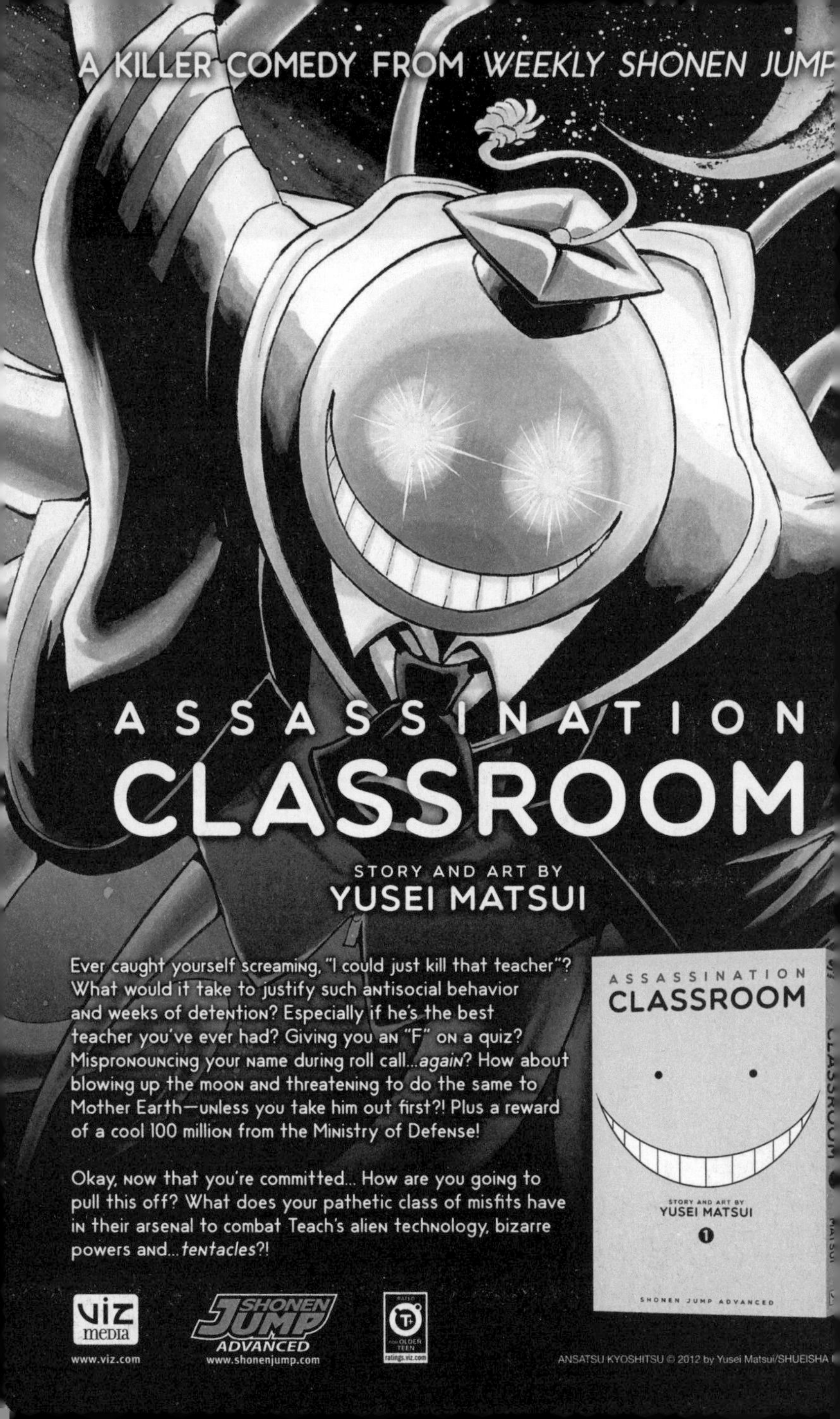
A KILLER COMEDY FROM *WEEKLY SHONEN JUMP*
ASSASSINATION CLASSROOM
STORY AND ART BY
YUSEI MATSUI
Ever caught yourself screaming, "I could just kill that teacher"? What would it take to justify such antisocial behavior and weeks of detention? Especially if he's the best teacher you've ever had? Giving you an "F" on a quiz? Mispronouncing your name during roll call...*again*? How about blowing up the moon and threatening to do the same to Mother Earth—unless you take him out first?! Plus a reward of a cool 100 million from the Ministry of Defense!
Okay, now that you're committed... How are you going to pull this off? What does your pathetic class of misfits have in their arsenal to combat Teach's alien technology, bizarre powers and...*tentacles*?!
ASSASSINATION CLASSROOM
STORY AND ART BY
YUSEI MATSUI
1
SHONEN JUMP ADVANCED
viz media
www.viz.com
SHONEN JUMP ADVANCED
www.shonenjump.com
RATED T+ FOR OLDER TEEN
ratings.viz.com
ANSATSU KYOSHITSU © 2012 by Yusei Matsui/SHUEISHA

YOU'RE READING THE **WRONG WAY!**

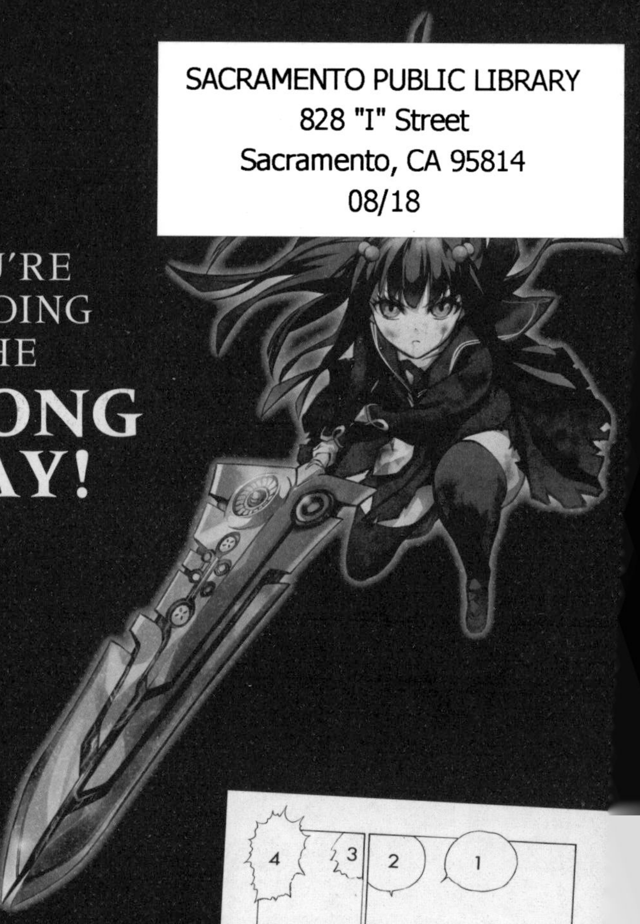

Twin Star Exorcists reads from right to left, starting in the upper-right corner. Japanese is read from right to left, meaning that action, sound effects and word-balloon order are completely reversed from English order.

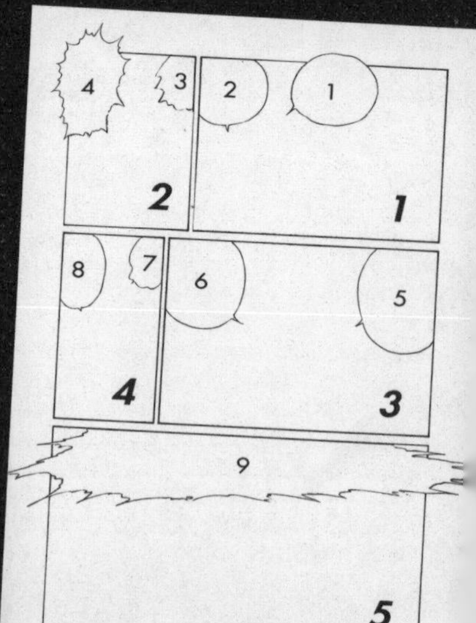
1
2
3
4
1
2
5
6
7
8
3
4
9
5
142